POWER TOOLS

for
Studio One 2

Volume 2

POWER TOOLS

for
Studio One 2

Master PreSonus' Complete Creation and Production Software
Volume 2

INCLUDES DVD-ROM!

Larry the O

HAL LEONARD BOOKS
An Imprint of Hal Leonard Corporation

Published in 2013 by Hal Leonard Books
An Imprint of Hal Leonard Corporation
7777 West Bluemound Road
Milwaukee, WI 53213

Trade Book Division Editorial Offices
33 Plymouth St., Montclair, NJ 07042

Printed in the United States of America

Book design by Kristina Rolander

Library of Congress Cataloging-in-Publication Data is available upon request.

ISBN 978-1-47687-468-5

www.halleonardbooks.com

Contents

CHAPTER 2
WORKING WITH VIDEO   31

CHAPTER 3
MIXING   41

CHAPTER 4
AUTOMATION   189

CHAPTER 5
MASTERING ON THE PROJECT PAGE

CHAPTER 6
SHARING YOUR WORK WITH THE WORLD

Acknowledgments

Well, here I am again. Writing my acknowledgments as if everything were finished for this book, when I still have a couple more months until it's all really wrapped up. Which brings me to my first acknowledgments: Group Publisher John Cerullo, Developmental Editor Bill Gibson, and Project Editor Bernadette Malavarca at Hal Leonard Publishing. Being thorough and being fast are two workflows I find difficult to reconcile with each other, but the HL folks somehow manage to hang with my, um, "challenging" production style, and produce a beautiful book from a mound of verbiage and screenshots. Thanks for that.

The cooperation of PreSonus is greatly appreciated, especially from Steve Oppenheimer (thanks, bro), Jonathan Hillman, Arnd Kaiser, Rick Naqvi, and a passel of others. I gotta slice uh malhai pie from the Hotel Pontchartrain for eechayou.

Focusrite Novation and Native Instruments also helped me out with generous loans of their equipment. Thanks for the favors.

Now it gets personal. Thanks to my wife, Angela, who gets up in the morning to go to a real job, while I crawl into bed just ahead of the sun with the light of the computer monitor still in my eyes. Mom, of course, made all of this necessary, a debt I can never properly repay.

And then there is Hammond D. Puppy, who has allowed me to sit in on countless sessions he has done with Studio One 2 while cranking out his tremendous legacy of country chart-toppers. Belly rub all night long, Hammie!

Finally, there are my friends at Moschetti Coffee, who really, REALLY know how to roast. You had a lot to do with this book getting done. Saint behind the glass smells coffee in the air.

Larry the O
Vallejo, CA

POWER TOOLS

for
Studio One 2

Volume 2

Introduction

WELCOME BACK!

If you're looking at this book, *Power Tools for Studio One 2*, volume 2, you probably have seen *Power Tools for Studio One 2*, volume 1, and know what this is all about. But I'm not taking any chances.

This book is the second of two volumes of the only comprehensive book about PreSonus' powerful Studio One 2 DAW software. Studio One was introduced in 2009 by PreSonus to provide a fast, easy-to-use DAW with powerful features and excellent sound. It is written by the same sharp programmers who brought you Nuendo and Cubase, so Studio One 2, while the newest major DAW to enter the market, is hardly a first-time effort.

Available in both Windows and Mac versions, Studio One's computer code is much newer than that of the other major DAWs, enabling the newest technologies to be incorporated at the lowest levels, for example:

- Drag-and-drop is in Studio One 2's DNA, so it is usable with a great many different functions in the program.
- Multiprocessor support has been in the program since its first beta version was created. This gives Studio One the ability to do real-time pitch shifting, resampling, time-stretching, and many other kinds of processing.
- Such Internet services as SoundCloud and Nimbit can be accessed directly from within the program. Once your mixes are finished, they can be uploaded right away with just a few mouse clicks.

Studio One's features, performance, and sound have created a fast-growing group of users around the world. And you are one of them, you clever person.

In Our Last Exciting Episode...

In *Power Tools for Studio One 2*, volume 1, I introduced the program and covered basic functionality like this:

- Introduction: A quick overview of Studio One, especially the features that provide its power and distinguish it from other DAW software, and of the contents of volume 1.

- Chapter 1—On Your Mark: Presented minimum system requirements for Studio One 2, selecting and connecting audio and MIDI interfaces, a first walk-through of Studio One 2, and getting some sound out of it.

- Chapter 2—Get Set to Record: Setting up to record, including the metronome, input monitoring, and headphone mixes.

- Chapter 3—Go! Recording with Studio One 2: Recording, playback, and overdubbing. Punching, loop recording, and layers.

- Chapter 4—Virtual Instruments and MIDI: Bundled virtual instruments (VIs), getting a drum groove going, recording MIDI Instrument tracks, and a first look at freezing tracks to free up CPU resources.

- Chapter 5—Basic Editing: An introduction to Studio One 2's editing tools and executing basic editing operations.

- Chapter 6—Advanced Editing: Deeper features for editing audio and MIDI, including fades, quantizing, meter and tempo changes, and time-stretching and compression.

What's in This Book?

Whereas *Power Tools for Studio One 2*, volume 1 got you off and running, volume 2 brings it on home like this:

- Introduction: What you are reading right now. Recaps volume 1, introduces volume 2, and identifies program features that have been released since volume 1 was written, which will be covered in this volume.

- Chapter 1—Working with Loops: A closer look at Studio One 2's features for making and using loops than was presented in volume 1. Includes coverage of Studio One 2's proprietary Audioloop and Musicloop formats.

- Chapter 2—Working with Video: While not created to be a high-end post production environment, Studio One 2 nevertheless allows working to picture. Features of the Video Player window, editing to picture, offsets, and more are discussed.

- Chapter 3—Mixing: Fun. Mixing is one of the best and possibly the most intricate parts of the recording process. Covers everything in Studio One 2's Mix view, including the mixer, panels, soloing, and monitoring, Event-level mixing (including Studio One 2's powerful Event FX feature), using control surfaces, bouncing and exporting mixes, and a host of mixing tips and techniques.

- Chapter 4—Automation: One of the most powerful mixing tools in the arsenal of any DAW, Studio One 2 has such extensive automation capabilities that the subject merited its own chapter. Recording, creating, viewing, and editing automation are all discussed.

- Chapter 5—Mastering in the Project Page: Studio One 2 offers mastering facilities as does no other DAW. This chapter covers all of the Project page's powerful features and, most especially, its unique integration with the Song page.

- Chapter 6—Sharing Your Work: You're done. Your music is entirely recorded, edited, mixed, and mastered. Now you want to get it out into the world, and this chapter will show you how to burn it to CD, export to DDP for submission to a duplication facility, create files for downloading, upload files to SoundCloud, PreSonus Exchange, and Nimbit.

- Chapter 7— The Latest and Greatest: Recent Developments in Studio One 2: Now Studio One 2 is in version 2.5. All of version 2.5's improvements in mixing, mastering, automation, and other areas covered by chapters 1 through 6 of this book have been incorporated into the appropriate chapters. Chapter 7 discusses important additions made to the areas covered in volume 1 during the writing of that book and this one. This includes macros, enhancements to comping, and much more.

- Appendices: There are always goodies that don't belong in the main text, and this is where to find those. "Appendix A—When Things Go Wrong" takes a swing at some of the more common problems users encounter and suggests some possible causes. I can't help you with bugs, but if only one session is saved by someone's finding an answer in this appendix, it will justify its inclusion in the book. Appendix B is PreSonus' developer documentation for the Audioloop and Musicloop formats. A little hardcore, but good reference material to have.

- Index: You have no clue how much work it is to create a good index, but it's all worth it if it enables you to quickly find the information you need when you're stuck in the middle of a session.

- About the Author: More frightening than science fiction because it's true.

WHAT'S NEW SINCE VOLUME 1?

It's a lot of work to flip back to chapter 7, so I'll tell you here what new developments you'll find there.

Macros

In volume 1 I discussed the great value of macros in increasing efficiency. I also mentioned that a Macros feature was in development for Studio One. Shortly after that volume went to press, the Macros feature was released. Although not especially difficult to use, this incredibly powerful feature bears some explanation, which you will find in chapter 7.

Exchange

Social media. We all use it with our friends, and it's only natural to use it with our professional colleagues as well. PreSonus Exchange is all about users' trading Studio One 2 data they've generated with other users. FX Chains, Presets, Soundsets, Extensions, Audioloops, pitch name lists…just about any kind of Studio One 2 data can be uploaded or downloaded. PreSonus uses Exchange to distribute Extensions and other data, as well. Best of all, it's accessed directly from Studio One 2's Browser and incredibly simple to use. I'll show you how in this section.

Nimbit

Nimbit is a technology that makes e-commerce a snap, selling music, merch, and even tickets to your gigs and events, as well as incorporating all of that into your Facebook page, website, or any of a number of services for reaching fans. PreSonus actually purchased Nimbit and integrated it directly into Studio One 2 with the free Nimbit Extension. The details are here.

Studio One Free

Well, you don't really need this because you already have Studio One 2, don't you? But there are still a few poor souls who haven't the heard the word yet, and if you know about the new Studio One Free, you might save them from making some other, less sensible choice of DAW. I'll tell you about Studio One Free, what it can do and what it can't.

Of course, these are just a few of the headline new developments. I couldn't possibly go over everything that has been added in chapter 7. But at www.powertoolsforstudioone.com (coming soon) I will be able to clue you in to all sorts of additional information and new developments, so check there for more, more, more.

MAC AND WIN

Studio One 2 is available both for Mac OS and Windows. As I explained in the introduction to *Power Tools for Studio One 2*, volume 1, most of the differences between the two versions are the same differences you usually see between the platforms: the Mac's Option key is Windows' Alt key, and so forth.

Along those same lines, considerable functionality in Studio One 2 is accessed by right-clicking. Some Mac mice have right-click buttons, some don't. When they don't, the equivalent is always Ctrl-click. But I will be making a *lot* of references to right-clicking and it just gets wearing to give the equivalent every single time. So I don't. I think everybody will figure it out okay.

Working with Loops

Studio One 2 is very facile in working with loops. Excellent tools exist to help you use and manipulate them, as well as create and save your own. Of particular note are Studio One 2's tempo syncing features, which can incorporate sophisticated time-stretching, and PreSonus' Audioloop and Musicloop file formats.

Loops can be imported in several recognized file formats from Studio One 2's Browser or directly from the Mac Finder or Windows Explorer. Loops containing tempo information can be auditioned in sync with the Song and manipulated in the Song to match tempo changes. Loops can also be transposed and tuned.

Once imported, loop files are not looped on playback. Aside from being aware of tempos and slices, loop files are played only a single time, as are other audio files. A loop file must be repeat-pasted into a track (usually using the Duplicate command) as many times as needed to fill the desired duration.

Many of the features used in working with loops were covered in *Power Tools for Studio One 2*, volume 1. In general, I have chosen to briefly summarize this information where it applies and provide a reference to the appropriate section in volume 1, rather than reproduce that text wholesale. Often, there are important details that are not mentioned here, so I recommend you do check the referenced sections of volume 1 to get the best results.

RECOGNIZED LOOP FILE FORMATS

Studio One 2 recognizes the following loop file formats:

- Audioloop: PreSonus' proprietary loop file format, described below.
- Musicloop: PreSonus' proprietary format for loops of music performance data, also described below.

- Apple Loops: Based on the AIFF file format, Apple Loops use lossless CAF compression.
- REX and REX2: Created by Steinberg, REX2 is one of the most widely supported loop file formats.

Studio One 2 cannot read ACID loop files directly, but because ACID files are based on the WAV file format, Studio One 2 can use them as audio files.

IMPORTING LOOPS

Auditioning Loops with the Preview Player

The Preview Player in Studio One 2's Browser lets you audition loop files in the Browser, looping them during playback, if desired, or even playing them back in sync with the Song. In addition to the compatible audio loop file formats listed above, Musicloop files also can be auditioned in the Preview Player. More information about the Preview Player can be found in the section "Auditioning in the Browser with the Preview Player" in chapter 2, "Get Set to Record," in *Power Tools for Studio One 2*, volume 1.

To listen through a collection of loops in context:

1. Locate the loops you wish to audition in the Browser.
2. Select the first loop you want to hear, and click the Loop and Play at song tempo buttons in the Preview Player.

Fig. 1-1: The Loop and Play at song tempo buttons.

3. Start playback of the Song.
4. When you reach the point where you want the loop to start, click the Play button in the Preview Player. The selected loop will start playing in sync with the tempo of the Song.
5. Use the up and down arrows to move through the list of loops. Playback of a loop starts as soon as it is selected.
6. When you find the loop you want, drag it in as follows.

Dragging a Loop to an Existing Track

A loop can be dragged from Studio One 2's Browser, the Mac Finder, or Windows Explorer and dropped into an existing track.

- If the tempo of the loop is readable and the Track Tempo field is set to Timestretch, it is synced to the tempo of the Song when it is imported.
- A loop will start playback from the location where you drop it. When you are dragging in a loop, a pop-up tool tip shows where the start of the loop will be if you release the mouse button at the current location.

Fig. 1-2: A loop being dragged into a track. Note the pop-up tool tip.

The Stretch Audio Files to Song Tempo Box

When a new Song is created, you can make the Tempo mode of all tracks default to Timestretch mode. This means that whenever you drag in an audio file containing tempo information, such as a loop, it will automatically be fitted to the Song tempo. To set the default Track Tempo mode to Timestretch:

1. Create a new Song. The New Song dialog opens.
2. Click the Stretch audio files to Song tempo box.
3. Each new track created will be set to Timestretch mode by default.

Dragging a Loop to Create a New Track

To create a new track for a loop, drag it and drop it into the track area of the Arrange view where there are no existing tracks, such as at the bottom of the area. A new track will be created and routed to the main output, and the loop will be placed at the location where the mouse button was released at the end of the drag.

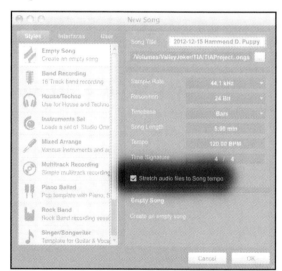

Fig. 1-3: The Stretch audio files to Song tempo box in the New Song dialog sets the default Tempo mode for new tracks to Timestretch.

Fig. 1-4: Dropping a loop in an unused portion of the Arrange view (such as below all existing tracks) creates a new track containing the loop. The track is also named for the loop.

Dragging a Loop from the Mac Finder or Windows Explorer

Any readable loop file can be dragged directly from the Mac Finder or Windows Explorer, instead of from the Browser, into an existing track or to create a new one.

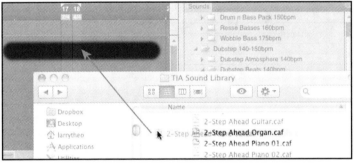

Fig. 1-5: Loop files can be dragged into the Arrange view directly from the Mac Finder or Windows Explorer.

Setting the Start Point Using Snap

Enabling Snap and setting the appropriate Quantize Value makes it easy to drop loops with precision. For more information on using Snap, see the section "Snap (Grid)" of chapter 5, "On the Cutting Room Floor: Basic Editing" in *Power Tools for Studio One 2*, volume 1.

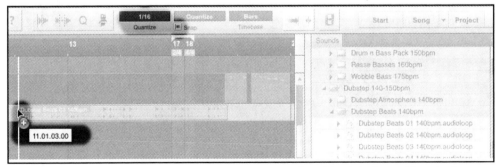

Fig. 1-6: When Snap is engaged, a loop will be snapped to the grid as it is dropped into the Arrange view. In this example, the grid is set to a sixteenth note, and the loop is being dropped on the beat, as shown in the tool tip.

LOOPS AND TEMPO

Studio One offers excellent facilities for tempo-locking, which is crucial in most loop applications. (Tempo-locking is alteration of a loop to match changes in the tempo of a Song.) For a thorough discussion of these facilities, see the section "Quantizing Audio" in chapter 6, "Advanced Editing" in *Power Tools for Studio One*, volume 1. I will simply recap the most important details here.

There are three components required for tempo-locking:

- The tempo of the music being locked must be known. This can mean the tempo is encoded in the file, that the tempo is inferred by Studio One 2, or that you enter the tempo directly.
- A mechanism for time-stretching audio to fit it to a tempo grid.
- A Quantize command to determine the grid to which the music should be locked.

Beat-Sliced Loops

Audioloops and REX files are both beat-sliced loop formats. In beat-sliced files, an audio file is effectively divided into a number of slices; think of isolating each snare drum hit into its own slice. Each slice can be quantized independently to achieve tempo-locking.

The difference between Audioloops and REX files is that, once dragged into Studio One 2, an Audioloop becomes an Audio Part, which can follow tempo changes or be quantized using time-stretching or not. Time-stretching is not available when performing these operations on REX files.

Audioloop files, REX files, and, for that matter, Audio Parts all store embedded tempo information.

QUANTIZING AUDIO PARTS

Audio Parts can be quantized like REX files, where start times are simply quantized to the grid, or they can be quantized to the grid with time-stretching applied to the slices to make them fit. The quantizing method is determined by the Stretch events checkbox in the Audio Part inspector.

To enable tempo-following for an Audio Part using time-stretching:

1. Select the Audio Part in the Arrange view.
2. Set the track Tempo mode field to Timestretch.
3. Click the Stretch events checkbox in the small Audio Part inspector that appeared when you selected the Audio Part.

To quantize an Audio Part using time-stretching:

1. Enable the Audio Part for tempo-following as described above.
2. With the Audio Part selected, press Q to invoke the Quantize command. The slices will be quantized to the grid using the Quantize value specified in the Arrange view toolbar, and time-stretching will be applied to make the slices fit.

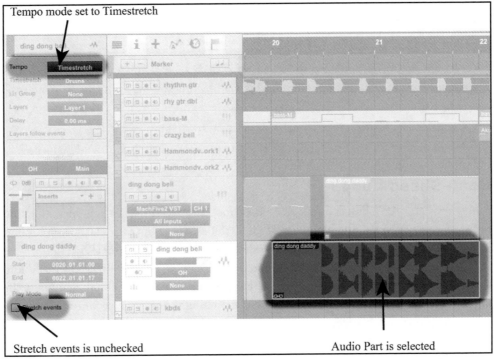

Tempo mode set to Timestretch

Stretch events is unchecked   Audio Part is selected

Fig. 1-7: When the Stretch events box in the Audio Part inspector is unchecked, the track Tempo mode is set to Timestretch, and the Quantize command is applied, slice start times are quantized, but the audio is unaffected. When the box is checked, time-stretching is applied to make the audio fit continuously (with no space between slices).

- To enable tempo-following for an Audio Part without using time-stretching: Follow the procedure above for enabling tempo-following, but uncheck the Stretch events box in the Audio Part inspector. Only start times will be changed to match tempo changes. To quantize the slices in an Audio Part without using time-stretching: Follow the procedure above for quantizing, but uncheck the Stretch events box in the Audio Part inspector. Only start times will be changed in fitting the slices to the grid.

Audio File (Non-Beat-Sliced) Loops

In beat-sliced loops, the work of segmenting the audio in the file has been done for you and the tempo is usually encoded in the file. Working with loops that are not in a beat-sliced format requires that Studio One 2 be told the tempo of the material in the audio file or figure it out for itself by analyzing transients in the loop.

Once the tempo is known, a loop can be tempo-locked in one of three ways:

• The loop can be time-stretched to fit a new tempo.
• Time-stretching can be applied based on Audio Bend markers in the file.
• Start time quantization or time-stretching can be applied to slices in an Audio Part.

TIP: Once a tempo has been set for an audio file, all Events based on that file will be affected by tempo changes. If this is not desirable, try using the Speedup field in the Audio Event inspector to fit an Event to the tempo with manual time-stretching.

For a detailed discussion of these topics, see the sections "Segmenting—Advanced Dividing" and "Time-Stretching (Compression/Expansion) and Quantizing Audio" in chapter 6, "Advanced Editing" of *Power Tools for Studio One 2*, volume 1. Brief summaries of these topics will be presented here.

TELLING STUDIO ONE 2 THE TEMPO OF A LOOP

There are four ways you can inform Studio One 2 of the tempo of an audio file:

• Enter the tempo in the File Tempo field in the Audio Event inspector. This is useful for loops where the tempo is given in the file name or documentation, but it is not encoded in the file. For more information, see the section "Audio Event Inspector" of chapter 5, "On the Cutting Room Floor: Basic Editing" of *Power Tools for Studio One 2*, volume 1.

Fig. 1-8: Entering a file tempo directly: Select the loop and enter the tempo into the File Tempo field of the Event inspector.

• Use Tap Tempo.
• Manually time-stretch the loop to fit the desired duration.
• Let Studio One 2 analyze the transients in the loop and infer the tempo from them.

SETTING TEMPO WITH TAP TEMPO

Tap Tempo allows you to show Studio One 2 the tempo, rather than tell it what it is. To use Tap Tempo to set the tempo of a file:

1. Be sure that the Tempo mode of the currently selected track is set to Don't Follow. If it is set to Follow or Timestretch, Studio One 2 will be trying to move and/or time-stretch Events on the track as you tap.

2. Start playback just before the passage with the tempo you want to use.

3. On each beat, click on the word "Tempo" beneath the Tempo field in the Transport bar. After a few taps, the tempo will be calculated and displayed.

Fig. 1-9: Click on the word "Tempo" in the Transport window to set a tempo with Tap Tempo.

For more information on Tap Tempo, see the section "Tap Tempo" of chapter 6, "Advanced Editing" in *Power Tools for Studio One 2*, volume 1.

SETTING TEMPO WITH MANUAL TIME-STRETCHING

To generate a tempo using manual time-stretching:

1. With the Arrow tool active, select the Event you wish to time-stretch.

2. Check that the Tempo field in the Track inspector is set to Timestretch.

3. Position the cursor over the end of the Event and hold down the Option + Cmd (Alt + Ctrl in Windows) keys. The cursor will change to a metronome icon next to the usual sizing cursor of an arrowhead and line.

4. If you want to size the Event exactly to the grid (that is, fit it to a precise musical or absolute time duration), be sure that Snap is active and that the desired Quantize Value setting is displayed in the Arrange view toolbar.

5. Drag while holding down Option + Cmd (Alt + Ctrl in Windows) to size the Event. As you drag, a pop-up tool tip will show you the duration of the Event in seconds and the tempo that will be assigned to the audio file if you release the mouse button at the current location.

6. Release the mouse button when the Event is at the desired duration.

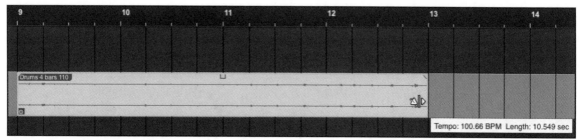

Fig. 1-10: A tempo can be assigned to a file by manual time-stretching. Simply set the track Tempo field to Timestretch, hold the Option and Cmd keys, and drag.

For more information, see the section "Manual Time-Stretching" of chapter 6, "Advanced Editing" of *Power Tools for Studio One 2*, volume 1.

DETERMINING TEMPO USING TRANSIENT DETECTION

In most pop music forms, notes are played on beats or common divisions of beats, such as quarter notes and eighth notes. Studio One 2 detects the transients of note attacks, uses them as indicators of where the beats are, and extrapolates the tempo from that. Impressive stuff. Transient detection is controlled in the Audio Bend panel.

To detect transients, use either of these methods:

- Right-click (Ctrl-click in Mac) on the Event in which you want to detect transients and choose Audio > Audio Bend > Detect Transients or choose Audio > Detect Transients from the main menu bar. The detection is entirely automatic from there.
- Select the Event in which you want to detect transients, open the Audio Bend panel, choose Standard or Sensitive from the drop-down menu in the Mode field of the Detection section of the panel, then click the Analyze button in the Detection section.

For more information on transient detection see the section "Transient Detection and Audio Bend" of chapter 6, "Advanced Editing" in *Power Tools for Studio One 2*, volume 1. For more information on the Audio Bend panel, see the section "The Audio Bend Panel" of chapter 6, "Advanced Editing" of *Power Tools for Studio One 2*, volume 1.

BEAT-SLICING AN AUDIO LOOP

If the material is suitable, you can turn an audio loop into a beat-sliced loop. The process is still based on transient detection, but, in this case, the loop is chopped into separate Events based on the locations of the transients. The resulting Events are then merged into an Audio Part, which can be used as is or exported to an Audioloop file.

There are three ways to beat-slice an audio loop:

- Use the Slice function in the Audio Bend panel.
- Slice at the grid lines.
- Use Strip Silence.

BEAT-SLICING USING THE AUDIO BEND PANEL

To beat-slice an audio loop with the Audio Bend panel:

1. Analyze the loop for transients, as described earlier in the section "Determining Tempo Using Transient Detection."

2. Set the Quantize Mode field in the Action section of the panel to Slice.

3. Select the Slice options as desired in the checkboxes below the Quantize Mode field. Note that checking the Merge box causes the beat-sliced Events to be merged into an Audio Part after slicing.

4. Click the Apply button in the Action section of the panel. The loop will be beat-sliced as specified.

Fig. 1-11: The Action section of the Audio Bend panel.

For more information on beat-slicing with the Audio Bend panel, see the section "The Audio Bend Panel" of chapter 6, "Advanced Editing" of *Power Tools for Studio One 2*, volume 1.

BEAT-SLICING AT THE GRID

Beat-slicing at the grid simply splits the selected Event(s) at quantization grid lines of the resolution specified in the Arrange view Quantize Value field. So, if Quantize Value is set to 1/8, the selected material will be split at eighth notes in the Song tempo.

This form of beat-slicing is not based on the content of the selected Event(s), but on the selected grid resolution. That is most useful if you are slicing a loop that is already at the Song tempo, at half the tempo or double the tempo, but it may produce interesting, if unusual, results if the loop is at a very different tempo than the Song.

To beat-slice a loop at grid lines:

1. Select the loop, which can be one or more Events.

2. Set the Arrange view Quantize Value field to the grid resolution at which you want to create new Events.

3. Right-click (Ctrl-click in Mac) on any selected Event and choose Event > Split at Grid from the contextual menu that drops down, or choose Event > Split at Grid from the main menu bar. The selected Event(s) will be split into separate Events at the specified resolution.

Fig. 1-12: Beat-slicing at gridlines is achieved using the Event > Split at Grid command.

BEAT-SLICING USING STRIP SILENCE

Fig. 1-13: The Strip Silence panel.

Strip Silence, which is accessed from the Strip Silence panel, is a method of breaking an Event into smaller Events based not on transient detection, but on detecting silences in the audio. The logic is that silences are the space between notes, so stripping out the silences leaves only the notes. Put another way, Strip Silence is probably the fanciest noise gate you are likely to encounter. The action of Strip Silence isn't really beat-slicing, but it can be useful in accomplishing the same goal if the nature of the source material is suitable.

So, what is "silence" and what source material is "suitable"? The success of Strip Silence in beat-slicing depends on how these two questions are answered.

The first question is answered by the settings made in the Strip Silence panel, which define what will be interpreted as a sound. Anything that does not meet that definition is presumed to be a silence and stripped out.

The answer to the second question, of what source material is "suitable," is simply that material in which it is easy to discern notes from silence. A reggae or '60s soul rhythm guitar track will probably work well, as those parts tend to be choppy so as to create the appropriate rhythmic feel. On the other hand, a bagpipe track (something everyone encounters on a nearly daily basis) would be quite difficult, because bagpipes sound continuously. (There are many reasons one could give for bagpipes being difficult, but that one applies here.) If there are no breaks between notes, the algorithm can't tell where one note stops and the next starts.

You might think that drum tracks are good candidates for Strip Silence, and they are, but a snare track, for instance, will require careful setting of the Strip Silence parameters to help the algorithm tell the difference between snare hits and bleed into the snare mic from the kick drum, rack tom, and/or hihat. Subtleties, such as ghost notes, will likely get lost in this process, so you will have a harder time using Strip Silence on, say, a jazz drum track than a country drum track. Open ride cymbals also pose a considerable challenge to sorting notes from silences.

To beat-slice using Strip Silence:

1. Select the loop or Events you want to split up.
2. Right-click (Ctrl-click in Mac) on any selected Event and choose Audio > Strip Silence from the contextual menu that drops down, click the Strip Silence button in the Arrange view toolbar, or choose Audio > Strip Silence or View > Additional Views > Strip Silence from the main menu bar. The Strip Silence panel will open.
3. Set the Strip Silence parameters as desired.
4. Click the Apply button. Silences will be stripped and the Event(s) will be chopped into smaller Events that are judged to be "sounds."
5. Usually, it will be necessary to do several iterations of undoing the Strip Silence action, adjusting the settings, and applying them again before getting a satisfactory result. Even then, some amount of adjustment to the results by hand normally is required.

Strip Silence is a sophisticated function that takes both understanding and experimentation to obtain the best results. For more information on Strip Silence, including explanations of the Strip Silence parameters, see the section "Strip Silence" of chapter 6, "Advanced Editing" in *Power Tools for Studio One 2*, volume 1.

Methods of Tempo-Locking

There are three ways tempo-locking can be achieved:

- Manual time-stretching.
- Auto time-stretching.
- Speedup (Event-level time-stretching).

Of these, only auto time-stretching makes use of the file tempo we so carefully determined in the last section, but it is the most elegant and useful of the three methods. The other two methods are good tools for those situations where auto time-stretching is not achievable; for example, with loops that are not rhythmic in nature or where transient detection is difficult.

MANUAL TIME-STRETCHING

Manual time-stretching to set a tempo was described earlier in the section "Setting Tempo with Manual Time-Stretching." If you have done this with your loop, it is possible for Studio One 2 to perform auto time-stretching on it. However, once a tempo for an audio file has been set, all Events based on that file will be affected by tempo changes. In cases where this is not desirable, you can opt to manually time-stretch a loop without generating or using a tempo for it. Manual time-stretching is accomplished using the Speedup setting in the Audio Event inspector.

To manually time-stretch a loop without generating a tempo:

1. With the Arrow tool active, select the Event you wish to time-stretch.

2. Position the cursor over the end of the Event and hold down the Option (Alt in Windows) key. The time-stretch cursor (a clock next to the usual sizing cursor of an arrowhead and line) will appear.

Fig. 1-14: The time-stretch cursor.

3. If you want to size the Event exactly to the grid (that is, fit it to a precise musical or absolute time duration), be sure that Snap is active and that the desired Quantize Value setting is displayed in the Arrange view toolbar.

4. Option-drag (Alt-drag in Windows) to size the Event. As you drag, a pop-up tool tip shows you the duration of the Event in seconds and the Speedup factor that will be applied if you release the mouse button at the current location.

5. Release the mouse button when the Event is at the desired location.

6. Alternatively, instead of dragging to set the duration, you can click in the Speedup field in the Audio Event inspector and enter a value.

For more information, see the section "Manual Time-Stretching" of chapter 6, "Advanced Editing" of *Power Tools for Studio One 2*, volume 1.

AUTO TIME-STRETCHING

Auto time-stretching is the preferred method of tempo-locking. Once a tempo has been set, all that needs to be done to engage auto time-stretching is to choose the optimal Timestretch material mode and set the Audio Track tempo mode. After that, tempo changes will automatically be followed.

For more information on auto time-stretching, and in particular, Audio Track tempo modes and Timestretch material modes, see the sections "Time-Stretch Material Modes" and "Auto Time-Stretching" of chapter 6, "Advanced Editing" in *Power Tools for Studio One 2*, volume 1.

AUDIO TRACK TEMPO MODES

The Tempo field in the Audio Track inspector sets the Audio Track tempo mode. There are three tempo modes:

- Don't Follow: Time-stretching is not performed automatically nor are Events moved when the tempo changes.
- Follow: When the tempo is changed, the start times of Events are moved in time to maintain their musical positions (bars and beats locations). No time-stretching is performed.
- Timestretch: When the tempo is changed, Events are moved in time to maintain their musical positions (that is, bars and beats locations), and time-stretching is applied to keep the Events in tempo.

To choose a tempo mode:

1. Select the track or track group that you want to time-stretch.
2. Click in the Tempo field of the Track inspector and choose the desired tempo mode.

TIME-STRETCH MATERIAL MODES

The time-stretch material mode optimizes time-stretching by indicating to the algorithm the nature of the signal. There are four time-stretch material modes in Studio One 2:

- Drums: Use for percussive material, especially unpitched instruments.
- Sound: A generic catchall for sounds that don't fit into any of the other categories. Chordal instruments, sound effects, and sections of instruments (such as string or brass sections) are good examples of what this mode might work for.
- Solo: Use for single-line instruments, such as vocals, brass, woodwind, single-line guitar leads.
- Audio Bend: Use with audio that has been segmented using transient detection and contains Audio Bend markers, as described earlier.

To choose a time-stretch material mode:

1. Select the track or track group that you want to time-stretch.
2. Click in the Timestretch field of the Track inspector and choose the desired time-stretch material mode.

THE AUDIOLOOP AND MUSICLOOP FILE FORMATS

Version 2 of Studio One 2 introduced the ability to read and write PreSonus' Audioloop and Musicloop formats. There's nothing you really need to know about these file formats to be able to use them; they just work. However, there are those who like to dig into how things work, and feel that they gain an understanding from this knowledge that is useful in their application. This section is for them. If you don't care what's under the hood, you can just skip this section, but should you ever change your mind, the information is here. If you *really* want the lowdown, the actual specification document is in appendix B, "PreSonus Audioloop File Format Specification."

To start with, there are a few important things to understand about these formats:

- A Musicloop file is nothing more than a special case of an Audioloop file. They are fundamentally the same, except that Musicloops contain some additional information.
- The Audioloop and Musicloop formats employ established file formats as much as possible: the Audioloop format is actually a particular kind of ZIP file, audio data is stored as a .wav or .flac file embedded in the Audioloop or Musicloop file, and MIDI/performance data is stored as a Standard MIDI File (SMF) embedded in the Musicloop file.
- Although the use of loops in music dates back to the early tape manipulation methods of electronic music in the 1950s, and loops see wide use in videogame sound effects and mobile applications, loop file formats today assume that loops are chunks of beat-oriented musical material. This does not mean they cannot be put to other uses, only that this assumption underlies many decisions about how loops are stored and the information that is stored with them.

If standard file formats are used, then why did PreSonus reinvent the wheel? Simply put, to allow these formats to contain additional information not stored in the established formats.

Audioloops

Audioloop files use a .audioloop file extension in their name. Here's what is contained in an Audioloop file:

- Audio data, stored as an embedded .wav or .flac file.
- The name of the embedded audio file.
- The original tempo of the audio in beats per minute (BPM).
- The time signature of the audio.
- Information about the slices, if it is a beat-sliced loop.

Audioloop files do not contain any automation or audio parameter data, such as volume or mute status.

Musicloops

Musicloop files use a .musicloop file extension in their name. Musicloop files contain everything that is contained in Audioloop files, plus:

- Performance data stored as a Type 0 or Type 1 (with a single track) Standard MIDI File (SMF).
- The performance data in the SMF is also stored in a proprietary XML file. Once again, this is done to enable storing additional data. In this case, that means the length of the loop, both in seconds and in musical terms.
- An audio file generated by bouncing the Instrument Part through the effects. This file is stored in the audio data section where Audioloops are stored in .audioloop files. The audio file is in either WAV or FLAC format.
- Preset data for virtual instruments (including multitimbral instruments) and effects plug-ins. As with audio data, preset data is stored in its original file format (the file extensions read: .aupreset for Apple Units, .fxb for VST2, .vstpreset for VST3, and .fxpreset for PreSonus plug-ins) embedded within the Musicloop file.

ACCESSING A MUSICLOOP'S COMPONENTS

One of the nice things about the Musicloop format is the ability to use its component parts individually. The instrument output was rendered to an audio file, which can be used apart from any of the other components, so even if the original instrument is not available, the Musicloop can be used. Similarly, effects presets can be used separately, as can the performance data.

To access the contents of a Musicloop file:

1. Navigate to the Musicloop file in the Sounds or Files tab of the Browser.
2. Right-click (Ctrl-click in Mac) on the file in the Browser and choose Show Package Contents from the contextual menu that drops down. A disclosure triangle will appear to the left of the file name.
3. Click the disclosure triangle to expand the contents of the Musicloop file and show its components.

Each component can be dragged out of the Browser and used individually. The audio file can be dropped in an Audio track to give you the sound and musical passage, whether you have the original instrument or not; drag a .mid or .music file to an Instrument track and edit the part or play it on a different instrument; the effects presets can be dragged to another channel to give it the same treatment. Tempo information

Fig. 1-15: Choosing the Show Package Contents command enables you to access and use each component of a Musicloop file individually.

lets you use it in different musical contexts. The ability to use the various bits of a Musicloop individually gives the format a lot of versatility and maximizes its value.

MAKING YOUR OWN LOOP FILES

Making Audioloop and Musicloop files couldn't be easier, so the hardest part of making your own loop files is creating the material and getting it to sound the way you want. This book isn't really about how to make loops, and there's plenty of good information available on that subject. So, I'm not going to go into detail here, but I will outline the process, give you some things to think about, and, of course, tell you how to turn your loop material into Audioloop and Musicloop files.

Making Audio Loops

Here's a basic step-by-step description of how to make a good audio loop:

1. Collect or record your source material. Perhaps it will be a single instrument, such as a bass loop, or it might be an entire ensemble, spread across multiple tracks, playing in a particular genre.

2. Decide how long you want the loop to be and arrange all of the source material to play the way you want. If you only want to hear shakers in the last four bars of an eight-bar loop, make sure they are placed in the last four bars and do not appear in the first four.

3. Select the entire loop, press the P key to loop the selection and snap it to the grid, or Shift + P to loop it without snapping to the grid. In most cases, you will want to loop it snapped.

4. Press the / (forward slash) key to make the loop active, if it is not already. For more information on setting up and controlling loop playback, see the section "Loop Playback" of chapter 3, "Go! Recording with Studio One 2" of *Power Tools for Studio One 2*, volume 1.

5. Now that you can hear your loop, it's time to make it sound the way you want. Adjust levels, make sure all of the Events have fades in and out so there are no clicks, make any tweaks to timing that are needed, and add the effects and processing you want. There are a number of issues to consider before your loop is finalized, which I will discuss in the next section, "Loop Considerations." Take a look at that before you commit your loop.

6. Once everything sounds great, export your loop to an Audioloop file, as discussed in the section "Exporting to a Loop File" below.

7. The last step is to check the exported file in Studio One 2 or another application to make sure it plays back properly. This is very important, as it is easy to have an artifact or problem that does not show up until the final loop file is put to use.

Loops can also be exported as standard audio files using any of the bouncing or exporting techniques described in channel 3, "Mixing" in this volume, but they will not contain slices, tempo, or any of the other additional information that Audioloop and REX2 files store.

One last word about exporting loops to audio files: People sometimes like to export loops as MP3 files. While this will often work just fine, MP3 is a block-based file format; that is, samples are handled in groups called blocks, making it impossible to be sample-accurate about loop points. In some cases, this results in clicks when the loop reaches its end and goes back to the beginning. There is no single technique for avoiding this, and there is not the room here for a full discussion of this, so just be aware that may happen with MP3 loops (as well as other compressed file formats).

LOOP CONSIDERATIONS

Making a good loop can be easy, but there are a number of considerations to bear in mind when doing so, some rather subtle. The more work you do with loops, the more issues you will encounter, but here are just a few examples to think about:

- Instrument and effects tails: If your loop is rendered with echo, long reverb, or instrument sounds with long decays, how are they handled at the end of the loop? Letting them be cut off sharp can sound just plain wrong. There are tricks that sometimes work, such as making the loop file be two repetitions excerpted out of several, so that the beginning of the loop actually contains the echo/reverb/instrument tails from the previous time through. But such tricks don't always work. Auditioning the loop with live effects can be misleading because the tails are always there, but the exported loop may sound very different.

- Loops with multiple instruments: Sometimes it is desirable to have the entire band in a loop file, but doing so eliminates any ability to balance, EQ, pan, effect, or otherwise handle instruments separately. You may want to build a loop in its entirety, then export each instrument to its own loop file, or have only a small number of carefully chosen instruments (e.g., drums and percussion) in a single loop file. One other strategy is to make a Musicloop instead of an Audioloop, which makes it simpler to keep instruments separate and be able to treat them individually.

- Another reason to think about multiple instruments in a single loop file is that some instruments respond well to time-stretching, whereas others may be best tempo-locked using a beat-sliced loop. Consider a loop file with drums and a synth pad: drums are better off in slices, which will fracture the pad sound.
- Loop length: If a loop is too short, it can have a sameness that gets boring. If it is too long, it limits the number of situations in which it can be used.

CREATING AN AUDIO PART FOR EXPORT

Only Audio Parts can be exported as Audioloop files, so your loop must be made into an Audio Part before it can become an Audioloop, even if it consists of only a single Event. While the actual procedure to make an Audio Part is simple, a bit of thinking ahead is warranted to ensure that the loop you end up with works the way you hoped it would. The crux of the matter is whether you want to end up with a beat-sliced loop, and, if so, making sure the slices are what they are supposed to be.

ARE YOU ON A NEED-TO-BOUNCE BASIS?

You may need to bounce some Events to new files if:

- Material spread across several tracks is supposed to be included in the loop file.
- The loop material exists in several Events on one track, but you want to end up with a loop file that is not beat-sliced. This may be the case if there are long sounds or effects tails in the loop, for instance.
- You want material spread across a number of Events on one track to end up as a beat-sliced loop file, but the existing Events do not correspond to the way you want the slices laid out. In this case, you will need to work your way through the material, selecting and bouncing all the Events intended to be in one slice, then moving on to select and bounce the Events for the next slice, and so on.

BOUNCING EVENTS TO FILES

To bounce Events to a new file:

1. Select the Event(s) you want to bounce to a new file.
2. Press Cmd + B (Ctrl + B in Windows), right-click (Ctrl-click in Mac) on any selected Event and choose Event > Bounce Selection from the contextual menu that drops down, or choose Event > Bounce Selection from the main menu bar. The selection will be rendered to a new file, which will appear as a new Event replacing the selected material in the track.

MERGING EVENTS TO AN AUDIO PART

Okay, all your ducks are in a row, as are the Event(s) destined to become a new loop file. There is only one more step before you can make that loop file, and that is to convert the material to an Audio Part.

To make a loop into an Audio Part:

1. Select all of the Events in the loop. If the loop is to be made from a single Event, then select only that Event.

2. Press the G key, right-click (Ctrl-click in Mac) on one of the Events and choose Event > Merge Events or Audio > Merge to Audio Part from the contextual drop-down menu that appears, or choose Event > Merge Events from the main menu bar. The selected material will be replaced in the track with an Audio Part.

EXPORTING TO A LOOP FILE

Whew! The first time you do it, it might seem that making your own loop is somewhat involved. However, you will find that by the second time, it doesn't seem like so much work, and by the fourth or fifth time, it's a breeze.

Studio One 2 can export your loop to either an Audioloop or REX2 file, and the only difference is where you drag the Audio Part.

To export an Audio Part to a loop file:

• To export to an Audioloop file: Drag the Audio Part to the Files tab of the Browser, right-click (Ctrl-click in Mac) on one of the selected Events and choose Audio > Export Audioloop from the contextual menu that drops down, or choose Audio > Export Audioloop from the main menu bar.

• To export to a REX2 file: Drag the Audio Part to the desired location in the Mac Finder or Windows Explorer. A REX2 file of the loop will be created where the Audio Part is dropped.

I strongly recommend that you check the exported file by importing it back into Studio One 2, dropping it into a track, duplicating it a few times, and playing it. In the case of REX2 files, you can play it in any application that can play them. Listen closely to the beginning and end of the loop to make sure it loops smoothly.

LOOPING A SAMPLE IN SAMPLEONE

Studio One 2's SampleOne virtual instrument provides one more way to create your own loop file. Here are a few reasons you might want to do this:

• To use SampleOne's filtering, modulation, and other synthesis facilities to process the audio material.

• To experiment with the loop at different pitches and playback rates. Doing this necessitates that special attention needs to be paid to what the tempo of the loop is.

- Interesting effects can be created by playing multiple notes simultaneously. The most obvious ploy is to play notes an octave apart, but other intervals can work, as well.

A loop created in SampleOne cannot be exported directly to a loop file; it must be played and then captured as audio as described below in the section "Exporting a MIDI Loop to an Audioloop File." For more information on SampleOne, see the section "SampleOne" of chapter 4, "Virtual Instruments and MIDI" of *Power Tools for Studio One 2*, volume 1.

Making a Musicloop

There are only two steps in making a Musicloop file:

1. Assemble the loop. When it sounds good looping in the program, you're ready. Have all your sounds stored as presets and the entire loop in a single Instrument Part. If your loop is made up of several Parts, select them all and press G to merge the Parts into a single Part.
2. Drag the Part to the Sounds or Files tab of the Browser, right-click (Ctrl-click in Mac) on the Part and choose Instrument Parts > Export Musicloop from the contextual menu that drops down, or choose Event > Export Musicloop from the main menu bar. A pop-up tool tip will show whether you are about to create a Musicloop file (the default) or a Standard MIDI File (SMF). If, for some reason, the MIDI file option is selected, pressing the Option key (Alt key in Windows) will change it to the Musicloop option.

That's all there is to it. You will see your new .musicloop file in the Browser.

EXPORTING A MIDI LOOP TO AN AUDIOLOOP FILE

If you want your loop to be audio instead of performance data, you need to turn your loop into an Audioloop file. This is only another step or two beyond making a Musicloop, but the audio has to be in the form of an Audio Part before it can be made into an Audioloop file.

1. Assemble the loop. If it sounds good, it is good.
2. Select the Part(s) in the Arrange view and press Cmd + B (Ctrl + B in Windows), right-click (Ctrl-click in Mac) on the Part and choose Event > Bounce Selection from the contextual menu that drops down, or choose Event > Bounce Selection from the main menu bar. The Part will be bounced to an Audio Event on a new track, and then muted.
3. Turn the new Audio Event into an Audio Part using the Merge to Audio Part command or the Audio Bend panel to detect transients, slice, and merge to an Audio Part.

For more information on Audio Parts, see the section "Editing Audio" of chapter 6, "Advanced Editing" in *Power Tools for Studio One 2*, volume 1.

4. Right-click (Ctrl-click in Mac) on the new Audio Part in the Arrange view and choose Audio > Audio Parts > Export Audioloop…from the contextual menu that drops down, or choose Audio > Export Audioloop…from the main menu bar. A Save dialog appears.

5. Name and save the Audioloop file.

MANIPULATING LOOPS

Inserting a Loop in a Track

Audioloops, Musicloops, and REX files do not play back as loops in Studio One 2, so it is necessary to replicate a loop file in a track as many times as you want it to play. This is accomplished using a repeat paste operation. There are two ways to perform repeat pasting.

The hard way:

1. Select the material you want to repeat paste.
2. Press Cmd + C (Ctrl + C in Windows), right-click (Ctrl-click in Mac) and choose Copy from the contextual menu that drops down, or choose Edit > Copy from the main menu bar to copy the material to the clipboard.
3. Position the play location where you want the loop to start.
4. Press Cmd + V (Ctrl + V in Windows), right-click (Ctrl-click in Mac) and choose Paste from the contextual menu that drops down, or choose Edit > Paste from the main menu bar to copy the material to the clipboard.
5. Choose Transport > Locate Selection End from the main menu to move the play location to the end of the material you just pasted.
6. Repeat steps 4 and 5 as many times as desired.

The easy way is to use the Duplicate command, which combines copy-and-paste in a single command:

1. Select the items and/or ranges you wish to duplicate.
2. Press D, right-click (Ctrl-click in Mac) on a selected item and choose Duplicate from the contextual menu that drops down, or choose Edit > Duplicate from the main menu bar.
3. Repeat step 2 as many times as desired.

For more information on the Duplicate command, see the section "Duplicating Items" of chapter 5, "On the Cutting Room Floor: Basic Editing" in *Power Tools for Studio One 2*, volume 1.

SHARED COPIES OF INSTRUMENT PARTS

If you are duplicating a loop that is an Instrument Part, the duplicate is independent of the original. If you edit the contents of one, the other will be unaffected. This is usually desirable when inserting loops, as it enables you to make variations in loop repetitions. However, it is possible to create duplicates that are linked such that editing the contents of any one of them changes all of them identically. These are called shared copies. For more information on creating and using shared copies, see the section "Shared Copies of Instrument Parts" of chapter 5, "On the Cutting Room Floor: Basic Editing" of *Power Tools for Studio One 2*, volume 1.

Explode Pitches to Tracks

There are some situations in which it is helpful to take pitches on one track and separate each pitch onto its own track. One example would be a drum loop for which you might want to assign the notes for different drums to sounds produced by different virtual instruments (VIs) or different presets. Another would be if you wanted the notes of chords recorded from a keyboard performance to be sounded by different instruments. Explode Pitches to Tracks does exactly this for Parts selected in the Arrange view: each pitch played in the selected Part(s) is given its own track. To explode pitches from one track to a track per pitch:

1. Select the Part(s) you want to explode in the Arrange view. If you are selecting multiple Parts, they do not all need to be on the same track.
2. Choose Event > Explode Pitches to Tracks from the main menu bar. A track will be created for each pitch played and the notes of that pitch moved to the new track.

Transposing and Tuning Loops

TRANSPOSING AUDIO LOOPS

Each Audio Event in Studio One 2 can be individually pitch-shifted using the Transpose and Tune settings in the Audio Event inspector. This processing is real-time and nondestructive, meaning that you can experiment and change your mind at any time. This is useful both in manipulating loops you have imported, as well as in creating your own loops. It is also easy to capture the pitch-shifting if you are creating your own loop file. For more information on the Event inspector Transpose and Tune fields, see the section "Audio Event Inspector" in chapter 5, "On the Cutting Room Floor: Basic Editing" in *Power Tools for Studio One 2*, volume 1.

Studio One 2 also has integrated support for Celemony Melodyne. For more information on Melodyne integration, see the section "Melodyne Support" of chapter 6, "Advanced Editing" in *Power Tools for Studio One 2*, volume 1.

As mentioned earlier, the SampleOne virtual instrument can also be useful in situations where changing tempo and pitch together is desirable.

To transpose or tune a loop:

- Select the Event or Events in the loop and set the Transpose or Tune field in the Event inspector to the desired value(s). All selected Events will assume those values.

To create a new loop file from the pitch-shifted loop:

1. Select the Event(s) in the loop.
2. Set the Transpose and/or Tune fields in the Event inspector as desired.
3. Press Cmd + B (Ctrl + B in Windows), right-click (Ctrl-click in Mac) on the loop and choose Event > Bounce Selection from the contextual menu that drops down, or choose Event > Bounce Selection from the main menu bar. The pitch-shifted selection will be rendered to a new file, which will appear as a new Event replacing the selected material in the track.
4. Convert the new Event to an Audio Part as described in the section "Creating an Audio Part for Export" earlier in this chapter.
5. Export the new Audio Part to an Audioloop file as described in the section "Exporting to a Loop File" earlier in this chapter.

TRANSPOSING MUSICLOOPS

Studio One 2 has quite a few tools for transposition at every level: track, Part, and note. It also offers scale snapping, which quantizes pitches to a chosen scale. Because Musicloops show up in tracks as Parts and are created from Parts, I only discuss transposing Parts here. For more information on transposing performance (MIDI) data, see the section "Transposing MIDI" of chapter 6, "Advanced Editing" in *Power Tools for Studio One 2*, volume 1.

THE TRANSPOSE DIALOG

The Transpose dialog can be used with selected notes in a Part in the Edit view, or on entire Parts in the Arrange view, though it offers few advantages over transposing a Part using the Transpose field in the Event inspector. However, transposition executed using the Transpose dialog box is reflected visually in the Edit view, which moves the notes to their new pitches, while the Transpose field in the Event inspector does not.

To transpose Parts using the Transpose dialog:

1. Select the Part(s) in the Arrange view that you want to transpose.
2. Right-click (Ctrl-click in Mac) on a Part and choose Transpose from the contextual drop-down menu that appears, or choose Event > Musical Functions > Transpose from the main menu bar. The Transpose dialog box will appear.
3. To transpose the selection by one or two octaves, simply click on one of the preset buttons in the Add/Subtract area in the top half of the dialog box.

4. To transpose the selection by some other number of semitones, drag the slider in the Add/Subtract area until the desired transposition is displayed, or simply click in the Transposition Amount field and enter the desired transposition value.

5. To set all notes in the selection to a single pitch, drag the slider in the Set All To area until the desired pitch is displayed, or simply click in the Set All To field and enter the desired note to which the selection should be transposed.

6. After setting the desired transposition, click on OK to execute the transposition.

Timecode Follows Loop

This setting determines how Studio One 2 acts when sending timecode from Studio One 2 to external devices equipped to sync to it while looping. The timecode can jump back when the loop does (Timecode Follows Loop is checked), or continue to be generated linearly (Timecode Follows Loop is unchecked), ignoring that the Song has actually looped back in time. By default, Timecode Follows Loop is active.

• To change how timecode addresses are transmitted when looping, open Preferences > Options > Advanced > MIDI and check or uncheck the Timecode Follows Loop box.

Working with Video 2

Studio One 2 offers video (movie) playback and basic capabilities for locking sound to picture. Note that Studio One 2 allows you to hear and/or import the audio from a movie, but it cannot save a movie with your finished audio.

Generally, when working to picture you will want to set the time base for your Song to Frames, so that the timeline corresponds to the picture location. Work to picture must be done by locking audio to the Video Player; it is not possible to lock Studio One 2 to an external timecode source.

QUICKTIME

Studio One 2 uses QuickTime as its video engine. This means that:

1. Studio One 2 can play any video format and codec that QuickTime can play, and that's a lot. One list of compatible formats and codecs is here: http://support.apple.com/kb/HT3775

2. There long have been QuickTime components available that have added codecs to those QuickTime could play natively, but the most prominent of these on the Mac, Perian, is no longer being developed.

3. While QuickTime is part of the Mac OS, you must download and install it on Windows machines. You can get it here http://www.apple.com/quicktime/download/.

TIP: Bear in mind that Apple often relocates information on its website, breaking old links. If any of these links do not work, search on the Apple site and you should be directed to a functioning link.

Once QuickTime is properly installed and functioning on your machine, Studio One 2's use of it will be completely transparent to you. Studio One 2 uses QuickTime on both Mac and Windows, running either 32-bit or 64-bit. One idiosyncrasy to be aware of as of version 2.5 is that, when running Studio One 2 as a 64-bit Mac application, it is not possible to extract the audio track from a movie.

THE VIDEO PLAYER WINDOW

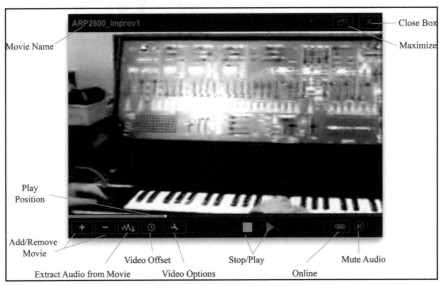

Fig. 2-1: The Video Player window.

Opening and Closing the Video Player Window

Open the Video Player window using any of these methods:

- Click the Video Player button in the Arrange view toolbar. The button is near the right side of the Song page, so you may need to widen the window if the button is not currently visible.
- Choose View > Video Player from the main menu bar.
- Import a movie into the Arrange view, as described below, and the Video Player window automatically opens. It will not open if you import into the Pool.

Close the Video Player window using any of these methods:

- Click the close box in the upper right corner of the Video Player window.
- Choose View > Video Player from the main menu bar to uncheck it.

Video Player Toolbar

All Video Player features are accessed from the toolbar at the bottom of the window. Unusually, none of this functionality is available elsewhere in the program.

The controls are all named in Fig. 2-1, but they are explained below in the context of how they are used, rather than having a section dedicated to each control.

Importing a Movie

IMPORTING A MOVIE INTO THE VIDEO PLAYER

Movies must be loaded into the Video Player to play. If no movie is loaded, when the Video Player is opened you will see a message that says (logically enough), "Movie Not Loaded." You can import a movie into a Song and load it into the Video Player using any of the following methods:

- Drag a movie file in a QuickTime-compatible format from the Files tab of the Browser to the track area of the Arrange view.

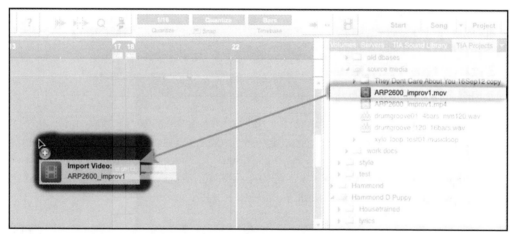

Fig. 2-2: Dragging a movie from the Browser into the Arrange view loads it into the Video Player window.

- Drag a movie file in a QuickTime-compatible format from the Mac Finder or Windows Explorer to the track area of the Arrange view.
- Click the + (plus) button in the Video Player window and navigate to the movie in the dialog that opens.

Fig. 2-3: Click the + (plus) button to load a movie into the Video Player.

Note that you cannot drag a movie directly into the Video Player window.

Importing a movie to the Video Player when a movie is already loaded simply replaces the existing movie with the new one. The existing movie is unloaded from the Video Player,

Fig. 2-4:
Click the
– (minus)
button to
unload a
movie from
the Video
Player.

but still available in the Pool. You can also choose to unload a movie without replacing it with another movie. An unloaded movie can be reloaded, if desired, by dragging it from the Pool into the Arrange view.

• To unload a movie, click the – (minus) key on the left end of the Video Player toolbar.

MOVIES IN THE POOL

Like audio files, movies that have been imported into a Song can always be found in the Pool. Movies can be added to the Pool and loaded into the Video Player from there. Adding a video to the Pool does not automatically load it into the Video Player.

To import a movie into the Pool, use either of these methods:

• Drag a movie file in a QuickTime-compatible format from the Mac Finder or Windows Explorer to the Pool in the Browser.

• Navigate to the movie in the Files tab of the Browser: Right-click (Ctrl-click in Mac) on it, and choose Import to Pool from the contextual menu that drops down.

To ensure that the movie (and all files used in the Song) are copied to the Song's Media folder, rather than referenced in their current locations, right-click (Ctrl-click in Mac) in the Pool, and choose Copy External Files from the contextual menu that drops down.

Sizing the Window

To size the Video Player window, use any of these methods:

• Move the mouse cursor over the lower right corner of the Video Player window until it turns into a finger, then drag to the desired size. Note that the image does not stretch, but maintains its aspect ratio. That means that stretching the window very wide when the video image is close to square will result in an image whose size is determined by the window height, which would be the shorter dimension.

Fig. 2-5: Effect of stretching the Video Player window.

- Click on the Video Options button in the lower left corner of the window and select Half Size, Default Size, or Double Size from the menu that drops down.
- Click the Maximize button in the upper right corner of the window to make it full screen. Clicking the Maximize button when the window is maximized returns it to its original size.

PLAYING MOVIES

Video Player Play/Stop Controls

Video playback is buffered to make it easier for Studio One 2 to keep picture and sound in sync. You might sometimes notice a brief hesitation in the start of movie playback while the buffer is filled, but as soon as that is done the picture will catch up to the sound.

- To start playback of a movie, click the Play button in the bottom center of the Video Player window. This button is entirely independent from playback of the tracks and starts only movie playback.

Fig. 2-6: The Movie Player Play button is independent of the Play button in the Transport bar, and starts only the movie playing.

Playing Movies and Tracks Together (Audio/Video Sync)

When you are working with movies, you will usually want to play the movie and the tracks in your Song together in sync with each other. To make audio and video play in sync:

Fig. 2-7: The Online button in the Video Player window makes picture and sound play in sync.

- Click the Online button (with the link icon) in the lower left of the window, if it is not already engaged. The button is colored blue when Online is engaged, and it is engaged by default. Starting playback of the Song now simultaneously starts playback of the movie (subject to the Video Offset, as explained in the next section, "Setting or Editing an Offset"), and the two are locked together.
- Clicking the Play button in the Video Player will not start playback of the Song. In fact, if the Video Player is not online, it is possible to start the Song playing and then click the Video Player Play button, with the result that the Song and the movie both play, but independently and not in any strict relation to each other.

Setting or Editing an Offset

There are many circumstances in which it is necessary for picture and sound to start playing at different times. Often, this is done to make some internal point in the sound match up to a particular frame of the movie. The difference in their start times is called an offset.

The offset represents the start time of the video relative to that of the tracks; a positive offset means the movie plays later than (lags) the tracks, whereas a negative offset means the movie plays earlier (leads) the tracks. The offset is expressed as a timecode, in hours:minutes:seconds:frames (hh:mm:ss:ff). The number of frames depends on the timecode format. For more information on timecode in Studio One 2, see the section "It's All About Timebase" in chapter 1, "On Your Mark," in *Power Tools for Studio One 2*, volume 1.

Set or edit an offset between movie and track playback times using either of these methods:

- Click the button with the clock icon to open the Video Offset window and enter a value. The range of frames values is determined by the frame rate chosen in the Preferences > Song Setup > General > Frame Rate field. Click in any field to make it active and enter the desired value. Use Tab to go between fields, or just click in another field to make it active and edit it. Click the OK button to apply the change.

- Click the button with the clock icon to open the Video Offset window, click any field to make it active, and use the + (plus) and – (minus) keys on the number pad to increment or decrement the value. Click the OK button to apply the change.

Fig. 2-8: The Video Offset window.

Muting Movie Audio

If the movie you have imported has an existing soundtrack, it can play when the movie does, in which case it is mixed with the tracks that are playing, or the audio in the movie can be muted. To mute the audio track in a movie:

Fig. 2-9: The Mute Audio button mutes the existing audio track in a movie file.

- Click the button with the icon of a speaker inside a circle with a slash in the lower right of the toolbar. The button is colored red when the audio is muted, which it is by default.

EDITING TO PICTURE

As audio for picture is all about the relationship between audio and video, Studio One 2 provides tools for scrubbing the picture while the play location follows (audio follows video) and for nudging audio and video together (video follows audio).

Scrubbing Video and Nudging

To scrub the movie and have the play location follow:

- Check that Online is engaged in the Video Player and drag the Play bar in the Video Player left or right to scrub the video earlier or later.
- With Online engaged, use any locating technique and the movie will follow. If the location point is before the start time of the movie (i.e., less than the Video Offset value), the movie will go to its first frame. For more on locating techniques, see the section "Locating" in chapter 3, "Go! Recording with Studio One 2" in *Power Tools for Studio One 2*, volume 1.

Video can also follow a marker being dragged, as described in the section "Using Markers with Video" below.

To nudge audio and have the video position follow:

1. Be sure that the Timebase field in the Arrange view is set to Bars.
2. Set the Quantize setting to the desired nudge duration.
3. Be sure that the Snap box is checked.
4. Set the Snap Type to Quantize.
5. Set the Snap Reference to Snap to Grid.
6. Press Option + Right Arrow (Alt + Right Arrow in Windows) or choose Edit > Nudge > Nudge from the main menu bar, or Option + Left Arrow (Alt + Left Arrow in Windows) or choose Edit > Nudge > Nudge Back from the main menu bar, to nudge the selected items later or sooner (respectively) in time by the Quantize value.

Using Markers with Video

Markers are an important resource when working to picture. Markers can be placed at locations where specific visual events needing sound, called hit points, occur in the movie. Here are a few tips for using markers with video; for more information on markers, see the section "Markers" in chapter 3, "Go! Recording with Studio One 2" in *Power Tools for Studio One 2*, volume 1.

- Markers can be "spotted" on the fly; that is, dropped into the Song while the Song and movie are playing. You might play through the entire movie, or maybe just part of it, dropping markers everywhere that you see a significant visual event you want to score with sound. It is usually necessary to go back and adjust the positioning of markers dropped on the fly to get the location exactly right.
- A more precise method of placing markers is to scrub the picture to the exact location where the marker should be while the movie is stopped, then drop a marker. This is slower than dropping markers on the fly, but eliminates the need to go back and adjust marker positions.

- When dropping markers at hit points, be sure the time base of the Marker track is set to lock the markers to absolute time locations. For more about this, see the section "The Marker Track" in chapter 3, "Go! Recording with Studio One 2" in *Power Tools for Studio One 2*, volume 1.

POSITIONING A MARKER BY DRAGGING WITH PICTURE CHASE
The simplest way to reposition a dropped marker to a precise moment in the picture is to drag the marker to the desired location while the picture follows the marker position.

To make video chase a marker while it is dragged, do either of the following:

- Click the Cursor follows Edit Position button in the Arrange view toolbar.
- Choose Options > Cursor follows Edit Position from the main menu bar.

Fig. 2-10: The Cursor follows Edit Position button makes picture chase a marker as it is dragged.

Note that it is actually the play location, not the mouse cursor, which is following the edit position.

EXTRACTING AUDIO FROM A MOVIE

If there is an existing audio track in an imported movie, it can be very useful to have direct access to it. To do so, the audio track must be extracted from the movie and placed into its own track.

Extract an audio track from a movie and place it in a new track using any of these methods:

Fig. 2-11: The Extract Audio button puts any existing movie soundtrack onto its own new track.

- Hold down the Cmd key (Ctrl in Windows) while dragging a movie into the Arrange view to extract audio from the movie to its own track without importing the video.
- Hold down the Option key (Alt in Windows) while dragging a movie into the Arrange view to import the movie and extract audio from the movie to its own track.
- Click the Extract Audio button (with the waveform icon) in the Video Player toolbar to extract audio from a movie loaded into the Video Player to its own track.

SAVING A MOVIE WITH NEW AUDIO

Studio One 2 does not allow saving movies with new audio. To integrate your audio into a movie, you must export the audio as a mix and then use a third-party application to integrate your new soundtrack into it. QuickTime Pro, in Mac or Windows, is likely the cheapest way to do this. (Okay, somebody knows where to download a free utility I don't know about…) Of course, nearly any video editing program that can work with QuickTime files can do this, too.

Mixing

WHAT IS MIXING?

Some would say that, next to writing a song, mixing is the most important step in recording. Whether you agree with that or not, the fact is, mixing is certainly a critical phase in production. Being as it's so important, let's be clear about what mixing is.

I like to use a cooking analogy. All of your tracking, overdubbing, sequencing, and editing amounts to gathering and prepping the ingredients for a dish. To say that mixing is simply balancing all of the recorded elements in the song is akin to saying that cooking a dish is nothing more than dumping the ingredients in a pan and heating them.

No, mixing is much more than that. Here are just some of the tasks that go into mixing:

- Level balancing
- Placement in the stereo sound field (panning)
- Tone shaping (EQ, etc.)
- Dynamic modification (compression, gating)
- Effects processing
- Ambience or reverb
- Stereo image enhancement

Of course, every mix does not require all of these things. Some mixes might be very simple, especially if a realistic, documentary style is the order of the day. Other mixes can be extremely elaborate and take a very long time to complete.

Mixes are often complicated by one or more of the processes being dynamic; for example, a guitar track that is at one level when it is behind vocals in verses, at another level when it plays a trademark riff during choruses, and at a third level for a solo. This is where automation comes in. Automation is the subject of the next chapter, but it is so much a part of mixing that it will pop up in spots throughout this chapter, as well.

Many people focus on the tools of mixing. These tools certainly are vital, but of equal importance are the monitoring environment, which determines how you hear your mix, and the process you use for mixing (which can vary widely from person to person and mix to mix). This is a chapter on mixing, not a book on it, so I will touch on these subjects, but not go into real depth. These are very deep subjects, though, and a great deal of information on them is available from a multitude of sources. I strongly encourage you to explore these sources and read as much as you can, then try out the things that seem interesting or apply to your work. After a while you will evolve your own style of mixing and gain a deeper understanding of how all of the pieces fit together.

SIGNAL PATHS AND ROUTING

At first blush, mixing could seem to be all about a single path that signals follow, coming into the mixer separately and being combined into the final (usually) stereo mix. Nothing could be further from the truth. In fact, mixing involves dozens of signal paths for various purposes: effects sends, submixes, parallel processing, and as many more as your imagination can devise.

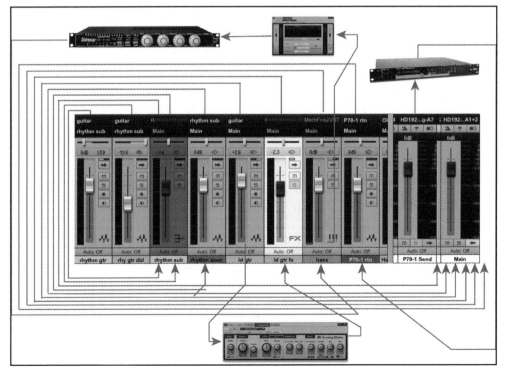

Fig. 3-1: A mix involves many different signal paths.

Mastering the concept of signal paths and the routing used to move signals through them as needed is a critical mixing skill. Understanding signal paths and routing is necessary for troubleshooting, solving creative problems, incorporating outboard processors, adding flair to your mixes, and, of course, determining what the final mix actually contains.

Virtual and Physical Inputs and Outputs in the Mix

One of the most important and powerful signal routing concepts in Studio One 2 (or any other audio software, for that matter) is the relationship between the software world of Studio One 2 and the physical world in which microphones, loudspeakers, and outboard processors exist. Inputs and outputs in the physical world appear as connectors on your audio and/or MIDI interfaces, whereas Studio One 2 has virtual inputs and outputs that are simply conceptual data routing schemes with no existence in the physical world.

As we have discussed in both this book and in *Power Tools for Studio One 2*, volume 1, the physical and virtual input and

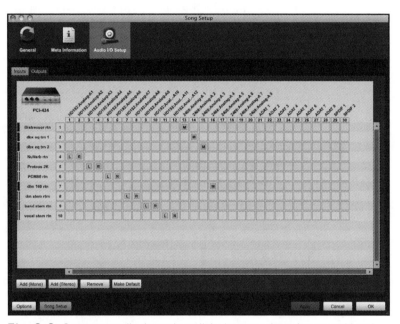

Fig. 3-2: Computer audio depends on links between the software world and the physical world. The Audio I/O Setup pane is one of the primary places this happens in Studio One 2, as it is where audio interface inputs and outputs are mapped to those created in Studio One 2.

output worlds meet in the Preferences > Song Setup > Audio I/O Setup pane, where the Inputs and Outputs tabs enable you to create, delete, and name virtual inputs and outputs, and route physical inputs and outputs to and from them. (Naming interface inputs and outputs is usually done in the control software provided by the interface manufacturer.)

But signal routing is not limited to connecting the physical and virtual worlds. Putting a reverb plug-in on an effects send, for example, is accomplished purely through software connections, specifically channel sends and FX or Bus channels. Similarly, submixing involves only routing channel outputs to a Bus channel and from there to the Main output. So, signal routing can involve hardware and software connections, or software connections only.

How does all this come into play in mixing?

The greatest emphasis on the meeting of the physical and virtual worlds comes when recording basic tracks and overdubbing, whereby microphones and electronic keyboards feed into the computer and software-generated headphone mixes need to come out. Software-only connections exist, but generally play a lesser role in this application.

Mixing flips this around. Physical I/O is used primarily for incorporating outboard processors, monitoring, and, possibly for final output if, for instance, you like to mix through a summing box and/or to analog tape instead of exporting a mix. Software-only connections, on the other hand, are used for all of the other purposes already mentioned: submixing, effects sends (for plug-in effects), virtual instrument (VI) returns, parallel processing, and so forth.

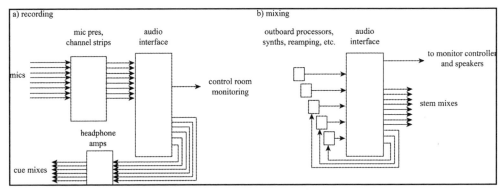

Fig. 3-3: During recording, interface I/O is used mostly for signal inputs and cue mix outputs. In mixing, interface I/O use is for integrating outboard gear, monitoring, and, sometimes, multichannel or stem outputs.

Software routing is not handled in a single pane, as are interface inputs and outputs, so there is no one place to go and see all of the routing. However, in many mixes so many different signal paths are in use that any display of the whole system would be incomprehensible anyway. This means that a lot of routing must be kept in your head. The fact that buses, inputs, and outputs can be all be named in Studio One 2 is what keeps the entire situation orderly, so be sure to take the time to name every signal path component as you set it up.

What Is a Bus?

Although we have been talking about buses and Bus channels quite a bit, this is a good time to discuss what a bus actually is. Simply put, a bus is nothing more than a signal path on which numerous signals can be combined. Sound familiar? Yup, each bus is just a separate mix. In fact, a traditional term for the final mix output on old-school analog mixing consoles was "the 2-mix bus," because Studio One 2's Main output is just a bus, albeit a special one.

Here are some of the uses for buses in Studio One 2:

- Effects sends: All of the buses in a Song appear in a drop-down menu in the Sends area of a channel. Each bus is returned into a Bus or FX channel with an effect inserted on it.
- Submixes: With a lot of channels going in a mix, it often becomes easier to handle the situation if related channels are combined into submixes before reaching the final mix.
- Folder track outputs: In the header of a Folder track is a field that accesses the bus list. Selecting a bus from the list routes the outputs of all tracks in the folder to the selected Bus channel. This is a very convenient way to create a submix.
- Stem mixing: Wait…why can't you just use the Export Stems command for stem mixing? Answer: Because Export Stems doesn't actually export stems, it exports individual tracks. *Stem* is just film-mixing terminology for a kind of final submix. Exporting stems instead of, or in addition to, a final stereo mix, is a technique that has also caught on in music-mixing circles. For information on how to do stem mixing in Studio One 2, see the section "Mixing Tips, Techniques, and Applications" later in this chapter.
- Parallel processing: One or more channels can be fed using channel sends to a Bus channel. The Bus channel, with one or more processing plug-ins inserted, is brought into the main mix alongside the original channels, creating a parallel signal path.

PREFADER/POSTFADER SENDS

When using channel sends, the option exists either to feed the bus with the signal after it has passed through the channel fader, or before. The difference is in the independence of the send: with a prefader send, the channel fader can be pulled all the way down and the bus will still receive signal from that channel, whereas the level going to the bus from a postfader send will vary as the channel fader is adjusted. For more information on prefader and postfader sends, see the section "Working with Sends" later in this chapter.

THE MIXING ENVIRONMENT

The mix you produce is shaped, if not determined, by your mixing environment. The oversimplified definition of the mixing environment I will use here consists of these three things:

- Monitoring: Loudspeakers, the room, and monitoring levels.
- Mix control: Do you mix with the mouse, a control surface, or both?
- Tools: Well, that's what most of this chapter is all about.

Monitoring

In the end, no one cares what microphones you recorded with, what plug-ins you used in your mix, or how many channels you had going. What people care about is how the music sounds; and if it sounds good, it is good. Sound, then, should be foremost in your mind when you are mixing. I don't mean digital signals or waveforms, I mean sound: moving air.

If your speakers lie to you, if your room obscures the truth, if you forget or ignore the fact that we hear differently at loud levels than at soft levels and differently over headphones or earbuds than over loudspeakers, then your mix will not be successful, which is to say that it won't sound the way you want. And you may not even find that out until it's too late and the damage is done. Get the message? Monitoring is critically important and worth all the attention and money you can afford to invest. Let's look at a few of the biggest concerns.

MONITOR LOUDSPEAKERS

Loudspeakers for studio monitoring are not like those you have in your house for listening. Their purpose is not to make music sound good; that's your job. The job of studio monitors is to render the signal as accurately as possible. Any coloration added to the sound by the speakers influences how you mix. Effectively, you are unintentionally mixing through an effects processor, which corrupts every judgment you make in mixing. Not good.

Loudspeakers are transducers, which means that they transform energy from one form to another. In the case of loudspeakers (and microphones), four forms of energy are actually involved: electricity, magnetism, mechanical motion, and acoustical. The upshot of this conversion activity is that loudspeakers are actually very inefficient devices, and it is darned hard to make them accurate. For a loudspeaker to be considered accurate, it must perform well in these regards:

- Frequency response: As commonly used, this term refers to the amount of variation in output from the loudspeaker at different frequencies given the same level of input at each of those frequencies. If a speaker puts out much less at 60 Hz than it does at 2 kHz, given the same level and type of 60 Hz and 2 kHz input signals, it does not have an accurate frequency response.

- Dynamic response: An accurate loudspeaker will exhibit the same response when playing loudly as it does when playing softly. We don't hear the same at loud levels as at soft levels, and the room you are in will respond differently at loud levels than at soft levels, but ideally, the loudspeaker should be the same in each situation.

- Time response: You've heard lots of talk about phase, and maybe you've found it confusing. Many discussions of phase are just plain factually wrong, which contributes to the confusion. (For instance, the so-called phase buttons found on many hardware and software mixing consoles have nothing whatsoever to do with phase. They actually control polarity reverse, a concept subtly but significantly different than phase.) Well, phase is actually nothing more or less than time delay. Generally, we use the term *phase* to discuss very short time delays, but one could correctly refer to a delay of three days as a phase difference! Loudspeakers can suffer phase corruption from many sources: mechanical, electronic, mathematical, and acoustical. Phase accuracy is one of the most difficult attributes to get right in a studio monitor. But there are other kinds of time response inaccuracies, too, such as transient response.

- Distortion: Literally, any difference between the sound that comes out of the loudspeaker and the signal that went in is distortion. Once again, distortion can be generated in numerous ways. It might be level overload of electronics, flaws in the mechanical movement of the loudspeaker driver, even just trying to have many different frequencies reproduced by a single driver can produce distortion.

All in all, making a loudspeaker that does well in all of these areas is a very difficult thing to do, which is why good studio monitors are expensive. When an inexpensive loudspeaker is advertised as a studio monitor, it is worth a careful and skeptical examination before you put your money down.

LOUDSPEAKERS AND TRANSLATION

But there's another part to the story of studio monitors. Although accurate monitors tell you how your mix really sounds, only visitors to your studio will actually hear your mix over studio monitors. Everybody else will be listening over earbuds, car speakers, computer speakers, or maybe home stereo speakers, none of which sound anything like your glorious monitors.

So how do you make a mix that sounds perfect in all of those different playback environments? Sadly, the answer is you can't. "Oh," say you, "then what in the world am I supposed to do?" The solution is compromise. You need to have some understanding of how your mix sounds in a variety of situations, and adjust the mix to achieve the best results possible across the greatest number of playback environments. A mix that sounds decent across a number of reproduction systems is said to "translate well."

There are two tactics for accomplishing good mix translation. One is that some studio monitors have the property of translating well. When it sounds good on a monitor that translates well, it is likely to sound good on many other systems. Why do some studio monitors translate well and others don't? I dunno. Maybe a speaker designer could tell you. Maybe not. Either way, engineers learn to correlate how what they hear from their monitors will translate to other systems.

The other tactic is much simpler and more obvious: If you want to know how your mix sounds on a number of systems…listen on a number of systems! They don't have to be accurate; in fact, the funkier the better. Studios usually have "rock and roll" monitors for this purpose, notably the infamous Yamaha NS-10M monitors. Listen in your car (studios have been known to have low-power, pirate FM transmitters so you can hear how it actually sounds when broadcast), on earbuds, use the built-in speakers in a computer monitor, take it to your house and listen there. Go to friends' houses and listen. The more places you listen, the better. Note the things that seem wrong in each environment and make adjustments back in the studio. I suggest using a light touch, though, because you are deliberately listening in bad environments.

Keep in mind that some things just can't be helped: your "big bass" mix just won't have big bass on earbuds because they simply are not capable of reproducing lots of low bass.

MONITOR PLACEMENT

Where monitors are located relative to the mix position is crucial. Ideally, loudspeakers should be in an equilateral triangle with the listening position. Many people mix with their monitors on a shelf just a couple of feet from their head. While many, many excellent mixes have been produced with this setup, there are a number of potential problems, including reflections off a mixing console or other surface directly in front of you or having the point at which sound from the monitors focuses fall well behind the listening position.

With small monitors, close-field monitoring such as this is logical, but with slightly larger, higher-powered monitors (for the sake of discussion I'll say this means monitors with a woofer 8 inches across or larger), midfield monitoring of 5 to 6 feet from the listening position will often give better results.

ROOM TREATMENT

The room in which you mix could arguably be considered the most important factor of all in getting a good mix. If your recordings are done with great mics and mic preamps, your software and plug-ins are all first-rate, and you have great studio monitors, but your room is acoustically horrible, you won't have any clue what your mix really sounds like.

Unfortunately, few of us can afford rooms with proper acoustical construction, and, worse, very few even consider it a priority to try to treat the room to improve the acoustics. Big mistake.

Most musicians understand the value of using material that absorbs sound, but many think that the more absorption there is in the room, the better it sounds. This is not so. Although absorption reduces many reflection effects, too much absorption makes the room feel too dry and gives it a "hushed" quality.

Less understood by musicians is diffusion, which occurs when sound strikes a complex surface. The sound is reflected, but not directly; it is broken up and sprayed around the room. While it is possible to buy excellent diffusers from a variety of sources, many common items found in a room, such a shelf filled with books, can provide very good diffusion. The best rooms for recording and mixing are not entirely dead with absorption, but also include some diffusion to keep some liveness. (Recording and mixing rooms will need different proportions and placement of absorption and diffusion.)

Plain old, garden-variety reflection is rarely something that needs to be added to a room, but it is not always evil. The key to the role of reflection in a mixing room is that it should not compete with the sound from the loudspeakers. First reflections from walls that reach the ear shortly after the sound from the loudspeakers can create imaging and coloration problems, but a little exposed wall area that creates reflection near the back of a room, for instance, might be no problem at all.

Next to avoiding too much absorption, the next most important thing to remember about room treatment is that everything in acoustics is frequency-dependent. An absorptive panel is effective over a range of frequencies, but no panel absorbs over all audible frequencies. Bass frequencies, in particular, need dedicated room treatment. Similarly, diffusers are typically effective at mid and high frequencies, but that is where they are most needed.

Absorption and diffusion are certainly not the only considerations in determining how your room affects your mixes. Room layout is also vital. Symmetricality is important, too: your mixing position should be as centered as possible, not close to one side wall. Avoid large obstacles, such as tall equipment racks, close to the mixing position.

There are many sources of information on room treatment, but not all of them give good information. I suggest consulting a number of different sources and paying particular attention to the ideas that recur across most or all of them.

Room treatment, like studio monitors, is one of the few areas of mixing that actually deal with sound. It is worth paying time, attention, and money to room layout and treatment.

MONITORING LEVEL

How loud should you be listening when mixing? Is there one proper monitoring level? It is common in creative pursuits, such as mixing, for there to be no single, correct answer to questions of technique, but there are considerations, points of comparison, and even some benchmarks for monitoring level.

As I have already stated, many things change with level: our perception, loudspeaker response, and room response, to name three of the biggest factors. While all of these are worth paying attention to, perception is really the most important of them. Human hearing is most sensitive to midrange frequencies, in large part to enable us to understand speech. At low levels, we don't hear high or low frequencies as well as at higher levels.

Let's use a little logic to decide which is better. If you listen loud while you are mixing, when you play your mix back at lower levels, it will seem deficient at both the high and low ends of the spectrum. On the other hand, if you mix mostly at low levels, when you turn it up it will have even more high and low end. Generally, people find high and low frequencies to be physically satisfying, so it seems that mixing mostly at low levels makes the most sense.

However, we face a situation similar to that of loudspeaker translation, in that listening at any one level exclusively narrows the circumstances under which the mix will sound good. Once again, variety is the answer. While low-level monitoring is what you should be doing most of the time, checking your mixes at both lower and higher levels gives the most complete picture of your mix.

Listening at high levels is very satisfying and good to do when you think you have a mix that is working nicely and want to get a "vibe" playback. Even more can be gained by listening at extremely low levels, however. One trick many engineers (including myself) use is to do some listening with the level so low the music is barely audible and notice which instruments are heard and which disappear. If the vocal, snare drum, and most important instrument (whether that is a trademark rhythm part or a lead instrument) can be heard, your basics are in place. As we have already said we don't hear high and low frequencies as well at low levels, there's no reason to be alarmed if the bass is not audible at such a low level.

By listening at different levels *and* on different loudspeakers, you will effectively be taking a broad survey of playback conditions that will give you a well-rounded sense of your mix. While level balance is the most obvious attribute that is revealed in this way, the impact of EQ, effects levels, and other aspects of the mix also become more apparent.

BENCHMARKING AT 85 (OR MAYBE 83)
There is no standard level for monitoring, but film mixing has long used a reference level of zero on the master meter producing an acoustical level of 85 dB SPL at the mixing position. The figure of 83 dB SPL was first proposed by Dolby, a company that has often strived to establish consistent references for production and, especially, film mixing. However, that reference level came to find broader use, including in music mixing. For the sake of convenience, many people use 85 dB SPL instead. While 2 dB is a noticeable difference in level, both 83 and 85 dB SPL are used as reference levels today, and either will work.

Again, it should be said that this is a good reference level, but by no means should it be the only level at which you ever work. In fact, some find 85 dB SPL to be uncomfortably loud as an average level. Still, it is a good practice to set up your monitoring system so that you can easily return to an 85 dB SPL reference level.

CALIBRATING YOUR MONITORING LEVEL
Setting up monitor level calibration using Studio One 2 is actually quite simple:

1. Create a new Song. Dedicating a Song to calibration keeps things simple and eliminates any possibility of confusion or problems that could arise by using a Song that has musical material in it.
2. Create a Bus channel.
3. Set your monitor level to very low or off.
4. Instantiate the bundled Tone Generator plug-in as an insert effect on the Bus channel and set it to generate the desired test signal. The Tone Generator plug-in is described in the section "The Tone Generator Plug-In" later in this chapter.
5. Set the plug-in and channel controls so that the meter on the Main output shows signal at zero on the scale.
6. With your measuring device held at ear level in the listening position, slowly raise the monitoring level until the measuring device shows a level of 85 dB SPL.
7. Mark the monitor level control so you can easily restore it to its current position.

The Tone Generator plug-in offers a variety of different test signal options. Which is the best to use? Probably the most popular for calibration purposes is pink noise. White noise contains all frequencies in equal amounts; pink noise is white noise weighted to have a slight rise in level in the amount of low frequencies. While white noise is statistically accurate, it does not reflect the fact that humans don't hear low frequencies as well as they do mid and high frequencies. Pink noise is intended to more closely reflect the sensitivity of human hearing. Some, notably well-known mastering engineer Bob Katz, contend that pink noise should be further modified by limiting its overall bandwidth.

Characteristics of human hearing must be accommodated on the measurement end, as well, so measurement of the reference level is often done using C weighting. A, B, and C weighting are discussed in the section "A, B, and C Weighting" later in this chapter.

Measuring monitoring level requires a calibrated system. It is quite tricky to calibrate a typical recording system, so it is best to use an outboard metering system. Many meters for measuring SPL are available, ranging from a ninety-nine-cent iPhone app, through a wide range of handheld instruments, all the way up to measurement tools costing thousands of dollars.

The old standby has always been a sound level meter from Radio Shack: http://www. radioshack.com/product/index.jsp?productId=12680845.

In general, the range for decent meters seems to start around $100, but the Radio Shack meter and one or two others are lower. Keep in mind that differences in cost of test and measurement gear usually correlate directly to the precision with which the measurement is made. Now remember that the *entire* point of making a measurement is accuracy, and it becomes clear the question is always how much accuracy is necessary for the measurement you are making. In the case of monitoring levels, absolute precision is not necessary, but I would hesitate to rely on an iPhone app for monitor calibration.

A, B, and C Weighting

There is much confusion about A, B, and C weighting, but it's really quite simple. They are three EQ curves applied in measurement devices to make their results more closely resemble what people hear. If you are making a measurement that is totally unrelated to perception (such as calibrating the output level of a device to be the same as its input level), then weighting curves are of no use to you. However, monitoring level calibration is all about human perception.

The idea behind having three curves is to reflect that human perception varies with level. A weighting was intended for environments where the measured level is relatively low, B was aimed at medium levels, and C weighting is for louder signals. A weighting saw (and still sees) tremendous use in environmental measurements, such as ambient noise levels in a community. Because such measurements are conducted very often, A weighting has always

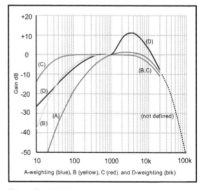

Fig. 3-4: The A, B, and C weighting curves were designed to make measurement results more closely match human perception. There are three curves to accommodate the variations in hearing sensitivity with level.

been the most used of the three curves, eventually often being applied even to louder signals for which it is not appropriate. For most audio production purposes, C weighting is the best fit, and so is often used when setting monitoring levels.

K-System

Devised by the aforementioned mastering engineer Bob Katz of Digital Domain, the K-System takes into account the headroom demands of different types of material in three presets:

- K-20: Provides for 20 dB of headroom, and is intended for music with wide dynamic range, such as orchestral music or film scores for theatrical presentation
- K-14: Provides for 14 dB of headroom, and is intended for pop music and most home applications
- K-12: Provides for 12 dB of headroom, and is intended for broadcast material, and other applications where audio generally is heavily compressed

Of course, these are guidelines, not hard-and-fast rules, so you should always choose the preset that is appropriate to the material with which you are working. The headroom is achieved simply by designating that the zero mark on the meter be at a level below the maximum signal that can be recorded.

If this was simply a matter of setting the zero point on a meter, however, it would accommodate headroom needs but would provide a rather inaccurate and not very useful monitoring situation, because the same monitoring level would show up differently on the meter for each preset. The key is to calibrate your monitoring environment to always produce the same acoustical level for zero on the meter, regardless of the preset.

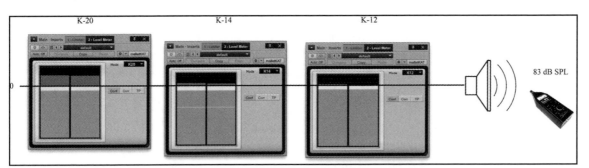

Fig. 3-5: The K-System is based on using differing amounts of metering headroom depending on the type of material, but, in all cases, setting zero on the meter to an acoustic output of 83 dB SPL.

TIP: The K-System specifies metering and requires that it be calibrated to acoustic output of the monitors. Because Studio One 2 does not control the level of your monitoring system, K-System presets cannot calibrate the entire system for the selected preset; they can only change the metering. When you select a K-System preset for a meter, you must manually calibrate the monitor level.

If you find yourself needing to use different K-System presets on a regular basis, try creating a Mixtool plug-in preset that applies an appropriate amount of gain for each K-System preset. For instance, let's say you often like to work with the K-14 preset. If you have calibrated zero on the meter to be 83 dB SPL, use a Mixtool preset with –2 dB of gain for the K-12 preset, and one with +6 dB of gain for the K-20 preset.

The K-System is a great way to deal with metering, but, on the whole, it fits more easily into mastering than in multitrack work, in part because most Studio One 2 mixer channels do not offer the K-System on their standard meters. Use caution when mixing K-System presets on Output channels with peak/rms scales on the other channel types, as it can mean expending a good deal of thought just to keep everything straight, especially if you are working quickly. Of course, you can always insert K-System metering on any channel with the Level Meter plug-in. When all channels use K-System metering, there should be no confusion.

There are three simple steps to implementing the K-System:

1. Access the K-System presets. For an Output channel, right-click (Ctrl-click in Mac) on the meter to bring up the contextual drop-down menu, which includes the presets. In the bundled Limiter plug-in, clicking one of the buttons below the metering reveals the presets. In the Level Meter plug-in, click the Conf (Configuration) button and click in the Mode field to see them.

2. Choose the preset most appropriate for the source material you are monitoring.

3. Set your monitoring level so that 0 on the meter produces 83 dB SPL at the mixing location, as described in the section "Calibrating Your Monitoring Level" earlier in this chapter.

Fig. 3-6: The K-System presets are available for Output channels simply by right-clicking (Ctrl-clicking in Mac) on the channel meter.

Listening Through "Final" Processing

During mixing, engineers are very concerned with how the material will sound when played back in the real world. I have already discussed loudspeaker translation in this regard, but it is common for mixes to receive additional processing before a listener hears the material. This might be additional gain maximization applied by a mastering engineer or as part of a broadcast (air, satellite, or Internet) signal chain.

To understand how that processing will affect the mix, it is common to insert a simulation of such processing on the Main output. How that processing gets used varies according to taste. Some engineers like to do most of their mixing through this "final" processing, occasionally bypassing it just to check what the "naked" mix sounds like, whereas others do the opposite, mixing mostly without the processing, but kicking it in now and then to check its impact. I tend toward this second school, because there is no guarantee your simulated processing in any way accurately reflects what will happen to your mix when it gets out into the cold world.

The one thing you do want to be sure of is that processing in the signal path purely for the purpose of simulating what might happen to the mix, is bypassed or removed before the final mix is exported or otherwise created. This is very important!

Mono Compatibility

Even today, there are situations where your mix will be listened to in glorious mono. Now, more than ever before, a multitude of mixing tools and techniques can result in significant changes in the mix if it is summed to mono. Thus, engineers will commonly check their mixes in mono as they go along.

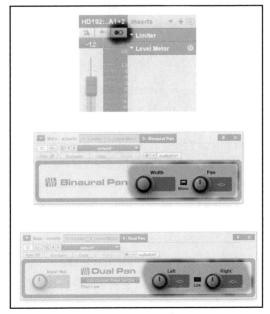

You can always choose to ignore cancellations and other artifacts that occur with mono summing, but, even if you make that choice, it is best to at least know the impact of it.

- To check for mono compatibility in Studio One 2, click the Channel Mode button on the Main output channel. When the button is engaged, it is colored red, indicating that the mix has been summed to mono.

- The Binaural Pan and Dual Pan plug-ins also both have facilities for folding a stereo channel down to mono.

Fig. 3-7: Signals can be put into mono with the Channel Mode button on Main Out (top), or in the Binaural Pan (middle) or Dual Pan (bottom) plug-ins.

Note that summing to mono still results in a two-channel output, but the same signal appears on both channels. Be sure to remember to disengage the Channel Mode button before you do your final mix export!

SETTING UP TO MIX

Mixing is a complex operation that goes smoothest when the way is prepared before mixing begins. Most of the preparation amounts to configuring Studio One and your Song.

Although it can take a surprising amount of time to do all of the following tasks, much more time is saved by the clarity and performance they promote.

Reset the Buffer Size

The Device Block Size field, found in the Preferences > Options > Audio Setup pane, is the buffer size parameter mentioned often in discussions of DAWs. When recording, it is best to set the buffer as small as possible to reduce latency, but when mixing, it is advisable to set it to a large value. A larger buffer demands less attention from your computer, leaving more processing power free for plug-ins, real-time processing, and other mixing facilities. I use a buffer size of 512 samples for mixing. For more information on this important parameter and how to set it, see the section "Understanding Buffer Size" in chapter 2, "Get Set to Record" of *Power Tools for Studio One 2*, volume 1.

Fig. 3-8: The Device Block Size field is important. Put briefly: Set it shorter for recording to reduce latency, and longer for mixing to ease processor strain.

Configure Interface I/O

When recording, most interface audio inputs are used for signals entering the computer, and outputs are mostly for monitoring. In mixing, interface I/O is used either to incorporate outboard processing gear, or to output the mix or mix stems.

Some needs will always arise in the moment, but if you have pieces of outboard gear you usually use, making both the physical and virtual connections in advance simplifies using that gear almost to the point that it is easy as using a plug-in.

You can choose to return outboard effects into Bus channels, but it is prudent to return them to Audio channels, so that their output can be captured into the Song. This makes it possible to execute mix adjustments at a later time when that equipment (or even simply the preset you are using) may not be available.

Monitoring Level Control

It is important to have a control for your monitoring level that follows the master fader, but is not part of the mix signal path. This allows you to check your mix

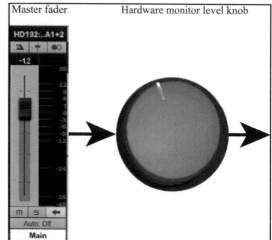

Fig. 3-9: A monitoring level control follows the master fader, but is not part of the mix path.

loud, soft, or anywhere in between, with no impact on the mix itself. Analog consoles have always had a Control Room level knob for this purpose.

A physical hardware control is what is needed for this purpose. Creating a monitoring level control in software is too tricky to be practical, and it is very difficult, if even possible, to grab and move a software control quickly enough if there is an urgent and immediate reason that the level needs to be turned down.

Many monitor control devices are available. I use PreSonus' Monitor Station, but there is also Mackie's Big Knob, Focusrite's VRM Box, and selections from Coleman Audio, Dangerous Music, and others.

Configure a Control Surface

If you are using a control surface to mix, there may be some configuration that can be done in advance to smooth the way. Although basic mixer functions, such as fader level, pan, solo, and mute, rarely need to be specifically configured, control of plug-ins may be another story. As with configuring interface I/O, you can't anticipate everything, but you probably have some favorite plug-ins (especially bread-and-butter EQ and compression) you know you are likely to use, and mapping controls to those plug-ins before you start mixing reduces the need to stop in the middle of a creative gesture to make a configuration.

Mix Organization

I'll say it one more time: The more you organize before you start, the more you can concentrate on creative concerns and not get slowed by technical overhead (although some techno-tweaking is unavoidable). The smartest method is to take the time to configure a Song the way you most often work and save it as a template. That way, a lot of your mix organization is in place from the moment you start recording, even if you don't use it until you get to the mix.

SIGNAL PATHS
Although a song or album can be quite different from any other you've worked on, most of us have methods we gravitate toward fairly regularly. Set them up in advance and you can always delete them if you don't need them. Here are some signal paths you might want:

- Submixes: I use drum, guitar, and vocal submixes in most tunes I do. In the case of drums it is because of the number of mics and the processing used; in the case of guitars, because there are usually effects and at least two tracks of guitar; in the case of vocals, because it can be nice to group lead and background vocals in a single submix. Create the Bus channels and route the channel outputs to them.

- Effects: Snare reverb, parallel compression on kick and snare, vocal delay—these are a few of the things I use often, so I create Bus channels for them. I might even instantiate the plug-in, if I have a feeling for which one I'm likely to want. I tend to set up send effects in advance more often than I set up insert effects.

• Outboard processors: To use an outboard processor as an insert effect (such as a nice analog compressor), instantiate the Pipeline plug-in and configure interface I/O for it. For send effects, set up the output channels to send to them and the Bus or Audio channels for their returns.

Studio One 2 will not let you create a feedback loop, for example, by routing buses, so don't be afraid to work fast when configuring your mix in advance.

NAMING

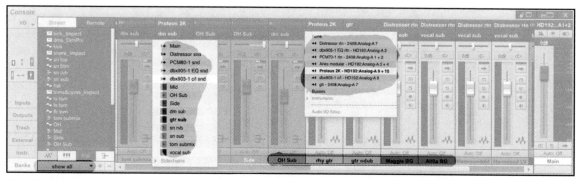

Fig. 3-10: Channels, inputs, outputs, and Console Scenes are all clearly named. Yes, it takes a lot of time to name everything, so do it once and save it as a template, and you'll thank yourself always.

While you are setting up all of those signal paths is the time to name them. Naming is painstaking work, but the gain from it cannot be overstated. Audio channels, Bus channels, Folder tracks, Automation tracks, interface I/O. Name them all. If you have alternative takes on different layers that you intend to evaluate in context while mixing, be sure to name those layers, too (if you did not name them when you recorded them). I put asterisks at the end of a layer name to mark it as the best take or the layer to use.

If you are using a control surface that has "scribble strip" displays, observe how it abbreviates names and take that into account as you name channels.

LAYOUT AND VIEW CONTROL
CHANNEL LAYOUT

A logical layout for channels will prove its value time and again while mixing. I tend to put all my submix Bus channels on the right side of the mixer, so they are near the Main output. Toward the left, I put channels contained in each submix next to one another. Bus channels with effects and FX channels go next to their source channels.

I use a lot of Folder tracks to collect related tracks under one "umbrella." Channels corresponding to tracks in a Folder track automatically appear next to one another in the mixer, which saves some configuration time.

When I start a mix, I spend a lot of time with individual channels on the left, but as the mix proceeds, I shift more and more attention to the submix masters on the right.

Fig. 3-11: A logical channel layout is essential to efficiency. This channel layout puts channels for recording stem mixes (only a few are showing) on the far right near the Main Out, submix masters just to their left, and individual tracks extending all the way to the left end. Dedicated effects, such as snare reverb, are grouped with the tracks that feed them.

VIEW CONTROL

When there are a lot of channels in a mix, you can spend a lot of time scrolling around to find the channels you want to work with. Often, you will be working with a relatively small subset of channels for a while, then move on to another subset. For example, you might start by working on drums, then move to vocals, then guitars, and so forth.

By controlling what is visible at any given time, visual clutter can be reduced, which helps maintain focus. There are several facilities for view control in Studio One 2:

- Folder tracks: Collapsing a Folder track gets a whole collection of tracks out of the way at once.
- Banks panel: This panel can control visibility of Audio, Instrument, FX, and Bus channels, individually or in groups by channel type.
- Console scenes: Console scenes are presets for the Banks panel, a snapshot of which channels are shown and which hidden. Set up console scenes in advance for drums, vocals, or guitars and instantly restrict your view to those channels by selecting a scene from the drop-down menu.
- Mix View panels: Show or hide Input and Output channels with buttons in the Console Navigation column on the left of the Mix view.
- Arrange View Track List: The Track List can be linked to the mixer so that they show the same thing. Well, almost. Automation and Folder tracks have no channels in the mixer, whereas Bus and FX channels have no tracks in the Arrange view. Once linked, selecting either a Track List preset or Console Scene changes both views.

THE MIX VIEW

The Mix view is where most of the mixing action happens. (Other important locations for mixing are Automation tracks and lanes, control surfaces, and plug-in editor windows.) The Mix view is often called the "Console" in Studio One 2. In *Power Tools for Studio One 2*, volume 1, I tried to avoid this inconsistency and talked about the "Mix view" or, when I was referring strictly to the section with channel strips, "the mixer." While that terminology was more consistent, it was at odds with the program UI where the term "Console" was used. It's a tough call, and in this volume I'm going to handle it a little differently. Hopefully, it will be more, rather than less, clear to you.

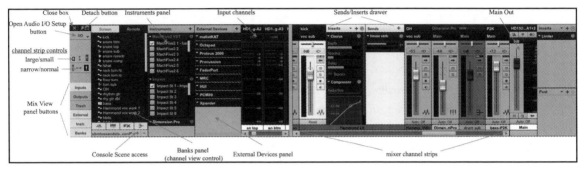

Fig. 3-12: The Mix view.

The mixer is the main area of the Mix view (Console). It contains channels for each Audio track and audio return channels for Instrument tracks. Note that there can be more than one Instrument channel for a single Instrument track, if the instrument being played is multichannel (has multiple audio outputs available) and more than one output is being used. For more information on multichannel instrument audio returns, see the section "Showing and Hiding Channels with the Mix View Panels" later in this chapter.

Opening, Closing, Detaching, and Reattaching the Mix View

With the exception of the close box in the following list, the methods for opening the Mix view are toggles, so any of these methods will open the Mix view if it is currently closed and close it if it is currently open:

- Press the F3 key.
- Click the Mix view select button below the Browser. The button is colored blue when the Mix view is open and gray when it is closed.
- Choose View > Console from the main menu bar. The command is checked in the menu when the Mix view is open and unchecked when it is closed.
- Like other panels and views, the Mix view can be detached and moved around independently, however, the detach button is located with the close box on the left side of the view, rather than on the right as with other panels and views.
- To detach the Mix view, click on the Detach button in the upper left corner next to the close box. The arrow on the Detach button will now point down and left.

Fig. 3-13: The Mix view select button.

Fig. 3-14: The Mix view can also be closed by clicking on the close box in its upper left corner.

Fig. 3-15: The Mix view Detach button.

- To reattach an editor to the integrated environment, click on the Detach button (if the arrow is pointing downward).

Sizing the Mixer

The mixer can be sized when it is detached, or set to large channel strips:

- To size the mixer vertically when it is set to large channel strips: Position the cursor over the top border, above the Inserts section, until the cursor icon turns to a double-headed arrow, then drag up or down to the desired height. You will encounter a minimum height if you are dragging down.

- To size the mixer vertically or horizontally when it is detached: Position the cursor over any border, until the cursor icon turns to a double-headed arrow, then drag up or down (from the top or bottom border) or left or right (from the left or right side border) to the desired size. You will encounter a minimum height if you are dragging down from the top or up from the bottom.

- To size the mixer vertically and horizontally simultaneously when it is detached: Position the cursor over any border, until the cursor icon turns to a hand with a pointing finger, then drag in any direction to the desired size. You will encounter a minimum height if you are dragging down from the top or up from the bottom.

Mix View Channel Types

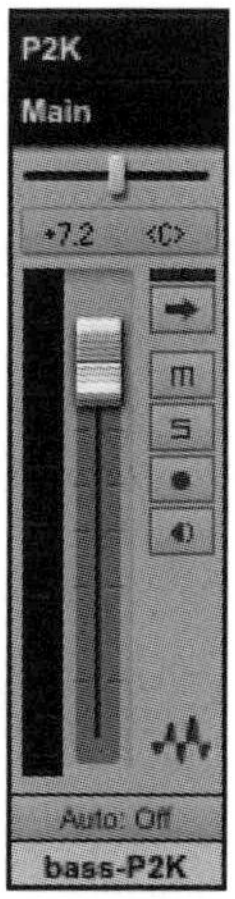

Studio One's mixer is populated first and foremost by channels. Mixer channels provide facilities for routing, combining, controlling such basics as level and pan, and adding both corrective and creative processing.

Fig. 3-16:
A stereo
Audio
channel.

TIP: Only Audio channels provide a one-to-one correspondence between tracks in the Arrange view and channels in the Mix view. Automation and Folder tracks do not show up as channels in the mixer, Instrument tracks may use more than one channel, and Bus and FX channels have no corresponding tracks.

AUDIO CHANNELS

Audio channels are the audio outputs of Audio tracks. There is a direct, one-to-one correspondence between Audio tracks in the Arrange view and Audio channels in the Mix view. In addition to Audio Events, Audio tracks can also contain automation data for their corresponding Audio channels.

INSTRUMENT CHANNELS

Instrument channels are the audio outputs of virtual instruments (VIs). VIs are played by MIDI/performance data in Parts on Instrument tracks, which also can contain automation data both for the VI itself (which may include some audio parameters), and for the Instrument channels.

Fig. 3-17: An
Instrument
channel.

BUS CHANNELS

Bus channels receive the outputs from submix or effects send buses. The output of a Bus channel can be routed to an output channel or another bus, including effects (usually compressor) sidechain inputs. Buses are also available as inputs to stereo Audio tracks, which is the easy way to capture audio from a Bus channel.

Busing facilitates subgrouping; for example, routing a background vocal submix and a lead vocal to a master vocal submix. The flexibility of Bus channels makes them particularly powerful tools. Bus channels are colored a darker gray than Audio or Instrument channels. For more information on buses, see the section "What Is a Bus?" earlier in this chapter.

FX CHANNELS

FX channels differ from Bus channels primarily in that FX channels have inserts but no Sends section. This is reflected in the fact that there is only a single indicator above the drawer open/close button. FX channels are colored the same dark gray as Bus channels.

Fig. 3-18: A Bus channel.

Fig. 3-19: An FX channel.

Fig. 3-20: An Input channel.

INPUT CHANNELS

Input channels bring audio from physical inputs into the mixer, by way of the Inputs tab of the Preferences > Song Setup > Audio I/O Setup pane, where physical inputs are mapped to Studio One 2's virtual inputs. Each input defined in Audio I/O Setup has a channel strip in the mixer (when the Inputs button in the Console Navigation Column is active) and appears in the list of Input channels available in the drop-down menu of the Input Select field on every Audio and Instrument channel in the mixer.

Input channels have a very different appearance than other channels. There are no channel strip controls at all on an Input channel, only the Input Select field, a meter, and the channel name.

OUTPUT CHANNELS

Output channels connect to physical outputs, by way of the Preferences > Song Setup > Audio I/O Setup pane, where physical outputs are mapped to Studio One 2's Output channels. Each output defined in Audio I/O Setup has a channel strip in the mixer (when the Outputs button in the Console Navigation Column is active) and appears in the list of Output channels available in the drop-down menu of the Output Select field on every Audio and Instrument channel in the mixer.

Output channels have a different appearance than Audio, Instrument, Bus, and FX channels, but, unlike Input channels, they do have some channel strip controls. Some of these controls are unique to Output channels, such as Post (postfader) inserts, which they have in place of sends, and metronome controls. They also have special metering options, which are discussed further in the section "Metering" later in this chapter.

Fig. 3-21: An Output channel.

Fig. 3-22:
Main Out.

MAIN OUT

Main Out is a special Output channel that is the default output for all other channels in the mixer. Generally, Main Out is the output used for monitoring and exporting the final mix. The position of the Main Out channel is fixed on the right end of the mixer. Aside from the two attributes of its position and it being the default output destination, Main Out is like any other Output channel.

Showing and Hiding Channels with the Mix View Panels

Channels can be made visible and invisible in groups or individually. Once you've selected a set of channels you want to see, you can store the selection as a preset. Presets make it easier to be looking only at the set of channels you need to work on at a different time.

INPUTS AND OUTPUTS

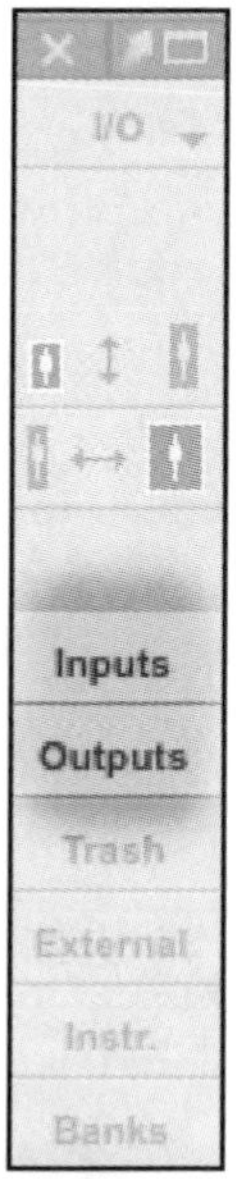

Input and Output channels can only be hidden or shown as a group, not individually.

- To show or hide all Input channels in the mixer, click the Inputs Mix View panel button in the Console Navigation Column on the left of the Mix view. When the button is colored blue, the Input channels are visible on the left of the mixer.
- To show or hide all Output channels in the mixer, click the Outputs Mix View panel button in the Console Navigation Column on the left of the Mix view. When the button is colored blue, the Output channels are visible on the right of the mixer, just to the left of the Main Out.

Fig. 3-23:
The Input and Output Mix View panel buttons show and hide Input and Output channels.

BANKS MIX VIEW PANEL

The Banks Mix View panel has two tabs: Screen and Remote. The Screen tab controls onscreen visibility of channels. The Remote tab is designed for use with control surfaces employing the HUI protocol. For more information about the Remote tab of the Banks Mix View panel, see the section "Mixing with Control Surfaces and MIDI Controllers" later in this chapter.

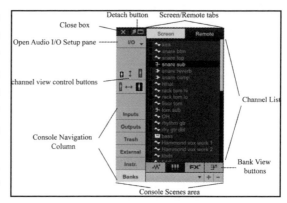

Fig. 3-24: The Banks Mix View panel.

There are three sections to the Screen tab: the Channel List, Banks view buttons, and the Console Scenes area.

THE CHANNEL LIST

The Channel List is a complete list of channels other than Input and Output channels. It can optionally display mini level meters and/or channel numbers on each line of the list. The visibility of mixer channels is set on an individual basis in the Channel List.

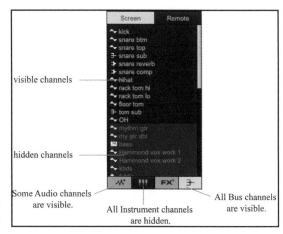

Fig. 3-25: Channels visible in the mixer are colored blue in the Channel List, while hidden channels are gray. Note the blue-gray Bank View button, indicating one or more hidden channels of that type.

- To show or hide an individual channel in the Channel List, click on its name. The line for the channel in the list is colored blue when the channel is visible, and gray when the channel is hidden. In addition, a Bank View button turns a blue-gray color when one or more channels of the type it controls are hidden.

- To show or hide mini level meters for all lines in the list, right-click (Ctrl-click in Mac) in the Banks panel and select View > Levels from the contextual drop-down menu that appears. These meters can really clear up the mystery when you are hearing channels that you're not seeing because they are hidden in the mixer.

- To show or hide channel numbers for all lines in the list, right-click (Ctrl-click in Mac) in the Banks panel and select View > Channel # from the contextual drop-down menu that appears.

Fig. 3-26: Mini level meters and channel numbers can be made visible by right-clicking (Ctrl-clicking in Mac) in the Banks panel.

BANK VIEW BUTTONS

The four Bank View buttons along the bottom of the Channel List are essentially an extension of the Mix View buttons in the Console Navigation Column, in that they show or hide all channels of the indicated

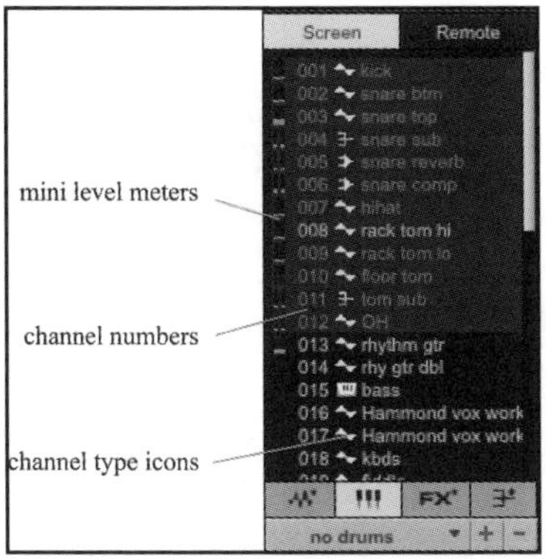

Fig. 3-27: Here the drum tracks are hidden in the mixer, but activity on them is indicated by the mini level meters in the Screen Channel List of the Banks panel.

Fig. 3-28: The Bank View buttons control visibility of Audio, Instrument, FX, and Bus channels (from left to right).

type: Audio, Instrument, FX, or Bus. If you are uncertain of the meaning of the icons, hovering the cursor over any button will make a tool tip appear that identifies the channel type controlled by that button. Don't be confused by the pop-up tool tip saying "Tracks" on the Audio channels button.

- When a Bank View button is colored blue, all channels of the indicated type are shown in the mixer. Click the button to hide all channels of that type.
- When a Bank View button is colored black, all channels of the indicated type are hidden. Click the button to show all channels of that type.
- When a Bank View button is colored blue-gray, one or more channels of the indicated type are currently hidden. Click the button to show all channels of that type.

Note that when one or more, but not all, channels of a type are hidden, it is not possible to preserve that selection in the list when switching to showing or hiding all of them. For example, if two Audio channels are hidden, hiding all Audio channels requires clicking the Audio Channel Bank View button twice: once to show all Audio channels, the second to hide them all.

CONSOLE SCENES AREA

The Console Scenes area allows creating, selecting, and deleting presets, each of which is a snapshot of which channels are shown in the mixer and which hidden. Console scenes (called "channel banks" in the Studio One 2

Fig. 3-29: The Console Scenes area.

manual) make it easy to switch between viewing selected sets of channels. For instance, you might have one Console scene for all drum channels, one for vocal channels, and one that is only submix Bus channels. This would make it easier to focus on each of these groups as you work on them.

To save a Console scene:

1. Click the + (plus) button to open the Store Preset dialog.
2. Enter a name into the Store Preset dialog that opens, and click the OK button. The preset name will appear in the Scene Select field in the Console Scenes area.

Fig. 3-30: Console Scenes are stored by the Store Preset dialog.

To select an existing Console scene:

1. Click in the Preset Select field and choose the desired Console scene from the drop-down menu that appears. If no menu appears, there are no saved Console scenes.

TIP: Console scenes store only the visibility of each channel. They do not capture which tab is selected or the visibility of level meters or channel numbers in the Channel List. Restoring a scene to the Remote tab originally made on the Screen tab changes only the channels on the Remote tab, restoring their visibility to that stored in the scene. In that situation, nothing on the Screen tab is affected.

To delete a Console scene:

1. Be sure the scene you want to delete is the currently active scene. If it is not, click in the Scene Select field and choose the desired scene from the drop-down menu that appears.

2. When the desired scene name is visible in the Scene Select field, click the – (minus) button. The scene will be deleted without a confirmation dialog, so be careful not to accidentally click this button.

LINK TRACK AND CONSOLE IN TRACK LIST

It is often convenient to show and hide a track in both the Tracks area of the Arrange view and the Console in the Mix view at the same time.

To link showing and hiding channels in the Arrange and Mix views:

Fig. 3-31: The Link Track List/Console button at the bottom right of the Arrange view Track List locks the Track List with the mixer, so that hiding a track hides the corresponding channel, and vice versa.

1. Open the Arrange View Track List by clicking on the Track List button above the track headers in the Arrange view.

2. Click the Link Track List/Console button at the right end of the Channel Type toolbar at the bottom of the Track List. Now, tracks or channels can be hidden or shown either in the Track List or the Banks panel in the Mix view and the change will be reflected in both views.

- Showing or hiding a Folder track in the Track List shows or hides all corresponding channels in the Console.

- If a Folder is collapsed, the tracks in it are unaffected by showing or hiding their corresponding channels in the Console. This makes it possible for the Arrange and Mix views to get out of sync, even when they are linked.

- Instrument tracks in the Track List are linked to their corresponding channels in the Channel List. Showing/hiding a track has the same effect on the channel and vice versa.

- For multitimbral VIs, showing or hiding any track in the Track List playing the VI causes the VI's first two audio outputs to be shown or hidden. Say there is a track playing an acoustic guitar sound on a sampler, which comes out the VI's first stereo pair of audio outputs, which are returned to a stereo Instrument channel. Another track on a different MIDI channel plays an electric guitar sound on the same sampler, which comes out the VI's second stereo pair of outputs and returns to another stereo Instrument channel. Hiding either track in the Track List hides the Instrument channel for the acoustic guitar sound in the Console, while the electric guitar channel is left unaffected.

Mix View Panels 2: More Mixer Configuration Features

The Mix View panels area has still more to offer in determining what you see in the Mix view. Channel strips can be set to be narrow or normal, vertically expanded or compact. External instruments and VIs can be configured from Mix View panels, and the Trash panel offers a powerful (and occasionally life-saving) mixer undo path.

EXTERNAL DEVICES PANEL

An External Device is any physical device that talks to or is talked to by Studio One 2. That includes control surfaces, keyboards, percussion controllers, sound modules, MIDI-controllable outboard processors, and so forth. The External Devices panel provides a single access point from which you can manage External Devices.

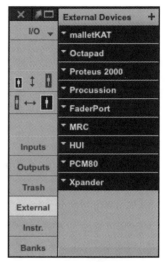

- To open the External Devices panel: Click the External button in the column of panel show/hide buttons in the Console Navigation Column on the left of the Mix view. The button will turn blue to indicate the panel is visible and a list of all External Devices currently known to Studio One 2 will appear.

- To add an External Device to Studio One 2 from the External Devices panel: Click the Add Device button with the + (plus) icon in the top right of the External Devices panel. The Add Device dialog will appear. For more information on using the Add Device dialog, see the section "Defining Your MIDI Devices and Control Surfaces" of chapter 1, "On Your Mark" in *Power Tools for Studio One 2*, volume 1.

Fig. 3-32: The External button in the Column Navigation List on the left, and the External Devices panel on the right.

- To edit the setup of an existing External Device: Click the arrow next to the device's name in the External Devices panel or right-click (Ctrl-click in Mac) on the device's name and choose Setup from the drop-down menu that appears. The Edit Device dialog will appear and the setup defined when the device was added can be changed as desired.

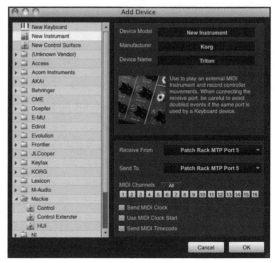

Fig. 3-33: The Add Device dialog.

- To open the Device Controller Map for an External Device: Double-click the device's name in the External Devices panel, click the arrow next to the device's name in the External Devices panel and choose Edit from the drop-down menu that appears, or right-click (Ctrl-click in Mac) on the device's name and choose Edit from the drop-down menu that appears. For more information on Device Controller Maps, see the section "Using Hardware Controllers with Studio One 2: Control Link" of chapter 4, "Virtual Instruments and MIDI" in *Power Tools for Studio One 2*, volume 1.

Fig. 3-34: A Device Controller Map for an External Device.

- To edit the Device Controller Map for an External Device with a Device Controller Map window open: Click the tab at the top of the window for the device you wish to edit. Its Device Controller Map will appear.

- To remove an External Device from Studio One 2: Click the arrow next to the device's name in the External Devices panel or right-click (Ctrl-click in Mac) on the device's name and choose Remove from the drop-down menu that appears. Note that External Devices are not local for each Song, but global for Studio One 2. Removing an External Device from the External Devices panel means that it will no longer show up at all in any Song in Studio One 2.

INSTRUMENTS

The Instruments panel displays all VIs instantiated in the current Song. Note that an instrument can be instantiated in the Song, but not used by any track.

- To open the Instruments panel: Click the Instr. button in the Console Navigation Column on the left of the Mix view. The button will turn blue to indicate the panel is visible and a list of all VIs currently instantiated in the current Song will appear.

Fig. 3-35: The Instruments Mix View panel shows all VIs instantiated in the current Song. It is also the place to enable and disable output channels in multichannel instruments.

- To add an instrument to the Instruments panel: Drag the instrument or a preset for it from the Browser to the Instruments panel, or click the Add Instrument button with the + (plus) icon in the top right of the Instruments panel and choose an instrument from the drop-down list that appears. If necessary, drag the scroll bar on the right of the list to locate the desired instrument in the list. Note that adding an instrument to the Instruments panel does not create a track for it in the Arrange view. A grayed-out instrument name in the Instruments panel indicates that no track in the Song currently uses that instrument.

- To deactivate an instrument: Click the Activate button to the right of the instrument's name in the Instruments panel. The button will turn gray to indicate that the instrument is no longer active, and the processing resources used by the instrument will be released. To reactivate the instrument, click the Activate button again. The button will turn brown to show that the instrument is active.

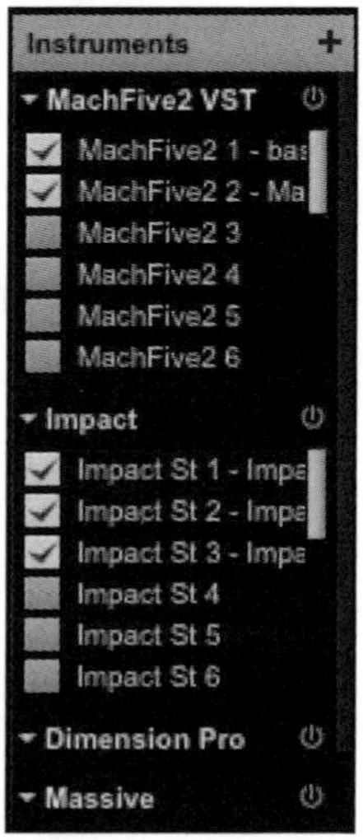

- To expand an instrument's display in the Instruments panel: Click the instrument's name in the Instruments panel, click the arrow to the left of the instrument's name and choose Expand from the drop-down menu that appears, or right-click (Ctrl-click in Mac) on the device's name and choose Expand from the drop-down menu that appears. If the instrument has multiple audio outputs available, or some other feature, such as a Bypass button, those options will appear below the instrument's name. Because not all instruments have such features, expanding the display for an instrument without appropriate features will have no visible effect.

- To collapse an instrument's display in the Instruments panel: Click the instrument's name in the Instruments panel, click the arrow to the left of the instrument's name and choose Collapse from the menu that drops down, or right-click (Ctrl-click in Mac) on the device's name and choose Collapse from the drop-down menu that appears. Multiple outputs and other features will disappear.

Fig. 3-36: Expand an instrument's display to access additional audio outputs, when they are available. Here, MOTU Mach Five and PreSonus Impact have both been expanded for output access.

- To open an editor window for an instrument: Double-click on the device's name in the Instruments panel, click the arrow next to the device's name in the Instruments panel and choose Edit from the drop-down menu that appears, or right-click (Ctrl-click in Mac) on the device's name, and choose Edit from the drop-down menu that appears. For more information on Instrument editor windows, see the section "The Device (Plug-In and Instrument) Editor Header" in chapter 5, "On the Cutting Room Floor: Basic Editing" in *Power Tools for Studio One 2*, volume 1.

- To open an editor window for an instrument when a Device editor window is already open: Click the tab at the top of the window for the device you wish to edit. Its editor window will appear.

- To rename an instrument from the Instruments panel: Click the arrow next to the device's name in the Instruments panel and choose Rename from the drop-down menu that appears, or right-click (Ctrl-click in Mac) on the device's name, and choose Rename from the drop-down menu that appears. The Rename Device dialog will appear.

- To store a preset for an instrument in PreSonus' proprietary .preset format: Click the arrow next to the device's name in the Instruments panel and choose Store Preset… from the drop-down menu that appears, or right-click (Ctrl-click in Mac) on the device's name, and choose Store Preset…from the drop-down menu that appears. The Store Preset dialog will appear. Enter a name and description for the preset and click the OK button to save the preset in Studio One's preset management system. For more information on saving presets, see the section "Preset Access" of chapter 5, "On the Cutting Room Floor: Basic Editing" in *Power Tools for Studio One 2*, volume 1.

- To add a track for an instrument from the Instruments panel, drag the instrument from the Instruments panel to the track area of the Arrange view. A new track will be created and assigned to the dragged instrument.

- To remove an instrument from the current Song, click the arrow next to the device's name in the Instruments panel or right-click (Ctrl-click in Mac) on the device's name and choose Remove from the drop-down menu that appears, or, if the Trash Bin panel is open, drag the instrument from the Instruments panel to the Trash Bin panel.

Fig. 3-37: All good dogs may go to heaven, but all deleted mixer parts go to the Trash Bin.

TRASH BIN PANEL

The Trash Bin panel adds some very powerful undo capabilities to the mixer. Any time a channel, plug-in, or VI is removed from the mixer, it gets added to the Trash Bin. Any item in the Trash Bin can be restored to its previous state at any time, with its configuration and all parameter settings intact.

- To open the Trash Bin panel: Click the Trash button in the column of panel show/hide buttons on the left of the Mix view. The button will turn blue to indicate the panel is visible and a list of all channels, plug-in effects, and VIs that have been removed from the current Song will appear.

- To restore a single item from the Trash Bin: Right-click (Ctrl-click in Mac) on the item in the Trash Bin panel that you wish to restore and choose Restore from the drop-down menu that appears.

- To restore multiple items from the Trash Bin simultaneously: Shift-click to select a range of items in the Trash Bin, or Cmd-click (Ctrl-click in Windows) to add individual items to the selection, right-click (Ctrl-click in Mac) on any selected item, and choose Restore from the drop-down menu that appears. All selected items will be restored to their respective previous states.

- To add a new item from the Trash Bin to the Song: Select an item in the Trash Bin and drag it to the Arrange or Mix view. A new item with the configuration and parameter settings of the item in the Trash Bin will be instantiated.

Fig. 3-38: The Trash button opens the Trash Bin, enabling access to deleted mixer items.

- To permanently remove a single item in the Trash Bin from the Song: Right-click (Ctrl-click in Mac) on the item in the Trash Bin panel that you wish to remove and choose Delete from the drop-down menu that appears.

- To permanently remove multiple items in the Trash Bin from the Song simultaneously: Shift-click to select a range of items in the Trash Bin, or Cmd-click (Ctrl-click in Windows) to add individual items to the selection, right-click (Ctrl-click in Mac) on any selected item, and choose Delete from the drop-down menu that appears.

- To permanently remove all items in the Trash Bin from the Song: Right-click (Ctrl-click in Mac) below the last item in the Trash Bin and choose Empty Trash Bin from the drop-down menu that appears.

Fig. 3-39: All items can be removed from the Trash Bin by clicking below the last item in the bin and choosing Empty Trash Bin from the drop-down menu that appears.

NARROW/NORMAL-WIDTH CHANNELS

The mixer can be compacted by making the channels narrow. Narrow channels come at the cost of having fewer controls accessible, but when you are editing, or even recording, it can be important to be able to show the largest number of channels, or to have the mixer take up less space onscreen. Channels cannot be switched individually; all channels are either narrow or normal.

- To toggle all Console channels between normal and narrow widths, click the Narrow/Normal button in the Console Navigation column.

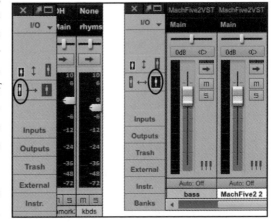

Fig. 3-40: Channel strips can be set to be Normal or Narrow width by the Normal/Narrow button.

SMALL/LARGE CHANNEL STRIPS

Channels can be viewed with the Inserts and Sends sections located vertically above the rest of the channel strip, instead of accessing them by opening the channel's Inserts and Sends drawer.

- To display large channel strips with Inserts and Sends at the top, click the Large/Small button in the Console Navigation column.

When the mixer is showing large channel strips with narrow channel widths, the top of the strip shows the level meter, rather than the Inserts and Sends section.

- To see the Inserts and Sends section when the mixer has large, narrow channel strips: Double-click on the meter and the Inserts and Sends section will replace the meter.
- To see the channel meter when the mixer has large, narrow channel strips: Double-click in the Inserts and Sends section (other than directly on a plug-in) and the meter will replace it.

Contextual Menu

The mixer is littered with contextual menus. Here's what you can find in them. I've tried to indicate commands that only show up in certain areas of the Mix view.

- Hide (Audio, Instrument, Bus, and FX channels): Choosing this command hides the channel in the mixer. To make it visible again, click the channel name in the Banks > Screen Mix view panel. If the Link Track List/Console button at the bottom of the Arrange view Track List is engaged, hiding the channel also hides the track, and vice versa. In that case, visibility can be restored in the Track List as well as the Banks > Screen tab.

- Show in Console: This command only appears when right-clicking (Ctrl-clicking in Mac) on a track header, Track inspector, or the Banks Mix View panel (Screens and Remote tabs). Choosing this command when right-clicking (Ctrl-clicking in Mac) on a track reveals the mixer channel associated with it. It can also be invoked by selecting the track and choosing Track > Show in Console from the main menu bar.

Fig. 3-41: The Large channel display puts the Inserts and Sends sections above the rest of the channel strip, instead of opening in a drawer on the channel strip's right.

- Show Track (Audio channels): Choosing this command when right-clicking (Ctrl-clicking in Mac) on an Audio channel reveals the track in the Arrange view associated with it.

- Group Selected Tracks/Dissolve Group (Audio tracks): This command groups all selected Audio channels and their associated tracks in the Arrange view. It works the other way, too; select tracks in the Arrange view and group them, choose this command, and the corresponding channels are grouped.

- Add Bus for Selected Tracks: This is an extremely useful command that actually should be called "Add Bus for Selected Channels," because it concerns routing in the mixer, not tracks in the Arrange view. To add a bus for selected channels: Select any combination of Audio, Instrument, Bus, or FX channels, right-click (Ctrl-click in Mac) on any channel, and choose Add Bus for Selected Tracks from the contextual menu. A new Bus channel is created and the outputs of all selected channels are routed to it.

- Add Bus Channel: Available in contextual menus almost everywhere in the mixer, other than those brought up by right-clicking (Ctrl-clicking in Mac) directly on a control, this command simply creates a new Bus channel with nothing assigned to it.

- Add FX Channel: Available in contextual menus almost everywhere in the mixer, other than those brought up by right-clicking (Ctrl-clicking in Mac) directly on a control, this command simply creates a new FX channel with nothing assigned to it.

- Audio I/O Setup: Available in contextual menus almost everywhere in the mixer, other than those brought up by right-clicking (Ctrl-clicking in Mac) directly on a control, this command opens the Preferences > Song Setup > Audio I/O Setup pane.

Creating and Managing Channels in the Mixer

ADDING CHANNELS

ADDING INPUT AND OUTPUT CHANNELS

Input and Output channels are added and deleted in the Preferences > Song Setup > Audio I/O Setup pane. Channels are created or destroyed as virtual inputs and outputs are created and deleted.

Fig. 3-42: The Add (Mono) and Add (Stereo) buttons in the Audio I/O Setup panel add Input or Output channels, depending on which tab you are on.

ADDING AUDIO AND INSTRUMENT CHANNELS

Audio channels are created when a new Audio track is added. There is no way to create additional Audio channels without creating corresponding tracks. Instrument channels are nearly the same story, with two differences.

First, whereas Instrument tracks contain performance (MIDI) data and not audio data, Instrument channels are the returns for the audio outputs of VIs. Unlike Audio channels, which carry the playback of recorded material (Audio Events), Instrument channels are carrying audio from live playback of a VI.

Second, multichannel instruments may have more than one corresponding Instrument channel. For more details on this, see the section "Mix View Panels 2: More Mixer Configuration Features" earlier in this chapter.

For more information on adding Audio and Instrument tracks in the Arrange view with the Add Tracks dialog, see the sections "Make a New Audio Track" of chapter 2, "Get Set to Record" and "Instrument Tracks" of chapter 4, "Virtual Instruments and MIDI" in *Power*

Tools for Studio One 2, volume 1, and "Get Set to Record" in chapter 7, "Update: What's New Since Volume 1" in this volume.

ADDING BUS CHANNELS
Create a Bus channel using any of these methods:

- Right-click (Ctrl-click in Mac) in the Mix view (Console) and choose Add Bus Channel from the contextual drop-down menu that appears. This creates a Bus channel but does not make any assignments to it.
- Select one or more channels, right-click (Ctrl-click in Mac) on any of them, and choose Add Bus for Selected Tracks, or choose Track > Add Bus for Selected Tracks from the main menu bar. This adds a Bus channel and routes the outputs of the selected channels to that bus. For more on routing channel outputs, see the section "The Channel Strip" later in this chapter.

TIP: Right-clicking (Ctrl-clicking in Mac) some locations in the Mix view, such as directly on an automatable control (e.g., the fader) or on a meter, will bring up a contextual drop-down menu appropriate to that location, rather than the general Mix view contextual drop-down menu. If you don't get the menu you want, just move the cursor over a different location and try again. On Input and Output channels, try clicking near the very top or bottom of its channel strip.

ADDING FX CHANNELS
FX channels can be created directly with a command in a menu, or as the result of a drag-and-drop operation. Create an FX channel using any of these methods:

- Right-click (Ctrl-click in Mac) in the Mix view (Console) and choose Add FX Channel from the contextual drop-down menu that appears. This creates an FX channel but does not make any assignments to it. See the Tip about right-click locations in the Mix view in the preceding section, "Adding Bus Channels."
- Drag an effect or effect preset from the Effects tab of the Browser to the Send area of any channel in the mixer. An FX channel will be created with the indicated effect instantiated on it, and a new send to that channel will be created in the Sends area of the channel strip. Note that you cannot drop an FX chain in a channel's Sends area, and that dropping an effect in a channel's Sends area when several channels are selected only instantiates the effect where it was dropped, not on all selected channels.
- Drag an effect or effect preset from the Effects tab of the Browser to any open area in the mixer. Frankly, you won't often find open areas in the mixer unless you either have very few channels in the mixer or the Mix view (Console) is stretched extremely wide.

DELETING CHANNELS
Delete channels from the mixer using these methods:

- Audio and Instrument channels cannot be removed from the mixer; their corresponding tracks must be deleted in the Arrange view or with the Track > Remove Track command in the main menu bar.

- Input and Output channels are created and removed in the Preferences > Song Setup > Audio I/O Setup pane, which can be opened by clicking the I/O button at the top of the Console Navigation Column.

- To remove a Bus or FX channel: Right-click (Ctrl-click in Mac) on the channel in the mixer and choose Remove from the contextual menu that drops down, or drag the channel to the Trash Bin Mix View panel.

- To remove multiple Bus or FX channels: Select the channels you wish to delete, right-click (Ctrl-click in Mac) on any of them and choose Remove from the contextual menu that drops down, or drag the channel to the Trash Bin Mix View panel. A confirmation dialog comes up listing the selected channels.

Fig. 3-43: To delete a Bus or FX channel, right-click (Ctrl-click in Mac) on it and choose Remove from the contextual menu that drops down. Input and Output channels are removed in the Audio I/O Setup pane, and Audio and Instrument channels are removed by deleting the tracks associated with them.

RENAMING CHANNELS

- To rename a channel: Double-click the channel name at the bottom of the channel strip and enter the desired name. Editing the name of an Audio channel changes the name of the corresponding track.

- Changing an Audio track name in the Track inspector or track header also changes the name of the corresponding Audio channel.

CHANGING THE COLOR OF CHANNELS

- To change the color used for a channel in the mixer: Click on the channel name at the bottom of the channel strip and choose a color from the palette that drops down. Note that changing the color of an Audio channel also changes the color of the corresponding Audio track, and vice versa.

Fig. 3-44: Click on the channel name in a channel strip to bring up the color palette, from which you can select a color for the channel.

MOVING CHANNELS IN THE MIXER

- Click in the blank area to the right of the channel fader and drag the channel left or right to the desired location.
- When tracks are rearranged in the Arrange view, the mixer attempts to follow suit, however, the mixer also has Bus and FX channels, which the Arrange view does not. Channel placement gets a bit more complicated with those, so the layout in the mixer will rarely match the track layout in the Arrange view.

SHOWING AND HIDING CHANNELS

There are three ways to show and hide channels in the mixer:

- Show and hide banks of different channel types with Show/Hide buttons at the bottom of the Banks > Screen tab. For more information on the Banks > Screen tab, see the section "Banks Mix View Panel" earlier in this chapter.
- Show or hide individual channels in the Banks > Screen tab.
- Right-click (Ctrl-click in Mac) on a channel strip and choose Hide from the contextual menu that drops down.

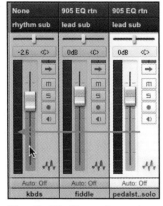

Fig. 3-45: Channels can be moved in the mixer simply by dragging. Note the blue line on the far left, which shows where the channel will end up.

Fig. 3-46: A channel can be hidden by choosing Hide from the contextual drop-down menu that appears when you right-click (Ctrl-click in Mac) on it.

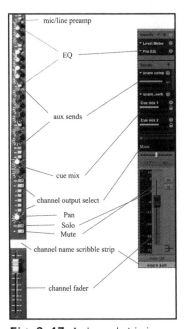

Fig. 3-47: A channel strip in the Soundtracs analog console at Studio Faire la Nouba, Vallejo, California, and an Audio channel strip in Studio One 2. It's easy to see how fully DAWs adopted the traditional channel strip architecture.

- mic/line preamp
- EQ
- aux sends
- cue mix
- channel output select
- Pan
- Solo
- Mute
- channel name scribble strip
- channel fader

The Channel Strip

Hardware mixing consoles consist of some number of identical vertical strips of controls, each one containing the available audio facilities for one audio input. These strips became known as "channel strips." Most DAWs, including Studio One 2, graphically emulate this layout.

However, just as hardware consoles have different facilities for input channels and matrix outputs, Studio One 2's different channel types also have different facilities and, hence, different channel strips. As well, channels in the mixer and related tracks in the Arrange view do not always feature the same controls. For instance, an Instrument track has an Input Monitor button, but the corresponding channel(s) in the mixer does not. The good news is that all channel strips have subsets of the capabilities of Audio channels, except for two features unique to Output channels. The title of the section describing each channel strip feature includes a list of the channel types that have that feature.

If you are unsure of the function of a channel strip control, hover the cursor over it and a pop-up tool tip usually will appear to identify it. Note that a few value displays or controls do not have tool tips.

Nearly all channel strip controls can be automated and/or adjusted from a control surface. For more information on automating parameters, see chapter 4, "Automation," in this volume. For more information on using control surfaces in mixing, see the section "Mixing with Control Surfaces and MIDI Controllers" later in this chapter, and the section "Using Hardware Controllers with Studio One 2" of chapter 4, "Virtual Instruments and MIDI" in *Power Tools for Studio One 2*, volume 1.

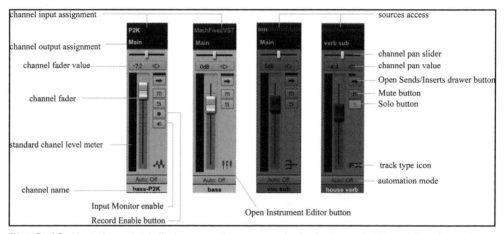

Fig. 3-48: Most channel strip features are the same on Audio, Instrument, FX, and Bus channels, but there are a few features particular to one channel type or another.

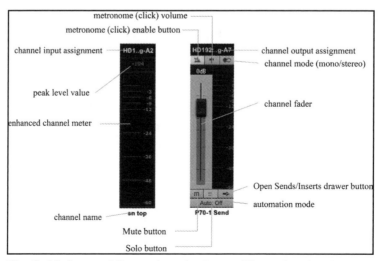

Fig. 3-49: Input and Output channel strips are different than the other channel types, but still share some common features.

CHANNEL STRIP SIGNAL FLOW

It is critical in mixing to understand the signal flow through your mixer. Fig. 3-50 shows the signal flow for a channel in Studio One 2's mixer. A few things are worth pointing out:

- The mixer illustrates its signal flow better when large, standard-width channel strips are used, because the channel is displayed vertically in almost the correct flow order. The channel size button is above the Mix View panel buttons.

- As a rule of thumb, signal flow is top to bottom through the channel strip. So, the insert effect in the second slot from the top is fed from the insert effect in the first slot, and, in turn, feeds the third slot.

- Sends and Cue mixes are all postinsert. Cue mixes are always prefader, as well, whereas Sends are switchable between pre- and postfader.

- The signal being recorded on the hard disk is preinsert. If you want to record with effects, you must insert them on the Input channel.

- Channel solo comes after the pan control and before the Mute button.

INPUT SELECT (INPUT, AUDIO)

One important upgrade in version 2.5 was the ability to select Instrument channel outputs, Bus channels, and ReWire channels as inputs to stereo audio tracks. This allows capturing audio from those sources.

- To select an audio input for an Audio or Input channel: Click in the Input field at the top of the channel strip and choose the desired input from the drop-down menu that appears.

- To select an Instrument or Bus channel as the input to a stereo audio track: Click in the Input Select field and choose a Bus or Instrument channel from the Buses or Instruments folders at the bottom of the menu that drops down.

SOURCE ACCESS (INSTRUMENT, BUS, FX)

Bus and FX channels are fed by submixes of one or more source channels. Any of these source channels can be accessed for editing from the Bus or FX channel strip. For Instrument channels, the instrument editor for the VI feeding the channel can be opened from the Instrument channel strip.

- To access a source channel for a Bus or FX channel, click in the Source field at the top of the channel strip and select the desired source from the drop-down menu that appears. The selected source channel will be highlighted in the mixer and its Sends/Inserts drawer opened. If no menu appears, there are currently no channels with a send to the Bus or FX channel.

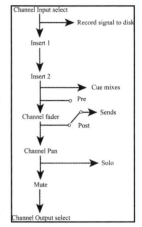

Fig. 3-50: Basic channel signal flow in Studio One 2's mixer.

Fig. 3-51: The channel size button switches the mixer between large (on the right, selected) and small (left) channel strips.

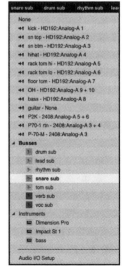

Fig. 3-52: Selecting a Bus channel as the input for an Audio channel.

- To open the Instrument editor for a VI feeding an Instrument channel, click in the Source field at the top of the channel strip. The Instrument editor will appear.

OUTPUT SELECT
(AUDIO, INSTRUMENT, BUS, FX, OUTPUT)

- To select an output for an Audio, Instrument, Bus, or FX channel, click in the Output field just above the pan control in the channel strip and select the desired Output or Bus channel from the drop-down menu that appears.

- To select an output for an Output channel, click in the Output field at the top of the channel strip and select the desired interface output from the drop-down menu that appears.

Fig. 3-53: Accessing a source channel for a Bus channel. Here, the rhythm guitar channel is being accessed from the rhythm submix Bus channel by clicking in the meterlike indicator at the top of the channel strip and choosing from the drop-down menu.

TIP: If you do not see the desired interface output in the drop-down menu of the Output field, open Preferences > Song Setup > Audio I/O Setup > Outputs and check or modify the configuration as needed.

CHANNEL VOLUME FADER
(AUDIO, INSTRUMENT, BUS, FX, OUTPUT)

The channel volume fader is the most basic way of controlling the level of a channel over a range of +10 dB to $-\infty$, where 0 dB = unity gain. The current volume value is shown in the Volume Value display immediately above the fader. When the track associated with a channel is part of a group, the channel volume fader will be affected by changes to any fader associated with the group. Adjust the channel volume fader using any of these methods:

Fig. 3-54: Selecting an output for a Bus channel.

- Drag the fader up or down to the desired value.

- When dragged, the fader value changes in steps of about a third of a dB. If you need finer resolution, Shift-drag and the value will change in steps of 0.1 dB.

- Cmd-clicking on a channel fader (Ctrl-clicking in Windows) will set it to 0 dB.

- Use a control surface to move the fader. When using the PreSonus FaderPort, the fader value will change in 0.1 dB steps. Using a standard MIDI controller, step size varies from about 0.7 dB at the low end of the fader to 0.3 dB near the top.

- Automate the channel volume.

Fig. 3-55: The channel volume fader and fader value.

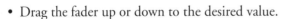

PAN (AUDIO, INSTRUMENT, BUS, FX)

The pan control positions mono signals in the stereo field and adjusts the channel balance for stereo signals. The pan value ranges from L100 (displayed simply as "L") at full left, through center (displayed as ""), to R100 (displayed as "R") at full right. The current pan value is shown in the Pan Value display below the right end of the pan control. The pan control is unaffected by track grouping. Adjust the pan value using any of these methods:

Fig. 3-56:
The pan control and pan value.

- Drag the pan control left or right to the desired value.
- Cmd-clicking (Ctrl-clicking in Windows) on a pan control will set it to center.
- Use a control surface to move the pan control.
- Click in the pan value field and enter a value directly.
- Automate the pan control.

SOLO (AUDIO, INSTRUMENT, BUS, FX, OUTPUT)

The Solo button mutes all other channels so that only the soloed channel is heard. This function is heavily used in mixing. A channel's Solo button is colored amber when the channel is soloed, and gray when it is not. Multiple channels can be soloed at once, and soloing a channel can affect soloing of other channels related to it. For more information on these issues, the meaning of a Solo button's being green, and important additional soloing features available in Studio One 2, see the section "Soloing" later in this chapter. When the track associated with a channel is part of a group, the Solo buttons of all channels associated with the group are always in the same state. If a group is created from all of the vocal tracks, soloing any track or channel associated with the group puts the Solo buttons on all associated tracks and channels into the same state. Solo a channel using any of these methods:

Fig. 3-57:
A channel Solo button. This channel is soloed.

- Select the channel you wish to solo and press the S key on the keyboard.
- Select the channel you wish to solo and click the Solo button on the channel in the mixer.
- Select the channel you wish to solo and use a control surface to solo it.
- Click the Solo button on an Audio or Instrument track in the Arrange view to solo the related channels in the mixer.
- Click the Solo button on a Folder track in the Arrange view to solo all channels in the mixer related to the tracks contained in the folder.

To unsolo a channel:

- Use any of the soloing methods just described on a soloed channel. The solo function will toggle and the channel will be unsoloed.

MUTE (AUDIO, INSTRUMENT, BUS, FX, OUTPUT)

The channel Mute button removes the channel's signal from its selected output and all sends to which it is routed. The Mute button is a toggle control; clicking it mutes the

Fig. 3-58:
The channel Mute button.

channel, clicking it again unmutes the channel. A channel's Mute button is colored red when the channel is muted.

When a channel is soloed, all other channels are muted. Unmuting a channel in that circumstance is the same as clicking its Solo button: the channel is added to any other soloed channels. Mute a channel using any of these methods:

- Select the channel you wish to mute and press the M key on the keyboard.
- Select the channel you wish to mute and click the Mute button on the channel in the mixer.
- Select the channel you wish to mute and use a control surface to mute it.
- Click the Mute button on an Audio track in the Arrange view to mute the related channels in the mixer.
- Click the Mute button on a Folder track in the Arrange view to mute all channels in the mixer related to the tracks contained in the folder.

To unmute a channel:

- Use any of the muting methods just described on a muted channel. The mute function will toggle and the channel will be unmuted.

GLOBAL SOLO AND MUTE

Fig. 3-59: The Global Solo and Mute buttons.

Global Solo allows all soloed channels to be unsoloed with a single action. Repeating the action restores the last soloed state. Global Mute performs the same function for muting.

To unsolo all channels with Global Solo, use any of these methods:

- Press Cmd + Shift + S (Ctrl + Shift + S in Windows).
- Cmd-click (Ctrl-click in Windows) the Solo button on any channel in the mixer.
- Click the Global Solo button in the upper left corner of the Mix view.

Performing any of these actions again restores the mixer to the last solo state. For instance, if all drum channels are soloed, Cmd-clicking (Ctrl-clicking) any Solo button will unsolo all channels, and Cmd-clicking (Ctrl-clicking) any Solo button again will return the mixer to having all drum tracks soloed.

To unmute all channels with Global Mute, use any of these methods:

- Press Cmd + Shift + M (Ctrl + Shift + M in Windows).
- Cmd-click (Ctrl-click in Windows) the Mute button of any channel in the mixer.
- Click the Global Mute button in the upper left corner of the Mix view.

Performing any of these actions again restores the mixer to the last mute state. For instance, if all vocal channels are muted, Cmd-clicking (Ctrl-clicking) any Mute button will unmute all channels, and Cmd-clicking (Ctrl-clicking) any Mute button again will return the mixer to having all vocal tracks muted.

INPUT MONITOR (AUDIO)

The Input Monitor button enables monitoring an Audio channel's selected input. Record-enabling an Audio track or Audio channel also engages input monitoring. Unlike the classic multitrack tape machine input monitoring model, in which you could switch between monitoring the input and any previously recorded material, Studio One 2's input monitoring simply mixes the input signal with any existing recorded material on the corresponding Audio track.

Input monitoring through Studio One 2 suffers from latency determined by the size of the channel buffer. Although this may not be a real problem if your computer can run with a small buffer, it is the reason for the spread of low-latency monitoring built into interfaces. For more about monitoring latency, see the section "Understanding Buffer Size" of chapter 2, "Get Set to Record" in *Power Tools for Studio One 2*, volume 1.

The Input Monitor button is a toggle control; clicking it engages input monitoring on the channel, clicking it again disengages input monitoring. The Input Monitor button is colored blue when input monitoring is engaged. Engage input monitoring for a channel with any of these methods:

Fig. 3-60: In mixing, the Input Monitor button often comes into use to monitor outboard equipment. Remember that, if you do not have interface-based low-latency monitoring, the Input Monitor function will have more latency the larger the buffer (Device Block Size) setting is.

- Select the channel on which you wish to monitor the input and press the U key on the keyboard.
- Select the channel on which you wish to monitor the input and click the Input Monitor button on the channel in the mixer.
- Select the channel on which you wish to monitor the input and use a control surface to engage input monitoring.
- Click the Input Monitor button on an Audio track in the Arrange view to engage input monitoring on the related channels in the mixer.
- Record-enable an Audio track or Audio channel using any method and input monitoring is also engaged.

For more about input monitoring, see the section "Monitoring" of chapter 2, "Get Set to Record" in *Power Tools for Studio One 2*, volume 1.

RECORD ENABLE (AUDIO)

The Record Enable button is not really a mixer function, it is for recording Audio tracks, but it appears on channel strips in the mixer for convenience. In the Mix view, only Audio channels have Record Enable buttons, but in the Arrange view Instrument tracks have them as well. That's because the Mix view is all about audio, and audio is only recorded on Audio tracks.

Fig. 3-61: The channel Record Enable button.

To arm a track for recording, use any of these methods:

- Select the track on which you want to record and press the R key. The Record Enable button will turn red to show that the track is armed.

- Click on the Record Enable button on the channel strip in the mixer.
- Click on the Record Enable button in the track header in the Arrange view.

To arm multiple tracks for recording, use any of the following methods:

- Click on the Record Enable button on the channel strip or track header of each track on which you want to record.
- Select all of the tracks on which you want to record by Shift-clicking on the track header in Arrange view or channel strip in Mix view, then press the R key or click on the Record Enable button on any of the selected tracks/channels.

METRONOME CONTROLS (OUTPUT)

Each output, including the Main output, has controls to turn the metronome on or off and set its level. This means that the drummer's Cue mix can have the metronome loud and clear, the bass player can have somewhat less metronome in his or her Cue mix, and the guitarist can play without a click. The metronome controls cannot be automated, so any changes to the metronome that need to happen while recording must either be done manually, or be captured in advance to a click track audio file, which is monitored in place of the metronome. Note that Studio One uses the terms *metronome* and *click* in different places, but they mean the same thing.

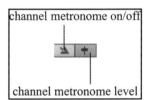

Fig. 3-62: Each Output channel, including Main Out, has its own metronome (click) controls.

To enable or disable the metronome in an Output channel:

- Click the Click On/Off button above the channel fader. When the button is colored blue, the metronome will be heard through that output. The button is a toggle; clicking it when the metronome is enabled disables the metronome on that channel.

To adjust the volume of the metronome:

1. Click and hold on the Click Volume button next to the Click On/Off button above the channel fader. The Click Volume fader will appear and the cursor will be placed over the current fader location.
2. Without letting the mouse button up, drag the Click Volume fader up or down to the desired level.
3. Release the mouse button when the Click Volume is set as desired.

CHANNEL MODE: STEREO/MONO (OUTPUT)

Studio One 2 makes it easy to switch stereo Output channels to mono to check for mono compatibility. Note that left and right channels are still being outputted, but both are carrying the same mono sum of the stereo signal. To audition a stereo Output channel in mono:

Fig. 3-63: It's easy to check mixes in mono with the Channel Mode button on Output channels.

- Click the Stereo/Mono button to the right of the Click Volume button above the channel fader. When the button is colored red, auditioning is in mono.

TIP: Although it turns red when clicked, the Stereo/Mono button on a mono Output channel actually does nothing.

INPUT AND OUTPUT CHANNELS

CREATING AND DELETING INPUT AND OUTPUT CHANNELS

Input and Output channels are audio facilities that connect directly to interface inputs, so they are created and deleted in the Inputs and Outputs tabs of the Preferences > Song Setup > Audio I/O Setup pane.

- To create an Input or Output channel: Open the Audio I/O Setup pane, go to the appropriate tab (Inputs or Outputs), and click the Add (Mono) or Add (Stereo) button.

- To delete an Input or Output channel: Open the Audio I/O Setup pane, go to the appropriate tab (Inputs or Outputs), select the Input or Output you want to delete, and click the Remove button. To delete multiple Input or Output channels at once, select them all, then click the Remove button.

RENAMING, SETTING CHANNEL COLOR, AND MOVING INPUT AND OUTPUT CHANNELS

- To rename an Input or Output channel: Double-click on the channel name at the bottom of the channel strip in the mixer or in the left column of the Audio I/O Setup window and enter the desired name.

- To set the color for an Input or Output channel: Click on the channel name at the bottom of the channel strip in the mixer and choose the desired color from the palette that drops down.

- To move an Input channel: Click on the meter and drag left or right to the desired position. A light blue outline will indicate what the new location will be.

- To move an Output channel: Click on the meter or in the fader area and drag left or right to the desired position. A light blue outline will indicate what the new location will be.

INPUT AND OUTPUT CHANNEL INSERTS

- To open the Inserts drawer on an Input channel: Double-click on the meter and the drawer will open on the right of the channel.

- To open the Inserts drawer on an Output channel: Click the arrow in the bottom right of the channel strip. The drawer will open on the right of the channel, the direction of the arrow will reverse to indicate it will close the drawer on the next click, and the button turns blue.

- Output channels have both prefader and postfader inserts; Input channels have no fader at all, so the inserts are neither!

SENDS (AUDIO, INSTRUMENT, BUS) AND INSERTS (AUDIO, INSTRUMENT, BUS, FX, INPUT, OUTPUT)

The process of mixing actually involves creating quite a few different mixes for various purposes, such as feeding effects. Most of these mixes are created using sends.

In Studio One 2, creating a Bus or FX channel actually creates both the channel in the mixer and the bus that is fed from sends on other channels. Fig. 3-64 shows how that works.

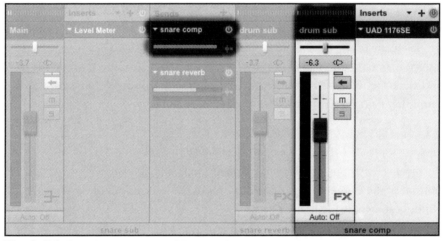

Fig. 3-64: Dragging the UAD1176SE plug-in from the Browser and dropping it in the channel Sends area creates a new FX channel with the plug-in inserted, and a send on the source channel to the effect.

By contrast, effects that will be dedicated to a single channel in the mixer can be inserted in the middle of that channel's signal path, eliminating the requirements for both a mix to feed them and a channel to return them to the mix. This is the purpose of inserts.

Note that signals flow through inserts from top to bottom, so reordering inserts can have a significant sonic effect. The order of sends on a channel, however, is purely cosmetic, so you can reorder sends to your heart's content and it will have no effect on the audio at all.

Inserts Versus Sends: Which to Use?

The question that always arises at this point is: When is it appropriate to use an insert and when a send? A quick look at the advantages of each will be instructive.

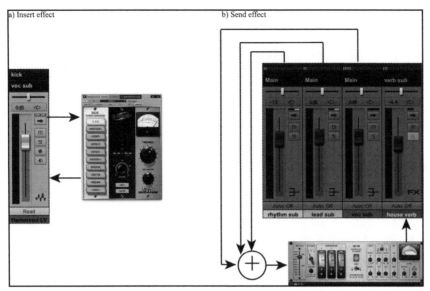

Fig. 3-65: An insert is useful for effects dedicated to a single source channel, while a send allows a mix of channels to feed an effect or submix.

If one or more plug-ins are going to be used only for one channel, such as distortion, EQ, and flanging for a lead guitar, then using an insert to place the effects directly in the guitar channel's signal path will generally be the best choice. On the other hand, if one or more plug-ins are intended to be accessible to multiple channels, such as a "house" reverb that you want heard on most of the tracks, then a Send will be needed, as it carries a mix of channels. Sends have many uses, to name just a few:

- Feeding effects, such as reverb, with a mix that is different from that being sent to Main Out.
- Cue mixes. Note that Output channels need to be configured as Cue mixes in the Outputs tab of the Preferences > Song Setup > Audio I/O Setup pane. For more information on configuring outputs as Cue mixes, see the section "Monitoring" in chapter 2, "Get Set to Record" of *Power Tools for Studio One 2*, volume 1, and the section "Cue Mix Outputs" later in this chapter.
- Splitting the signal to multiple signal paths (called multing). This could be for parallel processing, such as parallel compression, to create alternate mixes, or any situation where it is useful to send the same signal over more than one route.
- Generating surround and subwoofer sends for surround mixes. This is a clunky way to do surround (especially panning anything through the sound field), but it is how it was done on stereo mixing consoles for years just after surround came into common use.
- The Pipeline plug-in, used to integrate outboard processors with Studio One 2 Professional, uses an Output channel as a send and an Input channel as a return, but

is in the channel signal path as an insert effect. For more information on Pipeline, see the section "Integrating Outboard Devices: the Pipeline Plug-In" later in this chapter.

One other consideration is that an effects send can have greater flexibility in mixing processed sound with unprocessed sound than can an insert effect. Take the parallel compression example: few compressor plug-ins have wet/dry mix controls (although they were added to Studio One 2's compressors in version 2.5), making it extremely difficult to do parallel compression as an insert effect.

Accessing Sends and Inserts

The Sends and Inserts areas for each channel are stashed out of sight until they are needed. Reveal and hide the Sends and Inserts areas on a channel using these methods:

- Click the Expand button on the channel strip and a drawer opens on its right side, revealing the Inserts and Sends areas. Note that the Expand button on Audio and Instrument channels is near the top right of the channel fader, whereas on Output channels, it is on the right just below the channel fader.
- To open the drawer on an Input channel, double-click on the channel level meter and the drawer will open on its right side.
- To close all open drawers at once: Option-click the Drawer Open arrow on any open drawer. All drawers on all channels will close.
- Click the Small /Large channel strip button in the Console Navigation column on the left. Sends and Inserts will appear at the top of the mixer channel display.

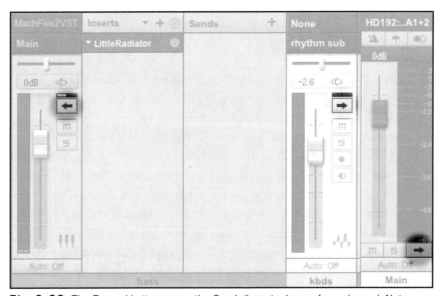

Fig. 3-66: The Expand button opens the Sends/Inserts drawer for a channel. Note that the Expand button is near the middle of Audio and Instrument channels, but near the bottom of Output channels. Double-click on the level meter of an Input channel to open its drawer.

Working with Inserts

ADDING, RENAMING, DEACTIVATING,
AND DELETING INSERT EFFECTS ON A CHANNEL

ADDING INSERT EFFECTS

Add Insert effects to a channel using any of the following methods:

- Drag an effect or effects preset from the Browser and drop it on a channel. If the channel already has any insert effects, the new effect will be inserted at the bottom of the list of effects. The effect can be dropped in the Inserts area of the channel, but it is not necessary to drop it there; dropping anywhere on the channel will work.

- If a channel already has insert effects, you can drag an effect or effects preset from the Browser and drop it at any position in the Inserts area of the channel. The new effect will be inserted at the position where it was dropped.

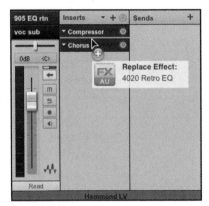

Fig. 3-67: An effect can be dropped anywhere in the middle of an existing list of insert effects. The blue line is indicating where the effect will end up.

- Open the Sends/Inserts drawer for a channel, click the + (plus) button at the top of the drawer, locate the desired effect in the drop-down menu that appears, and click it to insert it on the channel.

- Drag an effect or effects preset from the Browser and drop it anywhere on an Audio or Instrument track in the Arrange view. The effect will be inserted on the Audio channel in the mixer associated with that track. If the channel already has any Insert effects, the new effect will be inserted at the bottom of the list of effects.

- Drag an effect or effects preset from the Browser and drop it anywhere on a Folder track in the Arrange view. If a Folder track is assigned to an output (so that it is acting like a submix), the effect will be inserted on the Bus or Output channel selected for output. For Folder tracks with no output assigned, a new Audio track will be created in the Arrange view and the effect will be inserted on its associated channel in the mixer.

Fig. 3-68: An effect dropped on a Folder track is inserted on the Folder track's assigned Bus or Output channel, unless none is selected, in which case a new track is created and effect inserted on it.

When the Beat Delay, Groove Delay, Analog Delay, MixVerb, or Room Reverb plug-in is inserted into the first slot of the Inserts section of a Bus or FX channel, the Mix parameter gets set to 100 percent wet, and the Mix Lock (which, as the name suggests, locks the Wet/Dry Mix control) is engaged. These settings are saved with the Song, but are not associated with presets; they are neither saved with a preset, nor affected by loading one.

TIP: Effects inserted on Input channels affect signals being recorded from those inputs. If you wish to record through effects, this is the way to do it, but if you do not want the signal recorded with effects, insert the effects in the monitoring chain (which usually means on the appropriate Audio channel).

FX chains can be inserted on a channel as well, but they will replace any existing effects. For more information about FX Chains, see the section "Plug-Ins and Effects" later in this chapter. Insert an FX Chain on a channel using any of these methods:

- Drag an FX Chain from the Browser to a channel strip and drop.
- Drag an FX Chain from the Browser to the Inserts area of a channel strip.
- Click on the inverted triangle at the top of the Inserts area and choose the desired FX Chain from the drop-down menu that appears.

Fig. 3-69: An effect dragged from the browser can be dropped anywhere on the target channel.

- Drag an FX Chain preset from the Browser and drop it anywhere on an Audio or Instrument track in the Arrange view. The effects will be inserted on the Audio channel in the mixer associated with that track.

- Drag an FX Chain preset from the Browser and drop it anywhere on a Folder track in the Arrange view. If a Folder track is assigned to an output (so that it is acting like a submix), the FX chain will be inserted on the Bus or Output channel selected for output. For Folder tracks with no output assigned, a new Audio track will be created in the Arrange view and the FX Chain inserted on its associated channel in the mixer.

Fig. 3-70: Drop an FX Chain in the Inserts area of a channel to add an entire processing chain at once.

RENAMING AN INSERT

1. Right-click (Ctrl-click in Mac) on the effect you wish to rename in the Inserts section.
2. Choose Rename…from the contextual menu that drops down.
3. Enter the desired name and click OK.

Note that the name of the plug-in is unaffected; only the insert slot (the "Device") is being renamed. To make this totally clear, rename an Insert, then open the editor for the

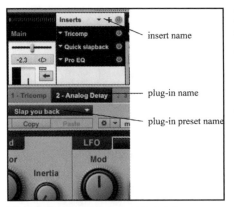

insert name

plug-in name

plug-in preset name

Fig. 3-71: Renaming an Insert only renames the "Device," but the plug-in instantiated in that device is unaffected.

plug-in. You will see that the "device" name is changed, but the plug-in editor looks the same otherwise.

DEACTIVATING AN INSERT EFFECT

The Insert Activate button is the same as (and linked to) the Activate button in the plug-in editor, which, when unchecked, actually unloads the plug-in code from memory. This is not a good parameter for automation because it can take a few seconds to load and unload processing code. The Bypass control in the plug-in editor is better for automation. For more information,

Fig. 3-72: The Insert Activate button causes plug-in code to be unloaded, not something you want to do if you will need to kick it back in quickly.

see the section "The Device (Plug-In and Instrument) Editor Header" in chapter 5, "On the Cutting Room Floor: Basic Editing" of *Power Tools for Studio One 2*, volume 1.

DEACTIVATING ALL INSERT EFFECTS ON A CHANNEL

- To deactivate all insert effects on a channel: Click the Activate button in the top right corner of the header in the Inserts area. The button will no longer be colored blue, and the Activate buttons on each of the insert effects will disappear, indicating all effects have been deactivated.

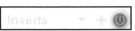

Fig. 3-73: The Activate button in the header of the Inserts area deactivates all inserts at once.

DELETING AN INSERT EFFECT

Delete an insert effect using any of these methods:

- Right-click (Ctrl-click in Mac) on the insert effect you wish to delete and choose Remove from the contextual drop-down menu that appears.
- Click the Trash button in the Console Navigation column to open the Trash Bin panel, then drag the insert effect you wish to delete to the Trash Bin. For more information on the Trash Bin panel, see the section "More Mixer Configuration Features" earlier in this chapter.
- To delete all insert effects currently on a channel, click on the inverted triangle at the top of the Inserts area and choose Remove All at the bottom of the drop-down menu that appears.

THE EFFECTS MICRO-VIEW

The PreSonus effects bundled with Studio One 2 offer an additional useful editing feature: the effects micro-view. The effects micro-view is an extremely compact editing panel that opens under the insert in the Inserts view, providing access to a small number of key editing parameters without the need to open a plug-in editor window.

Fig. 3-74: The effects micro-view lets you see and edit a few parameters for a plug-in in the mixer itself.

OPENING AND CLOSING THE EFFECTS MICRO-VIEW

Open or close an effects micro-view using either of these methods:

- Click on the name of the insert in the Inserts area for which you want to open a micro-view. The micro-view will drop down. Clicking the insert name again closes the micro-view.

- Click on the arrow to the right of the name of the insert in the Inserts area for which you want to open a micro-view and choose "Expand" from the drop-down menu that appears. The micro-view will drop down. Click the arrow again and choose "Collapse" to put the micro-view away.

EDITING PARAMETERS IN AN EFFECTS MICRO-VIEW

Since the point of the effects micro-view is its compactness, it is plain that the number of parameters viewable and editable in the micro-view has to be quite limited. Typically, two to five factory-chosen parameters, plus a Bypass checkbox, are available in the micro-view for an effect.

Most controls are value bars, as shown in Fig. 3-75. The range of some of these controls goes from zero to the maximum, but some have zero in the middle, from which it can be set to have a positive or negative value. An example of this is shown in Fig. 3-75.

Fig. 3-75: In this effects micro-view, Feedback is a positive/negative value bar, while Depth and Delay are zero-to-max value bars.

There are a few exceptions. The Compressor and Pro EQ plug-ins, for example, have editable graphic representations in their micro-views, as shown in Fig. 3-76; and display-oriented plug-ins, such as the Level Meter, include small meter displays.

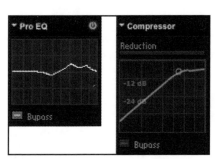

Fig. 3-76: The Compressor and Pro EQ are two examples of plug-ins that offer editable graphic displays in their effects micro-views.

As with any other parameter editing, the parameter value is always shown in the Control Link parameter display at the top left corner of the Song page as it is edited.

If you wish to see the current value of a variable control (such as a value bar) before editing it, just hover the mouse cursor over the parameter control. A pop-up tool tip will identify the control, and, for variable controls, will also display the current value. To edit a parameter value in an effects micro-view, use any of these methods:

Fig. 3-77: The current value of a parameter being edited in an effects micro-view is shown in the parameter display in top left corner of the Song window.

- If the control is a value bar, click at the desired position in the bar to set the value. Remember that some parameters have their zero point on the left of the bar, whereas others have it in the middle.

- Drag the value bar or parameter handle (usually a small circle) to the desired value.

- Cmd-click (Ctrl-click in Windows) on a value bar to reset it to its default value.

- Click in a checkbox control, such as Bypass, to enable or disable the parameter.

- Place the mouse cursor over the currently selected parameter's value in the parameter display in the upper left corner of the Song window and drag up or down to the desired value.

- Double-click in the value field for the currently selected parameter in the parameter display in the upper left corner of the Song window, enter the desired value, and press Return or Enter to complete the entry.

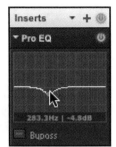

Fig. 3-78: A pop-up tool tip shows the current value of a control in an effect micro-view when you hover the cursor over it.

INSERT ORDER

As discussed in the section "Channel Strip Signal Flow" earlier in this chapter, signal flows from top to bottom in the Inserts area. The order of the inserts is therefore crucial to the sound. It is easy to rearrange the order of inserts, making it easy to experiment with different orders. Be warned that some experiments can produce very loud results, so you should turn your studio monitors down a bit before trying your experiments.

To rearrange the insert order, use either of these methods:

- Drag any insert from its current position in the list of inserts to the desired position. As soon as you start dragging, a blue line will appear at the bottom of the slot in the list where that insert is currently. As you drag up or down, the blue line will move to show you where in the list the insert will be if you release the mouse button at that point. No blue line appears when dragging an insert to the end of the list.

- When dragging an insert effect from the Browser or from another channel, you can drop it at any position in the chain.

REPLACING AN EFFECT OR COPYING AN EFFECT TO A DIFFERENT CHANNEL

Replacing one effect with another in an insert, or copying an effect from one channel to another, is a simple matter of dragging and dropping:

- To replace an insert effect with another effect, drag the replacement effect from the Browser (or another channel) and drop it on the insert containing the effect you wish to replace. A pop-up message will indicate the replacement, and the old effect will be moved to the Trash Bin.

• To copy an effect from one channel to another, simply drag it from the channel where it is currently instantiated to the one to which you wish to copy it. Remember that, if there are already insert effects on the target channel, the new effect can be dropped at any position in the list of inserts. The effect on the new channel will have the same settings as on the channel from which it was dragged.

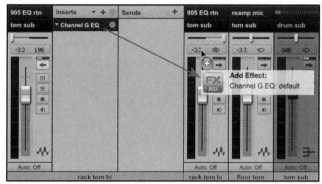

Fig. 3-79: Replacing an effect is as easy as dropping the new effect onto the old one.

Fig. 3-80: To copy an effect from one channel to another, simply drag it from the source channel to the target channel.

SHOW SOURCES

It is possible to examine Bus and FX channels to see the sources that feed them. Even better, any source can be accessed directly from the source list.

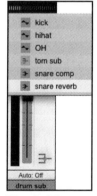

• The indicator that looks like a meter at the top of Bus and FX channels actually shows the number of sources feeding the channel. To see a list of the sources, click the indicator.

Fig. 3-81: Looks like a meter, doesn't it? This is actually a counter showing the number of sources feeding this channel.

• To access a source feeding a Bus or FX channel: Click in the indicator at the top of an FX or Bus channel and choose a source from the list that drops down. The selected source is revealed in the mixer.

Fig. 3-82: Click at the top of an FX or Bus channel to see a list of the sources feeding it.

• To hide or show all source channels feeding a Bus channel: Right-click (Ctrl-click in Mac) on the Bus channel and choose Hide Sources or Show Sources from the contextual menu that drops down. Note that if one or more of the sources is a Bus channel, such as a submix master, it will be hidden, but its source channels will not.

Working with Sends

ADDING, RENAMING, DEACTIVATING, AND DELETING SENDS ON A CHANNEL

ADDING A SEND

To add a send on a channel, use any of these methods:

- Drag and drop an effect or effects preset from the Browser into the Sends area of a channel. An FX channel is created with the effect instantiated on it, a send to that FX channel is created on the channel where you dropped the effect, and a plug-in editor is opened for the effect. The level of the send defaults to 6 dB below maximum.

- Click the Add Send button with the + (plus) sign at the top of the Sends area and choose an existing Bus, FX, Output channel, or Sidechain path from the drop-down list that appears. A send is created on the channel.

- Choose the Add Bus Channel or Add FX Channel command found at the bottom of most drop-down menus in the Mix view. Two examples of menus containing these commands are: the drop-down menu that appears when the Add Send button is clicked, and the contextual drop-down menu that appears when you right-click (Ctrl-click in Mac) in any Inserts or Sends area, or on most parts of the channel strip.

Fig. 3-83: The Add Bus Channel and Add FX Channel commands are in most drop-down menus in the mixer.

RENAMING A SEND

Sends cannot be renamed directly in the mixer, but they can be renamed from a menu in the plug-in editor window.

1. To rename a send, double-click on the send to open the plug-in editor window.
2. Click on the inverted triangle in the upper right corner of the window and choose Rename from the drop-down menu that appears.
3. Enter the desired name and click OK.
4. Click the close box in the upper right corner of the plug-in editor to close the window.

DEACTIVATING (MUTING) A SEND

The Send Activate button is different than the Insert Activate button. The Insert Activate button is the same as (and linked to) the Activate button in the plug-in editor, which, when unchecked, actually unloads the plug-in code from memory; however, the Send Activate button is actually only a Send Mute button. In fact, it is called Send Mute when automating it. Sends are activated by default, as indicated by their blue color.

Fig. 3-84: The Send Activate button does not unload a plug-in's code, but just acts as a send mute (Okay, an enable, to be precise).

- To deactivate (mute) a send, click the Activate button in the upper right corner of the send. It will turn black to indicate that the send has been deactivated. Click again to reactivate it.

DELETING A SEND
Delete a send using any of the following methods:

- Right-click (Ctrl-click in Mac) on the send name and choose Remove from the drop-down menu that appears.
- Click on the inverted triangle in the upper right corner of the send and choose Remove from the bottom of the drop-down menu that appears.
- Click the Trash button in the Console Navigation column to open the Trash Bin panel and drag the send to the Trash Bin.

TIP: Deleting a send on a channel does not delete the Bus channel it feeds. If you wish to remove the Bus channel as well as the send, use the methods described in the section "Creating and Managing Channels in the Mixer" earlier in this chapter.

EDITING SEND LEVEL AND PAN VALUES
Sends have only four editable parameters (not including renaming):

- Send level.
- Send pan (not present on all effects).
- Prefader/Postfader button. For more information on this see the section "Prefader and Postfader Sends" later in this chapter.
- Activate button. For more information on this, see the section "Deactivating (Muting) a Send" earlier in this chapter.

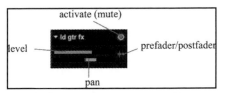

Fig. 3-85: Sends have four editable parameters, shown here.

To edit a parameter value, use any of these methods:

- To see the current value of the Send Level or Pan before editing: Hover the mouse cursor over the control. A pop-up tool tip will identify the control and display the current value.
- Click at the desired position in the value bar to set the value. Remember that some parameters have their zero point on the left of the bar, whereas others have it in the middle.
- Drag the value bar or parameter handle (usually a small circle) to the desired value.
- Cmd-click (Ctrl-click in Windows) on a value bar to reset it to its default value.
- Click in a checkbox control, such as Bypass, to enable or disable the parameter.

- Place the mouse cursor over the currently selected parameter's value in the Control Link parameter display in the upper left corner of the Song window and drag up or down to the desired value.
- Double-click in the value field for the currently selected parameter in the Control Link parameter display in the upper left corner of the Song window, enter the desired value, and press Return or Enter to complete the entry.

COPYING A SEND TO ANOTHER CHANNEL

- To copy a send to another channel, simply drag it from the source channel to the Sends area or channel strip of the destination channel. The send will be copied complete with level and pan (if present) settings.

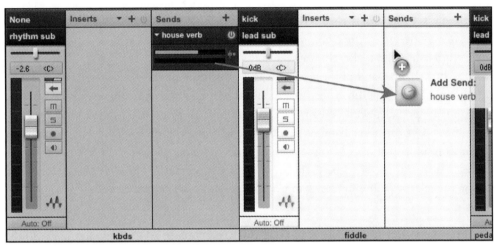

Fig. 3-86: To copy a send, drag it to the target channel.

STEREO VERSUS MONO SENDS

Bus and FX channels are all stereo, so sends that feed them are likewise all stereo. Output channels, however, can be configured in the Audio I/O preferences to be mono or stereo. This makes it possible to have a mono send, if one is needed, but only if it feeds a physical interface output.

To create a mono send:

1. If no mono output channel currently exists, open the Outputs tab of the Preferences > Song Setup > Audio I/O Setup pane.
2. Click the Add (Mono) button to create a new mono output.
3. Rename and reconfigure the new output as desired and click OK to close the dialog.
4. Create a new send on the source channel to the mono output, using any of the methods described in the section "Adding a Send" earlier in this chapter.

PREFADER AND POSTFADER SENDS

Fig. 3-87 shows that a send can be sourced either from a spot in the signal path just before the channel fader, or from just after it. This one detail is tremendously important because prefader sends are unaffected by the level of the source channel fader. The channel fader can actually be all the way down and an effect fed by a prefader send will still be getting signal, for example.

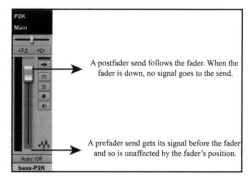

A postfader send follows the fader. When the fader is down, no signal goes to the send.

A prefader send gets its signal before the fader and so is unaffected by the fader's position.

Let's say you wanted to make it sound as if an instrument is receding into the distance. One good way to do this is to have the instrument fade-into a reverbed version of itself. A prefader send makes this easy: simply

Fig. 3-87: Prefader and postfader sends differ only in the point in the signal path at which they split off, but that one point is tremendously important.

create a Bus channel and put a reverb on it, feed from a prefader send, and slowly lower the channel fader. The direct instrument signal will fade out, but the reverb will still get fed from the prefader send and so you will continue to hear the reverbed version of the instrument. On the other hand, a postfader send would be preferable if you wanted the proportions of instruments being sent to an effect to mirror their relative levels in the mix.

Each send can be set to be prefader or postfader separately for each channel. A send can be prefader on some source channels and postfader on others. Sends are postfader by default.

- To make a send prefader on a channel: Click the Prefader On/Off button in the lower right corner of the send in the Sends area of the source channel. The button and level indicator both turn a light brown color when a send is prefader. When the level indicator is blue, the send is postfader.

THE SHOW DESTINATION COMMAND

It can be very convenient to jump from a channel on which you're working to an effect it is feeding through a send, but when the mixer has a lot of channels going, you can end up scrolling around trying to find the right Bus or FX channel. The Show Destination command solves this by making the destination channel immediately visible.

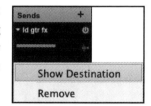

Fig. 3-88: The Show Destination command reveals the Bus or FX channel being fed by a channel send.

- To see the destination of any send, right-click (Ctrl-click in Mac) on the name of the send and choose Show Destination from the contextual drop-down menu that appears. The destination channel will be brought into view and selected.

Cue Mix Outputs

Performers need Cue mixes, and Cue mixes have their own needs. Studio One 2 treats Cue mixes as a special type of Output channel. They are different from Output channels in several ways:

- Channel cue sends (that is, the channel send to a Cue mix) are found in their own area of a channel to the right of the Sends area.

- In Large Console mode, the Cue mixes are found just below the Sends area.

- Cue mixes do not show up in the drop-down list of destinations in the Add Send sources list.

- Channel cue sends are always prefader.

CREATING, DELETING, AND USING CUE MIXES

- To make an Output channel into a Cue mix: Check the Cue mix box next to an output in the Outputs tab of the Preferences > Song Setup > Audio I/O Setup pane.

- To rename a Cue mix: Double-click the channel name at the bottom of the channel strip and enter the desired name.

- To change the color used for a Cue mix output in the mixer: Click on the channel name at the bottom of the channel strip and choose a color from the palette that drops down.

- To mute a channel Cue send: click the Mute Cue mix button in the upper right corner of the channel Cue send. The button will turn gray when the send is muted.

- To delete a Cue mix: Uncheck the Cue mix box next to an output in the Outputs tab of Preferences > Song Setup > Audio I/O Setup and it converts back to an Output channel.

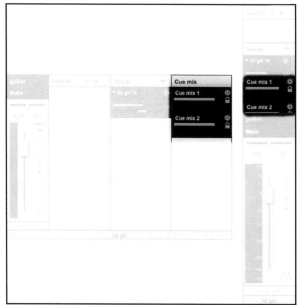

Fig. 3-89: Channel cue sends, when they exist in a Song, are located in their own dedicated area. When the mixer has small faders, cue sends are to the right of Sends area in the drawer that opens to the right of the channel strip. With large faders, cue sends are in their own section just below the Sends area.

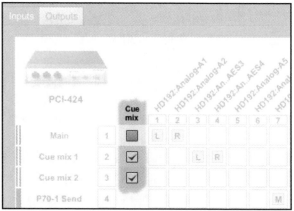

Fig. 3-90: Check the Cue mix box in the Audio I/O Setup pane to make an Output channel into a Cue mix.

- By default, volume and pan settings for a Cue mix on a channel are locked to the channel volume and pan settings. To unlock channel Cue send level and pan settings from the channel settings: Click the Lock level and pan to channel button (with the lock icon) in the channel Cue send. The lock icon is colored gray (and barely visible) when the Cue send and channel settings are unlocked from each other.

- To add effects to a Cue mix: FX and Bus channels have Cue sends, enabling effects to be routed to a Cue mix as sources, or click the Reveal arrow in the lower left corner of the Cue mix Output channel to open the Inserts drawer and insert an effect, prefader or postfader, as needed.

SOLOING

Soloing channels or groups of channels is an essential part of recording. Studio One 2 supplies a robust set of soloing functions to accommodate a variety of production needs.

Fig. 3-91: Deactivate the Lock level and pan to channel button and the send level and pan will be independent of channel level and pan settings. Cue mix 2 has been unlocked (notice the highlighted Lock button), and its level and pan differ from the channel level and pan. Cue mix 1 is still locked to the channel and shares the same settings.

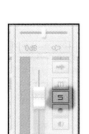

Fig. 3-92: A channel Solo button.

Channel Soloing

- Individual channels can be soloed using the Solo button on the channel strip.

- Multiple channels can be soloed at once.

- To add to the collection of soloed channels, simply click on the Solo button on each channel you want soloed.

- Solo follows pan in the channel signal flow, so soloing is in place in the stereo field, rather than in mono.

- All soloing includes effects. When a channel is soloed, the channels for each send used in the channel are also soloed.

- The Solo function is linked for all channels in a Group; soloing or unsoloing one channel makes all the other channels in the group do the same.

- Soloing a member of a submix (a group of inputs feeding a Bus or Output channel) also solos the submix master (the Bus or Output channel).

- Soloing an FX or Bus channel (such as a submix) also solos all source channels feeding it, as well as any Bus or Output channel it is feeding.

SOLOING WITH THE LISTEN TOOL

The Listen tool is a very quick and convenient soloing mechanism. An Audio, Instrument, or even Folder track can be played just by clicking on it with the Listen tool. To solo with the Listen tool:

Fig. 3-93: The Listen tool solos the material that it plays.

1. Press the 8 key on the main keyboard or click the Listen tool button in the Arrange View toolbar to select the Listen tool.

2. Click and hold anywhere in the track area of an Audio, Instrument, or Folder track you want to solo. Playback starts from the location clicked and continues until the mouse button is released.

Save Solo

Save Solo mode is often referred to as Solo Defeat in mixing consoles, but it's better described as Solo Protect, and maybe most accurately as Mute Defeat. Any channel in Save Solo mode will not be muted when a channel is soloed. This makes it easy to solo each instrument in turn and hear how it works with bass and drums, for instance. To set a channel to Save Solo mode:

Fig. 3-94: The green color of the Solo button shows that this channel is in Save Solo mode, which protects it from being muted when another channel is soloed.

- Shift-click the Solo button on each channel you want to be in Save Solo mode. The Solo button will turn green to indicate it is now in Save Solo mode. Each channel so selected will always be soloed when any other channel is soloed. FX channels default to Save Solo mode.

- Soloing a track or channel does not solo Bus or FX channels being fed from its sends, but FX channels default to Save Solo (Solo Protect) mode anyway.

- Output channels also default to Save Solo mode, but if an output is not in Save Solo, it will be soloed whenever a channel whose output is routed to it is soloed.

Global Solo

Global Solo enables all channels to be unsoloed with a single click or key shortcut (Cmd + Shift + S in Mac, Ctrl + Shift + S in Windows). For more information on Global Solo, see the section "Global Solo and Mute" earlier in this chapter.

Track Solo Follows Selection

Solo follows Selection is very useful when trying to figure out which track holds something you hear in a mix. Once enabled, selecting any track instantly solos it. Selecting multiple tracks solos them all, making it simple to try different groupings of tracks. Solo follows Selection is actually a track, not a channel, function. This means that:

- The function works just as well whether you solo a track in the Arrange view or its corresponding channel in the mixer, but it only works for tracks; Bus and FX channels cannot be soloed simply by selecting them.

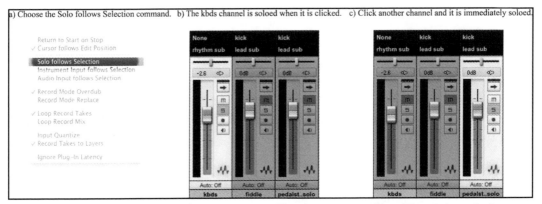

Fig. 3-95: The Solo follows Selection command is a fast way to audition different channels. As soon as a channel is selected, it is soloed.

- If a track's output is routed to a Bus channel being used as a submix, or even to an FX channel, the Bus (or FX) channel is automatically soloed when any channel with an output routed to it is soloed.

To enable Track Solo follows Selection:

1. Choose Options > Solo follows Selection from the main menu bar. The menu command will become checked to show the function is active.

2. One or more Audio or Instrument channels must be manually soloed before Solo follows Selection will work. You can solo a channel before or after choosing the Solo follows Selection command. Once a track has been put into Solo and the command is activated, selecting any Audio or Instrument channel(s) will cause it to be soloed.

Layer Solo

Although it is less often used in mixing than in recording and editing, it is worth mentioning Studio One 2's tools for soloing layers on a track in the Arrange view.

- To solo a layer: With all layers for the track expanded, click on the Solo button in the Layer header and play. Note that the Layer Solo button is independent of the Track Solo button, so you can solo layers and hear them with the track itself in isolation (soloed) or in context.

METERING

You've heard it said a million times that you should mix with your ears and not your eyes, and now it's a million and one. However, good metering is an excellent adjunct to listening. Signal analysis can be very helpful in diagnosing a problem you hear.

Peak Versus Rms Metering

Audio level is typically metered in two ways: peak and rms. Although more digital meters have peak response than rms, both are important and, in fact, a strong case can be made that rms is the more important of the two overall.

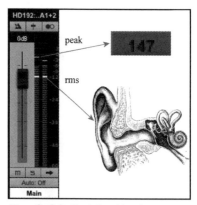

Fig. 3-96: Peak level is of use in setting levels so that they do not overload the equipment. Rms level is a better indicator of how loud it sounds to listeners.

So what's the difference and, more important, how does it apply to you and recording with Studio One 2? The difference is simple: Peak response looks at instantaneous signal level, whereas rms looks at the average level over a short period of time. A peak meter will show the maximum level from a note with a sharp attack, which can be considerably higher than the level over the rest of the note, which will be better shown by rms level. That means that you will see larger and faster fluctuations on peak meters, but get a better indication of overall level from rms.

The ear itself does a lot of averaging over time, so rms better approximates how a listener will perceive the loudness of a signal, but peak value is more important for ensuring proper recording. In short, the rms value of a signal is more important for people, whereas peak value is a concern for the equipment.

The desired recording level is one where the rms level is substantial, at least halfway up the meter in most cases, but the peak level never exceeds full level and clips. It is better to be conservative with your overall level setting than aggressive; the need to push levels as high as possible is a relic of the past now that we have 24-bit resolution in recordings (which is recommended whenever possible).

For some signals, the difference between peak and rms levels is small, in which case you have more slack in how you set the level and can put it fairly high, if you like. When the difference between peak and rms is large, however, you will need to set the level lower to avoid clipping peaks, or to introduce a limiter or other dynamics processor to keep peaks in bounds. The ratio of peak to rms values for a signal is called its crest factor. High crest factors suggest lower recording levels, and possibly dynamics processing later to tame peaks and bring up overall level.

TIP: If the analog signal entering your audio interface is too high, the signal will be recorded with clipping, something extremely difficult to undo or fix later. If you have a nice analog compressor or limiter, it will save you time and effort later to use it during recording. If you do not, it's better to be very conservative with your recording level, so as not to clip during recording, then apply compressor or limiter plug-ins later to shape the sound as desired.

You will find metering in Studio One 2 in four main places:

- Channel strips: Meter color and some details of response vary with channel type. Details of these are described in the rest of this section.
- Track headers: Audio and Instrument tracks have mini-meters to the right of the track header. Folder tracks have mini-meters if an output assignment has been made on it (making it act as a submix). With no output assignment, Folder tracks will not display a mini-meter.
- The Screen tab of the Banks panel can display micro-meters (really, really small) for Audio, Instrument, Bus, and FX channels, when the View > Levels option has been selected from the contextual drop-down menu in the Banks panel. For more information on the Banks panel, see the section "Banks Mix View Panel" earlier in this chapter.

Standard Level Metering

Studio One 2 provides basic level metering on every channel in the mixer, with more comprehensive options on Output channels. It also includes three metering plug-ins that provide even more analysis and display on any channel where it is needed.

Meters for stereo channels show both channels, so you can watch balance between the channels, as well as seeing where peaks appear on each.

PEAK HOLD (VU HOLD)

All level meters have peak hold capability, which Studio One 2 calls VU Hold, though it seems to have nothing to do with VU meters or response. Studio One 2's peak hold can be configured to any of three hold times.

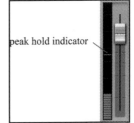

- To enable or disable peak hold in a channel: Right-click (Ctrl-click in Mac) on the meter and choose VU Hold from the contextual menu that drops down. When the command is checked, peak hold is engaged and can be seen as a single segment that stays highlighted in the meter for some time after the signal level drops below it. Peak hold is on by default.

Fig. 3-97: Peak hold in a channel meter.

- To set the peak hold time for a meter: Right-click (Ctrl-click in Mac) on the meter, choose the Hold Length submenu from the contextual menu that drops down, and select 2s (two seconds), 15s (15 seconds), or inf (infinite) for the hold time.
- To see a numeric readout of peak levels: Hover the cursor over a meter while there is audio playing through the channel. A pop-up tool tip will appear, showing you peak levels as well as the value represented at the cursor's current location on the meter scale.

AUDIO, INSTRUMENT, BUS, AND FX CHANNELS

Audio, Instrument, Bus, and FX channels all have mono or stereo level meters to the left of the fader, a clip indicator, and a pop-up tool tip when you hover the cursor over the meter that shows the last held peak level (at the time the cursor was brought over it) and the instantaneous level as numbers.

INPUT CHANNELS

Input channels have no channel strip to speak of (except for an Inserts section), so the whole channel strip is the meter. The meter shows peak level only, but a more extensive metering plug-in can always be inserted on the channel. There is a peak hold (VU Hold) option for the meter and a numerical peak level readout between the meter and the Input Select field.

Fig. 3-98: The level meter is to the left of the fader in the channel strip.

- To activate a meter peak hold function: Right-click (Ctrl-click in Mac) on the meter and choose VU Hold from the contextual menu that drops down, if it is not already checked.

- To set the peak hold time: With peak hold engaged on a channel, right-click (Ctrl-click in Mac) on the meter again and choose from the three durations in the Hold Length submenu: 2s (two seconds), 15s (15 seconds), and inf (infinite hold). A small blue bar on the meter will indicate the held level.

- Clicking in the meter brings up a pop-up tool tip that shows the meter marking where the cursor is located, and the difference in dB between the signal and the cursor location on the meter. You can move the cursor up and down to different levels.

Fig. 3-99: Input channels have no strip; they are pretty much all meter.

OUTPUT CHANNELS

Output channels, including Main Out, have fancier meters than other channels, with four available calibration presets:

- Peak/RMS
- K20
- K14
- K12

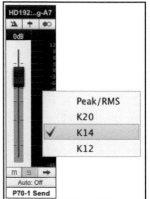

Fig. 3-100: Output channels offer K-System metering options.

Output channel meters have different coloring than channel meters, as well. With the Peak/RMS preset selected, the meters are a slightly lighter blue than channel meters, plus there are highlighted meter segments to show current peak and peak hold levels. With any of the K-System presets, average level is displayed in green for signals less than zero in the meter, yellow when the signal is greater than zero, and red when the signal is 3 dB over the zero mark on the meter.

PEAK/RMS PRESET

Output channels feature dual meters that simultaneously display peak and rms (average) levels. This kind of meter display is really the way to go, as you get both points of view at the same time. In general, you should be most concerned with watching peak levels to make sure nothing clips, but a healthy rms level is also a good thing. Peak/RMS is the default preset for Output meters.

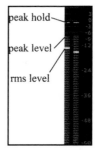

- To restore the Peak/RMS meter preset if it has been changed: Right-click (Ctrl-click in Mac) on the meter and choose Peak/RMS from the contextual menu that drops down.

Fig. 3-101: The Peak/RMS preset shows peak and rms values simultaneously.

The presence of the rms portion of the display gives rise to another parameter in the right-click drop-down menu: rms integration time (the amount of time over which the level is averaged).

- To set the rms integration time for an Output channel meter: Right-click (Ctrl-click in Mac) on the meter, choose the RMS Length submenu from the contextual menu that drops down, and select 0.6s (600 milliseconds), 1.8s (1.8 seconds), or 3s (three seconds) for the rms integration time.

K-SYSTEM PRESETS

Output channels also offer K-System presets, which constitute the other three preset choices. Remember, when changing K-System presets, to always make sure 0 on the meter corresponds to 85 dB SPL in the room.

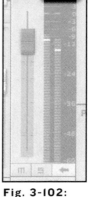

- To select a K-System preset: Right-click (Ctrl-click in Mac) on the meter and choose the K20, K14, or K12 preset from the contextual menu that drops down.

CLIP INDICATOR

Output meters have a clip indicator at the top of the meter. If the signal in the Output channel clips, the indicator turns red. The number of clipped samples is displayed in the indicator and is updated with the accumulated total throughout the Song.

Fig. 3-102: The Clip indicator at the top of Output channel meters shows whether clipping has occurred and, if so, how many samples have been clipped.

Metering and Analysis Plug-Ins

You could get to like this metering hoopla. Worse things could happen. If that does come about, you might find yourself wanting more detailed level metering and maybe even some other kinds of analysis tools. Well, Studio One 2 is ready for you, with a handful of PreSonus signal analysis plug-ins that can be inserted on any channel (or even an Event, if that were of use).

LEVEL METER

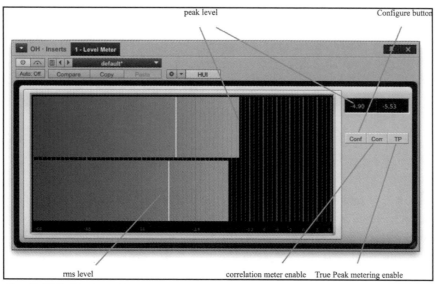

Fig. 3-103: The Level Meter.

The Level Meter plug-in provides a high-resolution meter than can be resized for the greatest visual detail, as well as set to horizontal or vertical orientation. The Level Meter offers a choice of simultaneous peak and rms metering or one of the K-System presets, plus a selection of configuration options.

The Level Meter is added to a channel using any of the standard methods for adding an insert effect. For more information on adding, removing, expanding, and deactivating plug-ins, see the section "Plug-Ins and Effects" later in this chapter.

SIZING AND ORIENTING THE LEVEL METER

The Level Meter can be sized to be as large as you want, all the way up to the full size of your screen, oriented horizontally or vertically. It can be made wider in horizontal orientation, taller in vertical orientation, or grown in both dimensions at the same time. However, a key point to understand is that the meter's orientation is a function of its size. When the Level Meter window (not just the meter area itself, but the entire window) is wider than it is tall, the meter is horizontally oriented, and when it is taller than it is wide, it is vertically oriented. Thus, orientation is changed by resizing.

- To make the Level Meter wider or narrower, position the cursor over the left or right edge of the window. The cursor will change to a horizontal double-headed arrow with a line between the arrows. Drag left or right until the meter is the desired width.
- To make the Level Meter taller or shorter, position the cursor over the top or bottom edge of the window. The cursor will change to a vertical double-headed arrow with a line between them. Drag left or right until the meter is the desired width.

- To resize the height and width of the Level Meter simultaneously, position the cursor over the lower right corner of the window. The cursor will change to a hand icon. Drag until the meter is the desired size.
- To change the orientation of the meter, resize it as desired until it is wider than it is tall for horizontal, or taller than it is wide for vertical orientation.

LEVEL INDICATORS

Level is displayed two ways in the Level Meter:

- In the meter area, it is shown as a dynamically changing color bar. The coloring is different for the Peak metering scale than for the K-System scales, as described in the next section, "Metering Scales and Options."
- A display above the Mode field displays the peak value numerically. The value is held for the specified peak hold time, and a red clip indicator on the right side illuminates if the signal goes into the red area of the meter area. The clip indicator can be cleared by clicking on it.

METERING SCALES AND OPTIONS

The Level Meter offers four metering scales: Peak (simultaneous peak/rms level display), or any of the three K-System presets. For more information on the K-System, see the section "K-System" earlier in this chapter.

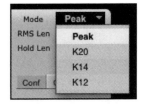

Fig. 3-104: The Level Meter offers the same four scale options as on Output channels.

To select a metering scale, use either of these methods:

- Click the Conf button to show the Meter Configuration parameters. Click in the Mode field and choose the desired metering scale from the drop-down menu that appears.
- Right-click (Ctrl-click in Mac) in the meter area and choose the desired metering scale from the drop-down menu that appears.

The color in the meter area changes as the level rises:

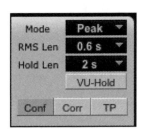

Fig. 3-105: The Conf button reveals meter configuration parameters.

- For peak level indication, the Peak metering scale uses a pale blue color from the bottom of the scale up to –6, when it fades to a pale gray. At –1 dB it becomes red. Rms level is indicated by a white line that is updated regularly.
- The K-System scales use green up to 0, then yellow to +4, and red above +4.

The Peak metering scale offers several options.

- To access the Peak metering scale options, click the Conf button.

- To set the rms integration time for the Level Meter: Click in the RMS Len field or, when the Level Meter is instantiated on a mono channel, right-click (Ctrl-click in Mac) in the meter area and select 0.6s (600 milliseconds), 1.8s (1.8 seconds), or 3s (three seconds) from the menu that drops down.

- To enable or disable graphical display of peak hold in the meter area: Click the VU Hold button or, when the Level Meter is instantiated on a mono channel, right-click (Ctrl-click in Mac) in the meter area and choose VU Hold from the menu that drops down. When the button is colored blue, VU Hold is engaged and can be seen as a single segment that stays highlighted in the meter for the specified hold time after the signal level drops below it.

- To set the peak hold time for the Level Meter: Click in the Hold Len field or, when the Level Meter is instantiated on a mono channel, right-click (Ctrl-click in Mac) in the meter area and select 2s (two seconds), 15s (15 seconds), or inf (infinite) from the menu that drops down.

- To show the phase correlation meter when the Level Meter is instantiated on a stereo channel: Click the Corr button. The button will turn blue and the correlation meter will appear beneath the meter area. A blue bar indicates the degree of correlation, and a numeric value is displayed to the right of the bar.

- TP (True Peak) metering: Clicking this button causes the peak level readout and clip indicator to show True Peak readings instead of peak sample value readings. For more on True Peak metering, see the next section, "True Peak Metering."

TRUE PEAK METERING

This is a bit on the "tweaky but worthwhile" side.

Called ISM (Intersample metering) in earlier versions of Studio One, True Peak (TP) metering monitors where intersample peak distortion is likely to occur. Intersample peak distortion is a sample-rate related distortion, in which the sample rate matches up with the stored waveform in a way that results in overload errors when the signal is converted from digital back to analog. This happens particularly in consumer playback devices that don't have as good quality D/A converters as your studio does. So, basically, it is one measure of how your mix will get screwed up on people's crappy playback devices. Minimize intersample peak distortion, goes the argument, and your music should sound better on all of those mobile devices everybody listens on.

If you are really interested in this sort of metering, consider downloading Solid State Logic's excellent and free X-ISM plug-in from this page, which also features an excellent explanation of the issue: http://www.solid-state-logic.com/music/X-ISM/.

SPECTRUM METER

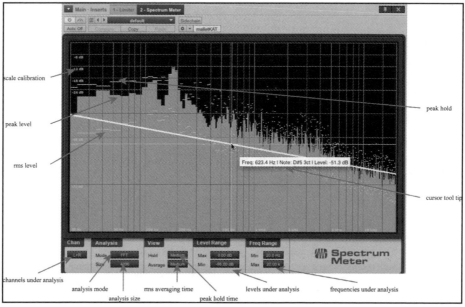

Fig. 3-106: The Spectrum Meter.

The Spectrum Meter is a high-resolution FFT analyzer with selectable display modes.

CURSOR AND TOOL TIP DISPLAY

When you move the cursor over the spectrum display area, three lines and a pop-up tool tip appear. The crosshairs and the tool tip indicate the cursor's X-Y location in terms of frequency (shown along the X axis), pitch (a translation of frequency), and level (shown on the Y axis). The slanted line that appears when the cursor is hovered over the spectrum display reflects a difference between measurement and perception.

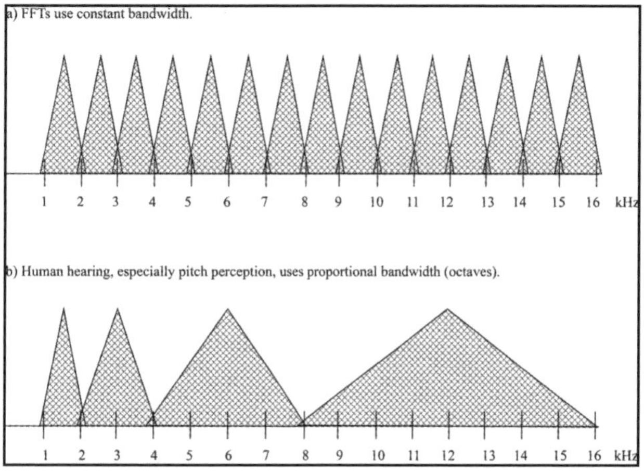

The issue is that FFTs, the measurement method used here, have bands of linear bandwidth, that is, each band spans the same number of Hz. Our hearing, on the other hand, is in many ways logarithmic. We like to hear in octaves (doubling or halving the frequency) and other proportional structures, which means that high octaves contain many more discrete Hz than low octaves do.

Map the linear FFT structure onto our logarithmic hearing structure, and the result is that higher FFT bands represent a smaller

Fig. 3-107: FFTs have constant bandwidth bands, but we hear pitch in octaves, which increase in bandwidth with frequency.

portion of an octave than do lower bands. As bandwidth goes down, so does the energy content displayed.

Bottom line: something that sounds pretty flat across the frequency spectrum looks on an FFT like it declines in energy as it goes up, because you are seeing individual bands but hearing octaves, which are much wider.

Whew. I did say it was tweaky, and if you got this far, good on ya.

SPECTRUM METER PARAMETERS
Here are the parameters in the Spectrum Meter.

- Scale calibrations: Octave, Third Octave, FFT, and FFT Curve analysis modes all put frequency on the X axis of the display, and amplitude on the Y axis. The Waterfall display puts frequency on the X axis and time on the Y axis, where the bottom of the window is the Now line. (The Z axis, color intensity, indicates amplitude.) Sonogram reverses the axes of the Waterfall display: time is on the X axis (with the Now line at the right side of the window), and frequency on the Y axis. Also, time in the Waterfall display runs bottom (present) to top (past), whereas in the Sonogram it runs right to left.

- Channel (L, R, L+R, L–R): Selects source signal for analysis. Click in this field and select the desired channel configuration from the menu that drops down. On mono channels, this is a read-only field.

- Analysis Mode (Octave, Third Octave, FFT, FFT Curve, Waterfall, Sonogram): The type of analysis display. Each presents a different view of the data. Click in this field and select the desired analysis mode from the menu that drops down.

- Analysis Size (512, 1024, 2048, 4096, 8192, 16,384, 32,768, 65,536): Sets the size of the analysis window. This field appears for all Analysis Modes except Octave and Third Octave. Click in this field and select the desired analysis window size from the menu that drops down. To grossly oversimplify, larger sizes give more accurate average levels but miss more transients and short-duration events. More discussion of this goes beyond the scope of this book, but plenty of great FFT primers can explain the tradeoffs of window size.

- Hold (None, Short, Medium, Long, ∞ [infinity]): When set to anything other than None, peak values are held, as indicated by white segments above the FFT display. Click in this field and select the desired peak hold time from the menu that drops down. The infinite setting does not freeze the display at a point in time; it simply holds the highest level that has occurred at each frequency.

- Average (None, Fast, Medium, Slow): Click in this field and select the desired averaging speed from the menu that drops down. When set to None, rms values are not displayed.

- Level Range Max (default = 0 dB): The highest level being displayed on the meter. Move the cursor over this field and drag up or down to the desired value, or click in the field and enter a value directly.

- Level Range Min (default = –120 dB): The lowest level being displayed on the meter. Taken together with Level Range Max, a window of dynamic range is defined for viewing. Move the cursor over this field and drag up or down to the desired value, or click in the field and enter a value directly.

- Frequency Range Min (default = 20 Hz): The lowest frequency being displayed on the meter. Move the cursor over this field and drag up or down to the desired value, or click in the field and enter a value directly.

- Frequency Range Max (default = 20 kHz): The highest frequency being displayed on the meter. Taken together with Frequency Range Min, a window of frequency spectrum is defined for viewing. Move the cursor over this field and drag up or down to the desired value, or click in the field and enter a value directly.

- Presets: Analyzer configurations can be stored as presets in the Device Editor header. A few factory presets are worth checking out, as well.

ANALYSIS MODES

- Octave: Octave-band measurement gives the big picture of spectral distribution, but is shy on detail.

- Third Octave: Third-octave analysis is intended to more closely approximate the way our hearing breaks up the frequency spectrum, but it does not reflect the fact that we don't hear all frequency bands equally well.

- FFT: FFT mode shows all bands of the FFT, giving it very high resolution.

- FFT Curve: This is an FFT display that is not filled under the line of current sample points, so all that is seen is the curve of current values.

- Waterfall: In this mode, the X axis is frequency, the Y axis is time (Y = 0 is "now," higher is older), and color intensity, the Z axis, represents amplitude. "Waterfall display," "sonogram," and "spectrogram" are, according to many sources, all exactly the same thing: a display of how frequency spectrum varies over time.

- Waterfall displays are often 3D projections, with amplitude on the Y axis and time along the Z axis. Graphically, that's a challenge to do in real time, so Studio One 2's waterfall is 2D. Looking at sonograms takes a little getting used to, but once you get it, you can get a lot of information reading them.

- Sonogram: This is the same thing as the waterfall display, but rotated for a different viewpoint. In the Sonogram mode, the X axis is time (with history on the left and the "now" line on the right), the Y axis is frequency, and, again, Z is color intensity, depicting amplitude.

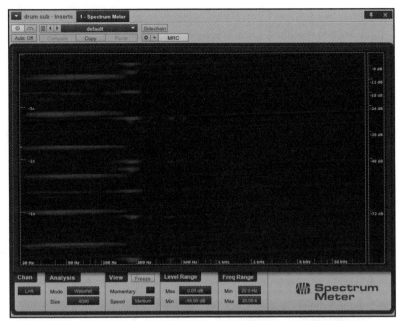

Fig. 3-108: The waterfall display, like Sonogram mode, shows how the amplitude of each frequency changes over time. In this waterfall display of a drum submix, it is easy to see the snare hits.

PHASE METER

The Phase Meter displays phase information in two different ways. The first is a goniometer, which displays a Lissajous figure.

Say what?

It's an X-Y display of the left and right channel signals that has been rotated a little, so that a mono signal (left and right carry the same signal) is a vertical line (note the axis labeled "M" in Fig. 3-109, a left channel signal is a 45-degree line going from upper left to lower right (labeled "L"), and a horizontal line indicates a phase or polarity inversion between the channels (one end of the X axis is labeled "S"; and the other end, "–S"). A healthy stereo signal produces something roughly approximating a wide vertical oval most of the time.

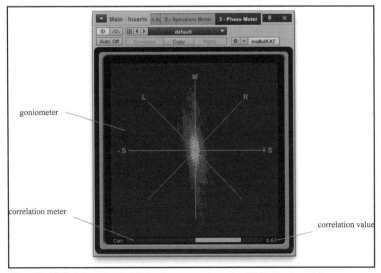

Fig. 3-109: The Phase Meter has a goniometer (X-Y display of the channels) and a correlation meter.

Below the Phase Meter is the Correlation Meter. Correlation is a measure of how similar the signals in the left and right channels are. If a signal is mono, the channels are highly correlated, which is indicated by the meter being mostly (or, for mono, fully) to the right. If there are totally different things in each channel, the channels are not well correlated, and the meter will deflect mostly to the left. A numerical readout on the right displays a correlation value; a value of 1 is mono. A typical stereo mix will stay a bit to the right, but will move around a fair amount.

SCOPE

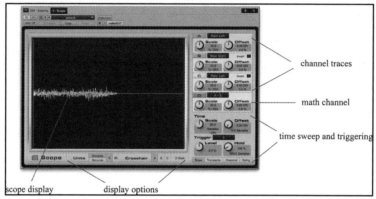

Fig. 3-110: The Scope plug-in is a serious measurement and analysis tool.

The Scope plug-in is no toy; it's a serious oscilloscope, suitable for many kinds of signal analysis. Its features include:

- Three color-coded channel traces with adjustable scaling and vertical offsets
- A math channel trace
- Flexible time sweep and triggering options
- Display scale options

An oscilloscope is a complex test tool that, while immensely useful, is not the primary focus of Studio One 2 or this book. Consequently, I will cover the features only briefly here.

CHANNEL TRACES (A, B, C)
Each channel trace has the following features:

- To disable a trace: Click the color-coded letter button next to the channel's controls. The button will turn gray to show that the channel is disabled. Click the button again to reenable it.

Fig. 3-111: Each channel has a disable button.

- To select a source signal for the channel: Click in the Source field and choose a signal from the menu that drops down. Choices are: Main Left (left channel of insert), Main Right (right channel of insert), Side Left (left channel of sidechain), or Side Right (right channel of sidechain).

- To invert the polarity of the signal on the channel (channels B and C only): Click the Invert box to the right of the Source field.

- To set the vertical deflection scale: Position the cursor over the Scale knob and drag up and down or side to side until the desired scale is reached, or click in the Scale field and enter a value directly. The range is from 200 percent of full-scale per division down to 1 percent per division, with the default being 20 percent.

Fig. 3-112: The Source field selects the signal flowing through a channel.

- To set the vertical offset of a trace: Position the cursor over the Offset knob and drag up and down or side to side until the desired vertical positioning is obtained, or click in the Offset field and enter a value directly. The range is +/– 100 percent, which is five divisions.

MATH CHANNEL (D)

The Math channel allows sum or difference signals to be observed.

- To disable the Math channel trace: Click the color-coded letter button next to the channel's controls. The button will turn gray to show that the channel is disabled. Click the button again to reenable it.

Fig. 3-113: The Invert box reverses the polarity of the signal.

- To select a source signal for the channel: Click in the Source field and choose a signal from the menu that drops down. Choices are: A-B, A-C, and B-C. Using the Invert boxes on the B or C channels allows summing instead of differencing.

- To set the vertical deflection scale: Position the cursor over the Scale knob and drag up and down or side to side until the desired scale is reached, or click in the Scale field and enter a value directly. The range is from 200 percent of full-scale per division down to 1 percent per division, with the default being 20 percent.

- To set the vertical offset of the trace: Position the cursor over the Offset knob and drag up and down or side to side until the desired vertical positioning is obtained, or click in the Offset field and enter a value directly. The range is +/– 100 percent, which is five divisions.

TIME SWEEP AND TRIGGERING CHANNEL (X AXIS)

The controls in this section affect the sweep generator, setting its parameters and triggering functions.

- To set the horizontal deflection scale for the time sweep: Position the cursor over the Scale knob and drag up and down or side to side until

Fig. 3-114: Time sweep and triggering controls.

the desired scale is reached, or click in the Scale field and enter a value directly. The units used for the scale value depend on whether Samples or Seconds has been selected in the scale display area. The ranges are: 8 to 8000 samples/division, or 0.17 to 166.7 milliseconds/division.

- To set the horizontal offset of the time sweep: Position the cursor over the Offset knob and drag up and down or side to side until the desired horizontal positioning is obtained, or click in the Offset field and enter a value directly. The units used for the scale value depend on whether Samples or Seconds has been selected in the scale display area. The ranges are: 0 to 80,000 samples or 0 to 1.67 seconds, which is 10 divisions.

- To set the trigger source: Click in the Trigger field and choose a source from the menu that drops down. Choices are: A, B, C, Ext (note), and Free.

- To set the trigger level: Position the cursor over the Level knob and drag up and down or side to side until the desired trigger level is reached, or click in the Level field and enter a value directly. The range is +/– 150 percent.

- To set the trigger hold time: Position the cursor over the Hold knob and drag up and down or side to side until the desired trigger hold time is reached, or click in either the percentage or units field and enter a value directly. The range is 0 to 1000 percent (0 to 8000 samples or 0 to 166.7 ms, depending on whether Samples or Seconds has been selected in the scale display area). Default value is 100 percent (800 samples or 16.7 ms).

- To set whether the time sweep is triggered by positive-going or negative-going edges of the signal: When the Slope button is selected (which it is by default), triggering occurs on the positive-going edge. Click the Slope button to deselect it and trigger off negative-going edges.

- To set triggering from transients: Click the Transients button to enable transient triggering.

- To limit triggering to a single sweep: Click the Oneshot button to engage it. When Oneshot is engaged, the first trigger fires a sweep, and the second trigger disables further triggering.

- To engage a one-trigger mask: Click the Retrig button. This will cause the scope to wait for a second trigger before sweeping.

UNITS SECTION

- To set the scope to display values in samples: Click the Samples radio button in the Units area. This affects the display of both trigger parameters and cursor position in the crosshair display.

Fig. 3-115: The units used in the scope's display are set in the Units section.

- To set the scope to display values in seconds: Click the Seconds radio button in the Units area. This affects the display of both trigger parameters and cursor position in the crosshair display.
- To set the crosshair display to show values as a percentage: Click the % (percent sign) radio button in the Units area.
- To set the crosshair display to show values in decibels: Click the dB radio button in the Units area.

CROSSHAIR SECTION

When the cursor is moved over the scope area, a pop-up tool tip shows the values at the current cursor position for the channel selected in this area. The appropriate color-coding is used to make it easy to understand at which channel's values you are looking.

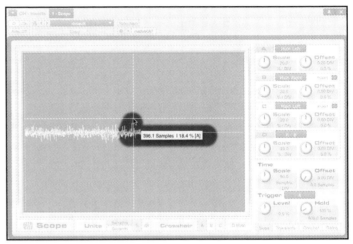

- To select a channel for crosshair display: Click the radio button for the channel whose values you wish to examine with the crosshair. Choices are: A, B, C, D, and Math.

Fig. 3-116: A pop-up tool tip shows the values at the current cursor position when the cursor is moved over the scope area.

TONE GENERATOR

The Tone Generator is a versatile signal generator, suitable for use as a test source, especially when used in conjunction with the Scope plug-in. You typically will want to insert the Tone Generator on a Bus channel dedicated to it, since when the Tone Generator is on, it

Fig. 3-117: The Tone Generator plug-in does much more than generate tones; it generates sweeps and noise signals. All controls are disabled when generating noise, except output level and the Off/Gated/On buttons.

precludes any other signal source on the channel. It can be useful to insert the Tone Generator on an Audio or Instrument channel if you are trying to calibrate or troubleshoot the channel in some way,

OSCILLATOR SECTION

- Waveform: Click in this field and choose the desired signal generator waveform from the menu that drops down. Choose from Sine, Saw. Rectangle, White Noise, and Pink Noise.

Fig. 3-118: The Oscillator section of the Tone Generator plug-in.

- To set the frequency of the signal generator: Click on the Frequency knob and drag up and down or left and right to the desired frequency, or click in the field to the right of the knob and enter a value directly.

- To engage anti-aliasing (Saw and Rectangle waveshapes only): The Anti-Alias option is checked by default to engage anti-aliasing. Click the Anti-Alias button that appears below the Waveform field when it shows Saw or Rectangle to disengage anti-aliasing.

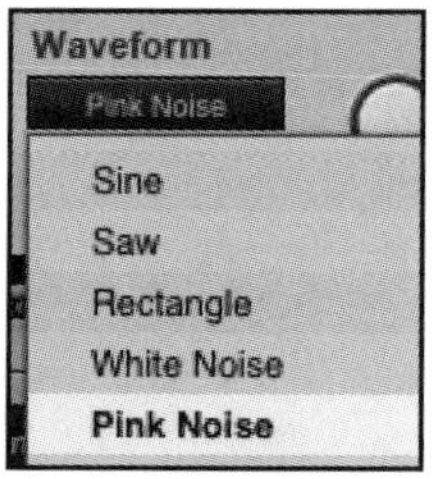

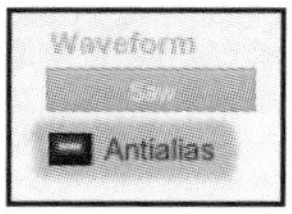

Fig. 3-119: Three periodic waveforms and two kinds of noise are available as source waveforms.

Fig. 3-120: Anti-aliasing for the Saw or Rectangle waveforms is accessed with this button.

MODULATION SECTION

The Modulation section generates frequency sweeps from the frequency set in the Signal Generator section to the frequency set in the Target Freq field over the time indicated in the Length field. The Wobble button enables frequency sweeps.

Fig. 3-121: The Modulation section creates frequency sweeps for the periodic waveforms in the Tone Generator.

The Modulation section applies only to the periodic waveforms: Sine, Saw, and Rectangle. No Modulation features are available when the Waveform is set to White Noise or Pink Noise.

- To enable frequency sweeps: Click the Wobble button to illuminate it. When the Wobble button is off, the oscillator pitch is constant.

- To make frequency sweeps logarithmic instead of linear: Click the Log Sweep button. When the Log Sweep button is off, sweeps are linear; when it is illuminated, they are logarithmic.

- To set the sweep duration: Click on the Length knob and drag up and down or left and right to the desired duration, or click in the field to the right of the knob and enter a value directly.

- Phase Shift: This parameter applies phase shift to the tone in the right channel when the Tone Generator is inserted on a stereo channel. It is disabled when the Tone Generator is inserted on a mono channel. To set the phase between channels: Click on the Phase Shift knob and drag up and down or left and right to the desired phase shift, or click in the field to the right of the knob and enter a value directly. A value of zero means the channels are in phase with each other; at a value of 100 the channels are 180 degrees out of phase with each other.

- To set the end frequency of the frequency sweep: Click on the Target Freq knob and drag up and down or left and right to the desired frequency, or click in the field to the right of the knob and enter a value directly. When Target Freq is set to a higher frequency than the Frequency knob, the Tone Generator performs an upward sweep; when it is lower than the Frequency knob, it is a downward sweep.

OUTPUT SECTION

- Off button: Disables the Tone Generator.
- Gated button: The Gated button enables the output of the Tone Generator to be turned on and off from an external source. To gate the output of the Tone Generator: Click the Gated button to illuminate it, create an Instrument track, and set its output to the Tone Generator. Note that when an Instrument track is assigned to the Tone Generator, there is no Instrument channel, so you cannot instantiate the Tone Generator on the Instrument channel.
- To set the output level of the Tone Generator: Click on the Level knob and drag up and down or left and right to the desired duration, or click in the field to the right of the knob and enter a value directly. The output level range is from −144 dB to +24 dB, where 0 dB produces a zero peak reading on Studio One 2's peak/rms meters.

Fig. 3-122: The Output section. Note the Gated button, which enables the test signal to be switched on and off by an external source, specifically, an Instrument track.

Third-Party Metering Options

If you want to go beyond the capabilities of Studio One 2's included metering, you can try third-party analysis plug-ins. There are also standalone analysis programs, but they are independent of, and, therefore not relevant to, a book about Studio One 2. Here are just a few examples of third-party analysis plug-ins:

- iZotope Insight
- Waves PAZ
- Blue Cat FreqAnalyst (free) and others (VST, AU)
- NuGen Audio Visualizer (VST, AU)
- Voxengo SPAN (VST, AU [free])
- Roger Nichols Digital's Inspector XL is an excellent metering suite that is no longer available, but if you find a copy of it somewhere, it runs just fine in Studio One 2.

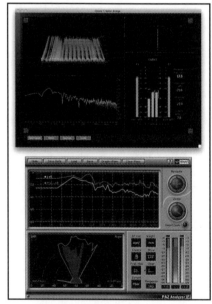

Fig. 3-123: iZotope Insight (shown here as part of the Ozone 5 Advanced suite, top) and Waves PAZ (bottom) are two of the available third-party metering options.

GROUPS

Studio One 2 offers the ability to group tracks, which, for mixing, enables the volume of all group members to be moved together by changing any one of its members. Note that grouping channels in the mixer is not supported, only grouping tracks in the Arrange view. This means it is not possible to include Bus, FX, or Output channels in a group.

Studio One 2's grouping scheme is basic, but can still be useful. Especially interesting is the ability to create a group of all of the tracks contained in a Folder track simply by clicking on the Group button in the Folder track's header. For more information on Groups, see the section "Track Groups and Folder Tracks" of chapter 5, "On the Cutting Room Floor: Basic Editing" in *Power Tools for Studio One 2*, volume 1.

MIXING WITH CONTROL SURFACES AND MIDI CONTROLLERS

Physical mixing consoles have several advantages over working entirely within a computer, including:

- Tactile controllers, such as faders and knobs, are generally better at making gestures than a mouse is, in large part because they are built to be operated by the fingers, over which we have pretty fine motor control.

- Physical mixers allow control of multiple channels simultaneously. Less channel selection has to be done; one simply reaches over to the desired channel and makes a change.

- Physical mixers make it easy to do A/B comparisons by muting one channel while simultaneously soloing another. This is generally a much more awkward maneuver in software.

Fig. 3-124: Control surfaces that can be used with Studio One 2 range from the inexpensive Korg nanoKONTROL2 (top) to the upscale SSL Matrix (bottom left). The original Mackie HUI was the first practical control surface, and its latter-day incarnation, Mackie Control Universal Pro (bottom right) is still popular. By the way, these are not shown to scale.

Given this, it is only natural that many people choose to use a control surface, which provides the tactile control features of a traditional mixing console. The Mackie HUI was one of the first viable control surfaces; today, numerous control surfaces are available, some of which are configured to emulate a traditional mixing console to one degree or another, and others that are designed with DJ use in mind. The ranges of price and capability are wide, from the Korg nanoKONTROL2, at well under $100, to the $25,000 SSL Matrix, which combines high-end control surface with high-end analog mixing functionality.

However, many personal studios don't even need as much as the nanoKONTROL2 offers; having all the controls for a single channel is enough, if they can be switched around quickly between all the channels you work with. A handful of single-channel control surfaces meet this need, one of which is PreSonus' own FaderPort. Although Studio One 2 plays nicely with many control surfaces, FaderPort obviously has an edge in providing well-integrated control.

FaderPort is covered here, but I also wanted to describe how Studio One 2 works with a multichannel controller, so I have included a section discussing Novation's ZeRO SL MkII controller as a control surface for Studio One 2. I chose this controller because it has multiple channels, is affordably priced, and is a popular line of controllers, as, in addition to the ZeRO SL, Novation also makes keyboard controllers with integral control surfaces. Each control surface will have its own capabilities and setup requirements; I give the ZeRO SL as one example of a control surface experience.

Here are a few of the most common tasks control surfaces are used for:

- Transport control, including punch-in and -out
- Channel select
- Channel fader and pan
- Channel mute and solo
- Automation mode control
- Plug-in editing
- Undo

Making a Control Surface Work with Studio One 2

CONTROL SURFACE PROTOCOLS

A control surface sends data to the software it controls about how its controllers are being manipulated. How that data is packaged is a very important question, because the DAW has to be able to understand what it's being told about the control surface. The format for this packaging is the control surface protocol.

The first protocol used was MIDI, which is still used by some control surfaces. MIDI is very general, so a mapping has to be created manually (or recalled from a preset). Mackie and Digidesign (now Avid) created a MIDI protocol for Mackie's HUI control surface that added two major features:

- It created fixed controller relationships. A fader on a MIDI control surface could send any MIDI controller message and be controlling any parameter. A HUI fader sends a fader-specific message, so it is always a fader, and the pan control sends a pan-specific message, and so is always a panner.

- It maintained dynamic channel assignment, which is to say, banks. A HUI hooks itself up to control the first eight mixer channels it finds onscreen in the DAW, and pressing the bank button moves it to the next eight visible channels. This made it possible to have many channels of virtual mixing controlled by only a small number of physical channel controls.

All of this was accomplished by using customizable MIDI SysEx messages, instead of standard MIDI continuous controller messages. Over time, other protocols have emerged, including Euphonix (now part of Avid, too) EuCon, and Propellerheads Remote.

The issue is whether and how much the DAW software supports a given protocol. Studio One 2 presently supports MIDI and HUI. Control Link is the means by which MIDI gets mapped into Studio One 2's parameters, while HUI controllers have "hard-wired" control of basic mixer functions (channel fader, pan, solo, and mute). HUI controllers are aware only of channels that are visible onscreen; the Remote tab on the Banks Mix View panel exists to manage this situation.

CONNECTIONS AND CONFIGURATION

The following steps are necessary to get working with Studio One and a control surface. This is a general procedure; the specifics can vary with the control surface and your system. Detailed examples are given in the sections "FaderPort," and "Novation ZeRO SL" that follow.

1. Physically connect the control surface. There are several possible connections between a control surface and your computer. For example, FaderPort and the Novation ZeRO SL are USB peripherals, the SSL Matrix uses Ethernet, and some control surfaces (especially older ones) may have MIDI connectors.

2. Install and configure any software that accompanies the control surface. Generally, if such software comes with the control surface, it is not required for general operation but adds advanced features. The ZeRO SL, for example, comes with Novation's Automap software.

3. Establish communications between Studio One 2 and the control surface by creating an External Device for the surface. For more information on creating External Devices, see the section "Defining Your MIDI Devices and Control Surfaces" of chapter 1, "On Your Mark" in *Power Tools for Studio One 2*, volume 1.

4. Map the controls on the control surface to parameters in Studio One 2. In some cases, some, or even most, of the parameters you will want to edit might already be mapped in the protocol (fader, pan, mute, and solo functions in the HUI protocol, for example) or in factory-supplied presets, whereas other situations may call for manually mapping basic mixing functions, as well as deeper editing controls such as plug-in parameters, to physical controls. Studio One 2's Control Link feature is useful for this.

5. If your control surface is using the HUI protocol, set up the Remote tab of the Banks Mix View panel to configure which channels are available for surface control. For more on this, see the section "The Banks > Remote tab" later in this chapter.

UPDATING CONTROL SURFACES WITH TRANSMIT VALUE

Control surfaces send messages to control such software as Studio One 2, but what happens if you move an onscreen control for a parameter controlled by the surface? If the control surface cannot be updated when an onscreen control is moved, then the surface and the software get out of sync and the controller is essentially useless.

Control surfaces that connect to the computer using USB, Ethernet, or another bidirectional networking interface usually have the ability to receive updates when an onscreen control is moved...as long as the software sends them, that is. Using Transmit Value mode for one or more controls in a Device Controller Map enables Studio One 2 to send updates to a control surface. Motorized faders and infinite-turn encoders get reset to match the incoming control data.

(MIDI, in its original hardware form, is a unidirectional interface, making such updating difficult. It is not impossible, however, and there have been surfaces that could communicate bidirectionally if you made a second physical MIDI connection for the messages returning to the surface. Still, you are much less likely to use Transmit Value with a control surface that connects to your MIDI interface.)

To enable transmission of messages to control surfaces for one or more controls:

1. Open the Device Controller Map for the control surface.
2. Click the MIDI Learn button to put the map into MIDI Learn mode.
3. Right-click (Ctrl-click in Mac) on a control you want to transmit and choose Transmit Value from the contextual menu that drops down. When the value of the parameter being controlled is changed by an onscreen control, messages will be transmitted to the control surface.
4. Repeat for as many controls as you want transmitting.

EXECUTING COMMANDS AND MACROS
FROM A CONTROL SURFACE

It is possible to assign a button in a Device Controller Map to execute a Studio One 2 command. The list of commands includes macros, so buttons on the controller can trigger the execution of commands or macros. To assign a button to execute a command or macro:

1. Open the Device Controller Map for the control surface.
2. Right-click (Ctrl-click in Mac) on a button in the map and choose Assign Command from the contextual menu that drops down. The Select Command dialog appears.

Fig. 3-125: Right-click (Ctrl-click in Mac) on a button control in the Device Controller Map and choose Assign Command to open the Select Command dialog.

3. Locate the command or macro you want to trigger and click the OK button to complete the assignment.

THE BANKS > REMOTE TAB

Probably the most widely accepted control surface protocol is the HUI protocol. To facilitate customizing which channels are controlled by a HUI-based controller, the HUI uses a scheme whereby it only controls channels that are visible onscreen. This allows you to have one screen set in which only submix masters

Fig. 3-126: The Select Command dialog.

Fig. 3-127: The Remote tab of the Banks Mix View panel is a list of channels that will be visible to a control surface using the HUI protocol. It is independent of the Screen tab, which determines what is actually seen in Studio One 2.

are visible, another in which all of the drum tracks are visible, and yet another that breaks out the half dozen attempts at a lead vocal onto different channels. Recalling one of these screensets puts those channels under the control of the surface. But what if you want to have submix masters under your fingers while seeing just the vocal takes onscreen? This is the purpose of the Remote tab of the Banks Mix View panel.

The Remote tab creates a "useful fiction" for a HUI-based control surface; it maintains a map for the surface of what channels are visible that may or may not be the same as the map of what really is visible in Studio One 2's mixer. (What really is visible is controlled by the Screen tab.) The control surface sees the map on the Remote tab, which, in our example, would show the submix masters as the only visible channels. Meanwhile, the Screen tab would show the tracks of vocal takes as the only ones visible. Note that the mixer displays whichever tab is selected; when the Remote tab is selected, only the channels visible to the control surface will be shown in the mixer.

FOOD FOR THOUGHT ABOUT CONTROL SURFACES

Control surfaces are not right for every need, and using them is not always completely seamless. Here are a few general points to consider:

- On the whole, control surfaces are better for editing, mixing, and transport control than for selecting items, which is more effectively done using a mouse.
- While it is usually difficult to access a DAW's menus from a control surface, it is sometimes possible to assign buttons on a control surface to send out a few characters of text—enough to trigger a keyboard shortcut in the DAW.
- Controlling basic mixer channel functions is usually straightforward, whereas plug-in editing is more complicated because of the large variation in parameters and implementations by the various plug-in makers. Although control surfaces can be valuable in editing plug-ins, you should expect to find idiosyncrasies and/or bugs with most of them when doing so.
- Control surfaces vary in their hardware capabilities. Some have motorized faders, some have touch-sensitive controls, some have endless turn knobs, some have all of the above. Each of these offers advantages and, sometimes, drawbacks. For instance, as useful as touch sensitivity is, if all of a surface's controls are touch-sensitive, it is very easy to brush a control accidentally and suddenly be editing a different parameter than you intended. Clearly, using a touch-sensitive control surface successfully demands that you be careful in your movements. On the other hand, without motorized faders, a surface cannot accurately reflect current channel levels.
- Controller resolution can vary with the controller, or, more often, with the protocol used to carry its data. For example, a MIDI controller linked to channel volume will produce a minimum fader value change of about 0.7 dB, while FaderPort can get steps as small as 0.1 dB. Depending on what is being controlled and a number of other facts, controller resolution can have an audible effect on how smoothly the mix changes.
- The value range of the controller may not have an understandable relationship to a parameter value in Studio One 2. For instance, a MIDI controller using a value range of 0 to 127 does not have an intuitive relationship with Studio One 2's channel faders, which are calibrated in tenths of a dB. Sometimes you just have to get the feel from repeated use and go from there.

FaderPort

As one would expect, PreSonus' FaderPort control surface communicates intimately with Studio One. FaderPort communicates via USB, rather than MIDI, and its presence is immediately recognized and configured by Studio One without your having to do one darned thing. It just does the right thing and shows up as an External Device available for control purposes.

Fig. 3-128: The PreSonus FaderPort controller provides a single channel of controls and is very smoothly integrated with Studio One 2.

FaderPort is designed to provide essential channel and automation controls, but it is not customizable (aside from a single User button), and must be mapped manually to edit plug-ins. This means that it is not highly flexible, but it is fast and intuitive to use. FaderPort includes the following controls:

- Touch-sensitive motorized fader for channel volume
- Infinite-turn pan pot
- Mute button
- Solo button
- Record Enable button
- Left/right select arrows: When Shift is off, these arrows step through channels in the mixer. Note that the arrows do not step through tracks in the Arrange view, so you can select Instrument channels in the mixer with FaderPort, but not Instrument tracks.
- Bank button: When the Bank button is off, using the arrow buttons to shift channels shifts the channel selected onscreen, as well as the channel being controlled by the FaderPort. The Bank button does not shift the active channel by a bank of eight channels.
- Output button: Switches FaderPort control to Main Out.
- Fader automation mode buttons: Read/Write/Touch/(Motor) Off.
- Windows view buttons: Mix, Project, Transport, Undo.
- Transport modes: Punch, Loop.
- User button: Assignable; no default assignment.
- Transport controls: Rewind, Fast Forward, Stop, Return to Zero, Play, Record.
- Shift key and shifted functions: Previous/Next (go to previous/next marker), Mark (drop a marker on the fly), Redo, Start (go to selection start), End (go to selection end).

- Footswitch input: Accepts a 1/4-inch phone plug. Default function is Transport Record.

ASSIGNING FUNCTIONS TO THE USER BUTTON AND FOOTSWITCH INPUT

The User button and Footswitch input can be assigned to do two things:

- Operate an onscreen switch through Control Link
- Trigger any command that appears in the Keyboard Shortcuts window

For more information on mapping a controller to an onscreen control with Control Link, see the section "Using Hardware Controllers with Studio One 2: Control Link" of chapter 4, "Virtual Instruments and MIDI" in *Power Tools for Studio One 2*, volume 1.

To map the User button or Footswitch input to trigger a command:

1. Double-click on FaderPort in the External Mix View panel. Its Device Controller Map will open.

2. Right-click (Ctrl-click in Mac) on the Footswitch or User button graphic in the Device Controller Map and choose Assign Command from the contextual menu that drops down. The Select Command dialog will appear.

3. Select the desired command to be triggered by the controller from the Select Command dialog, then click OK to dismiss the dialog.

Beyond the obvious front-panel functions, some hidden ones are useful to know about:

- To scroll the play location horizontally through the Song in the Arrange view: Hold the Shift button and turn the Pan knob.
- To shift through Arrange view tracks (instead of mixer channels): Press Shift and use the left and right arrow buttons.
- The Window View buttons show and hide Studio One 2 views: Mix shows/hides Mix view, the Proj button shows/hides Edit view, Trns shows/hides the Browser.

Fig. 3-129: To assign the Footswitch input or User button to execute a command, right-click (Ctrl-click in Mac) on the button for either in the FaderPort Device Controller Map, and choose Assign Command from the menu that appears.

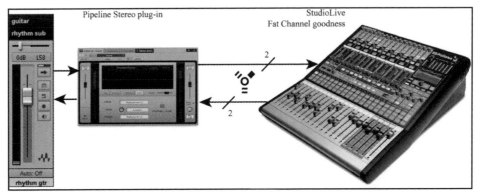

Fig. 3-130: PreSonus' StudioLive mixers cannot control Studio One 2, but they act like multichannel FireWire interfaces. StudioLive's channel and effects processing can be used by Studio One 2 using the FireWire channels. In this illustration, the Pipeline plug-in routes audio to and from the StudioLive via FireWire channels, so that the StudioLive's Fat Channel can be inserted on the Studio One channel.

StudioLive

StudioLive is PreSonus' range of digital mixers. StudioLive integrates with Studio One 2 as a FireWire audio interface, so audio can pass back and forth between them, showing up, like any other interface inputs and outputs, in the Preferences > Song Setup > Audio I/O Setup pane. However, StudioLive offers no control capabilities for Studio One 2.

Control Link

Control Link enables nearly any parameter in Studio One 2 to be controlled by standard MIDI controller messages. Any device that can generate these messages can be used to control Studio One 2. As I will discuss in the next section, "Novation ZeRO SL MkII," there are sometimes more efficient methods than mapping parameters one at a time in Control Link, but there also are control tasks in Studio One 2 that can only be accomplished that way.

Control Link can be used to change nearly any parameter in the program, from the mixer to plug-in processors to VIs, and it is pretty simple to operate. The basic process goes like this:

1. For each external device, create a map of the hardware controllers on it that you want to use.

2. Configure the map to have the desired types of controllers (sliders, buttons, and so on).

3. Create a link between a hardware controller and a software parameter.

For more information on Control Link, including creating Device Controller Maps and linking parameters to controls, see the section "Using Hardware Controllers with Studio One 2: Control Link" of chapter 4, "Virtual Instruments and MIDI" in *Power Tools for Studio One 2*, volume 1.

Novation ZeRO SL MkII

Novation makes a range of keyboard controllers, some of which incorporate control surfaces. The ZeRO SL MKII packages the control surface on its own, without a music keyboard. The control surfaces in the keyboard controllers work the same way as the ZeRO SL, so this section pertains to those, as well.

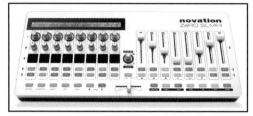

HARDWARE CONTROLS ON THE ZERO SL
The ZeRO SL consists of two sections. On the right are eight motorized, touch-sensitive faders, each with two buttons below. On the left is a section with a backlit LCD

Fig. 3-131: The Novation ZeRO SL MkII control surface is inexpensive and has impressive flexibility, but lacks motorized faders.

"scribble strip" display and eight channel strips, each with an infinite-turn pot (knob) controller, a fixed-rotation pot controller, a drum pad, and two buttons. The surface is completed by a crossfader, an infinite-turn "speed dial" pot, and a number of mode select buttons. The bottom row of buttons on the right side doubles as transport control buttons.

As most of the Songs you create in Studio One 2 are likely to have more than eight channels in the mixer, two of the drum pad buttons serve for bank-shifting left or right to access all of the channels.

The rear panel contains inputs for an expression pedal and a control pedal, plus MIDI ports (not needed for use with Studio One 2), including a MIDI In port.

SETTING UP THE ZERO SL TO USE WITH STUDIO ONE 2
There are only a few steps to get the ZeRO SL working with Studio One 2:

1. Install Automap software according to Novation's directions.
2. Connect the ZeRO SL to your computer. Although its MIDI connectors could be used for this, USB is the better choice.
3. Configure Automap for use with plug-ins in Studio One 2 according to Novation's directions. This is basically selecting Studio One 2 in the Automap software, clicking a button, and waiting while Automap does its thing. Automap offers the ability to enable or disable each plug-in for use with the ZeRO SL.

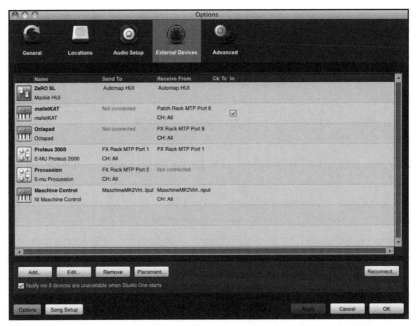

Fig. 3-132: The External Devices dialog, with the ZeRO SL HUI device at the top of the list.

Fig. 3-133: The Automap HUI choice in the Receive From/Send To field drop-down menu makes the ZeRO SL use the Mackie HUI protocol.

4. Create an External Device in Studio One 2 for the ZeRO SL. Create a HUI External Device, as Automap does not (yet) have a custom driver for Studio One 2. You can rename it, if you like, as I have in Fig. 3-132.

5. Click in the Receive From and Send To fields in the Add Device dialog and choose Automap HUI from the drop-down menu that appears for each. The ZeRO SL is now set up to control Studio One 2.

CONTROLLING STUDIO ONE 2 WITH THE ZERO SL
The ZeRO SL controls Studio One 2 in two different ways:

- Basic mixing and transport functions are controlled using the HUI protocol. Since the HUI protocol has been widely used for many years now, control of channel fader, pan, mute, solo, and record enable are seamless and require no setup.

- Plug-in editing is supported with a proprietary solution. Novation applies a software "wrapper" to VST and AU (in Mac) plug-ins that works with their Automap software, which is always running in the background. After installation, you will notice more plug-ins in the Effects tab of the Browser than before. There is now a second, "wrapped" version of each VST or AU plug-in, identifiable by the "-Automap" at the end of its name. This version of the plug-in must be used to edit it from the ZeRO SL. When you open a wrapped plug-in, most or all of the available parameters are already mapped to physical controls.

TRANSPORT AND MIXER CONTROL

- Basic transport (stop, play, record, rewind, fast forward) and mixer control (channel fader, pan, solo, mute, record enable) are essentially transparent to you; they just work.

- The faders and pots on the ZeRO SL are touch-sensitive but, because they are not motorized, are not immediately active. You must move the fader or pot until it passes through the position in its travel that corresponds to the current value of the parameter being edited. So, if volume for a channel is set to 75, but the fader on the ZeRO SL is near the bottom, the fader will have to be moved through the point in its travel that corresponds to 75. As soon as the fader goes through that point, it takes active control over the mixer fader's value. The fader will remain active as long as its position matches the parameter value, so if you move a second fader and then come back to the first fader without having moved it, it will still be active.

- Since Studio One 2 has a HUI External Device preset available, there is no need to set up a Device Controller Map. Of course, one exists, and you can see it by double-clicking on the ZeRO SL's name in the External Devices mixer panel.

- You must enable transport control on the ZeRO SL by pressing its transport button. This repurposes the bottom row of buttons beneath the fader, which otherwise is the Solo button for the channel. Thus, you are likely to be hitting the transport button often to pop in and out of transport control.

Fig. 3-134: The ZeRO SL uses the Device Controller Map for a Mackie HUI.

- The HUI Automap mapping can be edited to add additional functionality, such as setting loop/punch in and out points, enabling/disabling looping, return to zero, locating to markers, and so on. The simplest method is to assign available ZeRO SL controls to type Studio One 2 keyboard shortcuts. Remember that Studio One 2 macros can also be played from keyboard shortcuts. Refer to the Automap user manual for more information on programming the ZeRO SL.

PLUG-IN EDITING

As mentioned before, plug-in editing is a bit messier than basic transport and mixer control. Novation's Automap software maps hardware controls to parameters, just as does Studio

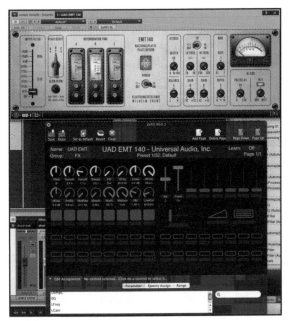

Fig. 3-135: Automap software controlling the Universal Audio EMT140 reverb plug-in.

One 2's Control Link. Why would you want to use Automap instead of Control Link? Mostly, because mapping takes time, so if Novation has already made a system that wraps and maps for you, it is probably most efficient to simply go with that.

Mappings for editing many plug-ins are supplied with Automap. If no mapping exists, Automap uses the list of available parameters it gets from the plug-in and tries to do its best to create a logical mapping.

If Automap's attempt is goofy, or if you have needs Novation's mappings don't satisfy, it still takes less time to use a preset as a point of departure and modify it than to build a new one from scratch. Of course, building from scratch is always an option, if necessary.

The plug-ins bundled with Studio One 2 are in PreSonus' proprietary format, not VST or AU, so Automap cannot access their parameters. No worries! As long as a control surface is capable of sending standard MIDI continuous controller (CC) messages when its controls are moved, the CC messages can be mapped by Control Link to the plug-in parameters. With the ZeRO SL, this is how it is accomplished:

1. An Automap Virtual MIDI mapping makes the ZeRO SL send standard MIDI continuous controller messages. The Automap manual describes how to do this.
2. Create a new Control Surface External Device in Studio One 2 for the ZeRO SL MIDI device. Select Automap MIDI in both the Send To and Receive From fields.
3. Create a Device Controller Map for the ZeRO SL MIDI external device.
4. Use Control Link to map ZeRO SL controls to PreSonus plug-in parameters.
5. The ZeRO SL must be in User mode with the Virtual MIDI mapping selected to edit PreSonus plug-ins.

PLUG-INS AND EFFECTS

One of the most important parts of mixing is processing with plug-ins and effects. Some plug-ins serve fundamental, "bread and butter" purposes (think EQ and dynamics), whereas others provide effects ranging from common tricks, such as flanging or delay, to exotic sound manglers, such as Waves Enigma, iZotope Iris, or any number of other unique processors.

Studio One 2 hosts three formats of plug-ins: VST (VST2 and VST3), Audio Units, and a proprietary format PreSonus uses for its own plug-ins that come bundled with the program.

Plug-ins are always inserted on channels or in Event FX chains. Even send effects are inserted on Bus or FX channels. A plug-in can be inserted on any kind of channel, but the placement is key to how it functions. For instance, a plug-in inserted on an Input channel is part of the recording signal chain, and the effect will be part of the recording. On the other hand, the same plug-in on an Output channel configured as a Cue mix will only be heard by someone monitoring that Cue mix; the effect will not get recorded or even be heard through the Main Out.

Studio One 2's system for plug-ins is both elegant and rich, offering lots of goodies, such as drag-and-drop functionality, automatic latency compensation, a flexible preset structure, Control Link to facilitate plug-in editing with control surfaces, the ability to store and recall entire FX Chains, an intuitive layout for the header of the Device Editor, and the Pipeline plug-in for integrating outboard processors nearly as easily as software plug-ins.

Bundled Plug-Ins

Studio One 2 comes with a solid collection of plug-ins that cover all of the basics and many advanced applications. For serious sound mangling or models of specific hardware, you will want to supplement the bundled set with selections from third-party plug-in makers.

While I would love to include detailed descriptions of every parameter of every bundled plug-in here, that is, sadly, beyond the scope of this book. I'll settle for a sentence or two of description about each one, in which I will try to highlight key features. The Studio One 2 Reference Manual has more detail, but a comprehensive guide will just have to wait for another day.

The bundled plug-ins are in PreSonus' proprietary format, which has a few implications:

- The bundled plug-ins use the PreSonus preset system. For more information on this, see the section "Editing Plug-Ins" later in this chapter.

- The bundled plug-ins do not make their parameter information available in a commonly used format. This makes it impossible for control surfaces to configure themselves to PreSonus plug-in parameters. Parameter editing from a control surface must be done by mapping MIDI controllers to parameters using Control Link.

Here's the list of bundled plug-ins:

- Ampire: A modeled guitar amp rig, including two channels, a baker's dozen of amp models, a rack of "stomp box" processors (with Pre/Post

Fig. 3-136: These are all of the PreSonus plug-ins bundled with Studio One Professional. Studio One 2 Artist and Producer include most of the PreSonus plug-ins; Studio One 2 Professional adds deluxe plugs, such as Multiband Dynamics and Pipeline.

controls!), a dozen cabinet models (plus the ability to add your own cabinet impulse responses), and three configurable virtual microphones. Many of PreSonus' top brass are guitarists (an instrumentally mixed metaphor, if ever there was one), so they care about this plug's sounding good!

- Analog Delay: A delay that models the behavior of tape delay units, such as tape saturation and speed slewing. Other features include the ability to sync to tempo, a very wide-range of delays (1ms to 3s, or whole notes to 1/64 notes), and filtering and stereo width control for the delays.

- Autofilter: A really interesting swept-filter processor, Autofilter offers two filters that can be configured in serial or parallel, and swept (cutoff and resonance) by an AR envelope, a tempo-syncable LFO, or both. The filters are versatile and the LFO includes a 16-step sequencer as one of its waveforms.

- Beat Delay: A tempo-syncable delay with filtering and stereo width control for the feedback.

- Binaural Pan: Varies the width of a stereo channel from mono to double-wide using an M-S (Mid-Side) approach.

- Channel Strip: A compact plug-in with a low-cut filter, simple compressor and expander, and a three-band EQ (HF and LF shelving filters, MF peaking filter).

- Chorus: A chorus/doubler with up to three voices, two-band EQ, stereo width control, and four LFO waveforms.

- Compressor: A full-featured rms compressor with variable knee threshold, a sidechain with filtering, adaptive release time, automatic gain compensation, and last but most decidedly not least, a mix control, allowing parallel compression to be done onboard. A useful, good-sounding plug-in.

- Dual Pan: A simple but highly utilitarian processor that allows setting input balance (in case one channel is simply louder than the other), a choice of five panning laws (curves that determine how sound travels from one side to the other), and individual pan controls for the left and right outputs.

- Expander: A flexible expander/gate with a filtered sidechain. With the right settings, this plug can be used as a downward expander (the most common use), upward expander (sometimes used in mastering to bring back over-squashed dynamics) or a range expander, which does not affect signals above or below the programmed range.

- Flanger: A basic flanger that is tempo-syncable.

- Gate: Gating is the extreme case of expanding, so what does the Gate plug-in offer that is different from the Expander? One very cool feature is the ability to generate a trigger output whenever the gate is opened. This trigger can be used as the MIDI (okay, "performance data") input to an Instrument track. This gives you one-step drum replacement: put a kick drum into this plug-in and it can extract a trigger you can then use to play a kick sample. The Gate plug-in also has a filtered sidechain that includes the ability to invert the envelope of an external sidechain input signal. Inverting the envelope of a sidechain input produces ducking. For instance, if the organ is fighting the lead vocal, put the organ through the Gate plug-in, feed the vocal to the sidechain input, engage Duck, and set the Range to something small, such as 3 or 4 dB. When the vocalist sings, the organ level will dip by a few dB to get it out of the way.

- Groove Delay (Studio One 2 Professional only): A monster groove tool, this plug-in provides four delay taps with independently variable level, timing, pan, filtering (with modulation), and feedback. There are several additional groove modification features, as well. I don't really have to say that it's tempo-syncable, do I?

- IR Maker: This is a specialized utility plug-in, not an effect. It is used to capture impulse responses that can be used with the bundled OpenAIR convolution reverb. The final output of an impulse response capture is a standard .wav file, which could be used with just about any convolution engine that lets you supply your own impulse responses. The penny version of how to use it is: set up an Output channel to send the test signal to the device from which you want an impulse response, connect the device's output to an Input channel, create an Audio track with the Input and Output channels you created as its input and output, and run the acquisition process. It's a little involved, but not really difficult. The Studio One 2 Reference Manual has a good discussion of how to go about it.

- Level Meter: A comprehensive meter for when the standard channel meter is not big enough or precise enough. The Level Meter plug-in is discussed in more detail in the "Level Meter" section earlier in this chapter.

- Limiter: A peak limiter with flexible metering, including K-System presets, soft clipping, and True Peak metering.

- Mixtool: A utility plug-in for solving common gotcha problems. Add up to 24 dB of gain, swap channels, invert the polarity of either channel, remove a DC offset…hey, this thing even has an MS (Mid-Side) matrix onboard.

- Mixverb: A basic and easy-on-the-processor reverb with a gate (if you *must* gate your reverb) and stereo width control.

- Multiband Dynamics (Studio One Professional): A full-featured processor with five bands of compression/expansion, range-based processing (that is, it can be configured to operate only over a specified level range), global offset editing (changing one parameter offsets that parameter on all bands by the amount the control is changed), variable knee, and, again, that beautiful wet/dry mix control that enables onboard parallel compression. This plug-in also has excellent and extensive metering capabilities, and uses phase-corrected summing to reassemble the signal on output.

- Open AIR (Studio One Professional): A convolution reverb that puts less demand on the processor than higher-end options, such as Altiverb, Open AIR is still quite flexible. The basic impulse response can be time-stretched to get longer or shorter decay times, a six-band equalizer enables tone shaping, and cross-feed features compensate for the fact that Open AIR does not do true stereo processing.

- Phase Meter: A goniometer and a correlation meter for monitoring phase relationships between stereo channels. The Phase Meter plug-in is discussed in more detail in the "Phase Meter" section earlier in this chapter.

- Phaser: Phasers sound similar to flangers, but flanging is achieved through time delay, whereas phasers use all-pass filters, which pass all frequencies at equal amplitude, but with different amounts of phase shift. The Phaser plug-in lets you set the number of filters up to 20 stages, as well as a frequency range within which all the filters are set.

- Pipeline Mono (Studio One Professional): The Pipeline plug-in allows outboard processors to be used as insert effects. Pipeline Mono sends and receives a mono signal. For more information on the Pipeline plug-in, see the section "Integrating Outboard Devices: The Pipeline Plug-In" later in this chapter.

- Pipeline Stereo (Studio One Professional): The Pipeline Stereo is the stereo send/receive version of the Pipeline plug-in. For more information on the Pipeline plug-in, see the section "Integrating Outboard Devices: The Pipeline Plug-In" later in this chapter.

- Pro EQ: A comprehensive equalizer with five bands of fully parametric EQ plus high-cut and low-cut filters, spectrum analyzer, individual band and composite curve displays, and a high-quality mode that gives better performance at a somewhat higher processor cost. Other nice touches include simultaneous peak/rms metering and an Auto Gain function that matches input and output signal power.

- RedlightDist: An analog-style distortion plug-in with six distortion models, high-cut and low-cut filters, and two variable distortion parameters.

- Room Reverb: A room emulator that takes the less common approach of supplying parameters that define a virtual space and the location of source and listeners in it, rather than parameters that describe the reverb itself. Although the parameters are somewhat less familiar, some very interesting effects can be squeezed out of this plug-in. I have had great results from layering it with a more conventional digital reverb.

Fig. 3-137: The Room Reverb interface lets you define the physical characteristics of a room and then renders the reverb of the room you described.

- Scope: An X-Y oscilloscope display with many features, including three input channels, a signal difference channel, triggering options, and more. This plug-in will either be a serious technical tool for you, a cool-looking multicolor light show, or useless. The Scope plug-in is discussed in more detail in the "Scope" section earlier in this chapter.

- Spectrum Meter: The Spectrum Meter provides real-time spectral analysis with selectable resolution. It is useful in identifying frequencies of interest, whether because there is too much or too little of them. The meter can display at octave, 1/3 octave, or "FFT" resolution. Actually, all of the displays are most likely based on FFTs, but the FFT setting allows specification of the window size. (If this makes no sense to you, you might want read up a little on FFT basics.) Analysis ranges can be specified for both level and frequency. The Spectrum Meter plug-in is discussed in more detail in the "Spectrum Meter" section earlier in this chapter.

- The Spectrum Meter also features a sidechain input. When a signal is sent to this input, the meter window gets split to simultaneously show the spectrum of the sidechain signal and the channel signal on which the meter is inserted, making for easy comparisons of spectra.

- Tone Generator: A versatile test signal generator, with three waveforms, pink and white noise, linear and log sweeps, gating, and a few other configuration parameters. The Tone Generator plug-in is discussed in more detail in the "Tone Generator" section earlier in this chapter.

- Tricomp: Tricomp is a semiautomatic multiband compressor. It has three bands of compression that can have program-dependent attack and release times, plus variable knee threshold and a saturation control to emulate classic leveling processors (such as the LA-2A). Although much less powerful than the Multiband Dynamics plug-in, Tricomp is much faster and easier to use.

- Tuner: The tuner looks like a standard guitar tuner, but there are some extra features. For one, it can be switched from the regular flat/sharp indicator display to a strobe-type display. It also shows the actual frequency played and the difference between that and the nearest note.

- X-Trem: X-Trem can be either a sophisticated tremolo effect or an autopanner. Tempo-syncable modulation is from one of four waveforms, or two 16-step sequencers.

Third-Party Plug-Ins

The story on third-party plug-ins is pretty short and sweet: They work. You'll run into some variation in implementations, and the occasional sloppy job of it, but, by and large, if your plug-in is in a supported format, you're good.

Studio One 2 supports the following formats:

- VST2
- VST3
- Audio Units (AU)
- PreSonus proprietary
- ReWire (not a plug-in format in the same sense, but worth including here)

TIP: Some manufacturers write multiprocessor support into their plug-ins, which can conflict with Studio One 2's multiprocessor code. If this happens, disable the multiprocessor support in the plug-in, if possible, and allow Studio One 2 to handle multiprocessor management.

Plug-In Latency Compensation

The nature of plug-ins (actually, of any digital signal processing) is that they unavoidably introduce a small amount of delay, referred to as latency. In most cases, the latency of a single plug-in is not enough to be objectionable, but when several plug-ins get stacked up, the latency can become a problem. Worse, unless every channel uses the exact same plug-ins in the same order, there is likely to be different latency on each channel. It's a mess, and the kind of the thing that computers ought to be able to deal with on their own. Fortunately, in many DAWs, including Studio One 2, they can. The best part is that latency compensation is automatic; there is nothing you need do to enable it.

For most people, that's the end of the story. However, there could conceivably be a circumstance in which it is desirable to disable the automatic compensation.

- To disable automatic latency compensation: Choose Transport > Ignore Plug-In Latency from the main menu bar.

Adding a Plug-In

Add a plug-in to a channel using any of these methods:

- Drag the desired plug-in from the Effects tab of the Browser to the channel; it will be added after any other effects already on the channel. An effect can be dropped anywhere on the channel, but dropping it in the Inserts area allows you to place it at a specific position in an existing chain of effects on the channel. If there are presets for the plug-in, dragging a preset instead of the plug-in itself causes it to be loaded along with the plug-in.

- Drag an effect to a track and it will be added to the Inserts area of the corresponding channel in the mixer.

- Click the Add Insert button with the + (plus sign) at the top of the Inserts area of a channel and select a plug-in from the menu that drops down.

- Drag a plug-in from the Inserts area of another channel. The plug-in will be instantiated on the destination channel with all of the settings of the plug-in on the source channel.

Fig. 3-138: This plug-in was dragged from the Browser and is being dropped in the middle of an existing processing chain.

- Drag or restore a plug-in from the Trash Bin to a channel.

Removing Plug-Ins

To remove a plug-in, use any of the following methods:

- Right-click (Ctrl-click in Mac) on the plug-in and choose Remove from the contextual menu that drops down.
- Drag the plug-in to the Trash Bin mix panel.
- To remove all plug-ins on a channel at once, click the arrow at the top of the Inserts section of the channel and choose Remove All from the drop-down menu that appears.

Copying Plug-In Settings

Plug-in settings can be copied from one instance of the plug-in to another using any of these methods:

- Drag the plug-in to another channel. A new instance of the plug-in will be instantiated with the same settings as the plug-in that was dragged.
- Click the Copy button in the Device editor header of the plug-in, open or create another instance of the same plug-in, and click the Paste button in the Device editor header.

- Save the plug-in settings as a preset, open or create another instance of the same plug-in, and load the preset you just saved.

Saving and Loading Presets

Preset access is discussed in detail in the section "The Device (Plug-In and Instrument) Editor Header" of chapter 5, "On the Cutting Room Floor: Basic Editing" in *Power Tools for Studio One 2*, volume 1.

THE PRESONUS PLUG-IN FORMAT

The PreSonus plug-ins bundled with Studio One 2 are in a proprietary format. This brings many advantages and a few limitations.

- Micro-view: PreSonus effects offer a tiny editor that appears directly in a channel's insert area in the mixer and offers access to a small number of key parameters for the effect, and sometimes even graphic displays. For more information on effects micro-views, see the section "The Effects Micro-View" earlier in this chapter.
- Editing from control surfaces: Control surfaces can edit plug-ins either using an established protocol that is part of the plug-in format, as with VST and AU plug-ins, or through standard MIDI continuous controller messages. Because PreSonus plug-ins are in a proprietary format, editing from a control surface requires making a Device Controller Map that assigns MIDI messages from a controller to plug-in parameters. For more information on Device Controller Maps, see the section "Making Device Controller Maps" of chapter 4, "Virtual Instruments and MIDI" in *Power Tools for Studio One 2*, volume 1.
- FX chains: You will find you often use the same series of plug-ins on certain sources. Two or more effects on a channel can be saved together as an FX Chain, then easily instantiated on a new channel. For more information on FX Chains, see the section "FX Chains" later in this chapter.
- Presets: PreSonus-format plug-ins can use the preset system built into the Device editor. For more information on the editor and preset system, see the section "The Device (Plug-In and Instrument) Editor Header" of chapter 5, "On the Cutting Room Floor: Basic Editing" in *Power Tools for Studio One 2*, volume 1.

Editing Plug-Ins

PreSonus and third-party plug-ins editors alike all appear framed by Studio One 2's plug-in/instrument editor header. The editor header is described in detail in the section "The Device (Plug-In and Instrument) Editor Header" of chapter 5, "On the Cutting Room Floor: Basic Editing" in *Power Tools for Studio One 2*, volume 1, but a few points important to plug-in editing will be recapped here.

OPENING THE DEVICE EDITOR

Open the Device editor using any of these methods:

- Press F11 or choose Track > Show Channel Editor from the main menu bar. Note that F11 conflicts with an f-key assignment for Exposé in Mac, and that this command will have no effect if there are no plug-ins on the selected channel when the command is chosen.
- Double-click the plug-in in the Channel (or Event FX) Device Rack.
- Right-click (Ctrl-click in Mac) the plug-in in the Channel (or Event FX) Device Rack and choose Edit from the contextual drop-down menu that appears.
- Add a plug-in to a channel.
- If a Device editor is open for a channel, other insert effects on the channel can be accessed for editing by clicking the appropriately named tab at the top of the Device Editor header.

THE DEVICE EDITOR HEADER

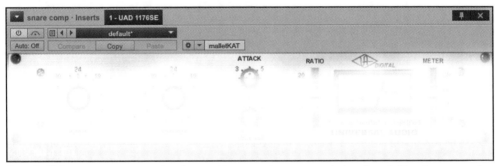

Fig. 3-139: The Device Editor header provides preset access, control surface linking, bypass, and more.

While every plug-in has its own user interface, they all appear within the same frame provided by Studio One 2. At the top of this frame, the Device editor header offers a set of functions for saving and loading presets, assigning control surface controllers to parameters, bypassing or deactivating the plug-in, and more. You will find some of this functionality, especially presets, described in later sections. For a complete discussion of the Device editor header, see "The Device (Plug-In and Instrument) Editor Header" section in chapter 5, "On the Cutting Room Floor: Basic Editing" of *Power Tools for Studio One 2*, volume 1.

PRESETS

PreSonus plug-ins use the preset system in the plug-in editor header. Whether third-party plug-ins use this preset system depends on how the plug-ins are implemented. For example, Universal Audio presets show up in the PreSonus preset system, whereas Waves and Sonnox plug-in presets do not. In most cases, presets you create can be stored using the editor header's preset system and, once stored, recalled later using it. However, if a plug-in has presets and they do not show up in the PreSonus editor's preset system, it is often the best policy to use the plug-in's own preset system for storing and loading presets. It adds a bit of "housekeeping" overhead to use more than one preset system, but it promotes more predictable performance.

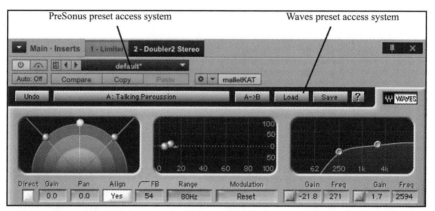

Fig. 3-140: The PreSonus preset access system lives alongside any third-party preset access system, such as this one from a Waves plug-in.

PRESET FORMATS

Studio One 2 recognizes the following preset file formats:

- .preset: PreSonus' proprietary format, used by the native plug-ins and VIs included with Studio One 2.
- .fxb: A VST preset bank format created by Steinberg (authors of the VST and VSTi plug-in formats), this type of file contains a set of presets that are loaded as a bank.
- .fxp: A VST preset format, also created by Steinberg, this type of file stores a single preset. This is useful for saving versions during development of a custom preset.
- .aupreset: A Mac-only format for Audio Units plug-ins.

LOADING PRESETS

There are four ways to load a preset:

- Select one from the Preset menu in the Device editor header.
- Drag a preset from the Browser to a channel.
- Use the preset system in a third-party plug-in.
- If a Device editor is open, double-clicking on a preset name for that device in the Browser will load the preset.

SAVING AND EXPORTING PRESETS

Presets can be saved and exported in the PreSonus preset system using any of these Preset Management menu commands:

- Store Preset: This command stores the preset as a .preset file to the chosen location with the name entered into the Save Preset dialog box and adds it to the Preset menu.

- Replace Preset: This command overwrites the currently loaded preset in its existing location, using the same name and the current parameter settings.

- Export VST Effect Bank: This command, available only for VST devices, creates a new .fxb file containing only one preset, using the current settings and the name entered in the Save As dialog box that appears. The preset will not appear in the Preset Select menu.

- Export VST Effect Preset: This command, available only for VST devices, creates a new .fxp file, using the current settings and the name entered in the Save As dialog box that appears. The preset will not appear in the Preset Select menu.

- Export AudioUnit Preset: This command, available only for Audio Unit devices, creates a new .aupreset file, using the current settings and the name entered in the Save As dialog box that appears. The preset will not appear in the Preset Select menu.

- Export Preset: This command creates a preset as a .preset file and saves it to the chosen location with the name entered into the Export Preset dialog box, but does not add it to the Preset menu.

- It is also possible to save presets using commands in the preset access system in a third-party device, rather than the PreSonus preset system.

Fig. 3-141: The Preset Management menu has commands for exporting presets to different formats, as well as storing presets.

COMPARE

The Device editor header offers a simple A/B comparison feature.

- The Compare button in the Device editor header automatically becomes active as soon as any edit is made to the last preset loaded. Click on the Compare button to toggle between the edited version (button is gray) and the original preset (button is blue).

Copying Effects Settings

Effects settings can be copied and moved without saving them to a preset, by either of these methods:

- Click on the Copy button in the Device editor header to copy the current settings to the clipboard, open a different copy of the same plug-in, and click on the Paste button in the Device editor header.

- Drag the effect in the mixer from the channel with the effects settings to be copied, and drop it on the same plug-in on another channel. If the plug-in does not exist on the destination channel, dropping the dragged effect in the Inserts area of the destination channel will instantiate the plug-in and load the settings.

Bypass Versus Deactivate

Bypass and Deactivate differ in this significant respect: Bypass provides smooth in/out switching (especially needed for automation) but does not free up the resources consumed by the plug-in, whereas Deactivate unloads the plug-in's computer code, freeing resources, but takes a moment to activate again. On the whole, use Bypass unless you have bounced a selection or for some other reason will not have need for the plug-in's processing for a while.

Fig. 3-142: The Bypass and Activate buttons.

- To activate or deactivate a device: Click on the Activate button. When the button is blue, the device is active.
- To bypass a device: Click on the Bypass button. When the button is red, the device is bypassed.

Sidechaining

Some plug-ins analyze an audio signal and from it derive a control signal that is then applied to control processing on the main signal path. For instance, in a compressor or gate, the input signal is watched for when it crosses a threshold, which initiates or concludes the compression or gating process on the main signal path. This control signal path is called a sidechain, and it is fed, logically enough, from a sidechain input, which, by default, uses the input signal.

There are many creative effects achievable using sidechains. Here are a few examples of common sidechain applications. It is a technique ripe with imaginative possibilities, so don't be afraid to experiment. As always, watch your monitor levels any time you do something that could cause unpredictable output levels.

- Ducking: The sidechain input initiates compression to lower the level of the signal when the sidechain signal is active. The classic ducking application is radio, where the signal is background music and the sidechain signal is the announcer's mic, so that the music level is decreased ("ducked") whenever the announcer speaks.

    However, ducking is useful whenever you want to get one thing out of the way of another. One more good ducking application is using a sung vocal as the sidechain input to a compressor where the signal is delay or reverb. When there are vocals, the effects are ducked to keep them audible and focused.

- Frequency-sensitive compression: An equalizer is inserted in the sidechain, which can be set to emphasize or deemphasize a specific frequency area. The result of emphasizing certain frequencies is that the compressor is more sensitive to those frequencies and goes into heavier compression on signals with a lot of energy at them.

  The classic application is de-essing, which relies on the fact that vocal sibilance occurs almost entirely in well less than an octave of the high-frequency spectrum. An EQ with boost at the relevant frequencies (usually around 5 kHz to 7 kHz) is inserted on the sidechain, causing the compressor to kick in and reduce gain when a signal has a lot of energy in the sibilance region.

  It can also be used to make a processor less sensitive to a given frequency region by cutting in the sidechain EQ. One example of this would be cutting low frequencies in the sidechain EQ to reduce pumping in the compressor.

- Cross-gating: The sidechain input causes a noise gate on the main signal to open and close. Think of a kick drum track triggering a gate on bass guitar to lock them up tight, or a snare drum track triggering a synth stab.

- Vocoding: An analysis/synthesis technique whereby the analysis signal feeds the sidechain input and the synthesis signal is in the main signal path. Because a spectral analysis is being performed (as opposed to the level analysis used in ducking and cross-gating), the tone of the main signal, not its dynamics, is modified.

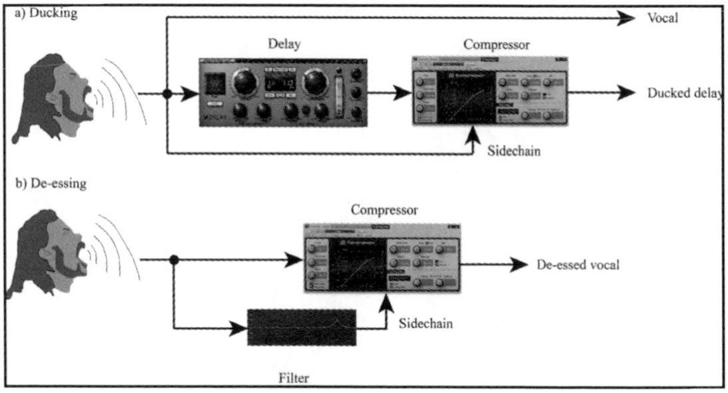

Fig. 3-143: Two popular applications for sidechaining. In a), a voice signal is triggering compression on a delay effect, ducking it by a few dB whenever the vocalist is singing. In b), we see de-essing: a filter has been inserted in the sidechain to emphasize high-mid frequencies, causing ducking when there is sibilance, which tends to be concentrated in that range.

SIDECHAINING FOR SPECTRAL COMPARISONS

Studio One 2 adds a twist to the sidechaining applications listed above. The Pro EQ and Spectrum Meter both include sidechain inputs that allow spectrum analysis of a second signal to be displayed simultaneously with the signal from the channel on which the EQ or meter is inserted. This makes it easy to compare spectra, if, for instance, you are trying to match an overdub to an original track, or, conversely, EQ a guitar and a voice to not be in each other's way spectrally.

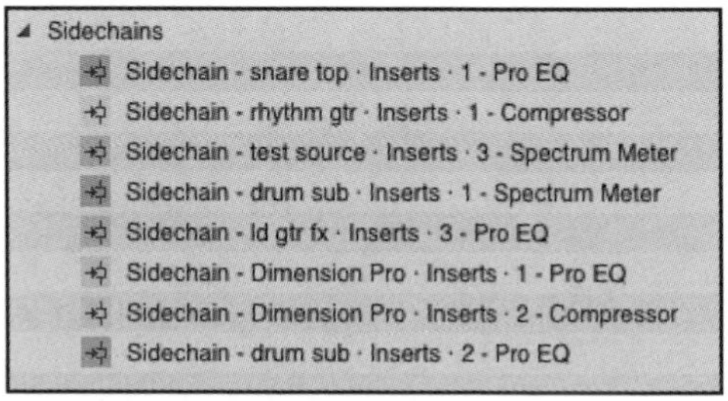

Fig. 3-144: At the bottom of this list of sidechains is the sidechain input for a Pro EQ plug-in. This enables two simultaneous spectrum analyzer displays (one for the channel signal and one for the sidechain signal) in the plug-in window.

ACCESSING SIDECHAINS

Sidechains are just buses that have predetermined destinations: the sidechain input of a plug-in. Consequently, sidechains are accessed in the same ways and places as buses. Anywhere you see a list of buses, active sidechain inputs will be in a subfolder called "Sidechains" (duh) at the bottom of the list of available buses. That means that channel sends or channel outputs can feed sidechain inputs. The one exception is that sidechain inputs are not available as output destinations for Folder tracks.

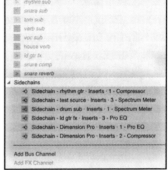

Assigning a signal to a sidechain may cause changes in the plug-in, such as activating a sidechain mode.

To access a sidechain input for a plug-in:

1. When adding a send, routing a channel output, or performing another assignment to a bus, move the cursor to the Sidechains folder at the bottom of the drop-down menu of available bus destinations and choose the desired sidechain input from the submenu that drops-down.

Fig. 3-145: Sidechains appear in a folder at the bottom of the list of available bus destinations.

FX Chains

An FX Chain can contain any plug-in, not just PreSonus plug-ins. All channel types have Device Racks into which an FX Chain can be loaded. Because an FX Chain is a complete Insert signal path, existing effects on a channel are replaced when an FX Chain is added to the channel.

CREATING, RENAMING, OR DELETING AN FX CHAIN

There are two ways to create an FX Chain from a set of insert effects on a channel.

Method 1:

1. Make the Effects tab of the Browser visible.
2. Move the cursor to the header at the top of the Channel Insert Device Rack, until the icon turns into an open hand.
3. Drag from the device rack header to the Browser.

Method 2:

1. Set up the chain of effects you want to store as an FX Chain.
2. Click on the triangle to the right of the "Inserts" legend in the channel's Device Rack and choose Store FX Chain from the drop-down menu that appears.

Fig. 3-146: The Store FX Chain command captures all of the inserts on a channel into a single preset.

3. Enter the name you want to give the FX Chain in the Store Preset dialog that appears. The FX Chain now appears in the list of presets in the FX Chains folder on the Effects tab of the Browser.

To rename an FX chain:

1. Right-click (Ctrl-click in Mac) on the FX Chain in the Effects tab of the Browser and choose Rename Preset from the contextual drop-down menu that appears.
2. Enter the desired name in the Rename Preset dialog that appears.

FX Chains are deleted from the FX Chains folder in the Effects tab of the Browser. Delete an FX Chain using either of these methods:

- Select the FX Chain you wish to delete in the FX Chains folder, press the Delete key, and click "Yes" in the confirmation dialog that appears.
- Right-click (Ctrl-click in Mac) on the FX Chain you wish to delete in the FX Chains folder, choose the Delete command from the contextual menu that drops down, and click "Yes" in the confirmation dialog that appears.

ADDING AN FX CHAIN

FX Chains can be added to any channel type. Add an FX Chain using any of these methods:

- Drop an FX Chain from the FX Chains folder in the Effects tab of the Browser on the Device Rack of a channel. Note that adding an FX Chain to a channel removes any existing effects on that channel.
- Click the triangle next to the "Inserts" legend in the Device Rack header on a channel and choose an FX Chain from the drop-down menu that appears.
- Drop an FX Chain from the FX Chains folder in the Effects tab of the Browser on a track in the Arrange view. Existing effects on the channel are replaced. Dropping an FX Chain where there is no track in the Arrange view creates a new Audio track and inserts the FX Chain on it.
- Create a new Audio track using the Add Tracks command, click in the Preset field in the Add Tracks dialog, and choose an FX Chain from the menu that drops down.

Fig. 3-147: Dropping an FX Chain on a track will instantiate the effects on the associated channel in the mixer.

FX CHAINS IN MUSICLOOPS

Among the pieces of information stored in a Musicloop file are the effects used on an instrument's audio returns in the mixer. (This assumes use of a VI; instruments that are external devices are returned to Audio channels, which are not captured in Musicloop files.) Multitimbral VIs may use multiple Audio channels for their returns, but the good news is that a Musicloop file will store FX Chains for *all* of the Audio channels used for an instrument's returns. For more about FX Chains in Musicloops, see the section "The Audioloop and Musicloop File Formats" in chapter 1, "Working with Loops."

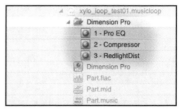

Fig. 3-148: Effects used on Instrument channels are saved as part of a Musicloop file.

Integrating Outboard Devices: the Pipeline Plug-In (Studio One Professional)

Have an amazing old compressor or high-end digital reverb? Like to be able to use it in your Studio One 2 Songs? That's what Pipeline is for. Pipeline is a plug-in that routes audio from a channel's insert chain to an interface output, then brings audio back from your outboard processor into an interface input and passes it on down the channel audio path, in short, an analog insert point. (Actually, the specified interface output could even be digital, but the majority of Pipeline applications are likely to be analog I/O connections.) With a little signal routing, Pipeline can also be used for send effects.

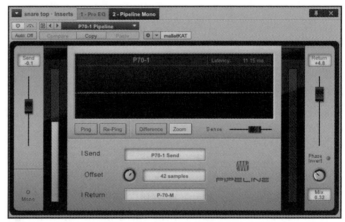

Fig. 3-149: The Pipeline plug-in, mono version.

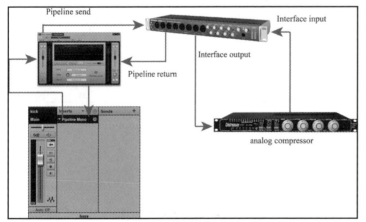

Fig. 3-150: Signal flow for a channel using Pipeline to integrate an analog compressor. An interface input and output are specified in the Pipeline plug-in, and the compressor is connected to the interface.

Pipeline's value is not simply that it provides an insert point for outboard equipment, but also that it includes a set of controls and diagnostic tools for optimizing the insert. Once set up for a specific device, the settings can be saved as a preset. The next time that device is used, it is only necessary to select its preset.

Pipeline can be instantiated on mono or stereo channels. The one thing it cannot do, however, is provide a mono send and a stereo return. For your mono-in/stereo-out processors, you will need a different strategy. For more information on using mono-in/stereo-out external processors, see the section "Integrating Mono-In/Stereo-Out Processors" later in this chapter.

SETTING UP AN ANALOG INSERT WITH PIPELINE

Here is the basic setup procedure for using Pipeline. More details about the features mentioned follow.

1. Open the Preferences > Song Setup > Audio I/O Setup pane and configure the inputs and outputs you wish to use as Pipeline sends and returns. Labeling these inputs and outputs appropriately will speed your workflow and reduce confusion.

2. If you create any new inputs or outputs in Studio One 2 to use with Pipeline, click Make Default before closing the dialog if you want this I/O configuration to show up in every Song you create.

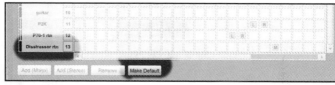

Fig. 3-151: In the Audio I/O Setup pane, create and name the inputs and outputs you will use with Pipeline. Click the Make Default button if you want these assignments to be part of every new Song document.

3. Patch the outboard device to the interface output(s) and input(s) you designated for its use. If the device has a bypass function, bypass it while setting up Pipeline.

4. Instantiate the Pipeline plug-in using any of the standard plug-in instantiation methods. Note that Studio One 2 allows you to insert Pipeline Stereo on a mono channel, but it doesn't work out well because you only have one of the send channels and one of the returns.

5. Click in the Send field and choose an interface output to use from the list that drops down.

6. Click in the Return field and choose an interface input to use from the list that drops down.

7. Click in the Device Label area above the signal scope and enter a label for the device.

8. Verify the signal path by clicking the Ping button to put Pipeline in Ping mode and clicking the Re-Ping button to send a short transient from Studio One 2 to the designated Send

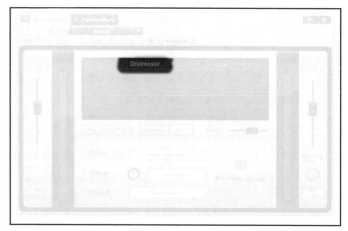

Fig. 3-152: Once you have selected the Send and Return connections, label the device in the Pipeline plug-in. Once the offset is determined, this setup can be saved as a preset.

output. Click Re-Ping as many times as needed to confirm that you see level through the entire signal path: on the interface output, outboard processor input, interface input, and Pipeline Return meter.

9. Adjust the Send and Return levels in Pipeline by either dragging the appropriate fader to the desired level, or clicking in the appropriate level value box and entering the desired level. The objective is to get the Send and Return levels as closely matched as possible on the meters, and achieve significant levels without clipping Pipeline, your interface, or the outboard processor (unless overloading the outboard processor is desirable). Watch the Send and Return meters in Pipeline, input and output meters on your interface, and any metering on the outboard processor for clipping.

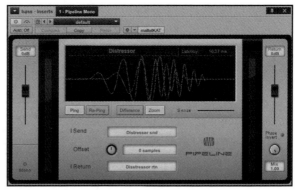

10. It will not always be possible to completely match Send and Return levels, but you can also use the master input and output level controls on the outboard device to match levels more closely, if it is proving difficult to do with Pipeline alone.

Fig. 3-153: Ideally, the two waveforms you see when pinging would be the same level. The levels match up pretty well in this example, but a good send/return level match is not always easy to achieve.

11. Set the Offset delay to minimize the phase (time) difference between Send and Return. For more information on setting the offset, see the section "Setting the Offset Time" later in this chapter.

12. Once the settings have been optimized, use the preset management features in the Device editor header to save them as a preset. It is a good idea to give the preset the same name as the label that was given the device, although they can always be different if there is a reason they should be.

13. Click the Ping button to exit Ping mode. The signal scope will now show the Send and Return waveforms.

14. Take the outboard device out of bypass.

15. Play the Song where there is audio on the track containing Pipeline and adjust the outboard processor as desired. Avoid changing the device's master input and output level controls, which you have just optimized.

16. Adjust the Output Mix control at the bottom right of the Pipeline plug-in for the desired dry/wet mix, with dry being the pre-Pipeline signal. This control makes it easy to do parallel compression with an outboard compressor, or just find the best balance of signal and effect.

17. Further slight adjustments to Pipeline settings may be required at this point.

The same Pipeline preset or I/O setup can be used on multiple channels. In this case, the Sends will be summed before being output and the return will be fed to all channels using that Pipeline setup. Be careful! Summing send signals can quickly result in a much higher send level.

TIP: There is no real-time rendering for Event FX. This means that Pipeline functions fine in an Event FX chain in Live mode, but when the Event FX are rendered, it is as if Pipeline were not there.

SETTING UP PIPELINE AS AN ANALOG SEND

Pipeline can be set up in a send arrangement, rather than as a channel insert. There are several reasons to do this:

- Multiple signals can be mixed with a high degree of control, then the mix sent to the outboard processor.
- Processing can be applied both before and after the outboard processor independently of processing on the source channels.
- In a send arrangement, Pipeline provides a compact solution for integrating mono in/ stereo out processors. While compact, it is not the most efficient method. For more information on how to accomplish this, see the section, "Integrating Mono-In/Stereo-Out Processors" later in this chapter.

The procedure for using Pipeline in a send arrangement is the same as using it as an insert, with only two differences:

1. Instead of instantiating Pipeline on an Audio or Instrument channel, create a Bus or FX channel and insert Stereo Pipeline on it. Because Bus and FX channels are always stereo, only Stereo Pipeline will ever be used in this arrangement.

2. Create Sends on the source channels to feed the Bus or FX channel.

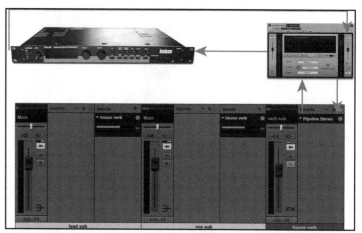

Fig. 3-154: The Pipeline plug-in can be used in a send arrangement by instantiating it on a Bus or FX channel and then creating channel sends to the Bus/FX channel.

SETTING THE OFFSET TIME

To make Pipeline as convenient and useful as inserting a regular software plug-in, it is crucial to compensate for any latency that occurs in the signal path. Pipeline automatically compensates for the latency introduced by your interface and displays the value in milliseconds in the Latency readout above the signal scope, but any other latency must be compensated for manually. One example might be an older digital device with analog inputs and outputs. The device's internal A/D and D/A converters will introduce some latency that cannot be compensated for automatically.

Pipeline lets you do this by providing a "ping" generator that outputs a short transient, and a signal scope that overlays the send and return pings. Latency compensation is applied until the two signals are right on top of each other (or as close to that as possible), indicating that they are effectively synchronous. Several options and helper functions are also included.

As mentioned earlier, the outboard processor should be bypassed while setting latency compensation.

To manually determine and apply the offset delay necessary to compensate for latency:

1. With the system prepared as described in the section "Setting Up an Analog Insert with Pipeline" earlier in this chapter, click the Re-Ping button to send a short transient through the signal path.

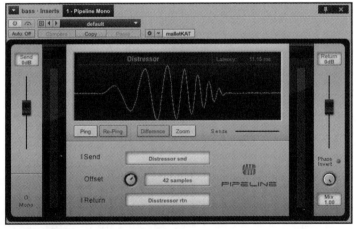

Fig. 3-155: The signal scope shows the ping as it was sent (the red trace) and as it was received (the blue trace), making the latency obvious. The objective is to set the offset time to match the two waveforms as closely as possible. Forty-two samples seems to be the magic number here.

2. Look at the resulting display on the signal scope and observe how far apart the send (red waveform) and return (blue waveform) signals are.

3. Click the Zoom button to expand the resolution of the display. This facilitates seeing the time difference in greater detail.

4. Slowly drag the Offset knob to add latency compensation. Positive values are used to compensate for latency; negative values introduce additional delay. Each time the knob is moved, a new ping is sent. As Offset increases, the blue (Return) waveform moves to the left; decreasing Offset moves it to the right. Move the knob until the waveforms are lined up as closely as possible. For very fine adjustment, you can click in the Offset value box and enter a value directly.

5. When the waveforms appear closely overlaid, click the Difference button to switch the signal scope to display the difference between the two waveforms and, if necessary, continue to adjust the Offset. When the amplitude of the difference waveform is as small as you can get it, the Offset is optimized. Fine-tuning the optimal Offset value can be performed by entering a value directly in a trial-and-error fashion, changing the value by perhaps three or less samples until the difference waveform is at its minimum.

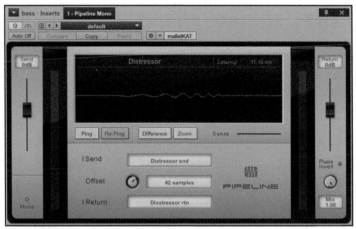

Fig. 3-156: Excellent cancellation can be achieved with this processor. The level of cancellation achievable varies between processors.

6. In some cases, it may be useful to experiment with clicking the Polarity Reverse button, which is labeled "Phase Reverse." (Unlike the Offset knob, the "Phase Reverse" button only inverts the polarity of the signal, with no impact on time delay.)

THE SENSE SLIDER

The Sense slider located just above the upper right corner of the signal scope is essentially a visual analysis aid. It sets a gating threshold for the scope when it is monitoring the channel signal (that is, when it is not in

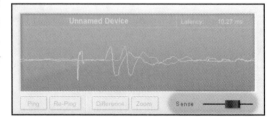

Fig. 3-157: The Sense slider gates the signal display to thin it out. On drum tracks, this makes it easy to compare how two drums are hitting relative to each other.

Ping mode). This can be useful in comparing the relative timing of several transient signals in a mix; for example, seeing how close the kick and snare are hitting in a drum mix. To simplify the signal scope display for transient comparison:

- While playing the Song, move the Sense slider until only the transients of the signal are visible. Moving the slider to the right increases the gating effect.

Fig. 3-158:
The Mix control provides easy parallel processing.

PARALLEL PROCESSING WITH PIPELINE

Pipeline's Mix control enables parallel processing to be accomplished right in the plug-in. Simply adjust the Mix knob to the desired proportion of send to return signal. When Mix is set to 0, the signal is all Send; when it is set to 1.0, the signal is all Return. It is sometimes worth experimenting with the polarity reverse button (labeled "Phase Reverse") and evaluating its impact on the sound.

PIPELINE IN THE FINAL MIX

When Pipeline is instantiated anywhere in a Song, exporting a mix automatically becomes a real-time operation, so that signals can be sent from Pipeline and the returns captured.

EVENT-LEVEL MIXING: EVENT FX

Most mixing happens at the track level, but Studio One 2 has a variety of features that operate at the level of Audio Events and Instrument Parts, and these can be powerful mixing tools.

In this section, I discuss Event FX, a feature that allows an entire processing chain to be created for a single Audio Event. The ability to apply processing individually to Events on a track enables you to make those Events either more closely match or differ more from others on the track. For example, an effect can be applied to a single word of a vocal, or a punch-in can be EQ'ed to make it blend more smoothly with the original track. Many processing tasks that can be done with automation can be done more efficiently with Event FX, especially since Event FX will always travel with the Event if it gets moved.

TIP: Event FX are not duplicated for shared copies; an Event FX chain applies only to the single Event on which it is instantiated

Automation at the Event level is also very useful in mixing. In chapter 4, "Automation," I discuss Event volume and Part automation.

Enabling Event FX

To enable Event FX:

1. Select the Event to which you want to add Event FX.
2. Press F4 or click the button with the i icon above the track header column to open the Inspector pane.

3. Click the Enable button next to the Event FX label just below the Event name in the Event inspector. For more information on the Event inspector, see the section "Inspectors" of chapter 5, "On the Cutting Room Floor: Basic Editing" in *Power Tools for Studio One 2*, volume 1. The Event FX insert rack will appear and the button label will change to Disable.

Event FX Device Rack Behavior

Once Event FX have been enabled for an Event, the effects in the Event FX device rack behave in all ways the same as channel insert racks in the mixer, including methods for:

- Adding, editing, and removing effects.
- Expanding and collapsing an effect micro-view.
- Deactivating and reactivating effects.
- Saving and loading presets and FX Chains.

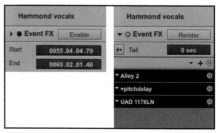

Fig. 3-159: The Event FX Enable button on the left, and the Event FX device rack on the right.

For more information on these techniques, see the section "Plug-Ins and Effects" in this chapter.

In addition to all of the standard methods for adding effects, an effect also can be added to an Event FX chain by Option-dragging (Alt-dragging in Windows) an effect from the Browser (or a channel) and dropping it onto an Event in the Arrange view or Audio Editor.

Unlike channel insert racks, Event FX device rack displays can be expanded and collapsed:

Fig. 3-160: Option-dragging (Alt-dragging in Windows) an effect from the Browser and dropping it on an Event in the Arrange view adds the effect to the Event FX chain.

- To expand or collapse an Event FX device rack: Click on the Event FX label or the disclosure triangle to its left in the Event inspector.

As soon as a plug-in is added to the Event FX insert rack after it has been enabled, the presence of effects in the rack is indicated in these ways:

- A small box labeled "FX" appears in the lower left corner of the Event in the Arrange view.
- The Enable button at the top of the Event FX area of the Event inspector changes its label to "Render."
- The "LED" indicator at the top of the Event FX area of the Event inspector becomes colored red.
- The Event FX insert rack can no longer be expanded.

Fig. 3-161: A collapsed Event FX Device Rack.

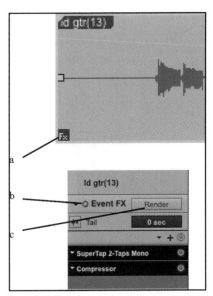

Fig. 3-162: Here are the signs that Event FX are present on an Event: a) a small "FX" box in the lower left corner of the Event, b) the indicator in the Event FX section of the Event inspector is colored red, c) the Enable button now says "Render."

Rendering Event FX

If Event FX are used on more than one or two Events, in addition to effects being used on channels, your processor is being asked to do a lot of real-time processing and will have to burn a lot of power to keep up. This burden can be reduced by rendering the Event FX,

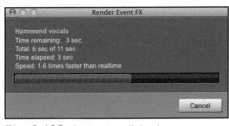

Fig. 3-163: A progress dialog keeps you updated about Event FX renders.

the equivalent of track freezing. This bounces the audio with effects to a file and disables the effects, so that their processing resources are released.

Rendering is easily reversed any time you want to adjust the effects, and it is sophisticated enough to have features for dealing with the extended Event length that results from reverb and delay effects.

To render an Event FX chain you have set up on an Event:

1. Select the Event.

2. If the Event FX result in a reverb or delay tail, set an appropriate Tail time as described in the next section, "Rendering Event FX with Delay or Reverb Tails."

3. Click the Render button at the top of the Event FX device rack. A progress dialog will appear as the effects are rendered, the button label will change to Restore, and the color of the "LED" indicator will change to blue.

To restore Event FX to real-time operation:

Fig. 3-164: Clicking the Restore button makes Event FX live again.

1. Click the Restore button at the top of the Event FX device rack. The rendered file is deleted, the rack reappears, and the color of the "LED" indicator will change to red.

RENDERING EVENT FX WITH DELAY OR REVERB TAILS

Many effects, most notably reverb and delay-based effects, will add to the length of the Event. These tails would simply be cut off if Studio One 2 always rendered to the exact length of the Event. Fortunately, this is not the case.

The Event FX Tail feature causes additional time to be added to the rendered Event, and a fade-out of the same duration to be added to the Event, as will be seen in the Event inspector Fade-Out field. Of course, this field is editable, so the fade-out can be set to any desired value up to the length of the Event itself.

Fig. 3-165: The Tail field allows you to specify a period of time that is added to the new file to capture delay and reverb decays.

- To add Tail extension when rendering Event FX: Move the cursor over the Tail field above the Event FX device rack and drag up or down to the desired value, or click in the field and enter a value directly. The specified value will be used when rendering is performed.

PROCESS VOLUME AFTER EVENT FX

Most of the time, Event FX will affect the volume of the Event. If you have specified Event volume for the Event, there will be a very different result if Event volume is calculated before the effects are rendered than if it is calculated after, which more often produces the best result. It is easy to tell Studio One 2 to render Event FX first and then render the Event volume:

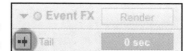

Fig. 3-166: The Process Volume after Event FX button renders the Event FX before calculating volume automation.

- To render Event volume after Event FX: Click the Process Volume after Event FX button to the right of the "Tail" label above the Event FX device rack. The button will turn orange to indicate it has been activated.

Live Event FX

It should be said that there is at least one circumstance in which it is desirable to let Event FX run in real time and put up with the burden on your processor, rather than rendering them. If you want to perform real-time control of one or more effects in the chain using Control Link, the effect(s) must be live. Once rendered, Event FX are playing back a bounced file, so parameters cannot be changed without restoring the Event FX chain to real-time processing.

FREEZING, BOUNCING, AND EXPORTING

Capturing audio is at the heart of mixing. Studio One 2 offers a number of different ways of creating audio files of your work. I have just discussed rendered Event FX as one method of capturing a section of audio. There are other methods of rendering selected audio, and, of course, the end product of all this mixing effort needs to be a final mix file, as well.

Bouncing a Selection

In the course of creating a Song, you may have done extensive editing to assemble a passage. Having worked hard to get every little bit where you want it, it is cumbersome to work with the whole passage. Wouldn't it be much easier if you could just make those pieces into a single entity? Bounce it! Bouncing is useful both for Instrument Parts and Audio Events, though there is a slight difference between bouncing the two of them.

When a selection is bounced to audio entirely within Studio One 2, such as when Audio Events and Instrument Parts playing VIs are bounced, the resulting file is always in 32-bit floating-point format. If it ever was necessary, most audio programs could open such a file.

TIP: It is important to note that bouncing a selection is not like freezing a track. All that is happening in a bounce is that the selection in the track is being combined into a single audio file; bouncing is not rendering audio from the channels in the mixer. No volume, pan, mute, or insert effect information is captured; you simply have one audio file where you had Instrument Parts or multiple Audio Events before.

BOUNCING INSTRUMENT PARTS

I suppose you could think of bouncing an Instrument Part as a kind of freezing method, but don't confuse yourself. Here are a few similarities between bouncing an Instrument part and freezing (transforming) a track or rendering Event FX:

- Bouncing a Part captures audio from a VI to an Audio Event.
- Bouncing renders the outputs of the Instrument channels, so it is rendering through the mixer and any effects on the channels.

And here are some differences:

- The VI is not disabled after the bounce.
- Only the selected Part is rendered (as with rendering Event FX), not the entire track (as in transforming).
- The Part is muted but not replaced by the audio.
- The audio is placed on a different track than the Part.

Of course, the Part may actually be playing an external device, in which case the process is even a little more different. I'll walk it all down.

BOUNCING PARTS THAT PLAY VIS

Bouncing a Part that plays a VI is the simplest case, because everything happens within Studio One 2. Further, Studio One 2 automatically handles a few details that must be dealt with manually in the other schemes for bouncing Instrument Parts I am about to discuss.

To bounce an Instrument Part that is playing a VI:

1. Select the Part or Parts you wish to bounce.

2. Press Cmd + B (Ctrl + B in Windows), right-click (Ctrl-click in Mac) on a selected Event and choose Event > Bounce Selection from the contextual menu that drops down, or choose Event > Bounce Selection from the main menu bar.

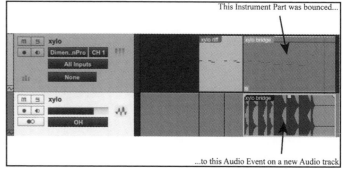

3. A new Audio track is created and the selection is bounced to the new track at the same time range as that of the source Part. The Part on the original track is muted.

Fig. 3-167: Bouncing a Part renders a VI's output to an Audio Event on a new Audio track.

When multiple Parts are selected, whether on one track or across multiple tracks, each Part is individually rendered to an Audio Event. All selected Parts on a track are rendered to Events on the same new Audio track.

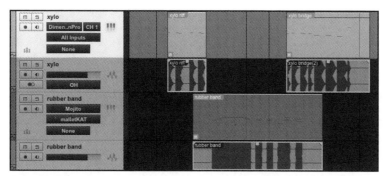

Fig. 3-168: Multiple Parts are bounced individually to new Audio tracks. Note that both Parts selected on the upper track are rendered to the same new Audio track below.

BOUNCING PARTS THAT PLAY EXTERNAL DEVICES

The significant difference between bouncing a Part that plays an external device and bouncing a Part that plays a VI, is that Studio One 2 captures a VIs output for you and puts it on a new Audio track. With an external device, you must physically return the external device's audio to your interface before you can capture it onto an Audio track.

However, there are two ways to capture audio from an external device, depending on whether your interface offers low-latency monitoring. Monitoring is obviously critical to writing or sound design with the device.

To bounce an Instrument Part that plays an external device when monitoring through an interface with low-latency monitoring:

Fig. 3-169: The Bounce Instrument Part dialog.

1. Select the Part you wish to bounce.

2. Press Cmd + B (Ctrl + B in Windows). The Bounce Instrument Part dialog will appear.

3. Check that the Track Name and Device Name fields are correct. (These fields are read-only.) If not, check whether you selected the correct Part.

4. Select the correct input in the Record Input field. Click the Play button and confirm that the correct Part is playing and that audio is showing on the Record Level Meter.

5. Click the Bounce Track button. The Part will get bounced to an Audio Event on a new Audio track by a real-time record and capture. After bouncing, the Part is muted.

6. You can select Parts playing VIs and Parts playing external devices and bounce them at the same time. The VI Parts will simply bounce, and the external device Parts will bring up the Bounce Instrument Part dialog.

When multiple Parts are selected on multiple tracks that play external devices, you can choose with the buttons in the Bounce Instrument Part dialog to bounce all Parts on all tracks, or step through the tracks and decide for each one whether to bounce or skip it:

- Bounce All: Bounces all selected Parts playing external devices, creating a new Audio track for the bounce(s) of each Instrument track. So, if you bounce two Parts from two tracks, two new audio tracks are created, each holding one part.

- Skip Track: When Parts are selected on multiple tracks that play external devices, clicking this button causes the track named in the Track Name field not to be bounced. The window then shows the next track that plays an external device.

- Bounce Track: When Parts are selected on multiple tracks that play external devices, clicking this button causes the track named in the Track Name field to be bounced, and the window changed to show the next track playing an external device.

Bouncing an Instrument Part when you are monitoring the external device through Studio One, rather than through low-latency interface monitoring, is a little different. The external device is heard as the input of an Audio track with input monitoring enabled. To capture the audio, you need only record enable the monitoring track and play the Part with Studio One 2 in record.

It would be easy if Studio One 2 had a Play Selection command, but Auto Punch provides a fine workaround.

1. Select a Part. Make sure either that there is enough length at its end to accommodate reverb or delay tails, or that you use the Range tool to make a selection that is long enough.

2. Press Shift + P or choose Transport > Set Loop to Selection from the main menu bar. Be sure loop playback is deactivated.

3. Press L or choose Transport > Locate to Selection from the main menu bar.

4. Record-enable the Audio track into which the external device is being returned.

5. Press I to activate Auto Punch.

6. Press * (asterisk) on the number pad or click the Record button in the Transport bar to start recording. Studio One 2 will capture audio from the external device as the Part plays.

7. Stop the transport once it has punched out and the Part has been "bounced" to an Audio Event.

8. To add postroll after the record area: Drop a marker the desired amount of postroll time after the end of the record area, right-click (Ctrl-click in Mac) on it, and check the Stop at Marker box. Playback will stop when it reaches the marker.

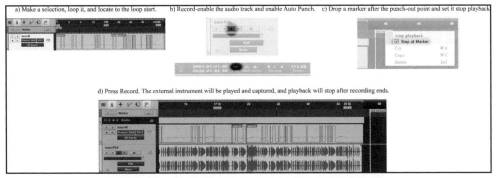

Fig. 3-170: Bouncing an Instrument Part that plays an external device. Note the postroll marker that stops playback after the punch, so you don't have to dive for the spacebar.

TIP: Buffer size does not affect the timing of the Part as it is recorded, but it does impact monitoring. Recording with a large buffer is easier on your computer, but if you are bothered by hearing the Part's playing late, reducing the buffer size will let you hear it correctly. However, since it is common to be bouncing Instrument Parts fairly late in the mixing process, when there may be lots of effects running, I recommend using the larger buffer size and then playing the new Event back to hear it in time.

BOUNCING PARTS THAT PLAY REWIRE INSTRUMENTS

If your ReWire instrument is correctly set up, bouncing an Instrument Part is the exact same procedure as when using a VI running in Studio One 2. For more information on using ReWire with Studio One 2, see the section "Using ReWire Applications with Instrument Tracks" of chapter 4, "Virtual Instruments and MIDI" in *Power Tools for Studio One 2,* volume 1.

To bounce an Instrument Part selection that is playing a VI through ReWire:

1. Confirm that the ReWire instrument is correctly configured in Studio One 2 and that audio returned from it into the mixer is audible.
2. Select the Part or Parts you wish to bounce.
3. Press Cmd + B (Ctrl + B in Windows), right-click (Ctrl-click in Mac) on a selected Event and choose Event > Bounce Selection from the contextual menu that drops down or choose Event > Bounce Selection from the main menu bar.
4. A new Audio track is created and the selection is bounced to the new track at the same time range as that of the source Part. The Part on the original track is muted.

BOUNCING AUDIO EVENTS

Bouncing Audio Events is easy, but it is important to remember what it accomplishes and what it does not:

- Bouncing combines all Events on a track that fall within the selected range into a single Event. Select an Event on beat 1 and another on beat 4, and all Events in between will be included in the bounce.

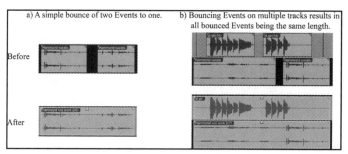

Fig. 3-171: a) A simple bounce of several Events on a track to a single Event. b) When Events are selected on multiple tracks, the range of time bounced is the same for all tracks.

- When Events on multiple tracks are selected, the range used for bouncing extends from the start of the earliest Event to the end of the one that finishes last. If Event 1 on Track 1 starts at bar 10 and Event 2 on Track 2 finishes last at the downbeat of bar 16, all Events on Track 1 between bar 10 and bar 16 will be bounced to a single Event, and all Events in that same range on Track 2 will be bounced to a single Event. Bounce range is global; you cannot have different bounce ranges for each track.

- Bouncing *only* combines the Events on the track; it does not capture the output of channels in the mixer, so no automation or effects are captured. Live Event FX are not captured, either.

- If you are bouncing a rhythmic sound that may need to follow tempo changes later on, you are probably better off merging the Events into an Audio Part than bouncing. On the other hand, if you have painstakingly comped a guitar solo together note by note, bouncing will put the whole solo into a single Event, as if it were performed in one pass, which can be much easier to deal with than a number of smaller Events.

Capturing Audio from Effects

It is often a good idea to capture effects output to Audio Events while mixing. Perhaps you are using an outboard processor you may not have access to later or that you want to apply to more than one track, or maybe you want to capture the output from an FX channel because you are going to finish mixing at another studio that does not have the plug-in that's on that channel. Whatever the reason, here are three ways to capture audio output from a processor to Audio Events.

USING PIPELINE TO
CAPTURE AUDIO FROM AN OUTBOARD PROCESSOR
The Pipeline plug-in was discussed in the section "Integrating Outboard Devices: the Pipeline Plug-In" earlier in this chapter. If Pipeline is set up to insert an outboard processor, the output of that processor will be captured when you export your final mix. However, if you wish to capture the processor's output on its own into an Audio Event, try this:

1. Insert and configure Pipeline with your outboard processor and confirm that the entire signal path is working.
2. Make a selection in the track. Be sure the end of the selection is long enough to accommodate delay or reverb tails.
3. Press Option + Y (or Alt + Y in Windows) or choose Transport > Set Start and End to Selection from the main menu bar. (An alternate method is to press Shift + P to set the loop markers.)
4. Solo the track.
5. Press Cmd + E (Ctrl + E in Windows) or choose Song > Export Mixdown from the main menu bar. Follow the directions for using the Export Mixdown dialog that are given in the section "Exporting (Bouncing) Mixes" later in this chapter to set up and execute the export. Be sure to select the appropriate Export Range (Between Song Start/End Markers or Between Loop Markers) for the type of markers you set. A real-time bounce that includes the Pipeline insert path will be executed, and a new mix file generated.

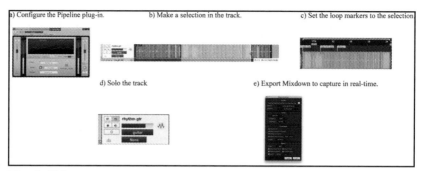

Fig. 3-172: Audio from an outboard processor fed by the Pipeline plug-in can be captured in real-time using the Export Mixdown command.

USING A SEND AND RETURN TO CAPTURE AUDIO FROM AN OUTBOARD PROCESSOR

There are times when Pipeline is not the best solution for integrating an outboard audio device. One example would be for processors that have mono inputs and stereo outputs. For these, the most straightforward solution is to use an Output channel as a send to the device, and return its audio to an Audio track, into which the effect can be captured:

1. Create a new mono or stereo output in the Outputs tab of the Preferences > Song Setup > Audio I/O Setup pane and map it to an interface output. It is a good idea to name it either for the processor it is feeding, or for its function ("snare rvb send," for example). An Output channel will appear in the mixer.

2. Create a new mono or stereo input in the Inputs tab of the Preferences > Song Setup > Audio I/O Setup pane and map it to an interface input. It is a good idea to make its name be the complement of the name you gave the output ("snare rvb rtn," for example).

3. Connect the physical inputs and outputs of the outboard processor to the interface inputs and outputs you just designated for its send and return.

4. Press T to open the New Track dialog, and create a new mono or stereo Audio track for audio returning from the processor. As the input to the track, select the input you just set up as the processor's return.

5. Add a send to the processor on every channel you want feeding it.

6. Record-enable the track (be sure Input Monitor is also enabled) and confirm that signal is being sent to and received from the device. If you have a problem, appendix A, "When Things Go Wrong," in this volume has suggestions for troubleshooting this signal path. Be sure no other channels are record-enabled, unless you also want to record to them now.

7. Press * (asterisk on the number pad) or click the Record button in the Transport bar to start Studio One 2 recording, and record the portion of the Song (or all of it) for which you want to capture processor output.

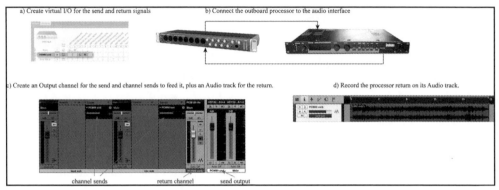

a) Create virtual I/O for the send and return signals   b) Connect the outboard processor to the audio interface

c) Create an Output channel for the send and channel sends to feed it, plus an Audio track for the return.   d) Record the processor return on its Audio track.

channel sends   return channel   send output

Fig. 3-173: The process for capturing audio from an external device using a send/return approach.

CAPTURING OUTPUT FROM EFFECTS ON BUS CHANNELS

Bus channels can be selected as inputs to Audio channels, making it easy to capture effects instantiated on those Bus channels.

TIP: If the Bus channel is being used for submixing, you will be capturing the entire submix, with effects, not just the effects output. If the Bus channel is only being used to host inserted effects, you will capture the effects return only.

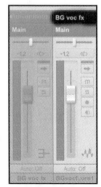

1. Press T to open the New Track dialog and create a new mono or stereo Audio track to capture audio from the processor on the Bus channel. As the input to the track, choose the Bus channel in the Busses folder in the drop-down Input Select menu.

2. Record-enable the track (be sure Input Monitor is also enabled) and confirm that you see signal from the Bus channel on the meter.

3. Press * (asterisk on the number pad) or click the Record button in the Transport bar to start Studio One 2 recording, and record the portion of the Song (or all of it) for which you want to capture Bus channel output.

CAPTURING OUTPUT FROM EFFECTS ON FX CHANNELS

FX channels are not available as inputs to Audio tracks, so to capture the output of an FX channel, you must route its output to a bus and capture the output of the Bus channel.

1. Right-click (Ctrl-click in Mac) on the FX channel in the mixer and choose Add Bus for Selected Tracks from the contextual menu that drops down. A new Bus channel is created, and the output of the FX channel is routed to it.

Fig. 3-174: Effects on Bus channels can be captured on an Audio track by selecting the bus as the Audio track's input. The BG voc fx bus has been selected as the input to an Audio track that will capture the effects to an audio file.

2. Capture the output of the Bus channel as described in the preceding section, "Capturing Output from Effects on Bus Channels."

Transforming (Freezing) Instrument Parts to Audio Events

Every DAW has some means of rendering tracks playing virtual instruments or using heavy-duty plug-ins, to free up the considerable processing resources these features consume. This is commonly referred to as "freezing" tracks. Each DAW has its own method of accomplishing this, and the various methods can differ in significant ways. Studio One 2's Track Transform commands are the way freezing is implemented in the program, and it is distinguished from other programs' freeze features in a very cool way.

In most DAWs, if you want to change the frozen track, you "unfreeze" it, which returns it to the state it was in when you froze it. In Studio One 2, after an Instrument track with Parts is transformed to an Audio track with Events, you can edit the audio, then transform the track back to an Instrument track, and it will (within reason) give you not the Instrument track as it was before transformation, but one that reflects the edits.

Transformation of Instrument tracks to Audio tracks is discussed in the section "Track Transform (Freezing Tracks)" of chapter 4, "Virtual Instruments and MIDI" in *Power Tools for Studio One 2*, volume 1. The basic procedure is quite simple:

1. Right-click (Ctrl-click in Mac) in the track header for the Instrument track you want to transform and choose Transform to Audio Track from the contextual menu that drops down, or choose Track > Transform > Transform to Audio Track from the main menu bar.
2. Click the boxes to set the options as desired.
3. Click OK and the Instrument track will be replaced with an Audio track containing Events that capture the VI's audio output.

CHANGES TO INSTRUMENT TRACK TRANSFORM SINCE VOLUME 1

Version 2.5 introduced enhancements to the Transform Instrument Track to Audio command. The Transform Instrument Track dialog has been changed from that shown in *Power Tools for Studio One 2*, volume 1, as can be seen in Fig. 3-175. The layout is cleaner and a brief description has been added for each option. Some processes are slightly changed, as well.

Here's a summary of the changes:

Fig. 3-175: The Transform Instrument Track dialog.

MULTICHANNEL INSTRUMENTS

Some VIs, samplers and drum machines in particular, can return multiple audio outputs, each to its own Instrument channel in the mixer. In the old Transform Instrument Track dialog, the Channel field allowed you to select which output would get rendered in that pass. That meant performing a transform pass for each output that was being used.

The new dialog makes things much simpler:

- The Channel field has been removed altogether.
- If an instrument is not multichannel, the Render All Channels box will not appear in the Transform Instrument Track dialog.
- To transform an Instrument track that plays a multichannel VI: Click the Render All Channels box to check it. An Audio track will be created for each active output of the instrument played by the track.
- If you leave the Render All Channels box unchecked when transforming an Instrument track that plays a multichannel instrument, only the channel showing in the Track inspector will be transformed.

REMOVE INSTRUMENT

- In version 2, Remove Instrument unloaded the instrument, to free resources, and moved it to the Trash Bin. With version 2.5, Remove Instrument unloads the instrument but, instead of moving it to the Trash, deletes it from the Song. However, if the Preserve Instrument Track State box is checked, the track can still be transformed back to an Instrument track with the original instrument and settings.
- If the instrument is used by any track other than the one being transformed, the Remove Instrument box is grayed out.

AUTOMATIC TAIL DETECTION

In version 2 (described in *Power Tools for Studio One*, volume 1), the Tail field allowed you to specify an amount of time to be added to the end of each Part on the track being transformed, to accommodate reverb and delay decays. This field is now called Fix Tail, and a new Auto Tail option has been added. Auto Tail watches the audio level and stops rendering once it has detected 100 ms of silence. Fix Tail and Auto Tail function as radio buttons: you can only do one or the other.

To manually specify a Tail duration:

1. Be sure the Auto Tail box is not checked.
2. Drag up and down over the Fix Tail field to the desired duration (from 0 to 30 seconds), or simply enter the value in the field.

To use Auto Tail:

1. Check the Auto Tail box.

2. Drag up and down over the Max Length field to set the desired maximum duration (from 0 to 30 seconds) for the tail, or simply enter the value in the field.

Fig. 3-176: When the Auto Tail box is checked, the Fix Tail field is replaced by the Max Length field.

UNDO AND RETRANSFORMING

It is often necessary to undo and redo a track transformation, or transform back and forth between an Instrument track and an Audio track, doing work in between. Version 2.5 cleans up both of these operations, doing a better job both of restoring settings and getting rid of extraneous files.

Transforming (Freezing) Audio Tracks to Rendered Audio

Similarly to transforming Instrument tracks to Audio tracks, the Transform Audio Track command captures the output from the Audio channel associated with the track for each Event on the track, freeing up resources consumed by hungry plug-ins, such as convolution reverbs. Unlike transforming Instrument tracks, however, insert effects are always removed; there is no option to leave them in place.

Fig. 3-177: The Transform Audio Track dialog.

To transform an Audio track to rendered audio:

1. Right-click (Ctrl-click in Mac) in the track header for the Audio track you want to transform and choose Transform to Rendered Audio from the contextual menu that drops down, or choose Track > Transform > Transform to Rendered Audio from the main menu bar. Note that if there are no insert effects on the Audio channel for the track, the command will not be available.

2. Click the boxes to set the options as desired.

3. Click OK and each Event on the track will be replaced with an Event that captures the Audio channel's output.

TRANSFORM AUDIO TRACK OPTIONS

Three options are available in the Transform Audio Track dialog:

PRESERVE REALTIME STATE

This is the equivalent of the Preserve Instrument State box in the Transform Instrument Track

Fig. 3-178: The Preserve Realtime State checkbox.

dialog. When checked, it preserves all of the settings of the insert effects, allowing the track to be transformed back to real-time audio.

FIX TAIL

As in the Transform Instrument Track dialog, this option lets you manually specify a duration added to the end of the audio to accommodate reverb and delay decays. The Fix Tail option does not appear in the dialog until the Auto Tail box is unchecked.

Fig. 3-179: The Fix Tail option.

1. Be sure the Auto Tail box is not checked.

2. Drag up and down over the Fix Tail field to the desired duration (from 0 to 30 seconds), or simply enter the value in the field.

AUTO TAIL

The extra time added for decays can be done automatically with Auto Tail:

1. Check the Auto Tail box.

2. Drag up and down over the Max Length field to set the desired maximum duration (from 0 to 30 seconds) for the tail, or simply enter the value in the field.

Fig. 3-180: Auto Tail adds time at the end of the transform to accommodate delay and reverb tails.

Exporting Mixes

This is the one you've been waiting for. After all is said and done, the end of mixing comes when you crank out a stereo file of the mix. The Export Mixdown dialog is where that job gets done.

Although the most obvious application of the Export Mixdown command is, as the command name says, to export a complete mix of the Song, the command is just as useful for exporting a selected portion of a Song, including a selection of tracks. You might choose to export a mix of an eight-bar loop three times: once with drums and percussion, once with rhythm instruments, once with lead instruments. By setting markers for the export region and soloing tracks you want to include (or muting ones you don't), it is possible to export any chunk of a Song desired.

Note that what you hear is what gets exported. If, for example, the drum tracks and/or channels have been hidden but the tracks are still active and audible, they will be included in the export.

The basic procedure for exporting a mix is here, followed by detailed descriptions of the settings in each area of the dialog.

Fig. 3-181: The Export Mixdown dialog.

1. Decide which markers you will use to designate the range for exporting, and set them to the beginning and end of the range. This will most often be the entire duration of the Song, but can just as easily can be any portion of the Song you want to export.

The markers that can be used are discussed in the next section, "The Export Mixdown Dialog."

2. Press Cmd + E (Ctrl + E in Windows) or choose Song > Export Mixdown from the main menu bar. The Export Mixdown dialog will appear.

3. Set the location to which you wish to save the mix and give the file a name.

4. Specify the file type, sample rate, and bit resolution.

5. Select which markers designate the range for exporting. This will most often be either the Song Start/End markers or the loop markers (locators). However, there are several other choices.

6. Choose the output channel that is being bounced, and choose from the other available options.

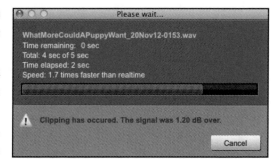

7. When all settings are as desired, click OK. Your mix will be exported. Oh yeah.

8. If clipping occurs during the export, a message will appear at the bottom of the progress dialog, as shown in Fig. 3-182. You can choose to abort the export at this point by clicking the Cancel button or let it continue.

Fig. 3-182: If clipping occurs during an export, this notice appears immediately, along with a Cancel button, in case you want to abort the export and fix the clipping problem.

9. After the export is completed, a dialog will inform you of the overload and by how much it exceeded the maximum allowable level. It also offers to delete the clipped mix file. (See Fig. 3-183) Reduce the master fader or take other action to reduce the level and try your export again.

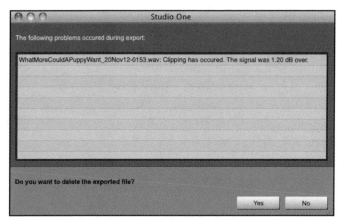

Fig. 3-183: When the export is complete, this dialog will appear if any clipping has occurred.

10. When you complete an export with no clipping, be sure to listen to the file to confirm it sounds right. Yee haw!

THE EXPORT MIXDOWN DIALOG

There are quite a few settings and options in the Export Mixdown dialog, but most of them are quite simple. The dialog is divided into labeled sections, so that is how I will discuss them.

LOCATION

- To set a location to which the mix file should be saved: Click the button with the ellipsis dots ("...") and navigate to the desired folder. The default location is the Mixdown folder inside the Song's main folder.
- Filename: Click in the Filename field and enter a name for the mix. As you will probably export a number of mix versions of a Song over the course of its production and mixing, it is a good idea to include the date and time in the name of each mix. The default file name is "Mixdown." Don't let that be your file name!
- Publishing: Click in the Publishing field and choose Upload to Nimbit or Upload to SoundCloud from the drop-down menu that appears, if you want to incorporate uploading to either of these sites as part of the export process. Very powerful!

FORMAT

Some formats offer options in fields that only appear when the related format is selected. When options that only apply to specific formats are discussed here, the applicable formats are shown in parentheses.

- File Format: Click in the File Format field and select a format for the mix file. Choose from WAV, AIFF, FLAC, Ogg Vorbis, or MP3. Some of these formats offer the following options:
- Resolution (WAV, AIFF, FLAC): Click in the Resolution field and choose the desired bit resolution from the drop-down menu that appears. .wav and .aiff files can be 8, 16, or 24 bits (linear PCM), or 32-bit floating point; .flac files can be 16 or 24 bits only.
- Samplerate: Click in the Samplerate field and choose the desired rate from the drop-down menu that appears. .wav, .aiff, and Ogg Vorbis files can be (in kHz) 11.025, 22.05, 44.1, 48, 88.2, 96, or 192; .flac files can be any of those rates except 192 kHz; .mp3 files can be 32, 44.1, or 48 kHz.
- Compression Level (FLAC): While FLAC is a lossless compression format, there are faster and slower ways to achieve compression. The cost of speed is not resolution, but space; faster algorithms (less compression) result in larger files than slower algorithms (more compression). To set the compression level: drag the Compression Level slider or click on the slider path to set the desired value, or click in the numeric field and enter a value between 0 and 8 directly.

- Variable bitrate (Ogg Vorbis): Ogg Vorbis can use either a variable or fixed bit rate, so Variable bitrate and Managed bitrate are radio buttons: you can choose one or the other. To use variable bit rate for your Ogg Vorbis file: Click the Variable bitrate button and drag the Quality slider or click on the slider path to set the desired value, or click in the numeric field and enter a percentage value (0–100) directly.

- Managed bitrate (Ogg Vorbis): To use a fixed bit rate for your Ogg Vorbis file: Click the Managed bitrate button. Click in the Minimum, Average, and Maximum bitrate fields and enter values between 64 and 320 kbps.

- Bitrate (MP3): Click in the Bitrate field and choose a rate of 64, 128, 192, 256, or 320 kbps.

Fig. 3-184: Available file format options vary with the format.

TIP: Note that Studio One 2 uses the abbreviation kBps for bit rates. kBps stands for "kilobytes per second," but these bit rates are actually in kilobits per second (abbreviated kbps).

EXPORT RANGE

This is where you choose which markers designate the range to be exported.

- Between Loop: Click this button to use the Loop Start and End markers (the locators) to designate the start and end times of the mix. A quick way to set these is to make a selection and then press Shift + P to loop the selection (or press P to snap the selection to the grid before looping it).

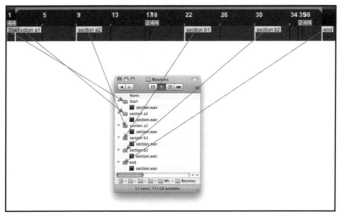

Fig. 3-185: Unlike all of the other options, the Between Each Marker option exports multiple files, as delineated by markers. The output is a set of folders named for the markers, each containing a file bearing the name specified in the Export Mixdown dialog. Because all of the files have the same name, renaming the files is recommended.

- Between Song Start/End Marker: Click this button to use the Song Start and End markers to designate the start and end times of the mix. A quick way to set these is to make a selection and then press Option + Y (Alt + Y in Windows) to set the Song Start and End markers to the selection.

- Between Each Marker: Clicking this button causes Studio One 2 to go through the Song marker by marker, exporting the area between each pair of markers as a separate file. The entire Song gets exported, but broken up according to marker placement. This is great for breaking a performance into files two or four bars long for use in looping.

- Between Selected Markers: Click this button to choose a pair of markers that designate the export range. Click in the field and choose a marker pair from the drop-down menu that appears. The list of marker pairs is the same as is used by the Between Each Marker option, thus Between Each Marker exports all of the marker-defined ranges in the Song, whereas Between Selected Markers chooses and exports a single one of them.

- Duration: This is a read-only field that shows the duration (in seconds or minutes and seconds) of the selected export range, that is, how long your mix file will be.

TIP: Note that file handling by the Between Each Marker option is unusual: rather than naming the files with the filename followed by the name of the marker from which it was created ("Mixdown-Marker 1," "Mixdown-Marker 2"), it creates folders named for each marker, and inside of each folder places a file with the name specified in the Filename field. This means you may end up with six or ten files that all have the same name and are differentiated only by the folder in which they reside.

O P T I O N S

Although this section is called "Options," the Output field, first in the section, is both mandatory and critical, as it selects the source of the mix to be captured.

- Output: Click in this field and select an Output channel to be the source for the export from the drop-down list that appears. For information on using this field for true stem mixing, see the section "True Stem Mixing" later in this chapter.

- Bypass Master Effects: Click this button if you monitor through "final processing" that you do not want included in the final mix file. Mastering engineers often request mixes with no final processing, and this box provides a quick and easy way to generate files for them without having to actually change anything in your mix.

Fig. 3-186: The Options section of the Export Mixdown dialog.

- Import to Track: Clicking this button causes the creation of a new Audio track with an Event containing the mix file, after the export is completed. A caveat: Be very careful to mute the track with the mixdown on it if you continue to work on the mix. Otherwise, you may be hearing the mix file combined with the live mix, which can be confusing and lead to a bad outcome the next time you try exporting a mix.

- Realtime Processing: If the Pipeline plug-in is used in your Song, mix exports will automatically be real-time. If Pipeline is not in the mix, but external instruments or processors are (and you have not captured their outputs), clicking the Realtime Processing button forces a real-time export that will capture audio from external devices.

- Close after export: Clicking this button simply closes the Export Mixdown dialog after the export is complete. If you are doing repeated exports, such as when doing true stem mixing as described in the section "True Stem Mixing" later in this chapter, you may wish to uncheck this box, which is checked by default.

- Overlap: Checking this box enables the Overlap feature. Overlap basically adds time to both the beginning and the end of the export range. When the Between Each Marker option is checked, overlap is added to each exported file.

- Overlap Amount: This field becomes active when the Overlap box is checked. Click in this field and enter a value between 0 and 10 seconds to be added to the beginning and end of the export range. If the export range is 8 seconds long and Overlap Amount is set to one second, the resulting file will be 10 seconds long: one second added to the beginning of the range and one second to the end.

Export Stems (Tracks)

As has already been mentioned, the Export Stems command does not actually export stem submixes. What it does is solo each track, one at a time, and export it to its own file, also a useful function. This is especially useful if you have written your song in Studio One 2, but it is being mixed on another DAW in another studio.

The Export Stems dialog has nearly the same settings as the Export Mixdown dialog, with a few differences and additions.

SOURCES

The Sources section contains a scrolling list of every track and channel in the Song. **Fig. 3-187:** The Export Stems dialog. Muted tracks and channels are grayed out and not available for export from this dialog. Because tracks and channels are on different lists, you can make mistakes, such as having a track checked and the corresponding channel unchecked. In most cases, Studio One 2 figures out what you really want and does the right thing, but it is possible to befuddle the poor program.

- Channels/Tracks radio buttons: These toggle you between viewing the list of channels in the Song and the list of tracks in the Song. Click the radio button for the list you wish to see.
- Select All/Select None buttons: Click the Select All button to check all available boxes on the currently displayed list. Click Select None to uncheck all boxes on the currently displayed list. The list not being displayed is unaffected by these buttons.
- Scrolling list with checkboxes: Check or uncheck boxes in the list to select the tracks and channels that will get exported. By default, all active tracks and channels are checked when the dialog opens. Hidden tracks or channels are checked by default as long as they are not muted.

LOCATION

The settings in this section are identical to those in the Export Mixdown dialog, as described in the section "The Export Mixdown Dialog" earlier in this chapter, except for the file name field. In the Export Stems dialog, the specified file name is used as the first half of the file name, with the track or channel name constituting the second half of the name, for example, "Mixdown-snare sub."

FORMAT

The settings in this section are identical to those in the Export Mixdown dialog, as described in the section "The Export Mixdown Dialog" earlier in this chapter.

EXPORT RANGE

The settings in this section are identical to those in the Export Mixdown dialog, as described in the section "The Export Mixdown Dialog" earlier in this chapter.

OPTIONS

The settings in this section are identical to those in the Export Mixdown dialog, as described in the section "The Export Mixdown Dialog" earlier in this chapter, with the following exceptions:

- There is no Bypass Master Effects option.
- Preserve Mono Tracks: Because Export Stems actually solos each track and exports it, it creates stereo files by default. Most of the time, though, it is preferable for mono tracks to be bounced to mono files. (The exception would be if stereo effects were inserted on a mono track.) By default, Preserve Mono Tracks is checked, so that mono tracks are exported to mono files. Uncheck this box to export all tracks to stereo files.

Other Methods of Exporting Audio from the Song Page

Two other methods of exporting audio are worth mentioning here:

- Select one or more Audio Events on a track and drag the selection to a location in the Files tab of the Browser. This is the equivalent of bouncing; no insert effects or Event FX are included.
- Adding the Song to a Project causes a mix to be exported to the Master folder inside the Song's folder. The Song Start and End markers designate the range that is exported.

MIXING TIPS, TECHNIQUES, AND APPLICATIONS

Mixing can be a very involved process. Studio One 2 is a toolbox, and its features are the tools you use, but the best results are achieved through the skillful application of them, the methods by which you employ them. In this section, I run through some of these methods to give you some ideas on how you can accomplish your mixing tasks. Some of this information has been given already, but I repeat it here to try to cast it in a larger picture of the mixing process.

Markers

Fig. 3-188: Markers have many uses in mixing, some of which are shown here.

Markers have many uses in mixing:

- Mapping out the song structure by marking the beginning of verses, choruses, bridges, solos, and other song parts.
- Flagging spots that need edits or repair work, such as wrong notes, missed beats, noises or artifacts.
- Placing reference points like the loudest and softest parts of the song.
- Setting locations where mix automation or adjustments are to be created.
- Setting locations from which to start playback and auditioning, for example, to facilitate comparisons between two or more spots in a Song.
- Designating start and end locations for operations like bouncing.
- Studio One 2 has a preroll feature, but not postroll. Postroll can be effectively created by placing a marker and setting the Stop Playback at Marker feature for it. See the section "Stop Playback at Marker" in chapter 7 for more information.
- Setting hit points for working to picture (that is, moments where there is visual action that needs to be highlighted by sound).

It is important to remember that in Studio One 2, markers can be locked either to musical position (bars and beats), in which case they move when a tempo change is added, or absolute position (minutes and seconds), in which case they are unaffected by tempo. However, this setting is global; all markers are always locked to the same reference. This means you cannot have a marker for a hit point in a video (which must stay locked to that absolute location) and also markers with musical functions that move with tempo changes as you try to compose to fit the picture and the hit point.

Versions

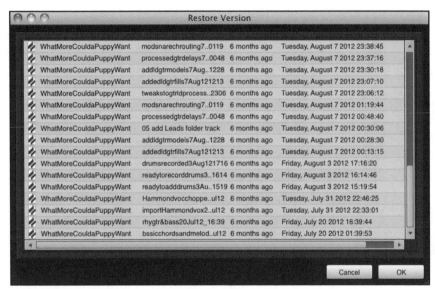

Fig. 3-189: Saving versions of mixes in progress and as delivered gives you a recallable history of the song's development, and a simple method of storing and recalling numerous mix variations.

Versions are extremely useful in mixing, because they allow you to save the state of the mix at a given point in time. When mixing, it is common to rethink something you already did, which might mean you want to return to a previous mix state. Perhaps you tried something that didn't work and want to just go back to where you were before you tried it, or maybe you just want to go back and copy an effects setting you had earlier but changed.

I save a new mix version as soon as I have done enough work that I would be annoyed to lose it. When I get to where I think the mix is done, I save the mix and call it "f1." Of course, that never ends up being the actual delivery version, so every version after that gets saved with a numbered "f" designation.

Versions are also useful when you need to have a full-length mix and a shorter (or longer) edit of the mix. The full-length mix is saved as a version, after which it can be used as the starting point for any number of edits.

Versions can also be used to save mix variations (vocal up, vocal down, bass up, bass down, etc.). These versions can be used in conjunction with a Project to make and burn multiple versions of a CD, to be able to hear which mix variation works best in context.

Developing Mixes Using Looping

Looping is a good tool for concentrating on developing the mix in a specific part of the Song. By setting loop markers around a particular range and letting it play looped, you can experiment with level changes, kick effects or EQ in and out, build the mix by adjusting one instrument on each pass, or simply focus on listening closely to something different each time through.

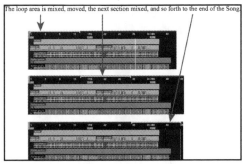

The loop area is mixed, moved, the next section mixed, and so forth to the end of the Song.

Fig. 3-190: Mixes can be developed a piece at a time by setting up a loop of, say, 30 seconds or so, mixing it, then using the Shift Loop command to move the loop forward, and continuing that way on through the Song.

The Shift Loop and Shift Loop Backwards commands can be particularly useful in working your way through a mix while automating. These commands do not appear in any menu; to use them you must find them in the Preferences > Options > General > Keyboard Shortcuts pane and assign shortcuts to them. Shift Loop moves the loop later in time by one loop length, meaning that the Loop Start marker is moved to where the Loop End marker was, and the Loop End marker is moved later by the length of the loop. Shift Loop Backwards, of course, does the inverse, moving Loop End to where Loop Start was, and Loop Start a loop length earlier.

1. Decide on a length of time that will be your "unit of currency" in mixing. For a very complex mix, this could be as short as 5 seconds; for a regular pop mix, you might want to mix a verse or chorus at a time, which might be eight or twelve bars.

2. Choose a place to start mixing. This might not be the beginning of the song; you may want to start with a verse or a chorus.

3. Set the loop markers to the range you want to start mixing, and make looping active.

4. Start playback and adjust the mix in the range until it sounds good.

5. Turn on Automation and write the levels you have.

6. When you like the way the range sounds, use the Shift Loop or Shift Loop Backwards command to move the loop.

7. Mix the next range until it sounds good. Continue shifting and mixing until the whole Song is done. Note that you can skip around by shifting the loop past a range without mixing it, then coming back to it.

8. Once you have gone all the way through the Song, you will need to either go through the Song from the beginning to end and make sure the transitions where loop markers were are smooth, or you can repeat the procedure with a longer loop that encompasses at least one of those transitions, and smooth them that way.

This technique will not often result in a final mix, but it is a fast way to put instruments in their proper relative proportions through the whole Song.

Capturing Audio

We have already discussed this, really, but it bears summarizing one more time because of how easily one can come to grief when audio is not captured. It is a good idea to make sure that everything in a mix is captured to audio before the Song is considered complete, and it is often a good idea to capture audio during the mix process, as well. I'm not saying absolutely everything should always be captured to audio (though that wouldn't hurt), but that capturing is a technique that can be beneficial when used liberally. Here are some reasons:

- External devices may not be available in the future if it is necessary to create more mixes.
- Even if an external device is available, it is possible the preset used in the mix might have gotten overwritten.
- VIs and some plug-ins consume substantial processor resources. In a mix that has a lot going on, it is possible to overtax your computer.
- When everything exists as audio, it is easy to transport the files to another studio, or even another DAW, for further work.
- Intensive edits are easier to handle as a single Event than as many smaller Events.

Here's what you should try to capture:

- Instrument tracks playing VIs.
- Instrument tracks playing external devices.
- Returns from external processors.
- External processors used by the Pipeline plug-in.
- Bus or FX channels used for send effects.
- Event FX.
- Complex edits, such as instrument solos, edited lead vocals, and tweaked drum tracks.

And here are tools Studio One 2 provides for capturing to audio:

- Capture Instrument tracks with the Transform to Audio Track command. See the section "Transforming (Freezing) Instrument Parts to Audio Events" earlier in this chapter.
- Capture insert effects on Audio tracks with the Transform to Rendered Audio command. See the section "Transforming (Freezing) Audio Tracks to Rendered Audio" earlier in this chapter.

- Render Event FX. See the section "Rendering Event FX" earlier in this chapter.
- Record returns from external processors used as send effects. See the section "Using a Send and Return to Capture Audio from an Outboard Processor" earlier in this chapter.
- Use the Export Stems command to capture each track to an individual file. See the section "Export Stems (Tracks)" earlier in this chapter.
- Use the Export Mixdown command on a selected range of a soloed track (or selection of soloed tracks). See the section "Exporting Mixes" earlier in this chapter.
- Record the outputs of Bus channels hosting send effects by selecting them as inputs to Audio tracks. See the section "Capturing Output from Effects on Bus Channels" earlier in this chapter.
- Record the outputs of FX channels by routing them to Bus channels and then recording them to Audio tracks. See the section "Capturing Output from Effects on FX Channels" earlier in this chapter.
- The Bounce Selection command. See the section "Bouncing a Selection" earlier in this chapter.

Submixing

Submixing is performed in Studio One 2 with Bus channels or Output channels. Like capturing audio, submixing is a technique that can be used a lot in a mix, and really should be whenever the channel count gets high. Here are some submixing applications:

- Combining drum tracks into a drum submix so that the overall level of the drums can be varied without changing the balance of individual channels.
- Managing background vocal tracks.
- Combining doubled or tripled vocal tracks.
- Applying processing to a mix of tracks, such as guitars or vocals.
- Send effects fed from a number of channels.
- Creating submixes for summing through an external analog mixing device. (This application would submix through Output channels.)
- Putting dedicated send effects under the same "roof" as the tracks feeding them. For instance, snare top and snare bottom tracks can be submixed with a dedicated snare reverb return.
- Parallel processing.
- Creating instrumental sections (brass, rhythm, etc.).
- True stem mixing.

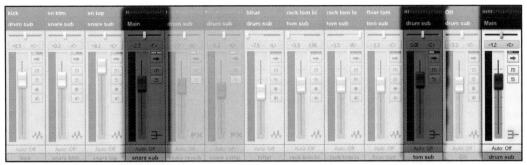

Fig. 3-191: Submixing organizes mixes and provides flexibility in handling the various elements. These drums use three submixes: one for snare, one for toms, and one that mixes these submixes with the rest of the drum tracks. Note that the snare reverb and snare comp tracks cannot be part of the snare submix because they are fed from sends on the snare sub channel.

Parallel Processing

If parallel processing is given a very generic definition, such as "any combination of original, unprocessed signal with processed signal," then even basic reverb and delay effects can be considered parallel processing. In Studio One 2, parallel processing can be achieved using any of these methods that might be available:

- Using a wet/dry mix control on an insert effect. While reverb and delay effects always have such controls, they can also sometimes be found in other plug-ins. The Compressor, Multiband Dynamics, and RedlightDist plug-ins bundled with Studio One 2 all have Mix controls.

- Use the Mix control in the Pipeline plug-in to accomplish parallel processing using an external processor.

- Create a Bus channel for the processing, then instantiate a send to the bus on each channel that you want to feed the effect. For example, you might create a Bus channel and instantiate a compressor on it, then instantiate a send to that bus on a drum submix Bus channel. Now, the drum submix Bus channel has the original submix, while the new effect Bus channel has the compressed version. Balance the two to taste.

- Duplicate a track and apply different processing to the copy than to the original. In the case of an Audio track, use the Duplicate Track with Events command. This method is not as good for Instrument tracks, as you need not only to make a copy of the track using Duplicate Track with Events, but also a new instantiation of the instrument (by dragging to the Instruments Mix View panel), plus make sure the instrument has the same sounds and settings as the original, and, finally, reassign the new track to the new instrument.

  (If you make a second instantiation of the instrument by dragging from the Browser to the new track, instead of dragging to the Instruments panel, Studio One

2 will ask if you want to replace the original instrument. If you choose to do that, the original instrument will be removed from the Song, leaving the original track with no instrument to play!)

Fig. 3-192: Simply put, parallel processing is mixing a processed signal back in with the original, unprocessed signal. Here, the kick and snare channels both have sends to the k_sn_comp bus. A Universal Audio 1176SE compressor is inserted on the k_sn_comp Bus channel, and the channel is brought into the mix with the source channels.

Reamping

Reamping is the process of playing a track back through an amplifier and speaker, and capturing the result. Reamping is easy to do virtually; simply insert an amp emulation plug-in on the channel. However, many people prefer using a real, physical amplifier in a real room, picked up by one or more microphones, gaining not only the benefit of the sound of an actual guitar amp, but also the ambience of the room.

The reamping idea is also used often in film sound, where it is referred to as worldizing. In that use, the amplifier and speaker are typically not chosen for their desirable distortion, as in reamping a guitar or synthesizer, but for accurate reproduction. In that application, the objective is mostly capturing ambience and the sense of moving air.

There are two methods of reamping with Studio One 2.

REAMPING WITH PIPELINE

Using the Pipeline plug-in for reamping is efficient and clean, but it has two significant limitations. One is that the send and return must be the same number of channels. A mono guitar track reamped using Pipeline must have a mono return. While mono room ambience can still be fine in many applications, if stereo ambience or multimiking are desired, Pipeline is not of much help. There is a workaround that can be useful in some situations, which is described in the section, "Integrating Mono-In/Stereo-Out Processors" later in this chapter.

The second limitation is that, until the reamped audio is captured, there is live audio running through the amp, the room, and the mic. If your studio room is separate from the control room, and there is no problem with leaving equipment set up, this may be no problem. If, however, like me, you have a studio that is all one room, you may wish to capture the audio sooner rather than later.

1. Configure an input and an output for Pipeline to use, connecting virtual I/O to interface I/O in the Preferences > Song Setup > Audio I/O Setup pane, mono if the source track is mono, or stereo if the source track is stereo.

2. Connect the interface output set up in the last step to the guitar amp.

3. Place a microphone in the sound field and connect the output of the mic preamp to the interface input set up for Pipeline.

4. Instantiate the Pipeline plug-in on the channel and adjust it to compensate for the delay in the signal path, as described in the section "Integrating Outboard Devices: the Pipeline Plug-In" earlier in this chapter.

5. Set the send level to the amp. The output level from most interfaces is well above that which a guitar amp input expects to see, so you will need to lower the Input level slider on the Pipeline plug-in until the amp sounds good. You may need to lower it quite a bit. If your interface has balanced outputs, be sure to use proper interfacing techniques to unbalance it before feeding it into the amp input.

6. Set the return level back to Studio One 2. First, you will want to set the mic preamp so that its output produces a healthy level on the interface's input level meter. It is better to leave a good amount of headroom than to see how close to the maximum level you can get. Next, observe the level returning into Pipeline and adjust it, if necessary.

7. When you export a mix, Studio One 2 will detect the use of Pipeline and perform the bounce in real time, capturing the reamped signal.

8. If you want to capture the reamped signal immediately, solo the track, use the Export to Mixdown command with the Import to Track option selected. After the export, rename the new track and mute the original track.

REAMPING AS A SEND EFFECT

The other method of reamping is to use an Output channel as a send to the amp, and return the mic preamp signal to an Audio track, into which it can be captured. There are two benefits to this approach. One is the ability to mix several source signals together for reamping, and the other is that the send can be mono and the return stereo, or even multitrack.

The procedure for this is described in the next section, "Integrating Mono-In/Stereo-Out Processors."

To reamp as a send effect:

1. Create an Output channel in the Preferences > Song Setup > Audio I/O Setup pane to use as a send to the amp.

2. Create an Audio track to receive the mic preamp signal.

3. Instantiate a send feeding the Output channel on every mixer channel you want to use as a source for the reamping.

4. Connect the interface output set up in the last step to the guitar amp.

5. Place a microphone in the sound field and connect the output of the mic preamp to the interface input set up as the input to the Audio track.

6. Record-enable the Audio track. Until levels are properly set, you might want to lower your monitoring level some, in case levels are too high at first.

7. Set the send level to the amp. The output level from most interfaces is well above that which a guitar amp input expects to see, so you will need to lower the level of the Output channel until the amp sounds good. You may need to lower it quite a bit, especially if there are several channels feeding it. If your interface has balanced outputs, be sure to use proper interfacing techniques to unbalance it before feeding it into the amp input.

8. Set the return level back to Studio One 2. First, you will want to set the mic preamp so that its output produces a healthy level on the interface's input level meter. It is better to leave a good amount of headroom than to see how close to the maximum level you can get. When the level reaching the interface is good, the level you see on the Input channel should be good, too. If it is not, the best place to adjust is frequently the mic preamp output.

9. Set the play location to the beginning of the material you want to reamp and start recording.

10. Stop recording at the end of the section you want reamped and your reamped audio is captured.

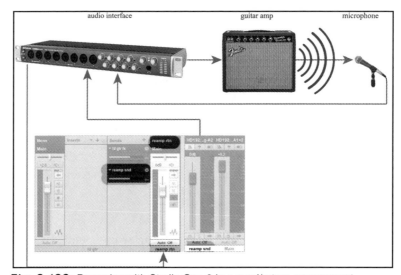

Fig. 3-193: Reamping with Studio One 2 in a send/return arrangement.

Integrating Mono-In/Stereo-Out Processors

Some outboard processors have mono inputs and stereo outputs. Integrating them is not as obvious as integrating mono-in/mono-out or stereo-in/stereo-out processors, but it is nevertheless easy to accommodate. Here are two ways to integrate mono in/stereo out external processors.

USING PIPELINE WITH MONO-IN/STEREO-OUT PROCESSORS

The Pipeline plug-in is set up to be either mono send/mono return or stereo send/stereo return, but there is a workaround that enables mono-send/stereo-return operation. To accommodate the stereo return, Stereo Pipeline must be used; however, it can only be inserted on a stereo channel:

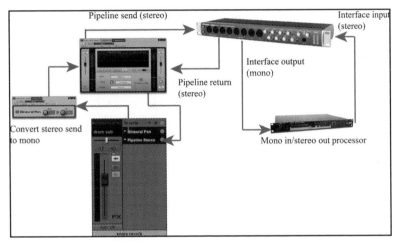

Fig. 3-194: Using the Pipeline plug-in with mono-in/stereo-out external processors. The Binaural Pan plug-in converts the stereo channel signal to dual mono. Both channels going out to the interface carry the same signal, so one output is used and the other left unconnected. The return path is stereo the whole way.

1. Configure a stereo input and stereo output for Pipeline to use, connecting virtual I/O to interface I/O in the Preferences > Song Setup > Audio I/O Setup pane.

2. Connect one of the interface outputs set up in the last step to the outboard processor. It does not matter which output you connect. The other output will go unused.

3. Connect the stereo outputs of the outboard processor to the interface stereo inputs set up to receive the return signals.

4. Create a Bus channel that will be used to host the Pipeline plug-in.

5. Instantiate the Binaural Pan plug-in on the Bus channel and click the Mono box. All signals, whether mono or stereo when they are sent to the Bus channel, are turned into mono.

6. Instantiate Stereo Pipeline below the Binaural Pan plug-in on the Bus channel.

7. In Pipeline, select the channel of the stereo interface output that is connected to the external processor input as the Send, and the interface input pair that is connected to the processor's outputs as the Return.

8. Adjust Pipeline to compensate for the delay in the signal path, as described in the section "Integrating Outboard Devices: the Pipeline Plug-In" earlier in this chapter.

9. Play the Song and balance the processor return with the original signal and the rest of the mix.

10. When you export the mix, it will execute in real time, capturing the audio running out of and back into Pipeline.

USING A SEND ARRANGEMENT WITH MONO-IN/STEREO-OUT PROCESSORS

The most intuitive way to integrate a mono-in/stereo-out processor is the old-school method, which is using a send arrangement:

1. Configure a stereo input and mono output for Pipeline to use, connecting virtual I/O to interface I/O in Preferences > Song Setup > Audio I/O Setup.

2. Connect the interface output set up in the last step to the outboard processor.

3. Connect the stereo outputs of the outboard processor to the interface stereo inputs set up to receive the return signals.

4. On the source channel, create a send to the output connected to the processor. Because it is a mono send, stereo signals will get collapsed to mono in the bus. If you want to send a mix of signals to the processor, create sends on each source channel and balance the levels.

5. Create a new stereo Audio track, and select the return inputs as the channel input.

6. Record-enable the new Audio track, making sure that Input Monitor is also enabled.

7. When you have the sound you want from the outboard processing, record the section you want to process and capture the processor return.

Using Studio One as an Effects Processor for a StudioLive Mixer

Because audio can be passed back and forth between Studio One 2 and a StudioLive mixer, Studio One 2 can act as an effects processor for the StudioLive. As with any live input, the effects return will be impacted by buffer latency, so endeavor to keep the buffer size low, as you would when recording.

StudioLive hard-wires its individual channels to the FireWire outputs, plus allows its stereo buses to be assigned to other slots. The FireWire returns are hard-wired to individual channels and activated by the FireWire Return button on each channel.

To pass StudioLive audio through Studio One 2 effects:

1. Map virtual inputs and outputs in the Preferences > Song Setup > Audio I/O Setup pane to FireWire channels coming from and going to the StudioLive to be the effects sends and returns.

2. Make a new Audio track, or Bus or FX channel to host the effects. Because Bus and FX channels are always stereo, a mono Audio track must be used to process a mono signal from the StudioLive.

3. Set the input on the channel to the virtual input set up to receive the effects send signal, and the output to the virtual output designated for the effects return.

5. If you are using an Audio track, Input Monitor must be made active. As previously noted, monitoring latency on Audio tracks is affected by the current buffer size.

6. Instantiate the desired effect(s) on the channel. Studio One 2 should be all set up at this point.

7. Press the FireWire Return button on the StudioLive channel receiving the effects return. You should now be able to hear your audio passing through the effects and back into the StudioLive.

Using a StudioLive Mixer as an Effects Processor for Studio One

Yes, it works the other direction, as well. StudioLive has Fat Channel processing on every channel, plus two effects processors, so it's not half-bad as an outboard processor.

To pass Studio One 2 audio through StudioLive processing:

1. Map virtual inputs and outputs in the Preferences > Song Setup > Audio I/O Setup pane to FireWire channels going to and coming from the StudioLive to be the effects sends and returns.

2. Use any of the methods already described for integrating outboard processors, with the one difference that virtual inputs and outputs are mapped to StudioLive's FireWire channels, rather than to physical interface I/O.

True Stem Mixing

Stem mixing originated in film mixing, which has long worked with high track counts. Tracks were submixed to reduce the number of elements that needed to be handled in a final mix. Each submix was then recorded as a separate mix, called a stem. A final mix consisted primarily of combining the stems. While Studio One 2's Export Stems command does not do this, true stem mixing is not at all hard to accomplish.

Stems make it very easy to go back after mixing is completed and make adjustments to the balance of the submixes, for example, bass up 2 dB, vocals down 1 dB (assuming you exported bass and vocals stems). Of course, to adjust an individual instrument in a stem, you have to go back to the full mix.

How many stems should you export? That is a good question with no single correct answer. If you export too few stems, you may find yourself needing to go back to the full mix frequently, something that might not be easy a while after the project was completed. This would suggest you might want to export an element you are likely to want to adjust, like the snare drum (with its reverb, parallel processing, and so forth) as its own stem, for instance. However, if you take this granularity too far, you hardly gain anything over using the full mix. The balance point is determined by the nature of the project and your mixing style and needs.

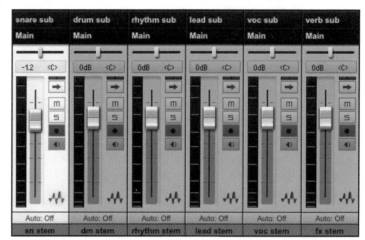

Fig. 3-195: There are several ways to set up true stem mixing in Studio One 2. This is one of them. Everything has been submixed into Bus channels, which are then selected as the inputs to Audio tracks, which capture the Bus channel outputs as stem mixes.

To create true stem mixes:

1. Create Bus channel submixes for each stem you want to export.

2. Create an Output channel for exporting stems.

3. Add a send to the Output channel on each of the Bus channels. Set the Send level to 0 dB and be sure it is set to be post-fader.

4. Solo one of the submixes. Studio One 2 is very smart about also soloing related effects returns and such, but it is worth taking a moment to look at the mixer and confirm that all the channels you want in the stem are soloed and the ones you don't want are muted.

5. Set the Loop Start and End or Song Start and End markers to the range you want to export. This will probably be the entire Song.

6. Press Cmd + E (Ctrl + E in Windows) to bring up the Export Mixdown dialog.

7. In the Output field, choose the stem export Output channel.

8. Set the rest of the options in the dialog as desired and export the mix.

9. Solo the next submix and export again. Repeat this process until all submixes have been soloed and exported. You now have true stem mix files.

As long as the Send levels were the same on every submix Bus channel, you will be able to drag all of the stem mix files into tracks of a new Song (or even port them to another DAW, if that is necessary) and the mix will be exactly the same as what you heard from the Main output. The files must be lined up to start at precisely the same time, but that can usually by accomplished simply by dragging all of the files to the beginning of the new Song.

Other techniques can be used for true stem mixing in Studio One 2, such as creating an Audio track for each stem and then selecting as the channel input a Bus channel carrying one of the stem submixes. Then, just record to the stem submix tracks while the mix plays and the stems are captured.

Making Alternate Mixes

It is common to make some, or even many, variations of a mix. This might be to produce "minus-one" versions for people learning a new song, or it might be to produce vocal up/down, bass up/down, and other mix variations made to provide choices in mastering. These mixes might be used in conjunction with the Project page, but the idea here is to give you a few different approaches to creating alternate mixes.

MIXES AS VERSIONS

The Versions command is the perfect tool for storing mix variations, especially since it stores the entire state of the Song, including VI sounds, effects, and so forth. Get the mix where you like it, then store it as a version with a name identifying its distinguishing characteristic. Remember that only the first twenty-four or so characters will be visible in the Restore Versions dialog. Repeat for each mix variation you need. Once that is done, you can restore any version and export a mix of it or update the mastering file in a Project.

MIXES AS LAYERS WITH ALTERNATE AUTOMATION

By creating layers containing different automation (and naming them appropriately), you can make it easy to create variations, especially of the instrument up/down variety. This requires that automation be used on the tracks that will vary.

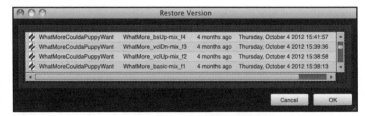

Fig. 3-196: Edits and alternate mixes can be stored as versions and accessed in seconds whenever they might be needed. This example shows a basic mix and vocal up, vocal down, and bass up variations.

For example, to create a vocal up (+1 dB) variation:

1. Make sure the vocal levels in the "standard" mix are preserved by enabling automation on the vocal track (or, more likely, on the vocal submix master), if it is not already. Rename the layer so you will remember it is the "standard" mix vocal levels.

2. Duplicate the layer on the vocal track and rename the new layer to something like "vocal +1 dB."

3. Select all volume automation in the layer and drag it to add 1 dB to all of the points.

4. Bounce the mix or update the mastering file as appropriate.

5. Repeat steps 2 and 3 to create additional variations. It is usually most straightforward to start from the "standard" mix layer each time.

Repeat this procedure for all tracks on which variations are needed. So, you might do the same procedure on the bass track, drum submix master, or other instruments for which you want to create variations.

The advantage of this method is it is easy to try different combinations, if desired, but the disadvantage is that there is considerably more to keep track of.

MAKE ADJUSTMENTS BY HAND

While the first two methods are the most versatile, especially in that they preserve each variation in some form, they are more trouble than might be justified if all you need to do is a few basic minus-one mixes or something similarly simple.

For minus-one mixes, the easiest route is simply to mute the instrument you don't want and export a mix or update the mastering file, as appropriate. For the next minus-one mix, unmute the first instrument and mute the second.

Automation

4

WHAT IS AUTOMATION?

Automation is a system for recording, playing back, and editing parameter control information. Automation does not tell the audio what to do; it tells the faders, knobs, and other controls what to do.

The ability to record and edit parameter data allows mix moves from simple to elaborate to be applied to almost any aspect of playback. Automation can be built up until there are dozens, even scores of parameters playing back under computer control at one time, enabling incredibly detailed mixes to be sculpted.

Automation either switches the state of a parameter, such as mute and bypass, or controls the dynamics of a parameter, such as volume and pan.

A Very Brief Automation Glossary

Getting a little terminology straight before we proceed will—hopefully—save us from confusion.

- Track automation: Automation of any parameter associated with an Audio or Instrument track. This includes channel volume, pan, and mute, send and insert effect parameters, instrument parameters, and MIDI continuous controllers for instrument automation. The instrument and plug-in parameters available depend on the manufacturer's implementation in the instrument or plug-in. Instrument parameters, in particular, can be named very differently on instruments from different manufacturers.

- Automation tracks: Some mixer items, such as Bus and FX channels, do not have corresponding tracks in the Arrange view. Automation of these is accomplished using Automation tracks. An Automation track does not contain content (Audio Events and Instrument Parts), only automation envelopes, but it can automate anything that is not being automated elsewhere. Audio tracks always carry channel volume, pan, and mute automation envelopes, so those are not available to add to automation tracks. However, if there are any insert effects on the track, they will be available (unless they have already been automated elsewhere), and channel volume, pan, and mute for FX and Bus channels will also be available.

- Part Automation lanes: Part automation is an alternative to Instrument Track automation. Part automation resides in one or two lanes located below the note display portion of the Music (piano-roll) Editor. The important difference between Part and Instrument Track automation is the fact that Part automation is contained in the Part itself, so if the Part is moved or copied, all of its automation will travel with it.

- Mixer automation: I use this term to refer to channel level, pan, mute, and send automation.

- Effect automation: Track automation for plug-in parameters.

Automation Envelopes (Breakpoint Automation)

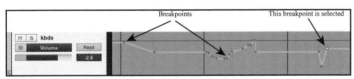

Fig. 4-1: A track automation envelope and its breakpoints.

Automation in Studio One 2 (and other DAWs) is most often viewed and edited as what is called "breakpoint automation": a series of points, each representing a parameter value at a point in time. To make these points more visually coherent, they are connected with line segments to form a shape. Because points usually represent the moment at which the value changes, or "breaks," from one value to another, they are called breakpoints. The ease with which these points are edited and the resulting shape altered has also brought about the name "*rubber-band editing*" to describe this method.

In Studio One 2, these shapes are called "automation envelopes." An automation envelope might contain only two points, if the parameter only changes value once in the Song, or it could be a very complex shape with hundreds of points describing automation moves. Curves are accomplished using many points placed so closely together that the resulting shape appears and, in nearly all cases, sounds, like the smooth change of a curve.

Nearly every parameter in the program, including plug-in and instrument parameters, can have automation envelopes. Recording automation performed on a control surface generates an automation envelope, which then can be edited either by directly editing the breakpoint automation or through more recording from the control surface.

HOW AUTOMATION ENVELOPES ARE CREATED

Automation can be created in any of these ways:

- Record in real time using a hardware controller, facilitated by three automation modes. This allows automation using tactile controllers, such as physical faders and knobs, and lends itself to using those controllers in automation record passes covering whole sections or even the entire song.

- Record in real time while manipulating onscreen controls with the mouse. Neither precise nor graceful, this ability is still nevertheless useful sometimes when a control surface is not available.

- Add manually by editing breakpoint automation curves (called envelopes in Studio One 2) using the Arrow tool. While it is possible to achieve the same automation as is accomplished with real-time recording (crucial if you have no control surface), automation envelope editing excels at very fast and precise changes, such as ducking a single syllable, contouring a word in which some parts of the word were considerably louder than others, or dropping a bypass or mute in a short break between notes or phrases.

- Draw automation with the Paint tool. Automation envelopes can be drawn freehand, or basic waveforms, such as sine and square, can be drawn in to create LFO-like modulation of a parameter, or generate a smooth controller gesture, such as a long parabola for a fade-in.

These four methods cover the majority of all automation needs. Real-time automation with control surfaces is often a good way to make a first pass through a song and get everything in the ballpark. From there, either real-time or envelope editing can be used to handle individual spots. Effects automation tends to use more envelope editing than real-time does because precision is often paramount.

EVENT ENVELOPES

The simplest form of automation in Studio One 2 is the Event envelope, which consists of the Event volume value and the Event fade-in and fade-out.

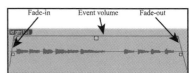

Fig. 4-2: An Event envelope consists of the fade-in, Event volume, and fade-out internal to an Audio Event.

- To set the Event volume: With the Arrange view set to show Event data (not automation data), move the cursor over the Event volume level (which defaults to full value, at the top of the Event) until the icon changes to a hand with a finger, and drag up or down to the desired level. A square handle sits on the Event volume line to make it easier to see.

- To create a fade-in or fade-out for an Event: Click on the triangular handle in the left (for a fade-in) or right (for a fade-out) corner of the Event and drag to create a fade of the desired length. The curve shape can be edited by dragging the square handle in the middle of the fade up or down.

Common Automation Tasks

The applications for automation are nearly endless, but here's a quick overview of the most common uses.

VOLUME RIDING

Moves can be recorded to maintain a consistent level, to bring out an important moment, or to deemphasize a passage or sound that is too prominent, such as pulling back some instruments during vocals or solos. Want the crunch guitar to be part of the bed during the vocal chorus but in your face during the instrumental hook? Volume automation is the simplest method to try.

Many times, volume automation can control peaks or other significant level variations with a less processed sound than using a compressor, as well as limiting the gain control only to those moments that need it, something harder to achieve using a compressor.

More time is spent generating volume automation than on any other parameter, and mixes commonly have highly involved automation on most or all tracks throughout a song.

SHOULD YOU USE A FADE OR AUTOMATION?

Fades and volume automation both control audio level, which leads naturally to the question of when you should opt for one, and when for the other. Here are a few things to consider:

- Fades are fast and convenient. They are created with a single keystroke and always travel with an Audio Event if it is moved. On the other hand, they are far less flexible than automation because fade shapes are simpler, and fades are only an option on Audio Events; there are no fades on Instrument Parts.

- Volume automation takes more time to create and does not always travel with the material to which it is applied, but its shape is arbitrary, which makes it more suitable than fades for many purposes. For example, fades can only occur at the beginning or end of an Audio Event, whereas volume automation can happen at any point and on almost any kind of track or channel.

MUTING

Muting of tracks, channels, sends, and returns is the next most common automation task. Tracks are brought in and out of a mix easily using mute automation, and spot effects are added by automating effects send muting. Sometimes muting can even be used to remove one note or part of a phrase.

Material can be just as easily taken out of the mix by deleting it from the track, but muting is very quickly changed or undone, should you change your mind. Thus, muting is of

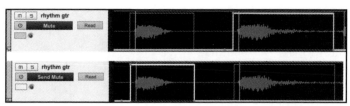

Fig. 4-3: Mute automation can be applied not only to channels, such as the rhythm guitar channel mute automation shown in the top example, but also to sends, such as in the bottom example, and to returns (not shown here).

particular value during writing or arranging, or any time changing one's mind is likely to occur. (We've probably all worked with people who can never seem to settle on what they like best. Mute automation was made for them.)

INSTRUMENT AUTOMATION

Both virtual instruments (VIs) and hardware instruments set up as External Devices can be automated with Studio One 2 and there's only a little difference between how automation is accomplished in the two cases. The most important principle to keep in mind is that there are two different automation targets for instruments: you can automate parameters on the instrument itself, or you can automate the audio returns from the instrument (Instrument channels for virtual instrument, Audio channels for External Devices) in the mixer. These are not the same thing! For instance, nearly every instrument has a master volume control that can be automated, but you will not see the channel fader for the instrument's returns in the mixer move an inch if you automate master volume, because the parameter you are automating is on the instrument, not its mixer channel.

Instrument parameters are automated using Instrument tracks. For VIs, you can add parameters directly from the Add Parameter dialog. For more on this, see the section "Automation Tracks" later in this chapter. Audio parameters of Instrument channels in the mixer can be automated on the associated Instrument track, as well, if the instrument is a VI.

Hardware instruments set up as External Devices require that their parameters be mapped to MIDI controllers in the instrument itself, then controlled using a Device Controller Map in Studio One 2. (Studio One 2 contains presets for a number of instruments, which are selected as part of setting up the instrument as

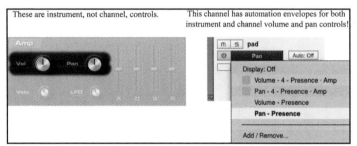

Fig. 4-4: Instruments often have audio parameters that should not be confused with mixer channel parameters that might perform the same functions. Keep straight on what you're automating or you can make a pretty mess for yourself.

an External Device.) I will give an example of this below, but for more information on Device Controller Maps, see the section "Using Hardware Controllers with Studio One 2: Control Link" of chapter 4, "Virtual Instruments and MIDI" in *Power Tools for Studio One 2*, volume 1. The Audio channels through which the instrument's audio is brought into Studio One 2 should be the target for mix automation.

Given that there are likely to be at least a few parameters available on both the instrument and its audio returns (such as volume, pan, and maybe even mute), how do you decide whether to automate the instrument or the mixer? There are no strict rules for this, but there are a few considerations. For most instruments, MIDI provides coarser control of volume and pan than the resolution of Studio One 2's mixer. If your pan move is simply jumping from the center to hard right or left, the difference in resolution may make little difference. On the other hand, if you are doing a pan sweep or a fine volume adjustment, automating the mixer is probably a better choice.

Another difference to consider is that you may want to record the audio from an external instrument into the Audio channels used for its returns, especially if you will be mixing somewhere other than where the external instrument lives. If you have automated audio parameters on the instrument itself, that automation will be "baked in" when you record the audio, whereas mixer automation can be changed after the audio is recorded. There are reasons to choose either of these paths, it's just important to be aware of the difference.

On the other hand, some instruments, such as Cakewalk's Dimension Pro, are multitimbral, but not multichannel, that is, they can play several sounds at once, each played by its own MIDI channel, but there is only one stereo output for the whole instrument. That means that automating volume separately for each timbre can only be done by automating the instrument.

EFFECTS AUTOMATION

How much time have you got right now? Well, it's going to take a lot more than that to cover everything you can do with effects automation, I'm afraid. This is a big, beautiful world so filled with interesting options many people get bogged down just playing around with the possibilities.

BYPASS AUTOMATION

Bypass automation lets you kick an effect in and out whenever you want. Throw a weird telephone filter on the vocals every chorus? Easy: just set up an EQ with the effect, drop a bypass automation point in at the start of the song to kick the effect out, a bypass defeat automation point at the start of every chorus to kick it in, and another bypass point to take it back out at the end of every chorus. Done.

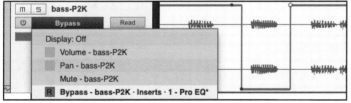

Fig. 4-5: Bypass automation lets you kick in a creative effect or corrective process only when it's needed. This bass part needed an EQ fix on a single note, so the EQ is automated to take it out of bypass just for that note, then it is bypassed again for the rest of the piece.

Bypass automation is also very useful in corrective applications. Perhaps a word or two was edited into a vocal track from another take that had a slightly different tone. The same EQ we used for our telephone effect could instead be set to a setting that matches the tone of the edited vocal to match the track vocal, and kicked in just for that word or two.

Of course, bypass automation is not limited to EQs! Any kind of plug-in, whether it is being used correctively or creatively, can be a target for bypass automation.

WET/DRY MIX

Wet/Dry Mix is a parameter found on many plug-ins. Automating this parameter lets you change the amount of effect being mixed in, as opposed to bypass automation, with which the effect is either in or out. Of course, the two could be combined so that each time bypass automation is used to bring in the effect, there is a different intensity of the effect set by the wet/dry mix.

Wet/dry mix automation will most often be used for insert effects, as achieving the same effect with a send effect usually amounts to automating the send return level. Wet/dry mix automation is one method for bringing an effect tail into the mix only at a selected spot, however, with some effects the perceived level goes down as more wet is introduced. The solution there is to automate output level in the effect (or the return level in the mixer) to compensate.

PARAMETER SETTINGS AND SWEEPS

Automating effects parameters is where the water really starts to get deep. You could automate the delay length in a beat-oriented delay, depth in a reverb, chorus rate, or filter cutoff frequency. Delay feedback, EQ settings that change for each passage, autopanning rate…I could go on forever.

Parameter automation takes the form either of stepping to a new value, or of some sort of dynamic gesture, such as a sweep. In either case, the audible effect of the change depends on a number of factors, including:

- The nature of the plug-in. It is difficult to dynamically change some reverb parameters, for instance.
- How the plug-in maker implemented automation control in their code. Not much to be done about that, other than figure out what works and what doesn't.
- Whether audio is running through the plug-in when the parameter is changed.
- Whether the effect is muted when the parameter is changed.

In short, not every parameter that can be automated should be. Trial and error will often be the way to sort it all out.

PAN AUTOMATION

There are plenty of situations where pan automation is useful, from simply locating instruments for different song sections, to movement effects. Panning effects are sometimes accomplished by selecting a waveform figure for the Pencil tool and drawing in pan automation. Another popular method is to perform pan moves on a control surface.

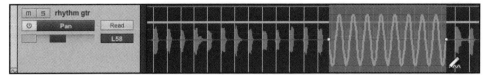

Fig. 4-6: Autopanning effects are easily created by automating panning with the function settings of the Paint tool.

VIEWING TRACK AUTOMATION

Automation can be viewed in the following places:

- On a track in the Arrange view that has been set to show automation, the display shows a single parameter at a time. On Audio tracks, the parameter automation envelope is superimposed over the Events on the track so that you can see how the envelope and the audio correspond. On Instrument tracks, the Part is not visible when automation is shown.
- An automation lane can be shown below the track for each automated parameter, making this the way to view multiple automation parameters for a track.
- Watch the GUI (graphical user interface) controls in the mixer and/or plug-in editor window. Automated controls and values move in real time to reflect their current values as automation is played.

Showing Automation on a Track or in Lanes

- To show automation on a track in the Arrange view, select the track and press A on the keyboard, click the Show Automation button in the toolbar just above the track headers, or choose Track > Show Automation from the main menu bar. All tracks switch from displaying audio or instrument data to displaying automation data (Show/Hide Automation is global). Click in the Automation Parameter field in the appropriate track header and choose the parameter you wish to see from the drop-down menu that appears. Press A again to toggle the track back to the audio/instrument data display.

- To show automation lanes below a track, right-click (Ctrl-click in Mac) on the track header in the Arrange view and choose Expand Envelopes from the contextual menu that drops down, or click the disclosure triangle on the track's line in the Track List.

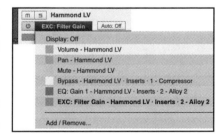

Fig. 4-7: The Automation Parameter field drop-down menu shows the track parameters for which automation envelopes already exist. The Add/Remove command at the bottom controls the contents of the list.

Put automation lanes away using any of these methods:

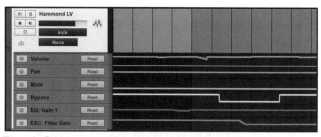

- Right-click (Ctrl-click in Mac) on the track header and choose Expand Envelopes in the drop-down menu that appears to uncheck the item.

- Click the disclosure triangle on the track's line in the Track List to collapse the list.

Fig. 4-8: Automation lanes (envelopes) can be displayed expanded below the track, just as layers can.

- Right-click (Ctrl-click in Mac) on any track header and choose Collapse All Tracks. This is global, so all automation lanes for all tracks are collapsed. This is the quick way to jump out of editing automation and back to other work.

Part Automation Lanes

Instrument parameter automation can be created and viewed in the Part Automation lanes shown at the bottom of the Music Editor. Automation created in this way is superimposed over the Parts in the track in the Arrange view.

TIP: Instrument automation changes parameters on the instrument, not on its audio channels in the mixer. Even though the parameter may be volume or pan, it refers to those controls on the instrument itself. However, if the right pane of a Track Automation dialog has an Audio folder, the parameters in that folder do refer to mixer parameters, not instrument parameters. Because Instrument channels in the mixer do not always correspond directly to tracks in the Arrange view, there may not be an Audio folder, in which case you will need to use an automation track to automate Instrument channels.

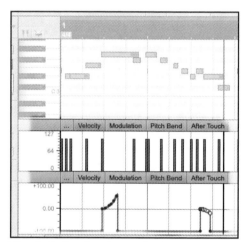

Fig. 4-9: Two Part Automation lanes are available below the Music Editor.

To open/close Part Automation lanes:

- Open an Instrument track into the Music Editor using any of the methods described in the section "Opening Events and Parts for Editing" of chapter 5, "On the Cutting Room Floor: Basic Editing" in *Power Tools for Studio One 2*, volume 1. A Part Automation lane will be below the note display.

- To show the second Part Automation lane, click the right Show/Hide Part Automation Lane button just below the lower left corner of the note display.

- Click the Show/Hide Part Automation Lane buttons to toggle between showing and hiding either of the Part Automation lanes.

For more information on Part Automation lanes, including how to edit in them, see the section "Instrument Tracks and Channels" later in this chapter.

Viewing the Value of an Automation Point

- To view the value of an automation point, just hover the cursor over it and a pop-up tool tip will appear showing the location (in the units selected in the Arrange view Timebase field in the toolbar), parameter name, and value for the point.

Fig. 4-10: A pop-up tool tip shows the value and location of an automation point when the cursor is hovered over it.

Automation Controls in the Track Header and Inspector

All track headers and inspectors (Audio, Instrument, Folder, and Automation) have an Automation section with a small number of very important automation controls. All of these settings apply only to the currently active parameter, meaning that Automation Mode, Envelope Color, and Automation Enable/Disable are all set on a per-parameter basis. The settings in the track inspector are the same ones that appear in the track header.

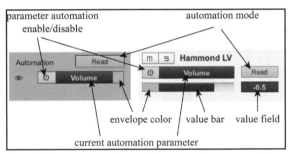

Fig. 4-11: Track headers and inspectors have a small but important Automation section.

- Parameter Automation Enable/Disable: Click this button to the right of the eye icon to enable and disable automation for the current parameter. When the eye icon is colored blue, automation is enabled for the parameter. Note that an automation envelope gives no visual indication of being disabled.
- Current Parameter: This field displays the parameter currently active for display, recording, and editing. To change to a different parameter, click in the field and choose the desired parameter from the drop-down menu that appears, or choose the Add/Remove command to add a new parameter for automation or delete automation for a parameter.

- Automation Mode field: To set the automation mode for a track, click in this field and choose the desired mode from the drop-down menu that appears. Choices are: Auto Off, Read, Touch, Latch, and Write modes. Note that nothing shows in this field when the Current Parameter field shows "Display Off." At least one parameter must be selected or added. For more on automation modes, see the section "Real-Time Automation with Control Surfaces and MIDI" later in this chapter.

- Parameter Envelope Color: To set the color for a parameter envelope, click in the color square to the right of the current parameter name and choose a color from the palette that drops down. Each automated parameter can use a different color for its automation envelope. A color code can really help keep things straight. For instance, you might set all volume envelopes green, all pan envelopes blue, and mute envelopes red. This helps avoid confusion when a lot of parameter automation is happening across a number of tracks.

- Value bar: The value bar displays the current value of the currently active parameter and moves in real time as the automation plays. When automation is playing between points on the envelope, the value bar overrides the automation, so dragging or clicking in the value bar will set the parameter to that value until the next point on the envelope is encountered, at which time it will jump back to playing automation.

- Value field: The value field is a text version of the value bar. Like the value bar, it is editable, but of limited use.

AUTOMATION TRACKS

Okay, let's make sure everything is clear. Automation in Studio One 2 is recorded onto and edited on tracks of any type. This is what is meant by "track automation." However, one type of track is devoted specifically to automation. These are called, naturally, Automation tracks, and they can contain automation for:

- Instruments, both virtual and external.
- Instrument return channels.
- Bus channels.
- FX channels.
- Output channels.
- Insert effects on any channel.

In other words, Automation tracks do not automate parameters for Audio channels (other than for insert effects) because they can already be automated on the corresponding tracks. Instrument parameter automation can be performed either on the Instrument's track or on an Automation track, as can automation of the mixer channels where the instrument is returned.

Fig. 4-12: Instrument parameter automation on an automation track.

A Few Uses for Automation Tracks

- Automating Bus channels, particularly those being used as submix masters.
- Automating FX channels.
- Automating Output channels.
- Organization: All submix masters could be controlled from one Automation track, for instance. If the submix envelopes are each a different color matching the color used for all of the channels feeding it (for example, the drum sub is the same green color as the individual drum tracks), automating can be very intuitive.

Creating or Deleting an Automation Track

To create an Automation track, use any of these methods:

- Press T to bring up the Add Track dialog, click in the Format field, and choose Automation from the drop-down menu that appears.
- Choose Track > Add Automation Track from the main menu bar.
- Click in the Current Parameter field and choose Add/Delete from the drop-down menu that appears. The Track Automation dialog opens. Click the Make New Automation Track button (+ [plus sign]) at the top of the window.

Automation Track Inspector

The inspector for an Automation track contains the following controls:

Fig. 4-13: The Automation Track inspector.

- Track color and name.
- Device name display. An Automation track might hold automation for several different devices, so this read-only field identifies the device associated with the currently active parameter.
- Duplication of the track header automation controls: Parameter Automation on/off, Current Parameter, Automation Mode, Automation Envelope color, Parameter Value bar, Parameter Value field.

CREATING AUTOMATION

There are five ways to create automation:

- Record automation in real time using a control surface. For more on connecting and using control surfaces, see the section "Mixing with Control Surfaces and MIDI Controllers" in chapter 3, Mixing.
- Non-real-time breakpoint editing of an automation envelope using the Arrow tool. For more on editing automation envelopes, see the section "Editing Automation" later in this chapter.
- Non-real-time breakpoint editing of an Instrument automation envelope in Part Automation using the Arrow tool.
- Draw automation using the Paint tool (including its functions, such as sine, saw, etc.).
- Copying automation from elsewhere and pasting it in. For more information on copying and pasting, see the section "Editing Automation" later in this chapter.

Automation for Audio and Instrument channels resides on the corresponding tracks in the Arrange view (although VIs can be automated as either Part or track automation). Bus, FX, and Output channels have no corresponding tracks, so their automation must be created on Automation or Folder tracks.

Adding an Automation Envelope

A parameter can be automated by adding an envelope for it to a track, which can be done in any of the following ways:

DRAG USING CONTROL LINK

The fastest way of making an automation envelope in Studio One 2 is, naturally, drag-and-drop, and Control Link provides the mechanism for doing it. For more about Control Link, see the section "Using Hardware Controllers with Studio One 2: Control Link" of chapter 4, "Virtual Instruments and MIDI" in *Power Tools for Studio One 2*, volume 1.

This technique only works reliably for mixer automation; with instruments, it depends on how the instrument was programmed. PreSonus instruments, of course, work just fine, as do many, but not all, third-party VIs. I have yet to find any third-party plug-ins that do not work using this technique.

If the parameter being dragged applies to an existing track, dragging the parameter to that track adds an automation envelope for it. Dragging the feedback parameter from a vocal delay to the vocal track creates an automation envelope for the delay on that track.

It is possible to drag Instrument channel audio parameters to Instrument tracks to create new envelopes, if the instrument in question is a VI. If it is an external device, the track and channel are not associated. If the parameter is not associated with a track, then a new Automation track is created, along with the indicated automation envelope.

Let's say I have recorded a drum kit, packed all of the individual tracks into a drum submix folder, and submixed it to a Bus channel by selecting that bus as the Folder track's output.

If I wiggle the channel fader on the submix Bus channel, and then drag the hand from the Control Link area to, say, the kick track, which has nothing to do with that fader, Studio One 2 will, instead, create a new Automation track and make an envelope on it. If I drag, instead, to the Folder track, Studio One 2 will create an envelope on that track because it is associated with Bus channel.

To add a new automation envelope using Control Link:

1. Move the control for a channel, instrument, or plug-in parameter so it appears in the Control Link display in the upper left of the Song page.

2. Drag the hand icon next to the parameter name in the Control Link display to the associated track in the Arrange view. A new automation envelope for the displayed parameter is created in the track. Audio parameters dragged to Audio tracks, as well as instrument parameters dragged to Instrument tracks, create new envelopes.

Fig. 4-14: Dragging a parameter from the Control Link area to a target track creates a new automation envelope for the parameter.

3. If there is no track corresponding to the selected parameter, a new automation track with an envelope for the displayed parameter is created.

MAKE AN ENVELOPE FROM A MIXER OR PLUG-IN CONTROL

- Right-click (Ctrl-click in Mac) on a control in the mixer or a PreSonus plug-in and choose "Edit <<parameter name>> Automation." A new Automation track will be created with an envelope for the selected control.

DRAG AN ENVELOPE FROM ANOTHER TRACK

Automation can be added to a track by dragging an automation envelope to it from another track:

1. Press the A key to switch the Arrange view to displaying automation data.

2. Prepare the target track by selecting or adding an automation envelope for the parameter you wish to control. Dragging automation copies the automation data, but does not create a new envelope where none exists, so if no automation parameter is showing on the target track, the drag-and-drop operation will not work.

3. Select the automation on the source track that you want to copy.

3. Press the 1 (number one) key to select the Arrow tool.

4. Move the cursor over an automation point on the source automation you want to copy. The icon will turn to a hand with a finger.

5. Hold down the Option key (Alt key in Windows) and the cursor will change to an open hand.

6. Drag the automation from the source envelope to the target envelope. As you drag, the cursor will be an arrow with + (plus sign) above it. You can drag to any location on the target envelope you wish.

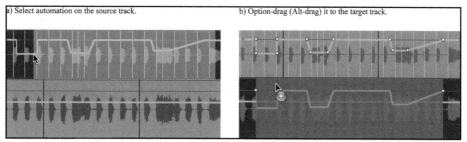

Fig. 4-15: A selection on an automation envelope for a parameter can be Option-dragged (Alt-dragged in Windows) from one track to another, as long as the destination track already has an envelope for that parameter.

ADD AN ENVELOPE FROM THE PARAMETER FIELD

1. Press A to show automation on tracks in the Arrange view or press F4 to open the Inspector pane.

2. Click in the Automation Envelope Select field in the track header or Track inspector and choose Add/Remove from the drop-down menu that appears.

3. The Track Automation dialog appears. Add the parameter using the Track Automation dialog as described in the next section, "Add an Envelope Using the Track Automation Dialog."

ADD AN ENVELOPE USING THE TRACK AUTOMATION DIALOG

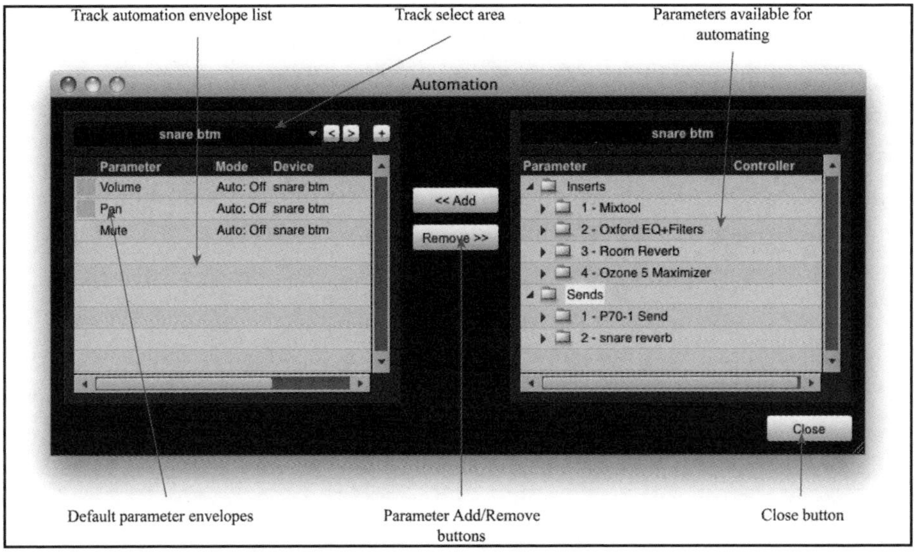

Fig. 4-16: The Track Automation dialog.

The Track Automation dialog (called the "Automation menu" in the Studio One 2 Reference Manual) lets you manage which parameters are automated on a given track. To open the Track Automation dialog:

1. Select the track on which you want to set up automation.
2. Press A to show automation, if the track is not already displaying it.
3. Click in the Automation Envelope Select field in the track header and choose Add/Remove from its drop-down menu. The Track Automation dialog will open.
4. Locate the parameter you wish to add in the right pane in the dialog.
5. Double-click the parameter to add it, or click it once to select it and then click the Add button to add it. The parameter will move to the left pane.
6. To remove an envelope, select it in the left pane of the dialog and click the Remove button.

TRACK SELECT AREA

At the top of the Track Automation dialog is the Track Select area, consisting of the Active Track field and three buttons. At any time, the dialog is managing automation parameters for the track named in the Active Track field.

    Use either of these methods to select a track for which you wish to add and remove automation parameters.

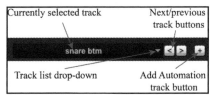

Fig. 4-17: The Track Select area of the Track Automation dialog.

Method 1:

- Click the Active Track field and choose a track from the drop-down menu that appears.
- Click the Next Track or Previous Track button to the right of the Current Track field to move ahead or back one track in the track list.

Method 2:

- To add a new Automation Track, click the Add Automation Track button (+ [plus sign]). A new Automation track will be added at the bottom of the Arrange view.

ADDING AND REMOVING PARAMETERS
IN THE PARAMETER MANAGER

The heart of the Track Automation dialog is the Parameter Manager, in which you add or remove automation parameters to or from a track.

The pane on the left shows existing automation envelopes for the selected track, the device each envelope plays, and the current automation mode for that track. The pane on the right shows all parameters available for automation on that track.

The Add/Remove buttons are the mechanism for moving parameters between the two panes.

To add an automation parameter to a track:

1. Select the track and press A to show automation.
2. Click in the Automation Envelope Select field and choose Add/Remove from the drop-down menu that appears. The Track Automation dialog will appear.
3. Navigate in the pane on the right to the parameter you want to add for automation. The right pane only displays parameters available to that track, so you will likely encounter a number of folders in the pane that appear to have nothing in them. In fact, they simply have nothing that can be automated on the selected track.
4. Double-click the parameter to move it to the left pane, or click it once to select it and click the Add button to move it to the left pane.

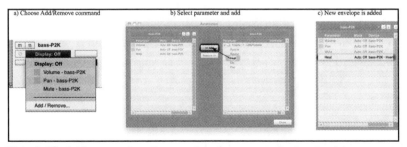

Fig. 4-18: Adding an automation envelope for a parameter to a track is as easy as a-b-c: a) Choose the Add/Remove command to open the Track Automation dialog. b) Find the parameter for which you wish to add an envelope and click the Add button. c) The parameter moves to the left pane. Note that clicking on the color bar will open a color palette, if you wish to select a different color for the envelope.

5. Multiple parameters can be moved at once by Cmd-clicking (Ctrl-clicking in Windows) each parameter to add it to the selection, then clicking the Add button. A range of adjacent parameters can be selected by clicking on the first parameter in the range and Shift-clicking on the last.

To remove a parameter from automation:

1. Navigate in the left pane of the Track Automation dialog to the parameter(s) you want to remove.

2. Click the parameter to select it, or Cmd-click on multiple parameters to add each to the selection. Ranges of parameters can be selected by Shift-clicking.

3. Click the Remove button and the parameters will be moved back to the right pane.

ADD ENVELOPES FOR ALL TOUCHED PARAMETERS

The Automatically add envelopes for all touched parameters checkbox in the Automation tab of the Preferences > Options > Advanced pane applies when a control surface is being used for automating parameters. For more information on automating with control surfaces, see the section "Real-Time Automation with Control Surfaces and MIDI" later in this chapter.

Fig. 4-19: The Automatically add envelopes for all touched parameters preference is for use with control surfaces having touch-sensitive controls.

ADDING AN ENVELOPE IN A PART AUTOMATION LANE

While mix, instrument, and plug-in automation all are created and edited in tracks, instrument automation can also be created in the Part Automation lanes below the note display of an Instrument Part in the Music Editor. Only VI parameters are available in Part Automation lanes; mixer channel parameters are automated in the corresponding track in the Arrange view.

Part automation differs from instrument automation done on the track in that Part automation is a component of the Instrument Part and travels with it, if the Part is moved.

Two Part Automation lanes can be displayed, but each lane can contain automation for several parameters. There are two ways to add an envelope to a Part Automation lane for automating an Instrument parameter.

Method 1:

1. Open the Music Editor for the track and Part you want to automate by selecting the track and pressing F2 or double-clicking a Part in the track to open it in the Music Editor.

2. Click the Add/Remove button (labeled "...") in the parameter bar to the left and just above the Part Automation lane.

3. The Part Automation dialog opens. It is essentially the Parameter Manager portion of the Track Automation dialog and is used in exactly the same way to add an envelope to the Part Automation lane.

4. Once a new envelope has been added, a tab for it will appear in the parameter bar above the Part Automation lane.

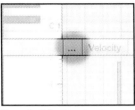

Fig. 4-20: The Add/Remove button for a Part Automation lane.

Method 2 (for use with VIs only):

1. Move the control on the VI for the parameter you want to automate. It will appear in the parameter display on the left of the Control Link area at the top left of the Arrange view.

2. Drag the hand icon at the top of the Control Link area and drop it in the Music Editor for the track. A new automation envelope for the parameter will be added to the Part.

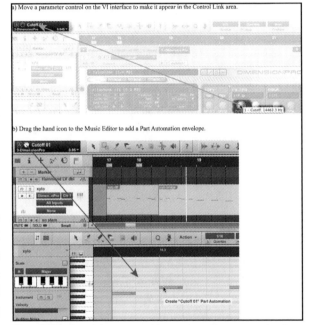

Real-Time Automation with Control Surfaces and MIDI

Control surfaces were discussed in detail in the section "Mixing with Control Surfaces and MIDI Controllers" in chapter 3, "Mixing." One of the primary uses of control surfaces in mixing is as automation controllers. An experienced hand with a control surface can record a significant amount of automation in a single record pass, then quickly edit and polish the automation until only the fastest and most precise moves remain to be executed using a mouse.

Fig. 4-21: A quick way to add an automation parameter for a VI to an Instrument Part is to move the VI control you want to automate so that it appears in the Control Link area, then drag the hand icon into the Music editor.

Control surfaces are used to write both mixer and instrument automation. Mixer automation is for audio parameters, whether in a channel or its plug-ins. Instrument automation controls parameters on the instrument itself. This can include audio parameters, such as volume and pan, but these are separate from the volume and pan controls on the Instrument channels in the mixer, and, in fact, both could be automated. In most instances, this is not recommended, however, because it becomes difficult to keep track of where a given volume change is happening, and the two could conceivably be automated to more or less cancel out each other's effect. Staying aware of when you are working with mixer automation and when instrument automation is the best guard against ending up lost in a baffling maze of interactive automation changes.

The basic procedure for automating with a control surface is:

1. Map controllers on the control surface to Studio One parameters.

2. Add automation envelopes for the parameters you wish to automate. This and step 1 can happen in a single short process with Control Link.

3. Set the Automation Mode for one or more automation envelopes to one of the writing modes (Write, Touch, or Latch).

4. Locate to where you want to start writing and put the transport into playback. Of course, automation also can be written while recording, if you like.

5. Move the controllers to write automation as desired. Multiple parameters can be written in a single pass, and, with a touch-sensitive controller, it is possible to drop in and out of writing automation on the fly.

6. When the automation write pass is complete, change the Automation Mode to Read, unless you are going to continue writing from the current location. This prevents inadvertent overwriting of existing automation.

7. Repeat as desired for other envelopes.

Before attempting to write automation using a control surface, controllers on the surface first must be mapped to the envelopes you want to write.

ABOUT AUTOMATION MODES AND AUTOMATION ENABLE/DISABLE

- The Automation Enable/Disable button available for each automation envelope affects automation playback only. If the Automation Mode for an automation envelope is set to Write, automation for that parameter will be written when the transport is in motion, even if automation has been disabled for that envelope.

Fig. 4-22: The Automation Enable/Disable button only affects whether or not the associated automation envelope will play back.

- The basic mixer channel parameters (volume, pan, mute) change automation modes together. When one is in Write mode, they all are. This is important to keep in mind, because writing pan automation also overwrites volume automation. Plug-in parameters, however, behave differently; their automation mode is independent of that of any other automation envelope.

- All automation envelopes set to a writing mode (Write, Touch, Latch) are written whenever the transport is in motion. For this reason, be careful when using Write mode, because envelopes you are not viewing but are set to Write will start to be overwritten as soon as playback begins.

If you are trying to automate only one parameter and do not want others overwritten, there are a few ways to avoid the problem. Here are two:

- Create a new automation track and record automation onto it, then drag the automation envelope to its intended track, as described in the section "Drag an Envelope from Another Track" earlier in this chapter.

- Use Touch and Latch modes as often as possible. That way, an envelope should not get overwritten unless a controller linked to it is moved.

RECORDING INSTRUMENT PART AUTOMATION

When creating automation for third-party VIs, the parameters available for automating are the ones the VI maker chooses to reveal to Studio One 2. Parameter control might be established through HUI protocol, a template supplied by the control surface manufacturer, or maybe using standard MIDI continuous controller (CC) messages.

- If you are using a HUI-based control surface, the mapping is done for you in Studio One 2's HUI driver. You're ready to plug and play.

- If you're using some other control surface, you will need to use Control Link to map controls to parameters.

Working with external instruments, you may want to record standard MIDI CC messages on an Instrument track. Here are the steps:

1. Using the mapping facilities in the external instrument, map a controller number to a parameter you want to automate in the instrument.

2. Create an automation envelope on an Instrument or Automation track for the controller number you want to record.

3. Using the mapping facilities in the control surface, assign a control to send the controller number you are automating.

4. Open the Device Controller Map for the control surface in Studio One 2 and add the control, if needed. If a control sends out MIDI CC7 messages in one of the control surface's onboard presets, but the same control sends out CC10 in another of its presets, the Device Controller Map needs to have a control for each of those controller numbers.

5. Now that the controller is linked into Studio One 2 and parameter control has been mapped to the same controller number, all that needs to be done is to use Control Link to connect the two. Move the control on the control surface, select the parameter so it shows up in the Control Link display, and click the link button. The controller should now be able to write automation for the selected MIDI CC number.

For more on mapping with Control Link, see the section "Using Hardware Controllers with Studio One 2: Control Link" of chapter 4, "Virtual Instruments and MIDI" in *Power Tools for Studio One 2*, volume 1, and the section "Mixing with Control Surfaces and MIDI Controllers" in chapter 3, "Mixing," of this volume.

Recording automation in real-time on a third-party VI is accomplished like this:

1. Press A to make the tracks in Arrange view show automation data.
2. Use the Automation drop-down in the track header to add an envelope for the parameter you want to control.
3. Use Control Link to map your physical controller to the VI parameter.
4. Put the track into an Automation Write mode (Touch, Latch, Write).
5. Start the transport and perform the automation as desired.

CONTROLLER CONSIDERATIONS

Physical controllers have their own characteristics, which can be very different from controls in Studio One 2 because they are more mechanical in nature.

- Knobs: Controllers either have "endless" pots (encoders, actually) that rotate all the way around, or fixed travel, with a start and a stop in the rotation, which is what we are used to from the analog world. Endless encoders are better for scrolling through lots of values, while fixed travel can be better for performed gestures.
- Touch sensitivity: Touch-sensitive controls make it easy to be spontaneous in grabbing different parameters, and for dropping in quick moves.
- Motorized faders: Without motorized faders, a positional "pickup" system has to be used to coordinate the position of the fader with the starting parameter value, which is less intuitive than faders that are always at the correct position. However, motorized faders add substantially to the cost of a control surface.
- Feel: Each controller is different in terms of the physical sensation of operating it. Both the hardware and software chosen by the control surface manufacturer play roles in determining how expressive or accurate a control surface is.
- Controller software: Some controllers come with mapping software or programs that expand the controller's capabilities in some way. Bundled software can bring versatility and power, but adding layers of software increases the complexity of the system, which, in turn, increases the chances of bugs or odd behavior, or the need to do reconfiguration elsewhere to make everything run smoothly.

AUTOMATION MODES

Although many aspects of automation as it evolved in the 1970s, '80s, and '90s are gone forever (and good riddance to some of them), some structures that were based more on fundamental automation needs than on the automation technology of the time remain, automation modes key amongst them. Automation modes define how the automation responds to moves on a control surface. Each automation envelope (that is, each parameter being automated) has its own automation mode setting. In some automation systems, a track automatically goes back to reading automation as soon as the transport is stopped. In Studio One 2, an automation envelope maintains its automation mode until it is changed by you. There are five automation modes available for Studio One 2 tracks:

- Off: Disables automation for the currently active parameter and all related parameters (for instance, all other parameters in that plug-in).

- Touch: Press K on the keyboard to select Touch mode on a selected track. Unsurprisingly, Touch is an automation write mode for use with touch-sensitive controllers. Any time a controller is touched, automation is written as long as you are touching that controller. As soon as you stop touching the controller, the parameter switches back to playing back the existing automation. Touch mode is excellent for making adjustments to a number of selected spots in a single pass through the Song.

- Read: Press J on the keyboard to switch to Read mode for the envelope currently displayed on each selected track. Read mode is just automation playback. Repeated presses of the J key toggles between Read mode and Auto: Off.

- Write: The basic automation write mode, Write overwrites existing automation. While Write mode is mostly intended for recording from a control surface, it does record from Studio One 2's GUI, so you can record changes to an onscreen control using the mouse. Automation is written as long as the transport is playing. Write mode is useful for writing automation through the whole song.

- Latch: Latch mode plays existing automation until a controller (or an onscreen control) is moved, at which point it begins recording automation. Automation continues being written for as long as the transport is playing. Use Latch mode when you need to drop in at a certain point and record automation from there until the transport is stopped.

One other common automation mode is not (yet) implemented in Studio One 2, and that is Trim mode. When recording in Trim mode, the automation does not record the controller value directly, but instead uses it as an offset to the existing automation. If you created a complex volume envelope for a particular word in the vocal, Trim mode will shift the whole envelope up or down with the movement of the controller, making the word louder or softer without changing the shape of any of the complicated existing automation.

There really isn't any clever way to fake Trim mode in Studio One 2. The best workaround is to select all of the automation points you want to trim and then drag up or down by the desired amount, as described in the sections "Selecting Automation" and "Editing Automation" later in this chapter.

SETTING THE AUTOMATION MODE FOR A TRACK

Set the automation mode for a track using either of these methods:

- With automation showing on the track for which you want to set the automation mode, click in the Automation Mode field on the right of the track header and choose the desired mode from the menu that drops down.

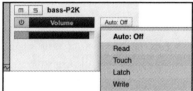

- With automation showing on the track for which you want to set the automation mode, click in the Automation Mode field just above the parameter name in the Automation section of the Track inspector, and choose the desired mode from the menu that drops down.

Fig. 4-23: Choosing an automation mode from the drop-down menu in the Automation Mode field of the track header.

RECORDING AUTOMATION WITH A CONTROL SURFACE

To record automation using a control surface:

1. Be sure the control surface is properly installed and configured to control Studio One 2.

2. Map one or more controls on the control surface to the parameter(s) you want to automate.

3. Set the Automation Mode to Write, Latch, or Touch, as needed. The workflow for performing automation can be sped up by having all the automation modes (including "Off") mapped to keystrokes on the QWERTY keyboard, or controls on the control surface.

4. Select the parameter you want to automate on the track or Part. Automation will be recorded even if you don't do this, as will be the case if you automate multiple parameters in a single pass. However, if you are automating only one parameter, selecting it on the track makes its automation visible as it is recorded. It can be confusing to be recording automation without seeing it onscreen.

5. Start Studio One 2 playing. Automation will be written according to the current automation mode, which controls you operate, and how they are mapped. When you are skilled at using your control surface with Studio One 2, it is possible to automate on a number of channels and parameters in a single, real-time, automation recording pass.

6. When automation recording ends, because you either stop the transport or let go of a controller while using Touch mode, the parameter immediately returns to its value before automation recording began. Studio One 2 does not have a "fadeback" or "return" mode that creates a smooth transition back.

TIP : When automation is in Write or Latch mode, the automation mode does not change to Read when the transport stops. This means that putting the transport back into motion after completing the automation pass will continue writing automation for enabled parameters, overwriting existing data.

REHEARSING AUTOMATION MOVES

Studio One 2 lacks any kind of rehearsal facility for automation, but there are workarounds:

- When an automation envelope is between automation points during playback, you are free to change the value of any parameter and it will stay where you put it until another point is encountered on the parameter's envelope. When the next point is read, the jig is up: the parameter jumps to the value of the new point. If you need to find the right level or move to add to an area that has little automation, this can serve as a crude method for rehearsing the automation.

- Pressing the J key to toggle Read mode. If the Automation Mode is set to Off before rehearsing, the J key effectively turns automation on and off.

CREATING AND DELETING AUTOMATION WITH THE ARROW TOOL

The Arrow tool is extremely useful in automation, as it allows you to add, delete, select, and move automation points. Selecting and moving are both simple drag operations described in detail in the section "Editing Automation" later in this chapter. Remember that automation modes do not apply; they are only for use with control surfaces.

To insert automation points onto an envelope with the Arrow tool:

1. Display the desired automation envelope on a track as described in the section "Selecting Automation" earlier in this chapter. The envelope will be sitting at the current value of the parameter.

2. Choose the Arrow tool if it is not already active in the Arrange view.

3. Move the cursor over the automation envelope at the time in the timeline at which you want to insert an automation point. The cursor will turn to a hand icon.

4. Click to insert a point at the current value shown on the envelope, or click and drag to insert a point and set it to a desired value and time. A pop-up tool tip shows the location and value at the current cursor position. Release the mouse when the point is at the desired location and value.

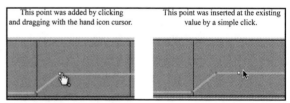

Fig. 4-24: Adding automation points with the Arrow tool. On the right is a point added by a simple click. It is inserted at the existing value. You can also click and drag to create a new point at a different value.

CREATING AUTOMATION WITH THE PAINT TOOL

The Paint tool allows automation to be drawn into a track. Drawing freehand is the first thing that comes to mind when one speaks of drawing automation, and the Paint tool certainly allows freehand drawing. But it is more versatile than that, and offers eight different settings, including the Transform setting, which is discussed in the section "Editing Automation" later in this chapter.

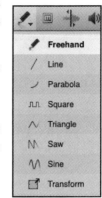

- Freehand: As the name indicates, this setting lets you just draw as your heart desires.
- Line: Draws a single straight line segment.
- Parabola: Draws curves. Because this setting does not create symmetrical functions, what it draws looks (and sounds) to me more like a logarithmic or exponential curve.
- Square: Draws a square wave.
- Triangle: Draws a triangle wave.
- Saw: Draws a sawtooth wave.
- Sine: Draws a sine wave.
- Transform: Scales selected automation. See the section "Editing Automation" later in this chapter.

Fig. 4-25: Settings for the Paint tool simplify creating automation envelopes through drawing.

DRAWING LINE AND CURVE AUTOMATION WITH THE PAINT TOOL

The first three settings (Freehand, Line, Parabola) draw lines and curves for automation envelopes. To draw a line or curve in an automation envelope:

1. Select the track or Instrument Part you wish to automate.

2. Show automation and add an automation envelope for the parameter you want to automate, if one does not already exist, as described in the section "Add an Automation Envelope" earlier in this chapter.

3. Click in the lower right corner of the Paint tool button in the Arrange (for track automation) or Edit (for Part automation) view and choose the desired setting from the drop-down menu that appears.

4. Drag in the automation area of the track or lane from the location and value at which you want to start drawing to the location (horizontal drag) and value (vertical drag) at which you want to finish.

For freehand drawing you may simply draw the shape you want; the Line and Parabola settings scale what they draw to fit between the start and finish points. Option-dragging (Alt-dragging in Windows) with the Freehand tool draws straight lines, just as does the Line setting.

If you draw over existing automation, the Paint tool will overwrite it in the area through which you drag, and if your dragging starts at a value different from the existing automation at that location, it will simply step directly from the value of the existing automation to the value of your start point.

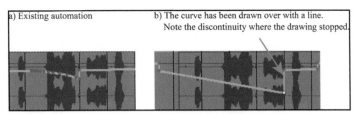

Fig. 4-26: Drawing over existing automation with the Paint tool replaces the old with the new, but can leave a sharp discontinuity at the point where the drawing stops, if the stopping point differs in value from the existing values.

DRAWING AUTOMATION USING FIGURES (WAVEFORMS)

The Paint tool includes four waveform settings: sine, triangle, square, and sawtooth. These functions, called "figures" in the Studio One 2 manual, are useful for dropping LFO-like modulation of a parameter into an automation envelope. This could be sine wave control of level to create tremolo, sawtooth automation of the delay time on a flanger to get a custom sweep, or square wave modulation of an instrument's pitch to get a trill effect. To draw a line or curve in an automation envelope:

1. Select the track or Instrument Part you wish to automate.
2. Show automation and add an automation envelope for the parameter you want to automate, if one does not already exist, as described in the section "Add an Automation Envelope" earlier in this chapter.
3. Click in the lower right corner of the Paint tool button in the Arrange (for track automation) or Edit (for Part automation) view and choose the desired setting from the drop-down menu that appears.
4. Drag in the automation area of the track or lane from the location and value at which you want to start drawing to the location (horizontal drag) and value (vertical drag) at which you want to finish.

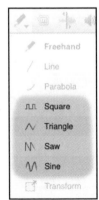

Fig. 4-27: The Paint tool's "figures" (waveforms) can be used to draw in LFO modulation (as illustrated in Fig. 4-6).

The waveform uses the starting value as the centerline of the waveform. Vertical dragging scales the waveform amplitude. While dragging, the cursor's vertical location indicates the maximum or minimum value; clicking and dragging down makes the starting value the maximum, whereas clicking and dragging up makes it the minimum.

If you draw over existing automation, the Paint tool will overwrite it in the area you drag, and, if your dragging starts at a value different from the existing automation at that location, it will simply step directly from the value of the existing automation to the value of your start point.

To change the frequency of a waveform:

- After dragging until at least one cycle of the waveform is in the track or lane, hold down the Option key (Alt in Windows) and continue to drag. The frequency of the waveform changes.

TIP: When changing the frequency of a waveform, as soon as you hold down the Option (Alt) key, it fixes the number of cycles of the waveform to what you drew up to the point you pressed the key. The frequency changes, but the number of cycles is fixed. Another method for accomplishing this is to draw in the waveform, then select it and use the Transform setting, as described in the section "Editing Automation" later in this chapter, to change the frequency and amplitude of the waveform.

What Studio One 2 does not provide, however, is a way to set a frequency for the waveform before drawing it in, so that you can fill a specific time period with a wave at a chosen frequency.

PLAYING BACK AUTOMATION

An automation envelope actively controls a parameter if its Automation Mode is set to "Read," or if it is set to "Touch" or "Latch" and no control has been moved since playback started. To set an automation envelope to read automation:

1. Show automation in the track or Part.
2. Click in the Automation Envelope Select field and choose the desired automation envelope from the drop-down menu that appears.
3. Click in the Automation Mode Select field and choose "Read" from the drop-down menu that appears. The track will now only read automation for that envelope.

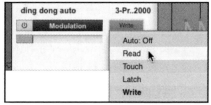

Fig. 4-28: Setting an automation parameter to Read mode.

If an automation envelope is enabled (that is, the automation mode is not set to "Auto: Off"), clicking anywhere on the timeline will cause the automated parameter to jump to its value at that point.

SELECTING AUTOMATION

To select a single automation point on an automation envelope:

1. Display the desired automation envelope on a track.
2. Choose the Arrow tool if it is not already active in the Arrange view.
3. Click a point on the automation envelope to select it.
4. To change the selection to the next automation point on either side of the currently selected point, use the left or right arrow key. Repeated presses step the selection through the points on the automation envelope.

To select automation points in a range of time:

1. Display the desired automation envelope on a track.

2. Choose the Arrow tool if it is not already active in the Arrange view.

3. Drag across the range of time you want to select. Vertical placement is ignored; all points within the range of time will be selected.

4. To make a range selection across multiple adjacent tracks, be sure that all of the tracks are showing automation and that the desired automation envelope is active on each of the tracks. Then, simply extend your drag across all of the tracks you wish to include and all automation points in the range on any of the tracks dragged across will be selected.

5. To add to a selection or select discontiguous areas, hold down the Shift key and drag over the area you wish to add to the original selection. You can add an adjacent range, a discontiguous range, or a range on a different track to the original.

To select automation points in multiple automation envelopes:

1. Right-click (Ctrl-click in Mac) in the track header for the track you wish to automate and choose Expand Envelopes from the contextual drop-down menu that appears. All automation envelopes will appear in lanes below the track.

Fig. 4-29: Dragging over automation points selects them. You can add to the selection by Shift-dragging.

2. Drag across the range of time and envelopes that you wish to select.

3. A selection across multiple envelopes can be added to just like any other: drag across multiple tracks (which may also be expanded) to extend the selection across multiple tracks, Shift-drag to add to a selection.

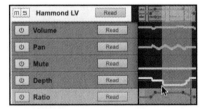

To select automation points in multiple layers of a track:

Fig. 4-30: Selecting automation across a number of envelopes.

1. Right-click (Ctrl-click in Mac) in the track header for the track you wish to automate and choose Expand Layers from the contextual drop-down menu that appears. All layers on the track will appear in lanes below the track.

2. Drag across the range of time and layers that you wish to select.

3. A selection across multiple layers can be added to just like any other: drag across multiple tracks (which may also be expanded) or envelopes to extend the selection, Shift-drag to add to a selection.

EDITING AUTOMATION

Moving Automation

On the whole, moving automation is as simple as dragging or cutting and pasting.

AUTOMATION FOLLOWS EVENTS

By default, the Automation follows events option in the Automation tab of the Preferences > Options >Advanced pane is selected. This makes automation local to an Audio Event, that is, when the Event is moved, automation underlying it moves with it.

Fig. 4-31: The Automation follows events option in the Automation tab of the Preferences > Options >Advanced pane is selected by default, which enables automation to travel with the Events to which they apply when the Events are moved.

AUTOMATION AND EDIT RESOLUTION

When dragging automation, some moves are fairly broad, whereas others require great precision. Studio One 2 provides several different ways of varying the resolution with which you can modify automation.

- Track size: The larger the track is in either dimension, the more screen space is available for dragging automation. That screen space gets put to use by enabling greater resolution. If you are zoomed far out and try to move automation in time or value, the smallest step available will be much larger than if you zoom in very close to that same area. For greater editing resolution, zoom in horizontally or make the track larger vertically (to edit timing and value, respectively).

- Shift key: Holding down the Shift key while dragging engages higher resolution. Taking advantage of this typically requires fine movement.

- Automation Point contextual menu header: Right-clicking (Ctrl-clicking in Mac) on an automation point drops down a contextual menu. The Value field in the header of this contextual menu can be edited to directly input a value for that point. For more information on the contextual menu see the section "The Automation Point Contextual Menu" later in this chapter.

CHANGING THE LOCATION OF AN AUTOMATION POINT

1. Display the automation envelope on which you wish to move one or more automation points.

2. Click on the automation point you want to move and drag it horizontally to the desired location. You can simultaneously change its value with vertical dragging. A pop-up tool tip shows the current location and value of the point as you drag. Release the mouse button when the desired location is displayed. If you drag the point beyond other points on the track, they will move along with it, but they will revert to their previous positions if the point is dragged back.

CHANGING THE LOCATION OF
A SELECTION OF AUTOMATION POINTS

1. Display the automation envelope on which you wish to move one or more automation points.

2. With the Arrow tool selected, drag over the range of time in which you want to select automation points to move.

3. Use any of the methods described in the section "Selecting Automation" earlier in this chapter to modify or add to the selection, or to extend it across multiple tracks, layers, or envelopes.

4. Click on any selected automation point and drag to the desired location and value. All selected points will follow, maintaining their relationships to one another.

Here are a few more important points about dragging automation:

- When automation points are dragged either down to the bottom (value = 0) or left side (time = 0), the selected points will collapse into each other as you continue to drag past the boundary.

- When automation points are dragged to the top (value = max), the drag is stopped as soon as any point reaches the maximum value. The points do not collapse; it simply becomes impossible to drag any higher.

- To constrain dragging to either the horizontal or vertical axis: Cmd-drag (Ctrl-drag in Windows) the selected automation points horizontally or vertically to the desired values or locations. Be sure to release the mouse button before releasing the Cmd (Ctrl) key.

CUT/COPY/PASTE AUTOMATION

Automation is easily cut or copied and pasted. Since it is not possible to drag automation to a different track, layer, or envelope, copy-and-paste is the way to move automation between tracks, layers, or envelopes. Of course, it is just as good for duplicating or moving automation on a single track. Automation is pasted at the play location, so to paste it into a track at the same location as on the track where it was written, you must place the play location at the location of the first automation point you are moving.

Option-dragging (Alt-dragging in Windows) a selection of automation points makes a copy, just as with most data.

MOVING AUTOMATION TO THE SAME TIME
ON ANOTHER TRACK, LAYER, OR ENVELOPE

To copy or move automation to the same location on another track/layer/envelope:

1. Select the automation points you want to move.

2. Press Cmd + C (Ctrl + C in Windows) to copy the data to the clipboard.

3. Put the cursor over the first automation point in the range and note its location from the pop-up tool tip that appears.

4. Select the destination track, layer, or envelope.

5. Press Cmd + T (Ctrl + T in Windows) and enter the location of the first automation point in the Go to Time dialog. Press Enter to go to the specified location.

6. Paste in the automation data. The first automation point will get pasted at the cursor location, which is the proper starting point.

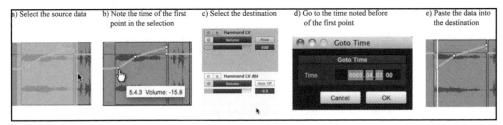

Fig. 4-32: A technique for moving automation to a different track. The same technique works for moving data to a different layer or envelope. It can also be useful when the same data needs to get moved to multiple tracks or envelopes.

Modifying Automation Values

CHANGING THE VALUE OF AN AUTOMATION POINT

Change the value of an automation point using any of these methods:

- Display the automation envelope on which you wish to change the value of one or more automation points. Click on the automation point you want to change and drag it vertically. You can simultaneously change the point's location with horizontal dragging. A pop-up tool tip shows the current location and value of the point as you drag. Release the mouse button when the desired value is displayed.

- Right-click (Ctrl-click in Mac) on the automation point. A contextual drop-down menu will appear with the value selected. Enter the desired value and press the Enter key to terminate entry.

- Select an automation point on an envelope, hold down the Option key (Alt in Windows) and use the up and down arrow keys to modify the value. While the size of the value change with each press of an arrow key depends on the parameter being automated, they tend not to be small steps; for instance, with volume the value changes about 6.5 dB with each press of the arrow key.

Fig. 4-33: A pop-up tool tip shows the current location and value of an automation point as you drag it.

CHANGING THE VALUES OF A SELECTION
OF AUTOMATION POINTS

When you change the value of a selection of automation points, you are essentially performing the same operation as the Trim mode found in most automation systems, which is to offset the whole collection of selected points.

DRAGGING A SELECTION OF AUTOMATION POINTS

1. Display the automation envelope on which you wish to change the values of one or more automation points.
2. With the Arrow tool selected, drag over the range of time in which you want to select automation points to change.
3. Use any of the methods described in the section "Selecting Automation" earlier in this chapter to modify or add to the selection, or to extend it across multiple tracks, layers, or envelopes.
4. Click on any selected automation point and drag to the desired value and location. All selected points will follow, maintaining their relationships to each other.

When automation points are dragged either down to the bottom (value = 0) or left side (time = 0), the selected points will collapse into each other as you continue to drag past the boundary.

When automation points are dragged to the top (value = max), the drag is stopped as soon as any point reaches the maximum value. The points do not collapse; it simply becomes impossible to drag any higher.

USING A SCROLL WHEEL
TO CHANGE AUTOMATION POINTS

Automation values can be changed with a scroll wheel, rather than dragged:

1. Select automation points as described.
2. Hold down the Option key (Alt key in Windows) and move the cursor over the selected automation until the icon turns to an open hand.
3. Without letting the Option (Alt) key up, turn the scroll wheel to move the selected points up or down to the desired values.
4. Release the Option (Alt) key when you reach the desired values.

NUDGING AN AUTOMATION POINT

A single selected automation point can be nudged earlier or later using the left and right arrow keys:

1. Select an automation point.
2. Click the left or right arrow to nudge the point. With Snap off, the point is nudged 1 ms at a time; with Snap on, the point is nudged by the Quantize Value set in the Arrange view.

THE AUTOMATION POINT CONTEXTUAL MENU

A small but useful contextual menu is available for each automation point. It is brought up by right-clicking (Ctrl-clicking in Mac) directly on an automation point, and contains four functions:

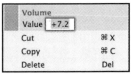

Fig. 4-34: The Automation Point contextual menu.

- To set the color of the automation envelope: With the menu displayed, click on the color bar and choose the desired color from the palette that drops down.

- To edit the value of the automation point: When the menu is displayed, the value for the automation point is selected in the Value field. Use a scroll wheel, if your mouse has one, to increase or decrease the value, or enter a value directly. If the automation Value field is not selected, you can place the cursor over the Value field and drag up or down to the desired value, as well.

- The parameter controlled by the automation envelope (read-only).

- Cut, Copy, and Delete commands: These do the obvious: cut, copy, or delete the automation point.

MODIFYING AUTOMATION WITH THE TRANSFORM SETTING

The Transform setting for the Paint tool (referred to in the manual as "the Transform tool") offers a very fast and intuitive way of manipulating automation data through scaling. Put briefly, the selection you make with the tool becomes enclosed in a box with handles you can drag. The automation in the box is scaled to fit the dimensions of the box.

Fig. 4-35: The Transform setting of the Paint tool is found at the bottom of the Paint tool drop-down menu.

If you drag a handle vertically, you increase the range of values used by the automation, thereby increasing the impact of the automation. Drag a handle horizontally and you change the amount of time over which the modulation in the box occurs.

Say you have drawn in some triangle wave modulation with the Paint tool for an LFO effect, then selected it with the Transform setting. Dragging vertically will increase the depth of the LFO effect, whereas dragging horizontally lowers the LFO rate while expanding the modulation to cover a larger range of time.

But that's not all the Transform setting does. By dragging on the right handle, it is also possible to rotate the automation (!), or make its intensity increase or decrease over the course of the selected data. These distortions are easily grasped visually.

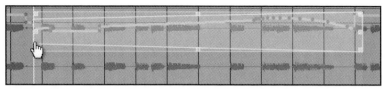

Fig. 4-36: Automation data selected using the Transform setting of the Paint tool is enclosed in a yellow box with eight handles. Dragging the handles distorts the data in useful ways.

To select automation data for modification with the Transform setting:

1. Display the automation envelope on which you wish to scale the automation data.
2. Right-click (Ctrl-click in Mac) in the lower right corner of the Paint tool icon in the toolbar and choose the Transform setting at the bottom of the menu.
3. Drag over the ranges of time and values that you want to modify. The ranges being selected will be highlighted in a deep yellow box. When you release the mouse button, the area you dragged over will be enclosed in a box with eight handles: one at each corner and one in the middle of each side.

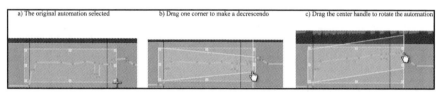

Fig. 4-37: Dragging one of the handles in the middle of a vertical side allows rotation of the selected automation. Dragging a corner handle allows crescendos and decrescendos to be quickly added.

- To modify the intensity of selected automation data using the Transform setting of the Paint tool: Click on the handle in the middle of the top or bottom of the box and drag up or down to increase or decrease the range of values used by the selected automation. There is no effective difference between using the top handle and the bottom one.

- To skew or rotate the selected automation: Click on the handle in the middle of the left or right side and drag as desired to rotate the selected automation. The side you are dragging moves, while the opposite vertical side remains fixed, thus the automation rotates around the opposite side. Note that dragging one side past the other causes the automation to be reversed.

- To create crescendo and decrescendo effects on the selected automation: Grab one of the corner handles and drag up or down to lengthen or shorten the side. The opposite side does not change, so the selected automation is distorted to increase or decrease in intensity over the course of the selection. There is no effective difference between grabbing the top corner handle and the bottom corner handle for a side.

CHANGING THE COLOR OF AN AUTOMATION ENVELOPE

Like tracks, Parts, Events, and other elements, automation envelopes can be color-coded. Change the color of an automation envelope using any of these methods:

- With the envelope you want to color showing in a track in the Arrange view, click in the Parameter Color field to the left of the Parameter Value bar in the track header and click on a color from the color palette that drops down to choose it.

- With the envelope you want to color showing in a track in the Arrange view, and the Inspector pane open, click in the Parameter Color field to the right of the parameter name in the Automation section of the Track inspector, then click on a color from the color palette that drops down to choose it.

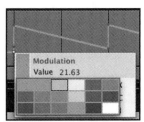

Fig. 4-38: One way to set the color of an automation envelope is to right-click (Ctrl-click in Mac) on a point on the envelope, click in the Parameter Color field, and choose a color from the color palette that appears.

- Right-click (Ctrl-click in Mac) on any automation point on the automation envelope you want to color, click on the Parameter Color field in the header of the contextual menu that drops down, then click on a color from the color palette that drops down to choose it.

DELETING AUTOMATION

Deleting an Automation Point

To delete an automation point from an envelope using the Arrow tool:

1. Display the desired automation envelope on a track as described in the section "Selecting Automation" earlier in this chapter.
2. Choose the Arrow tool if it is not already active in the Arrange view.
3. Click the point on the automation envelope that you want to delete to select it.
4. Press the Delete key to delete the point, or press Cmd + X (Ctrl + X in Windows) or choose Edit > Cut from the main menu bar to cut the point.

Deleting Automation Points in a Range

1. Display the desired automation envelope on a track as described in the section "Selecting Automation" earlier in this chapter.
2. Choose the Arrow tool if it is not already active in the Arrange view.
3. Drag over the range of the automation envelope that you want to delete to select it.
4. Use any of the techniques described in the section "Selecting Automation" earlier in this chapter to extend the selection to other tracks, layers, envelopes, or discontiguous ranges.

5. Press the Delete key to delete the points in the range, or press Cmd + X (Ctrl + X in Windows) or choose Edit > Cut from the main menu bar to cut the point.

DISABLING AUTOMATION

There is no global on/off control for automation in Studio One 2, but automation can be disabled for related parameters on a track, or for just a single parameter.

Disabling Related Parameters

What are related parameters? All of the parameters for a plug-in would be considered related, and disabling automation for one parameter would disable all of them. In terms of basic channel functions, volume, pan, and mute are considered related.

Disable related automation parameters for a track using any of these methods:

- With automation showing on the track on which you want to disable related automation, press J on the keyboard. If the track is in Read mode, pressing J will disable automation. If it is in Touch, Latch, or Write mode, pressing J will change it to Read mode, and a second press of J will then disable automation.

- With automation showing on the track on which you want to disable related automation, click in the Automation Mode field on the right of the track header and choose Auto: Off from the menu that drops down.

- With automation showing on the track for which you want to disable automation, click in the Automation Mode field just above the parameter name in the Automation section of the Track inspector, and choose Auto: Off from the menu that drops down.

Fig. 4-39: Setting the Automation Mode field to Auto: Off disables the displayed parameter and all related automation.

Disabling Automation for a Single Parameter on a Track

Disable automation for a single parameter on a track using either of these methods:

- With automation showing on the track on which you want to disable related automation, click on the Automation Enable/Disable button to the right of the parameter name in the track header. The button is colored the same as the background of the track header when automation is disabled. Click the button again to enable it; the button will turn dark blue when it is enabled.

- With automation showing on the track on which you want to disable related automation, click on the Automation Enable/Disable button to the right of the parameter name in the Automation section of the Track inspector. The button is colored the same as the background of the inspector when automation is disabled. Click the button again to enable it; the button will turn dark blue when it is enabled.

Fig. 4-40: The Automation Enable/Disable button disables only the displayed parameter.

SUMMARIZING A FEW KEY AUTOMATION POINTS

I will summarize here some key points about automation on each potential target.

Audio Tracks

- Audio tracks have a direct relationship with Audio channels, so automation for Audio channels is done on the corresponding track.
- By default, Audio tracks have volume, pan, and mute envelopes available. That can be changed in the Automation tab of the Preferences > Options > Advanced pane.

Instrument Tracks and Channels

- Automation can be performed on a track, or on individual Instrument Parts.
- Volume, Pan, and Mute parameters are VI, not Audio channel, controls, unless they are in the Audio folder for the track. Similarly, effects parameters are for effects in the VI, unless they are found in the Audio > Inserts folder in the Track Automation dialog.
- Part automation can be created, viewed, and edited in the Part Automation lanes at the bottom of the Music Editor.
- Part automation is local, meaning that when the Part is moved, the automation goes with it.
- Program changes can be automated either by performing them while in an automation write mode, or using the Arrow tool to edit the automation envelope. Neither method is ideal, but both can work.

TIP: It is possible to add VI parameter automation in an Instrument track or as Part automation in the Music Editor. Automation will only be local to the Part and travel with it when the Part is moved if it is added as Part automation. The same parameter added in the Arrange view as track automation will remain where it is when a Part is moved.

Automation and Folder Tracks

- Automation tracks can automate any parameter that is not already being automated on another track. This includes the ability to automate Bus and FX channels.
- Folder tracks behave like Automation tracks, automating any parameter not handled elsewhere. However, the output assignment function on Folder tracks, which sets up submixing of the tracks in the folder, makes them the logical place to automate submix masters.
- Bus, FX, and Output channels must be automated on an Automation or Folder track.

ADVANCED AUTOMATION PREFERENCES

To access the advanced automation preferences:

1. Press Cmd + , (comma) (Ctrl + , [comma] in Windows) to bring up the Preferences window.
2. Click the Options button and choose the Advanced pane.
3. Click the Automation tab on the Advanced pane.

There are a small number of automation preferences, but they are worth noting:

- Automation follows events: Engaged by default, unchecking this box means that when an Event is moved, the underlying automation will be left where it is, instead of moving with the Event.
- Disable events under automation envelopes: Most often, it is desirable to avoid accidentally changing Events or Parts while editing automation. This box is engaged by default; unchecking it allows both Events or Parts and automation to be edited at the same time.
- Automatically add envelopes for all touched parameters: When one or more tracks are in Touch mode, touching a controller causes an envelope to be added for the parameter it controls, if one does not already exist. This makes it easy to improvise and capture the result.

Fig. 4-41: Advanced Automation preferences are few in number, but highly useful.

- Default envelopes for new Audio tracks: These three boxes (Volume, Pan, Mute), all checked by default, determine what automation envelopes are created for an Audio track when it is created.

AUTOMATION CPU COSTS

1. To see how much processor power is being used for automation: Click on the Performance meters in the Transport bar or choose View > Performance Monitor from the main menu bar. The Performance Monitor window will open.
2. The Automation meter will show the percentage of available processing power being consumed by automation.

AUTOMATION TECHNIQUES

Here's a few tips on how to execute some common automation techniques in Studio One 2:

Fadeback

It is difficult when writing automation to finish at exactly the right value to match the rest of the automation envelope after the point where writing is completed. In Studio One 2, this results in a sharp discontinuity, as the last written value is followed immediately by the value that existed before writing.

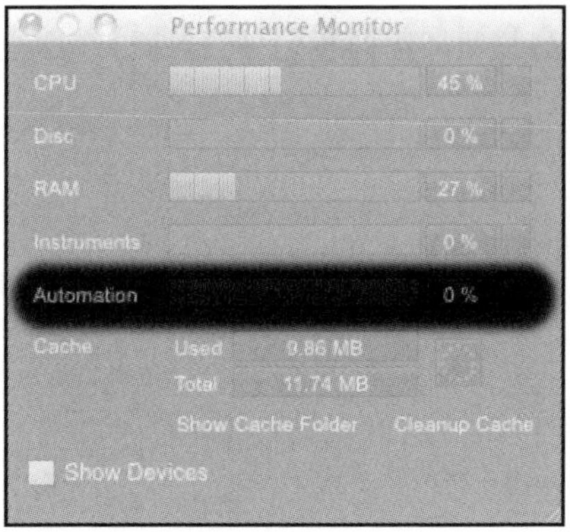

Fig. 4-42: The Automation meter in the Performance Monitor window shows how much of the available processing is currently being consumed by automation. Looks like we're doing okay here!

Console automation systems before personal computers conquered the studio traditionally had a feature called fadeback to deal with this problem. With fadeback engaged, when automation writing ended, a smooth ramp would be written at the transition point from the last point of automation to the first point that follows the point where writing stopped.

Studio One 2 does not have a fadeback feature (yet), but there is an easy workaround, which is to use the Paint tool to manually draw in a smooth transition. The Parabola setting of the Paint tool can produce excellent results in this application.

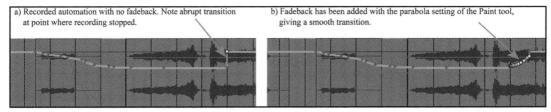

a) Recorded automation with no fadeback. Note abrupt transition at point where recording stopped.

b) Fadeback has been added with the parabola setting of the Paint tool, giving a smooth transition.

Fig. 4-43: Fadeback was an old-school automation feature for providing a smooth transition where automation writing was exited. In Studio One 2, smooth transitions can be drawn in.

Rehearsing Automation Moves

If you are automating with a control surface, it is like a performance. With a DAW, you could record every attempt you make at writing automation and undo or edit it if it does not turn out as you like. However, you might be trying to make a number of automation moves in a single pass, or you might be trying to capture an expressive gesture into automation. It can be effective to rehearse your moves before writing them, in some situations, more effective than recording and editing with a mouse.

Rehearsing automation moves is the same as rehearsing a punch-in (well, it is rehearsing a punch-in on the automation!). For it to work, automation cannot be playing back for the parameter while you are trying to rehearse it.

There is no rehearsal feature in Studio One 2 that facilitates this, so the best solution is to be sure the automation mode for the parameter is set to Read before you start the pass, then, where you want to rehearse your move, press the J key to toggle the parameter to Auto: Off, and make your move.

1. Map controllers to all of the parameters you want to automate.
2. Set all of the parameters to Read mode.
3. Select all of the tracks you are automating. Only selected tracks will be toggled by the J key.
4. Start playing before the point where you want to start rehearsing your automation moves.
5. When you get to where you want to start automating, press the J key. The parameters will toggle to Auto: Off.
6. Perform the automation moves you want to rehearse. Stop the transport when you're done.

Dropping into Writing

Sometimes it is necessary to drop into writing automation on the fly. This is where Touch and Latch modes shine, if you have a touch-sensitive control surface. You can set the envelope(s) you wish to write to Touch or Latch mode before you start your writing pass, or start the pass in Read mode and use key shortcuts to change modes while the transport is rolling.

Either way, no automation is written until you touch the controller mapped to the parameter. In Touch mode, you can drop in and out of writing automation at will; in Latch mode, once writing starts, it continues until the transport is stopped.

Fade-outs

Probably the most commonly performed automation task is a fade-out at the end of the song. It's also probably the easiest automation to do:

1. Map a controller to the Main Out fader volume.
2. Right-click (Ctrl-click in Mac) the Main Out fader and choose Edit Volume Automation from the contextual menu that drops down. A new Automation track will be created with an automation envelope for Main Out fader volume.
3. Set the envelope to Latch or Touch mode. (This assumes you have a touch-sensitive controller.)

4. Start playing somewhere before the fade-out is to begin. I recommend listening to enough of the Song to get a feel for the overall volume and flow. Otherwise, the fade may sound good on its own but wrong in the context of the entire piece.

5. Make your fade-out when the time comes. Let the transport run for a few seconds after the fade-out is done, just for cleanliness.

Mastering on the Project Page

Mastering in Studio One 2 Professional takes place on the Project page. Whereas the Song page is a multitrack environment, the Project page is optimized for dealing with no more than two stereo pairs of channels at a time. However, it supports those pairs with both global (master) and local (per Song) processing, robust metering options, numerous final output and publishing options, and, uniquely, the ability to flip back and forth between the realms of mixing and mastering.

The Project page is a feature found only in Studio One Professional.

WHAT IS MASTERING?

Mastering has long been a mysterious process to musicians, and sometimes, even to engineers. Mastering studios are less numerous than recording, sound design, or mixing facilities, the equipment seems similar to that in recording studios (EQs, compressors, etc.), yet mastering studios often seem to use equipment of a different ilk. And mastering studio rates are very high compared to recording studio rates.

What is mastering and what makes it so special? Once you have created and mixed your music, mastering is the final stage before the music is released. Four basic operations take place during mastering:

- Sequencing and assembly of the songs into an album. (This assumes the songs will be released as a collection and not simply as a series of singles.) The order of songs, the timing between them, and creating fades or crossfades (in the case of segues) of the desired shape and length for each song are all performed in mastering.
- No matter how consistent the production of a group of recordings, there are always some differences in how individual songs sound. This is often deliberate and desirable, but usually it is desirable for the songs to sound like a coherent collection, especially when

released as such, as in an album or soundtrack. Mastering is where individual songs are given (hopefully) slight adjustments so that levels from song to song are consistent and tonal differences between songs are not excessive. It would be rare, indeed, for an album to feel good when one song has massive bass and another with similar instrumentation and musical feel has very little. (A well-recorded and mixed album would not have such disparity between songs, but an anthology or other collection could.) So, bringing overall coherency across songs is one purpose for mastering.

- Mastering is the last opportunity to fix problems in the recordings. We would all like our recordings and mixes to turn out perfect, but producing music can be an involved enterprise, and anything from running out of time to less-than-perfect acoustics to bad decisions can result in problems in the final mixes. Mastering engineers generally prefer not to have to perform major surgery, but it is without question part of mastering to make necessary repairs. Last-minute edits and even the addition of a bit of reverb are also common tasks in mastering.

- It is never a good idea to choose to leave things to be fixed in mastering, partly because it is an expensive way to go, but even more because once all the tracks are mixed, the mastering engineer's options are far more limited than the mixing engineer's were. The most common example is mixes that have had the life squeezed out of them from too much compression being applied, often at the insistence of the artist. Resist that temptation; it ties the mastering engineer's hands, and the mastering engineer is just as capable of adding that apparent loudness if you still feel you need it when mastering happens.

- Every medium in which music is delivered has its own characteristics, and mastering is where your mixes get optimized for each medium in which your music is to be released. Music destined to be issued as a CD is mastered differently than music that will be downloaded as MP3 files. If you are releasing on vinyl, yet another set of considerations comes into play. Mastering engineers often consider making your music sound its best in each release format to be the most important aspect of their jobs.

Because mastering is the last step in music production, mastering studios use gear of the absolute highest precision (and, often, highest cost), and have rooms that are purpose-built and feature excellent acoustical characteristics. Mastering engineers also work with finer resolution than is commonly employed in recording and mixing, making adjustments of less than 1 dB of level or a few Hz of EQ frequency.

The Mastering Process

As with any other aspect of music creation, there are no absolutes when it comes to the mastering process, especially in the order in which functions are performed, but music mastering for albums usually involves these steps, more or less in this order:

1. Importing the mixes: Mastering houses receive materials in many formats, including individual .wav or .aiff files, analog tape, audio CD-Rs, and more. Some projects arrive in multiple formats, perhaps even using multiple sample rates. The mastering engineer sorts through it all so that the final, mastered product is consistent.

2. Sequencing: This is not the same kind of sequencing as you do with MIDI instruments. In mastering, sequencing is the process of putting the songs into the desired order for the album.

3. Spacing: This refers to the interval of time between songs. Spacing is important to the flow of the album.

4. Level setting: Levels of the songs in an album should be consistent and proportional. You would not want one song to be so much louder than the others that the listener has to dive for the volume control when it comes on, nor would you want a ballad with one voice and an acoustic guitar to have the same level as a song with a full band. As mentioned earlier, level adjustments in mastering can be quite fine.

5. Editing: Edits may be performed for a number of reasons in mastering. Perhaps a shortened version is needed as well as a full-length version of a song, or maybe the final mix turns out to have a flaw in one spot that can't be corrected, so an edit is made to extract a better version of that spot from an alternate mix.

6. Fades and crossfades: Transitions are important. Sometimes a fade-out is deliberately left for the mastering stage, other times a shorter fade-out might work better with the sequencing and spacing. Crossfades are constructed either for edits or segues.

7. Processing: This is a big area, discussed in the next section in this chapter, "Processing in Mastering." Processing can be added individually to each song (called track processing), but mastering almost always includes global, or "master" processing, which is applied to the final stereo output.

8. Song/Project interaction: This one is kind of a trick answer. During mastering, a mastering engineer may request that the artist go back to the mixing engineer and have some changes done, but only in Studio One 2 is it a simple, integrated process to go back and forth between mixing and mastering. For more information on this, see the section "Song/Project Integration" later in this chapter.

9. Creating final output in delivery format(s): This is the end of the line, where the final mastered product is created. In the case of CD releases, the manufacturing stage still needs to occur, but that should simply be a faithful transfer of the master to a pressed disk. If your release will be in multiple formats, such as CD and MP3 for download, masters for each format are created at this stage.

10. Uploading: Studio One 2 offers additional options not traditionally found in a mastering studio, specifically the ability to publish your finished masters directly by uploading them to SoundCloud or Nimbit directly from within the program. This is an exciting new advance.

PROCESSING IN MASTERING

As in mixing, processing is applied in mastering both for corrective and creative purposes. Corrective processing might be EQ to give tonal consistency across all of the songs, or maybe to reduce the prominence of an overly loud instrument. Limiting might be applied to tame unruly peaks, or repairing clipped samples from peaks so unruly they literally went over the top. Creative processing examples include widening the soundstage, gain maximizing, multiband compression (a tool also used for corrective purposes) to add punch, EQ for low-end "beef," and so forth.

To help you get your head around the wide world of mastering processing, here's a brief categorical summary of the types of processing applied in mastering:

- Tonal
- Dynamic (broadband compression, peak limiting, leveling, gain maximization, multiband compression, upward expansion)
- Frequency-selective (for example, on HF or LF only)
- Soundstage modification or ambience (including MS processing and reverb)

MAKING A NEW PROJECT

To create a new Project, use any of these methods to bring up the New Project dialog:

- Press Cmd + Shift + N (Ctrl + Shift + N in Windows).
- If no Project is currently open, click on the Song page Project quick-access button.
- Choose File > New Project from the main menu bar.
- Select Create a new Project from the Start page.
- Choose Song > Add to Project > New Project <<song name>> from the main menu bar.

The New Project Dialog

Your Project is given basic definition in the New Project dialog.

CHOOSING A PROJECT SAMPLE RATE

The choice of a sample rate is the one decision that cannot be changed later, so it merits some consideration. The two things to think about are the sample rate of the individual source files/Songs, and what the primary target medium is.

If you are creating a CD that may be repurposed for other media later, 44.1 kHz may be the best

Fig. 5-1: The New Project dialog. The button labeled with an ellipsis ("...") is the Location button, for setting where the Project will be stored.

Project sample rate. If you are doing audio for video (such as DVD), 48 kHz may work better. If your primary delivery medium is digital download, then the sample rate does not matter so much as the bit rate you choose for the MP3 files when you export them.

But what if your primary target is DVD and the Songs were all produced at 44.1 kHz? In that case, rather than have to worry about upsampling all of the individual files to 48 kHz, you would be better off mastering at 44.1 kHz and then doing a single sample rate conversion (SRC) on the final mix file.

What about if your source files are a mix of sample rates? As in the Song page, when a Song or file is added to a Project with a different sample rate, Studio One 2 does real-time SRC on it. This is not desirable for mastering, as real-time SRC is not likely to be as high quality as non-real-time SRC, which can take the time to apply a more powerful algorithm.

If sample rates are mixed in your source files, you should choose one of the sample rates (usually the highest of them), and convert the files to that rate. Here's a method for doing that:

1. Create a new Song.
2. Import all of the source files to it that are not at the Project sample rate.
3. Select all of the newly imported source files in the Pool.
4. Right-click (Ctrl-click in Mac) on any of the files and choose Convert Sample Rate from the contextual menu that drops down.
5. Drag the converted files into the Project.

Professional mastering engineers usually convert source files to a high sample rate, such as 96 kHz, and perform mastering using that sample rate, to maintain precision during processing. Downsampling is done as the last step, to the rate needed for each delivery medium. Studio One 2 is capable of working at high sample rates, and mastering is the best place to consider using them.

However, high sample rates and plug-ins made for mastering can seriously tax a computer. If you are uncertain how fast your computer can work, try a few tests before committing to a project at a high sample rate. Most modern computers can handle working at high sample rates, as long as they have relatively fast disk drives and a high-bandwidth connection to them.

USING THE NEW PROJECT DIALOG

1. Click in the Project Title field and enter a name for the Project.
2. Click the Location button and navigate to the place in the file system where you want to store the Project. The default location is the Projects folder inside the user data location specified in Preferences > Options > Locations > User Data > User Data Location (a.k.a. Studio One\Projects). Another good approach is to create a folder for the Project and all of the Songs and other files pertaining to it, an album folder.

3. Click in the Sample Rate field and choose a sample rate from the menu that drops down. For more information on deciding on a Project sample rate, see the previous section, "Choosing a Project Sample Rate."

DELETING A PROJECT

There are two ways to delete a Project:

- Delete the Project folder in the Mac Finder or Windows Explorer.
- Navigate to the Project folder in the Files tab of the Browser, right-click (Ctrl-click in Mac) on the folder and select Delete Folder from the contextual menu that drops down. You can also choose to open the folder and use the same method to delete the Project file itself.

WELCOME TO THE PROJECT PAGE

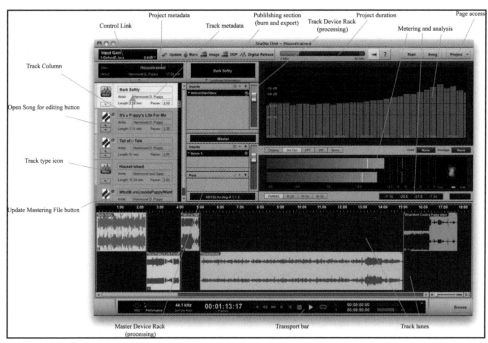

Fig. 5-2: The Project Page.

The Project page is unique to Studio One 2 Professional. There are certainly other excellent desktop mastering environments, but what really sets the Project page apart is its integration with the Song page, which, for the first time, enables fast, seamless switching between mixing and mastering environments to make adjustments.

The Project page also offers excellent metering and analysis, including ITU-standard loudness and True Peak metering, separate track and master processing, drag-and-drop sequencing, and versatile final output options, which are discussed in detail in chapter 6, "Sharing Your Work."

Basic Project Page Mastering Workflow

The mastering paradigm is a tad different than the multitrack production environment of the Song page. On the Song page, many elements are combined into a single stereo output file. On the Project page, activity is focused on assembling complete mixes into a sequence; there is minimal combining. Consequently, instead of having lots of tracks, there is really only one track on the Project page, though it's displayed as mixes alternating between two Track Lanes for easier visualization, especially of overlaps and relative timing. This alternation between lanes is called "checkerboarding."

That brings me to a terminology difference between the Song and Project pages. On the Project page, a track is not a playlist in a lane, as on the Song page, but a mix file that is more equivalent to an Audio Event on the Song page. The entire Project is the playlist.

Most important, in the end, is that mastering is the final stage of preparation for release of the material. This places heavy emphasis on metering and analysis of the signal; tasks peripheral to

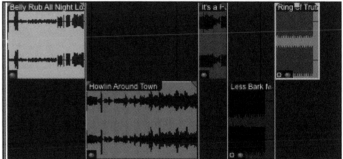

Fig. 5-3: Checkerboarding is a technique in which material is spread over two (or more) tracks for ease of handling and processing. On the Project page, checkerboarding is simply a display feature to make the layout of tracks easy to grasp visually.

the audio production, such as entering metadata; and optimization for and output into multiple release formats. The Project page has tools for all of these jobs.

Most people perform the same tasks when mastering, but not always in the same order. Although some tasks require steps to be performed in a specific order, the sonic aspect, which is the most creative part of the mastering job, can be approached in many ways. Tasks are frequently interwoven: having made a repair, you might give the track level a tweak and adjust the spacing a bit.

Keeping in mind that the steps may not be segregated as discretely as this list might suggest, and that every step is backed up by close metering and analysis, here's one workflow that works:

1. Add tracks to the Project: Tracks can be imported audio files, Studio One 2 Songs, or a combination of the two. Songs from the Song page become Tracks on the Project page.

Songs and files can be dragged from the Browser, Mac Finder, and Windows Explorer. You may even need to acquire the audio from analog tape or some other source.

2. Rough in the sequencing: Move tracks into the order you anticipate by dragging them in the Track Column. If you move them in the Track Lanes instead, you can also play with the spacing. It is easy to change sequencing and spacing at any time, which is good, because they often do change, sometimes substantially, before the album is done.

3. Audition the material: You need to hear what you are working with. The realities of different mastering situations will dictate how much time you can spend on this, but the entire rest of the mastering process can be significantly more efficient, and produce a better result, if you know going in what basically is going on with the material.

4. Rough in levels and spacing: All the music is present and in some kind of order. Look at the waveforms and jump around during playback to the largest waveform you see in each song. Bring levels from cut to cut roughly into proportion, using the fader in the Track Column. The loudest song should be the standard the others are measured against.

5. While you're at it, take at least a rough whack at finding appropriate amounts of time between each cut. Don't feel like it needs to be close to right; once again, it's about bringing some kind of order where there was none before.

6. Listen again, this time making note of issues. No, I mean really take notes: where the issues occur and what they are. Listen for flaws in the audio (flaws in performance should have been dealt with in mixing), disturbing differences in instrumental balance from song to song, cuts or moments that differ significantly from the rest of the album. Notice the things your ear just doesn't like.

7. Now we get down heavily. Got your issues list from the last step in front of you? Perform all edits, fades, repairs, noise removal, and mix adjustments, as needed, to satisfy the items on the list. Open Songs for editing and adjust the mix, bounce complex edits, do whatever needs to be done to work out the kinks in all the material and get everything clean.

8. Focus on dialing in spacing. You might already be there, if you've been adjusting it all along, but, if not, try and get the flow of the album working at this point. Drag tracks in the Track lanes, auditioning transitions. You'll make further tweaks between now and when you finish, but if you get this step right, there won't be a lot of them, and they are unlikely to be large deviations.

9. Apply EQ on each track that needs it for overall tonal matching across cuts and any repair that remains. As on the Song page, processing can be dragged in from the Browser directly to the track or master processing device rack.

10. Sweeten to taste, adjusting sound stage, ambience, multiband compression, exciter, hair restoration, whatever. Don't overdo it; you could blow the whole thing right here. Depending on the nature of the sweetening, it might be applied at the track level or globally, as master processing.

11. Add dynamic processing: limiting, leveling, upward expansion, gain maximization. Many people add this earlier in the process. Some people apply dynamics at both the track and master processing levels, some only use master processing. You'll have to learn for yourself what works for you. Again, I caution you not to overdo it.

12. Export to final delivery formats, whichever you might choose. If you are having CDs made, find out from the CD manufacturing house whether they would rather get a disk image, DDP file set, or a burned disk. Upload to SoundCloud or Nimbit. You're done!

Project Page Overview

THE TRANSPORT BAR

Fig. 5-4: The Project page Transport bar.

Fig. 5-5: The Project page Browser.

The Transport bar appears below the Project page, exactly as it does on the Song page. For more information on the Transport bar, see the section "The Song Page" of chapter 1, "On Your Mark" in *Power Tools for Studio One 2*, volume 1.

BROWSER

The Browser on the Project page is slightly different than the Song page browser. First, there are only two tabs at the bottom: Effects and Files. The Files pane has two tabs at the top: the Files tab at the top displays your computer's file system, whereas the Studio One tab displays items in your Studio One User Data folder.

Fig. 5-6: The Track Column provides access to opening Songs for editing and entering metadata, as well as its being a quick and easy place to resequence a Project.

TRACK COLUMN

Once you have imported files and/or Songs to your Project, you will see them listed in the Track Column. The order of items in the list reflects their order in the Track lane.

PROJECT METADATA

At the top of the Track Column are three Project metadata fields:

Fig. 5-7: The Project metadata fields.

- Disc: Click in this field to enter the name of the finished album. The Disc field supplies a name for the entire work that is independent of the Project name. It is used as part of the folder name created when a Digital Release is generated.

- Artist: Click in this field to enter the Project-level Artist name. Artist names can also be entered for each track, but this field is used as part of the folder name created when a Digital Release is generated.

- Length. Length shows the length of the entire project. It is not an editable field.

TRACK HEADERS

- To change track sequence order: Drag a track header to the desired position in the running order.

Fig. 5-8: Track headers in the Track Column.

- Track icon: The track icon shows whether the track is an audio file (and, if so, what format) or a Song.

- Track name: Click in this field to change the track name. The contents of this field will be used as the track name in the final release format.

- Artist: Click in this field to enter an artist name for the track. If no name is provided, the Project Artist name will be used for the track on exports. This makes it easy to create compilations or collections of cuts for digital release, with the correct artist name for each track, plus an album name.

- Pause field: Pause is most easily edited by dragging in the Track Lanes, but clicking in this field allows direct entry of a value from zero to 10 seconds. The default value is two seconds.

- Length: This read-only field gives the length of the track.

- Edit Song button: This button with a wrench icon appears only on tracks on which Songs were imported (as shown by the Song document logo). Click this button to open the Song for editing.

- Metadata Show/Hide button: Clicking this button causes an extended collection of track metadata fields to appear or, if they are already visible, disappear. For more on metadata in the Project page, see the section "Metadata" later in this chapter.

TRACK LANE AND TIMELINE

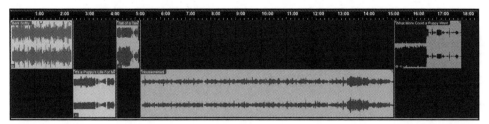

Fig. 5-9: The Track lane. It looks like two tracks, but that's primarily for show; it functions as a single playlist.

The bottom portion of the Project page is the Track lane. When you import files or songs, you will see them show up in the Track lane as Audio Events with waveform displays. There are actually two Track lanes, and Studio One 2 alternates between them, placing one track on the top lane, the next on the bottom lane, then back on the top, and so forth. This is called checkerboarding, and it makes it easy to adjust the tracks in time relative to each other, overlapping them if desired.

The timeline at the top of the Track Lane shows where each track fits in time in the context of the Project. The Track Lane incorporates track Pause times as time added onto the start of the track. When a track is moved in the Track Lane, its pause moves with it. Note that Pause is always positive, when there is overlap, the field shows a zero value.

ZOOMING AND SIZING THE TRACK LANES
- To zoom horizontally: Drag the Horizontal Zoom bar in the lower right corner, or use any of the techniques for horizontal zooming in the Song page, including pressing W to zoom out and E to zoom in, dragging up or down in the timeline, and choosing zoom commands from the View menu in the main menu bar.
- To size the track lanes vertically: Drag the divider bar at the top of the Track lanes up to enlarge the lanes.
- To zoom the waveform in and out vertically: Click the Data Zoom box in the lower right corner of the Track lanes and drag the fader that appears up or down.

LOOPING IN THE TRACK LANES
Looping works on the Project page just as on the Song page:

- Set the Loop Start and End markers by Cmd-clicking (Ctrl-clicking in Windows) and Option-clicking (Alt-clicking in Windows), respectively, in the timeline, or click one or more tracks and press Shift + P to set the loop. You cannot drag to select a range and then set the loop to that.
- Activate or deactivate looping by pressing the / (forward slash) key.
- The Shift Loop and Shift Loop Backwards commands work, as well.

TRACK AND INDEX MARKERS

The Project page has two kinds of markers besides the loop start and end markers:

Fig. 5-10: The Project page has the two kinds of markers used on CDs: track start to mark the beginning of a track, and track index markers for locations internal to a track.

- Track Start: A track start marker is dropped automatically at the beginning of each track and is always there.
- Track Index: Move the cursor to the bottom of the timeline, until the icon turns to the Paint icon, and click to drop an Index marker. In practice, Index markers do not see a lot of use.

Note that Track and Index Markers are only used when burning a CD, or exporting an image file or DDP file set. When exporting a digital release, manually placed Track Markers are ignored and separate files are only rendered for actual Tracks, as listed in the Track column.

It is not possible to drop positional markers to note locations for reference and comparison in the mastering process.

TRACK DEVICE RACK

The Track Device Rack is the Project page's equivalent to the Song page's Track inspector channel strip, with the difference that the Track Device Rack is the only place these functions are available on the Project page; there is no mixer on the Project page, and so there is no mixer channel strip as there is on the Song page.

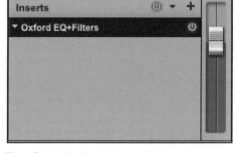

Fig. 5-11: The Track Device Rack.

In the Track Device Rack, you can set the level of the selected track with a fader (which can be controlled from a control surface), and insert signal processing and effects plug-ins, just as in the Song window mixer. Track inserts are prefader.

MASTER DEVICE RACK

The Master Device Rack is similar to the Track Device Rack just above it, with two big differences. First, every track in the Project plays back through the processing on the Master, and, second, in addition to the prefader inserts, there is a section for inserting postfader processing.

Fig. 5-12: The Master Device Rack. Note the postfader inserts section.

Finally, at the bottom of the Master Device Rack area is a drop-down menu for choosing the interface outputs through which the Project will play.

METERING AND ANALYSIS

The metering and analysis section of the Project page consists of a spectrum analyzer, high-resolution level meter, and phase analyzer, all reporting on the Master output (postfader). The features of these meters on the Project page are, with only a few small exceptions, the same as the Spectrum Analyzer, Level Meter, and Phase Meter plug-ins discussed in the "Metering" section of chapter 3, "Mixing." Please refer to that section for more information on and detailed discussion of these metering functions.

TIP: The plug-ins can also be inserted on any track in the Project page or on the Master, either prefader or postfader. The plug-ins can be resized, but built-in metering cannot. Although sizing a meter larger does not change the signal analysis at all, it can improve visibility of the metering resolution, letting you see detail better, especially if you work with multiple monitors.

SPECTRUM ANALYZER

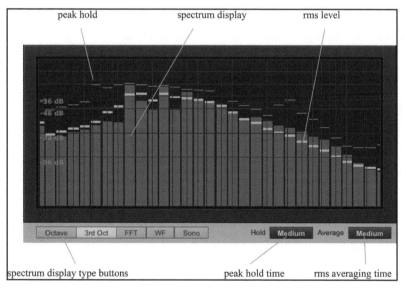

Fig. 5-13: The Project page Spectrum Analyzer.

The Spectrum Analyzer offers most of the same functionality of the Spectrum Analyzer plug-in. The buttons in the lower left corner of the Spectrum Meter select between five different types of spectrum display. To select a spectrum display type, click one of the five buttons:

- Octave: Displays the spectrum in octave-wide bands.

- 3rd Oct (1/3 Oct): Displays the spectrum in 1/3-octave-wide bands.
- FFT: Actually, all five kinds of spectral display are based on FFTs, but this setting shows all of the FFT's bands. The Spectrum Analyzer plug-in offers FFT configuration parameters not available in this display.
- Waterfall: "Waterfall display," "sonogram," and "spectrogram" are, according to many sources, all exactly the same thing: a display of how frequency spectrum varies over time. In this mode, the X axis is frequency, the Y axis is time (Y = 0 is "now," higher is older), and color intensity, the Z axis, represents amplitude. This is essentially the same display as the sonogram, but with the axes flipped.
- Waterfall displays are often 3D projections, with amplitude on the Y axis and time along the Z axis. Graphically, that's more of a challenge to do in real-time, so Studio One 2's waterfall is a 2D projection. Looking at sonograms takes a little getting used to, but once you get it, you can get a lot of information reading them.
- Sono: A sonogram shows time on the X axis and frequency on the Y axis. Amplitude is represented by color intensity.

The Spectrum Meter has two other settings:

- To select a peak hold time for the meter: Click in the Hold field and select the desired peak hold time from the drop-down menu that appears. The choices are: short, medium, long, and infinite.
- To select an rms averaging period: Click in the Average field and select the desired averaging rate from the drop-down menu that appears.

As the cursor is moved through the meter area, a yellow crosshair shows the cursor position. As well, a pop-up tool tip shows the values at the current cursor position.

Using the FFT setting, a blue line follows the cursor, going roughly from upper left to lower right. This is essentially a reminder that FFTs do not work as our ears do. An FFT calculates using a window of constant bandwidth, but our ears tend to hear things in relationships, especially octaves, which increase in bandwidth with frequency. This discrepancy distorts your view of how energy is distributed across the spectrum. Under these circumstances, a flat frequency response appears as a diagonal line...the blue line mentioned earlier. Generally, when you watch the meter while a Song plays, the response should approximate the blue line.

LEVEL METER SECTION

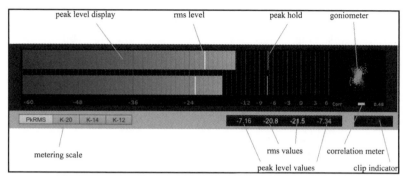

Fig. 5-14: The Level Meter section of the Project page.

Below the Spectrum Analyzer is the output Level Meter section. This section incorporates both level and phase metering. The level meter has identical functionality to the Level Meter plug-in, but it cannot be independently sized and has a slightly different layout. The Level Meter section has the following components:

- Horizontal stereo level meter: Displays levels according to the selected metering scale (peak/rms or K-System). To select a metering scale: Click one of the buttons in the lower left corner of the Level Meter section. Choices are: PkRMS (simultaneous peak and rms level display, 0 on meter is 6 dB below full-scale), K-20, K-14, and K-12.

- Level readouts: Beneath the stereo level meter are four numeric readouts. The outer two are colored blue and give the last held peak levels for the left and right channels, while the inner readouts show rms levels. So, looking from left to right, the readouts show: peak L, rms L, rms R, and peak R.

- Clip indicator: To the right of the level readouts, in the lower right corner of the Level Meter section is a clip indicator that turns red if clipping occurs. The indicator stays red until it is clicked to reset it.

- Goniometer: To the right of the stereo level meter is a goniometer with the same function as that in the Phase Meter plug-in.

- Correlation meter: Beneath the goniometer is a reeeeeeallly small correlation meter, like the one in the Phase Meter plug-in.

LOUDNESS INFORMATION

At the top of the Track Device Rack, a Loudness Information drop-down menu is available, in which you can detect loudness for the Track. Dynamic Range, R128 Loudness, left and right channel peaks,

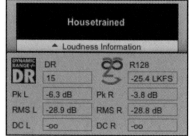

Fig. 5-15: The Loudness Information area displays the results of the loudness analysis Studio One 2 can perform for each track, based on definitions in recommendations from the EBU and ITU.

rms, and DC levels are measured and displayed here. This information can help when making level balance decisions from Track to Track across the Project.

These measurements are taken from loudness measurement recommendations by the EBU (European Broadcast Union recommendation R128) and ITU (International Telecommunications Union recommendation ITU-BS-1770-1). For more information on these measurements, investigate those recommendations.

View loudness information for a track on the Project page using either of these methods:

- Click the Show/Hide Loudness Information button at the top of the Track Device Rack. When the Detect Loudness button appears, click it to start loudness analysis.
- Right-click (Ctrl-click in Mac) on a track in the Track Column or in the Track Lanes and choose Detect Loudness from the contextual menu that drops down.

Once the loudness analysis is done, there will be values for the parameters in the loudness information area:

- DR (Dynamic Range): The dynamic range of the track.

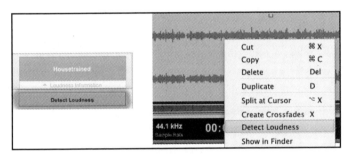

Fig. 5-16: Two ways to invoke loudness calculation: the Detect Loudness button (left) and command (right).

- R128 (Program loudness in LKFS): This field shows the objective measurement of loudness specified in the EBU and ITU recommendations just discussed.
- Peak-L and Peak-R: These are the peak levels for each channel in the track, given in dBFS (full-scale).
- RMS-L and RMS-R: These are the rms levels for each channel in the track, given in dBFS (full-scale).
- DC L and DC R: This is the amount of DC offset in each channel.

To see Maximum True Peak Level, which is also part of the EBU and ITU recommendations, insert the Level Meter plug-in and click the TP button. The Project page level meter does not display TP.

PHASE METERING

The phase meter displays phase information in two different ways. The first is a goniometer, an X-Y display of the left and right channels signals that has been rotated a little, so that a mono signal (left and right channels carry the same signal) is a vertical line. A healthy stereo signal produces something like a wide vertical oval most of the time.

Below the phase meter is a correlation meter. Correlation is a measure of how similar the signals in the left and right channels are. If a signal is mono, the channels are highly correlated, which is indicated by the meter being mostly (or, for mono, fully) to the right. If there are totally different things in each channel, the channels are not well-correlated, and the meter will deflect mostly to the left. A numerical readout on the right displays a correlation value; a value of 1 is mono. A typical stereo mix will stay a bit to the right, but will move around a fair amount.

LEVEL METER CONTEXTUAL MENU

The level meter can be configured through a contextual drop-down menu. Right-click (Ctrl-click in Mac) on the meter and the contextual menu drops down, with these settings available:

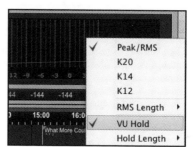

- Scale: Choose one of these values to select a metering scale for the level meter. Choices are PK/RMS, K12, K14, and K20.

- To set the rms integration time for the level meter: Right-click (Ctrl-click in Mac) on the meter, choose the RMS Length submenu from the contextual menu that drops down, and select 0.6s (600 milliseconds), 1.8s (1.8 seconds), or 3s (three seconds).

Fig. 5-17: The Level Meter can be configured by choosing settings in the contextual menu that appears when you right-click on it.

- To enable or disable peak hold for the level meter: Right-click (Ctrl-click in Mac) on the meter and choose VU Hold from the contextual menu that drops down. When the command is checked, VU Hold is engaged and can be seen as a single segment that stays highlighted in the meter for some time after the signal level drops below it. Peak hold is on by default.

- To set the peak hold time for a meter: Right-click (Ctrl-click in Mac) on the meter, choose the Hold Length submenu from the contextual menu that drops down, and select 2s (two seconds), 15s (15 seconds), or inf (infinite) for the hold time.

INFO PANEL

Fig. 5-18: The Info panel on the Project page is the same as on the Song page, except, of course, different mouse actions are available.

This panel (called Info View in the Studio One Reference Manual) displays mouse options available given the current cursor location. On the Project page, the Info panel only works when the cursor is located in the Track Lanes.

To read more about the Info panel, see the section "Arrange View Info Panel" in chapter 5, "On the Cutting Room Floor: Basic Editing" of *Power Tools for Studio One 2*, volume 1.

- To open the Info panel, choose Views > Additional Views > Info View from the main menu bar or click on the ? (question mark) button in the Project page toolbar.

PUBLISHING

At the top center of the Project page is the publishing section. This will be the last stop in mastering your Project. The right portion of the Publishing section gives a horizontal bar display of the duration of your Project relative to the space available on a CD.

Fig. 5-19: The publishing section of the Project page is the end of the trail. This is where you choose and begin output to a delivery medium.

To the left of the duration display are five buttons. The Burn, Image, DDP, and Digital Release buttons initiate output of your finished Project in the indicated format; the Update button is located there merely because it was the only place left to put it.

For more information about publishing your Project, see chapter 6, "Sharing Your Work."

MANAGING PROJECTS

Opening and Closing Projects

Open an existing Project using any of these methods:

- Click on the Project's name in the Projects or Recent Files tabs of the Start page.
- Double-click the Project file in the Mac Finder or Windows Explorer.
- Choose File > Open in the main menu bar, navigate to the Project, and click the Open button to open it.
- Drag a Project file from the Files tab of the Browser, Mac Finder, or Windows Explorer to anywhere on the Project page. This simply opens the Project, it does not create any relationship between the Project opened and the current Project into which it was dropped.

Close a Project using any of these methods:

- Press Cmd + W (Ctrl + W in Windows).
- Choose File > Close from the main menu bar.

Switching Between Open Projects

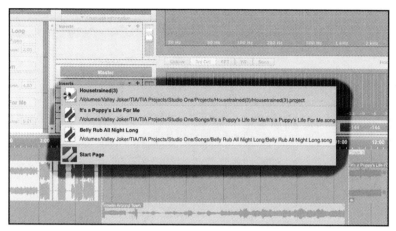

Fig. 5-20: Ctrl-Shift-tab steps you through a list of open documents. It's a very quick method of switching back and forth between documents.

- Hold down the Ctrl and Shift keys and press the tab key to bring up a list of open documents. Without releasing either the Ctrl or Shift keys, press tab repeatedly to step through the list, until the Project you want is highlighted. When you release the Ctrl and Shift keys, you will be switched to that Project.
- Click the arrow next to the Project quick access button in the upper right corner and select the desired Project from the list of open Projects that drops down.
- Choose View > Projects from the main menu bar and select the desired Project from the list of open Projects that drops down.

Switching Between the Song and Project Pages

- Hold down the Control and Shift keys and press the tab key to bring up a list of open documents. Without releasing the Control and Shift keys, press tab repeatedly to step through the list, until the Song or Project you want is highlighted. When you release the Control and Shift keys, you will be switched to the selected Song or Project.
- Click the arrow next to the Song or Project quick access button in the upper right corner and choose the Song or Project to which you want to switch from the list of open documents that drops down.
- Choose View > Projects or View > Songs from the main menu bar and select the Project or Song to which you want to switch from the list of open Projects or Songs that drops down.
- In a Project, open a Song for editing using any of the methods described in the section "Song/Project Integration" later in this chapter.

Versions in the Project Page

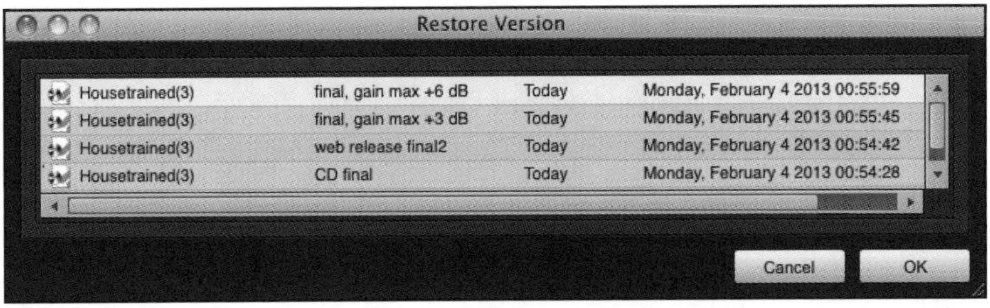

Fig. 5-21: Versions can be useful on the Project page to store variations of the Project.

The Versions command is just as useful in mastering on the Project page as it is in mixing on the Song page. Some of the things you might store as versions include variations in:

- Track order.
- Versions of edits.
- Amount and type of dynamic processing.
- Processing chains.
- Track balance.

Of course, you may also save versions for the most obvious reason of all: because you did enough work that you'd be upset to lose it.

SONG/PROJECT INTEGRATION

One of Studio One 2's most exciting features is the integration of the Song and Project pages. In other mastering environments, if it becomes clear it is necessary to go back and make some mix adjustments, all of these steps must be executed:

1. Quit the mastering environment.
2. Open the mixing environment.
3. Make the mix adjustments.
4. Export a new mix file.
5. Quit the mixing environment.
6. Open the mastering environment.
7. Import the new mix file.
8. Replace the old mix with the new one.

Man, I'm tired already!

By contrast, Studio One 2 lets you open a Song directly from the Project, make the necessary adjustments, and choose one command that returns you to the Project page with an updated mix in place. That's more like it.

Add Songs, Not Files, to the Project

The key to Studio One 2's integration of Songs and Projects is in adding Songs to the Project, rather than mix files. Projects handle mix files just fine, and if you are mastering files that were not created as Studio One Songs, or you simply don't have the Song files and all of the associated files available, that is what you will do. But mix files contain no link back to the environment in which they were created. Songs do, which is what allows the Project page to open Songs for editing and then update the mastering file, all without direction from you.

Songs can be added to Projects using any of the methods described in the section "Tracks and Track Sequencing" later in this chapter.

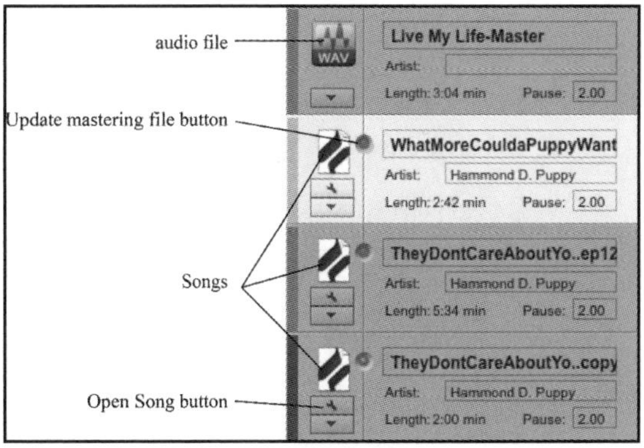

Fig. 5-22: Ideally, all of your Projects would consist solely of Songs. In practice, there will be files, as well, as in this example. Note the Open Song and Update mastering file buttons on the Song tracks.

Opening a Song for Editing from the Project Page

Open a Song for editing using either of these methods:

- Click the Edit Song button with the wrench icon below the source format icon in the track entry in the Track Column.
- Right-click (Ctrl-click in Mac) on the track entry in the Track Column or the track in the Track lanes and choose Edit Song from the contextual menu that drops down.

Fig. 5-23: The Edit Song button opens the Song document and switches you to the Song page to begin your edits.

Updating Mastering Files

Once mix adjustments have been made, it is time to update the mix on the Project page. When a Song is imported to a Project, Studio One 2 automatically exports a mastering file, a mix file linked to the Project page. This link is what enables opening a Song for editing, but it also allows keeping track of whether the mastering file is current with the state of the mix in the Song.

When the mastering file used on a track in the Project is not current with the Song, a red indicator appears in the track header in the Track Column. The mastering file then needs to be updated, which can be done from the Song page or the Project page.

One thing to keep in mind is that anything that would prevent Studio One 2 from successfully exporting a mixdown will also foul up a mastering file update. That means problems from simple clipping to missing files will be a problem. Make sure the mix is working right in the Song before you try to update the mastering file.

Fig. 5-24: A mastering file that needs updating is shown by a red indicator in the track header in the Track Column.

UPDATING A MASTERING FILE FROM THE SONG PAGE

- To update a mastering file from the Song Page, choose Song > Update Mastering File from the main menu bar. A dialog will appear while the new mix is exported to the mastering file.

Fig. 5-25: The progress dialog for a mastering file update initiated from the Song page.

UPDATING A MASTERING FILE FROM THE PROJECT PAGE

To update the mastering file for a track in the Project page, use either of these methods:

- Click the red Update Mastering File indicator in the track's header in the Track Column.
- Right-click (Ctrl-click in Mac) in the track's header in the Track Column and choose Update Mastering File from the contextual menu that drops down.

A bounce dialog will appear and keep you informed as the update occurs:

Fig. 5-26: The bounce dialog that appears when updating a mastering file gives lots of information about the update and its progress.

When an update is completed, you see a dialog with the details:

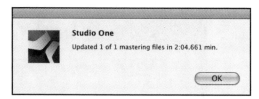

Fig. 5-27: This is what you'll see when an update succeeds. It's a happy occurrence.

PROBLEMS WHILE UPDATING

As was already mentioned, anything that would cause problems with the mix if you were playing or exporting it will mess it up when you update a mastering file.

If clipping occurs during a bounce, a notice appears at the bottom of the Update Mastering File progress dialog with the details. Click the Cancel button to abort the bounce, so that you can make the necessary adjustments and try again.

Missing files or even inadequate processing power (too many expensive plug-ins and instruments) can cause failure of the bounce, as will be reported by the dialog in Fig. 5-29:

TIP: Be sure to deal with the complaints of this dialog, or you will never be able to get a successful mastering file update. If you cannot locate a missing file, be sure to remove it.

UPDATING ALL MASTERING FILES

When a Project is opened, Studio One 2 checks that the Project has the most current mix of every Song that has been added to it. If it does not, the Update Mastering Files dialog appears, offering the capability to update one or more mastering files for tracks that do not have the most current mix.

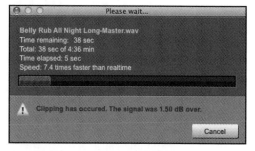

Fig. 5-28: The bounce dialog informs you the moment a clip occurs and offers the option of canceling the update, so that you can fix the problem.

Fig. 5-29: Mastering file updates can fail if there are unresolved problems in the Song, such as a missing file.

1. Open the Project. If all mixes are not the most current, the Update Mastering Files dialog appears.

2. To update mastering files for all tracks, confirm that the boxes on the left of the dialog are all checked and click OK. A new mastering file will be generated for each track listed in the dialog.

3. Uncheck the boxes for tracks whose mastering file you do not want to update. If you have reason to believe one of the updates might fail, uncheck it and let the rest update, then deal with the problem child.

4. Click the OK button and all tracks with checked boxes will get updated mastering files.

Updating of all files can also be invoked manually.

- With the Project open, choose Project > Update Mastering Files from the main menu bar. The Update Mastering Files dialog will appear.

TRACKS AND TRACK SEQUENCING

Fig. 5-30: The Update Mastering Files dialog enables you to select for which Songs new mastering files will be generated.

On the Project page, track lanes are the equivalent of what the Song page calls tracks, and Tracks on the Project page are the parallel concept to Audio Events on the Song page. For an album production, track sequencing is the process of putting tracks in order and adjusting their spacing to have a suitable pause between them (or not, if you are looking for a segue or overlap).

The first step, of course, is getting all of the tracks into the Project.

Adding Tracks (Songs and Files) to the Project

The difference between adding a track by importing a Song and adding it by importing an audio file is that importing a Song provides access to Studio One 2's Song page/Project page integration.

Mastering environments usually "checkerboard," alternating placement of tracks between the two track lanes.

ADDING A SONG TO A PROJECT
Add a Song to the Project using any of these methods:

- Drag the Song document you wish to add to the Project from the Files tab of the Browser, Mac Finder, or Windows Explorer to a Track Lane or the Track Column. The document can be dropped at any position in the order that you wish. Note that dragging from the Browser to the metering area opens the Song for editing, but does not add it to the Project.
- Right-click (Ctrl-click in Mac) in the Track Column and choose Import File from the contextual menu that drops down. When the Import File dialog appears, navigate to the desired Song file and select it. It will be added after the last track in the Project.
- Choose Project > Import File from the main menu bar. When the Import File dialog appears, navigate to the desired Song file and select it. It will be added after the last track in the Project.

ADDING AN AUDIO FILE TO THE PROJECT

Audio files are added to the Project using the same methods as for Songs (drag-and-drop or the Import File dialog). Any audio file format recognized by Studio One 2 can be imported. When MP3 files are imported, uncompressed .wav files are created from them for the Project page's use.

HANDLING DIFFERENT SONG AND PROJECT SAMPLE RATES

Ideally, the sample rate of the Project and all of the Songs or audio files will be the same. It is often the case, however, that mixed sample rates are contained in the same project. For example, you might have recorded at a 48 kHz sample rate but now want to make a CD, which requires 44.1 kHz audio.

There are several approaches you can take if all of your material is not at the same sample rate as what you would like for a Project sample rate:

- If all of the material is at the same rate, but it's not what you want for the Project, work at the sample rate of the source files and do sample rate conversion to the target rate on the mastered file(s) at the end of the process.
- If the rates are mixed, choose one rate to work at and sample rate convert the rest to that rate in non-real time. Often, mastering engineers upsample everything to a high sample rate, such as 88.2 kHz or 96 kHz, master at that rate, then convert to whatever target rates are needed.
- Allow Studio One 2 to sample rate convert files in real time. Because non-real-time SRC can be better than real-time SRC, this is probably not the way to go for final releases, but for interim versions for evaluating different track orders and the like, this option can be fast and convenient.

Editing Songs at a different rate than the Project should be avoided to the degree possible, because going back and forth between sample rates can confuse some interface drivers and cause annoying behavior.

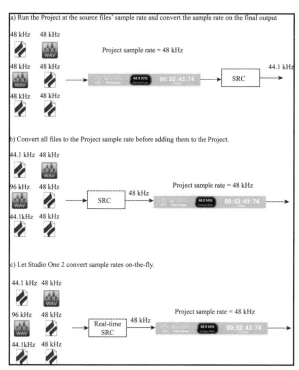

Fig. 5-31: Three methods of handling mixed sample rates in a Project. In a), the Project is run at the sample rate of the source files and the final output is converted to the desired sample rate. In b), files are brought to the same sample rate through off-line SRC. In c), Studio One 2 performs SRC in real-time, as needed, to bring all of the tracks to the Project sample rate.

Removing Tracks

Remove a track from the Project using any of these methods:

- Select the track in the Track Lane or the Track Column and press the Delete key.
- Right-click (Ctrl-click in Mac) on the track in the Track Lane and choose Delete from the contextual menu that drops down.
- Right-click (Ctrl-click in Mac) on the track header in the Track Column and choose Remove Track from the contextual menu that drops down.
- Choose Project > Remove Track from the main menu bar.
- Multiple tracks can be removed at once by selecting them and then using any of the above methods to remove them.

Enabling and Disabling Tracks

Disabling a track removes it from the timeline, but leaves it in the Track Column, labeled as disabled. If you are playing around with which tracks to include or trying to hear different transitions between tracks, disabling can be more convenient than removing the tracks.

Fig. 5-32: A disabled track is removed from the timeline, but remains visible in the Track Column, marked as being disabled.

Disable a track using either of these methods:

- Right-click (Ctrl-click in Mac) in the track header in the Track Column and choose Disable Track from the contextual menu that drops down.
- Select the track and choose Project > Disable Track from the main menu bar.

To disable multiple tracks at once, select them all and then use either of the above methods.

To enable a disabled track, use either of the methods above and choose Enable Track from the menu.

Track Sequencing

The primary tasks to be accomplished in track sequencing are establishing the running order and the spacing between the tracks. Tracks in the Project are reordered in the Track Column, while spacing can be determined in the Track Column or Track Lanes.

ORDERING TRACKS

When a track is moved, other parameters associated with it, notably the pause time before the track starts playing, move along with it. Pauses and other parameters for the other tracks move appropriately, as well. Checkerboarding is also automatically managed when the tracks get reordered.

- To reorder a track in the Track Column, click on its track type icon and drag the track to the desired position in the running order.

SETTING SPACING

- Drag a track in a track lane. All tracks following the dragged track will move with it, properly maintaining their spacing. This method allows overlapping of tracks. As you drag, the Pause field changes to reflect the current spacing, until there is overlap.
- Click the Pause field in the track's header in the Track Column and enter the pause value directly. Pause cannot be less than zero, so it is impossible to create overlap through direct value entry in the field.

Fig. 5-33: Tracks are reordered in the Track Column by dragging.

If you create overlap between tracks, you will typically want to create a crossfade between them. For more information on crossfades, see the next section "Edits, Segues, Fades, and Crossfades."

EDITS, SEGUES, FADES, AND CROSSFADES

With the tracks in order and having the desired spacing, the transitions from one to the next are the other major component in determining how the whole album flows. The mechanics of transitions involve fade-ins and fade-outs and crossfades for overlapping tracks and segues.

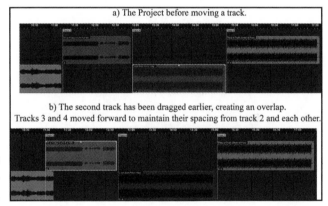

Fig. 5-34: When a track gets dragged, all tracks following it move with it, maintaining their spacing.

Trimming a Track Start or End

The start and end of any track can be edited in the Track Lanes, but they behave a little differently from each other.

Tracks behave as if their pause times were simply the first part of the track, so when the track end is trimmed, other tracks following it retain their time relationship with it based on their Pause times: as the end of a track is trimmed, the start time of the next track moves to maintain the same pause length between them.

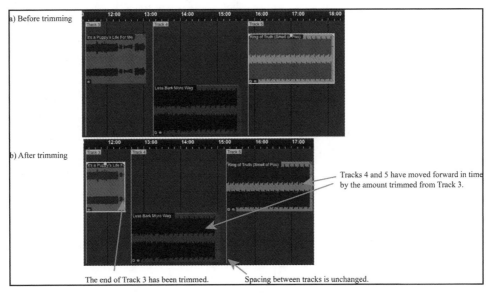

Fig. 5-35: When the track end is trimmed, all the following tracks move as well, maintaining their spacing.

Trimming a track start has the same effect; the track and all that follow it move to maintain their specified spacings.

To trim the start or end of a track:

• Position the cursor over the start or end of the track you want to trim until the cursor icon becomes an arrowhead with a line, then drag as desired. The Track Length readout in the track's header in the Track Column will update to show the new length of the track.

Splitting Tracks

Tracks can be split into pieces. This could be useful for separating the songs in a live recording, or even to create an edit (although the Song page is a more graceful editing environment). To split a track:

1. Place the play location where you want to split the track.
2. Press Option + X (Alt + X in Windows) or choose Edit > Split at Cursor from the main menu bar.
3. The track is split and immediately checkerboarded; however, the transition at the split will play seamlessly until you do something to modify it. The fade-in of the first half of the split track is replicated in shape and duration on the second half, so that both halves have identical fade-ins.

Editing Example

Let's run through a quick edit, so you can get the idea:

1. Find the edit in point in your audio example (Fig. 5-36).

2. Place the play location at the edit in point and press Option + X (Alt + X in Windows) to split the track at the cursor. The checkerboarding will immediately adjust.

3. Find the edit out point and drag the front edge of the (new) track back to it. When you let go of the mouse after dragging, the later track will jump forward so that it immediately follows the first part of the track.

4. If a crossfade is desired, drag the second track earlier to create some overlap, then press X to make the crossfade.

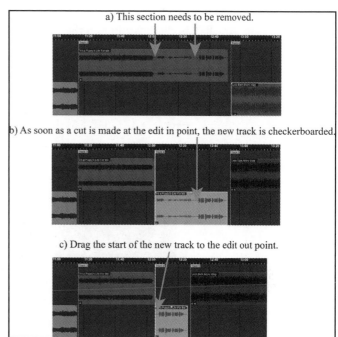

a) This section needs to be removed.

b) As soon as a cut is made at the edit in point, the new track is checkerboarded.

c) Drag the start of the new track to the edit out point.

Fig. 5-36: Making a simple edit in the Track Lanes. Make a cut at the edit in point; the new track will be checkerboarded. Next, trim the start of the new track back to the edit out point. The track and all tracks following it will move to maintain their specified spacing.

Creating Fade-Ins and -Outs

Fade-ins and -outs for tracks are created in exactly the same way as fades on Audio Events on the Song page. To add a fade-in or fade-out to a track:

• Position the cursor over the top left corner (for a fade-in) or top right corner (for a fade-out) of the track and drag the square handle in the corner to make a fade of the desired duration, then drag the handle in the middle of the fade to adjust the fade curve. For more information on creating fades, see the section "Fades" of chapter 6, "Advanced Editing" in *Power Tools for Studio One 2*, volume 1.

Fades on different tracks are entirely independent. If a track is dragged until it overlaps another track, there will be no effect on the fades on either. Even if multiple tracks are selected, editing a fade affects only that fade on that track.

Creating Crossfades

Crossfades on the Project page differ from those on the Song page in a couple of ways:

- On the Song page, crossfades most often occur between overlapping Events on a single track. Checkerboarding on the Project page means that crossfades always occur across track lanes.

- On the Song page, crossfades are interactive: move part of a crossfade and some other aspect changes in response. On the Project page, crossfading is a quick way to create complementary fades on two tracks at the same time, but once created, they are simply two separate fades. Modifying the fade-out has no impact on the fade-in, and vice versa.

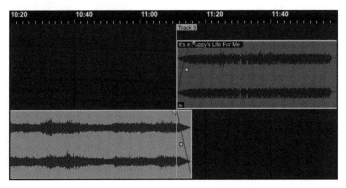

Fig. 5-37: Crossfades on the Project page differ slightly from those on the Song page. For one, they occur across track lanes, and, for another, the fades are entirely independent, as opposed to the interaction seen on the Song page. Note that the crossfade curve shapes are different for the two tracks that overlap.

To create a crossfade between two tracks:

1. Position the two tracks with the desired overlap.

2. Press X, right-click (Ctrl-click in Mac) on either of the tracks and choose Create Crossfades from the contextual menu that drops down, or choose Project > Create Crossfades from the main menu bar.

3. To create crossfades on more than two tracks at a time, select all of the overlapping tracks you want crossfaded and press X, right-click (Ctrl-click in Mac) on either of the tracks and choose Create Crossfades from the contextual menu that drops down, or choose Project > Create Crossfades from the main menu bar. Crossfades will be created everywhere two selected tracks overlap.

CROSSFADE CURVE SHAPES

There are a few things to be aware of relative to how crossfade curve shapes work on the Project page:

- Because the fades constituting a crossfade on the Project page are actually independent of each other, the crossfade shape of each part of the crossfade can be edited separately from the other.
- When creating a crossfade, a track will receive a fade with the default linear fade shape if the track had no fade before crossfading. However, if the track had a fade at some time since the program was booted, the fade it gets from crossfading will have the same shape as its previous fade.
- On a CD, the CD track start will fall where the track starts in the Project, meaning that the CD track will start where the track begins fading in.

TRACK LEVELS

The level of a track on the Project page is controlled in two places:

- The track fader to the right of the Inserts section of the Track Device Rack
- The track level set in the Track Lanes

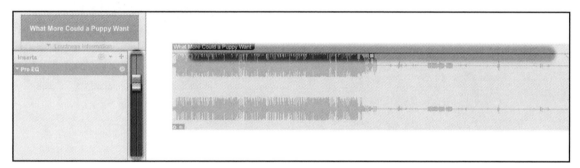

Fig. 5-38: Track level is controlled by both the track fader (left) and the track level in the Track lane (right). The two operate independently, so be careful or be confused.

These two adjustments are totally independent of each other; changing the track level in the Track Lanes will not move the fader at all, in fact, the track level can be all the way down and the fader could still be up full. By the same token, the track level could be full up; and the fader, all the way down. Either way, you'd hear nothing, which is rarely what one is looking for in these situations.

Of course, any other level controls in a track's insert effects will also have a say in the track's overall level.

Having noted all of this interactivity of level controls, to set the level of a track, use one or both of these methods:

- Drag the fader in the Track Device Rack up or down to the desired level. Hovering the cursor over the fader pops up a tool tip showing the current fader setting; the tool tip is also visible as you drag the fader. The fader setting is also shown in the Control Link area in the top left corner of the page.

- Hover the cursor over the current track level in the Track Lanes, which will be at the top of the track, if it has not been moved from its default position. When the cursor icon turns to a hand with an extended finger, click on the square handle in the track level line and drag up or down to change it. As you drag, a pop-up tool tip shows the track level, as well as how much it has changed since you started dragging. The waveform display will scale larger and smaller as the level is changed.

TRACK PROCESSING

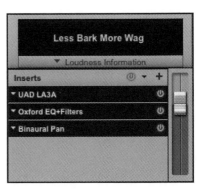

As well as track level control with the Track Column fader and the Track Lane track level envelope, each track also has an insert section for adding processing, the Track Device Rack. While there are, of course, no rules, tradition has it that this processing is not typically effects-oriented. While a bit of ambience might be added, most processing in mastering falls into three categories:

Fig. 5-39: The Track Device Rack works exactly like a channel Device Rack on the Song page.

- Corrective: Often EQ or dynamics to compensate for or control some anomaly.

- Matching: Anything that adds coherence to a collection of tracks. It might be EQ or ambience, but the objective is to reduce radical dissimilarities across tracks (unless, of course, contrast is the objective).

- Enhancing: Basically, anything that isn't done to fix a problem or increase blending across tracks qualifies as enhancement. Stereo image width modification, gain maximization, exciters, and multiband dynamics are all examples of processing used for enhancement.

The Inserts section behaves exactly as does the Inserts section of a channel strip in the mixer on the Song page, including preset and FX Chain management, and both global and local deactivation of plug-ins. For more information on the Inserts section, see the section "Sends and Inserts" in chapter 3, "Mixing."

Using External Processors with Pipeline

The Pipeline plug-in is available on the Project page to make it easy for you to incorporate all your lovely outboard processors. Pipeline used on the Project page works exactly as on the Song page, which is described in the section "Integrating Outboard Devices: the Pipeline Plug-In" in chapter 3, "Mixing." Also as on the Song page, using Pipeline forces your export to be real time so as to capture the audio from the outboard processors.

Copying Track Processing to Another Track

Just like in the mixer on the Song page, plug-ins can be copied from one track to the other.

- To copy a single plug-in to another track: Drag the plug-in from the Track Device Rack of the source track to the track header in the Track Column of the target track. The plug-in, with all of its settings, will be copied to the end of any existing insert processing on the target track.
- To copy an entire FX Chain to another track: Move the cursor to the top of the processing chain, until the cursor icon changes to a hand, then drag and drop the FX Chain onto the track header in the Track Column of the target track. A pop-up tool tip will confirm that you are dragging the whole FX Chain. Note that the FX Chain will replace any processing existing on the track.

MASTER PROCESSING

In addition to each track having its own Track Device Rack, at the end of the signal chain is the Master Device Rack. All tracks play through the Master Device Rack, so master level and processing affect all tracks.

There are four components to the Master Device Rack:

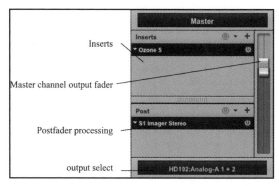

Fig. 5-40: The Master Device Rack is where global processing (which applies to all Songs in the Project) is performed.

- Master channel output fader: The global level control for the entire Project. As with the Track Device Rack, the level of the Master fader is shown as you adjust it in a pop-up tool tip, and in the Control Link section in the top right corner of the window.

- Inserts section: Just like all of the others, these are prefader inserts. As with other Inserts sections, the header of the section includes an Activate All button that allows deactivating all prefader inserts.

- Post section: This is where the Master Device Rack differs from Track Device Racks. This is another insert effects area that follows the fader (postfader). Be very careful not to create overloads in the Post section because it is the last step in the chain, so there is nothing downstream to catch overloads. The header of the section includes an Activate All button that allows deactivating all postfader inserts.

- Output select: Click in this field and choose the interface outputs through which you are monitoring the Project.

TIP: If you are using dithering in a third-party plug-in, such as iZotope MBIT+ or Waves IDR, insert the plug-in in the Post section of the master processing and disable the Use dithering for audio devices and file export option in the Audio tab of the Preferences > Options > Advanced pane.

METADATA

The Project page hosts a collection of metadata fields for each track in the Track Column, plus a few Project metadata fields at the top of the Track Column. This metadata gets stored in any export format designed to store it, most notably MP3 files. Because this is the information that comes up when someone listens to your music online or in a download, it is a good idea to give metadata a little TLC and make sure it is all filled out correctly.

Project Metadata

The Project metadata is quite simple, in fact, it is just three fields:

- Disc: Click in this field to enter the name that will be used by all export formats as the album name.

- Artist: Click in this field to enter the name of the artist for the Project.

- Length: This is a read-only field that displays the duration of the entire Project.

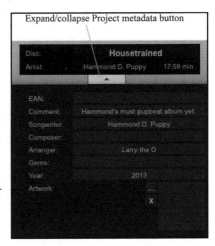

Fig. 5-41: The Project metadata fields.

EXPANDED METADATA

- To access expanded Project metadata: Click the arrow at the bottom of the Project metadata section.

The expanded Project metadata fields are the same as those described for Track expanded metadata, except for the first field:

- EAN: The International Article Number. Technically, the EAN is barcode, and the number shown in this field is the Global Trade Item Number (GTIN).

Track Metadata

More metadata fields are available for each track. If a track was added by importing a Song, the Project automatically imports any metadata defined on that track's Song page.

The Project page defaults to showing only basic metadata, but the track metadata area can be expanded to show several more fields.

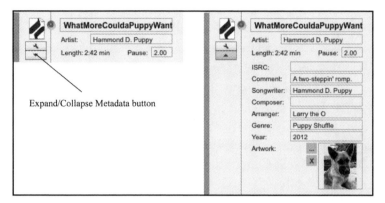

Fig. 5-42: When the metadata display is collapsed, only the title and artist fields can be set. However, the expanded metadata view offers many more metadata fields.

BASIC METADATA
When I say "basic," I'm talking about just two fields:

- Track title: Click in this field to rename the track. Don't worry; this won't confuse updates to the mastering file. Updates still refer to the Song by the name of the Song document, not the track title on the Project page.
- Artist: Click in this field to name the artist for this track. This field is entirely independent of the Project Artist metadata field. The default for this field is the name entered in the Artist field in the Artist Profile (metadata) area on the Start page.

This area also includes two read-only fields:

- Track length: The duration of the track. Remember that mastering files are made based on the placement of the Song Start and End markers in the linked Song.
- Pause length: The time between the end of the previous track and the beginning of playback of the next track. This time is generally handled by Studio One 2 as time added to the start of the Song.

EXPANDED METADATA
- ISRC code: The International Standard Recording Code is a code that identifies the rights holder for a recording, as well as the recording itself. ISRC codes are created

by registering at http://www.usisrc.org (in the US) to obtain a registrant code, then issuing a code for each recording. ISRC codes enable tracking of airplay for each recording.

- Comment: Click in this field to enter a text comment. Note that the Comment field will allow you to enter a substantial quantity of text, but there is no way to enlarge the view of the field, making it impossible to read or edit a long comment.
- Songwriter: Click in this field to enter the songwriter for the track. You will typically use either this field or the Composer field, but not both.
- Composer: Click in this field to enter the composer of the track. You will typically use either this field or the Songwriter field, but not both.
- Arranger: Click in this field to enter the arranger of the track.
- Genre: Click in this field to enter the musical genre for the track. While there exists a list of commonly used genre names, it does not appear here, so you must enter the genre manually. The default for this field is the value entered in the Genre field in the Artist Profile (metadata) area on the Start page.
- Year: Click in this field to enter a date for the track. If the track is a Song, the default for this field is the date given in the Song metadata (Song Information dialog).
- Artwork (image): To add a .png or .jpg image to the track metadata, click on the Select Image button, labeled "…" (ellipsis), located by the top left corner of the image area and navigate to the location where the image is stored. To remove the image from track metadata, click on the Remove Image button, labeled X, directly below the Select Image button.

FINAL OUTPUT

When everything is just as you want it, you are ready to export your final product. In mastering, this can often be a multistep process, as there may need to be exports in several formats, a number of mix variations (for instance, vocal up/vocal down, or bass up/down), and perhaps even different edits.

Studio One 2 offers a number of options for output of your finished Project, which are detailed in chapter 6, "Sharing Your Work."

The Project page is not just for the final mastering stage of your album; it is just as useful for works-in-progress. The Project page can help you create and upload the latest versions of Songs after each recording session, make "minus-one" mixes for musicians' reference, compare different mixes in progress, and much more.

Sharing Your Work with the World

The point of making music in Studio One 2 is for people to be able to hear it. Studio One 2 offers a rich set of choices for exporting your material and getting it out into the world. This eliminates the need to open a different application to convert your finished Project to the various formats demanded in today's music market.

Studio One 2 also offers direct upload capability not only to SoundCloud, but to Nimbit (which is a PreSonus company) as well as downloading from both of those and PreSonus Exchange, a venue for PreSonus and Studio One users to make materials available to others in the Studio One 2 community.

Remember that most of these facilities are as useful for works in progress as for finished works. As you develop an album, you may want to burn reference CDs or MP3 files to post, and the Project page makes it easy to create these throughout the course of production.

BURNING AND EXPORTING

Burning CDs

1. Click the Burn button in the Project page toolbar, or choose Project > Burn Audio CD from the main menu bar. The Burn Audio CD dialog appears.

2. Insert a blank CD into the drive and close it. In a few seconds, the dialog will indicate the presence of a blank disk, as shown in Fig. 6-1.

3. Configure the parameters in the Burn Audio CD dialog as desired. For more information on these choices, see the next section, "The Burn Audio CD Dialog."

Fig. 6-1: The Burn Audio CD dialog. A blank disk has been inserted and all that needs to be done to create a CD is to click the Burn button.

4. Click the Burn button and sit back. A progress dialog will show you how your burn is proceeding, and will vanish when the CD is done.

Studio One 2 can burn a CD from a Project that is not at a 44.1 kHz sample rate and 16-bit resolution, but it has to do sample rate conversion and dithering on the fly. This can work fine for reference CDs of works in progress. For example, if you are recording at 48 kHz but want to burn CDs of the latest versions of the songs for yourself or others to review, you might have a 48 kHz Project, because the Songs are all at 48 kHz, but you can burn a CD and Studio One will take care of the conversions and housekeeping.

This is not a good way to approach sample rates in final mastering situations. In those cases, it is best to convert sample rates before mastering, preferably with a high-quality, non-real-time converter.

THE BURN AUDIO CD DIALOG

The Burn Audio CD dialog offers the following features:

- Device: Click in this field and choose a disk-burning device from the drop-down menu that appears.
- Speed: Click in this field and choose a burn speed from the drop-down list of available speeds that appears.
- Options: Three checkboxes offering utility functions, which are detailed in the next section, "Burning Options."
- Disk control: Erase (for rewritable disks) and Eject.
- Burn control: Clicking the Burn button burns a CD, naturally, while the Cancel button dismisses the dialog.

BURNING OPTIONS

CD burning is not a foolproof process. There are several ways that a burn can fail. The Options area of the Burn Audio CD dialog contains three utility functions intended to reduce the risk of a failed burn. You may never need any of these, but if you have problems burning CDs, you should give them a try.

- Test Write: When checked, this box causes a series of tests to be run before burning to confirm that the resources exist on your computer to successfully execute burning a CD.
- Use Burnproof: When a CD is burned, the data is streamed into a buffer, which is the source for the data used in the burn. If data is taken out of the buffer faster than it is filled, a buffer underflow error occurs, which, with some burners, causes the burn to fail. The Burnproof option attempts to prevent buffer underflow. This option is checked by default.

- Use Temporary Imagefile: This option is essentially an even more drastic approach than the Burnproof option to solving the problem of inadequate data flow. When this box is checked, a complete disk image is created, from which the burn is executed, guaranteeing that all of the data will be available.

Disk Image

A disk image is a good way to transport all of the data of a CD without actually burning a disk. There are a number of common formats for disk image files, the most common being a .wav or .bin file accompanied by a .cue file. The .cue file is a text file containing metadata that describes the structure of the file, whereas the .wav or .bin file contains the actual audio data. Studio One 2 uses the .wav + .cue format.

To create a disk image:

1. With the Project fully prepared, click the Disk Image button in the Project page toolbar or choose Project > Make Image dialog from the main menu bar. The Make Image dialog appears.
2. Configure the parameters in the Make Image dialog as desired. For more information on these choices, see the next section, "The Make Image Dialog."
3. Click the OK button and sit back. A progress dialog will show you how generation of your image is proceeding, and will vanish when the image is done.
3. In the specified location you will find a .wav file and a .cue file, both having the name of the Project document. Although the .wav file contains all of the audio in your Project, you should be sure to keep the .wav and .cue files together at all times to retain usefulness as a disk image. It is common to create a folder to hold them both.

THE MAKE IMAGE DIALOG
The Make Image dialog is divided into four sections: Location, Format, Options, and Publishing. Here are the fields:

- Location: To set the location to which the disk image files will be written, click the button with the legend "…" (ellipsis), and navigate to the desired destination folder.
- File format: Click in this field and select the desired format for the audio file from the list that drops down. The available formats are: WAV, AIFF, FLAC, Ogg Vorbis, and MP3. Most of these formats display additional format parameters when selected. For more information on these parameters, see the section "Exporting Mixes" in chapter 3, "Mixing.".

Fig. 6-2: The Make Image dialog.

- Resolution: Click in this field and select the desired bit depth for a single sample from the list that drops down. The available options vary with the selected format, as described in the section "Exporting Mixes" in chapter 3, "Mixing.".

- Samplerate: Click in this field and select the desired sample rate from the list that drops down.. The available options vary with the selected format, as described in the section "Exporting Mixes" in chapter 3, "Mixing."

- Realtime Processing: This forces a real-time bounce to accommodate the use of outboard processors whose output needs to be captured in real time.

- Publishing options: This is the first place SoundCloud and Nimbit integration appear. This section contains three, mutually exclusive options: Do not publish, Upload to Nimbit, and Upload to SoundCloud. Uploading to Nimbit or SoundCloud can only succeed if you have set up an account and access to it has been established. Uploading to both SoundCloud and Nimbit in a single pass is not possible from this dialog, but uploading to these services is easily accomplished using the Servers tab of the Project page Browser, as described in the section "The Browser > Files > Servers Tab" later in this chapter.

DDP

DDP (Disc Description Protocol) is a format devised and introduced by Doug Carson Associates to provide a robust disk image format for delivering final media to replication facilities for manufacturing. Although replication facilities vary in their preferences for the format in which they receive material, most will accept DDP files. DDP is not a single file, or even two files like the Disk Image option, but a small set of files.

To make a DDP file set for your Project:

Fig. 6-3: The DDP button in the Project page toolbar.

1. Click the DDP button in the Project page toolbar or choose Project > Make DDP Image…from the main menu bar. A confirmation dialog appears showing the destination for the file set.

2. Click the OK button and Studio One 2 will create the file set inside a folder named "<<Project name>> DDP." Be sure to keep all of these files together or the set will not validate at the replication facility.

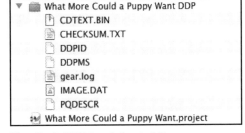

Fig. 6-4: DDP is a full set of files.

Digital Release (Individual Files)

Downloading individual songs has quickly climbed in popularity as people's method of obtaining music. Digital delivery requires that each track in the Project be outputted to a separate file, rather than a composite form, like an album. Clearly, spacing and crossfades are no longer of consequence in this case; however, fades are still included as part of the track. You will want to deal with this issue before generating files for digital release. One tool that can help is the Versions command, which enables you to save one version for CD, disk image, and DDP release, and a different version with fades altered or removed for digital file release.

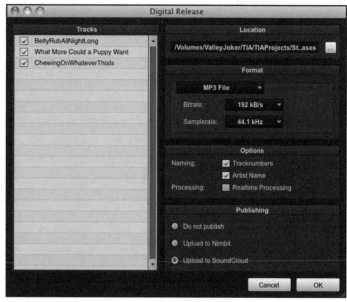

Fig. 6-5: The Digital Release dialog.

To generate files for digital release:

1. Click the Digital Release button. The Digital Release dialog appears.
2. Confirm that boxes are checked in the Tracks list on the left of the dialog for all tracks you want to export as files.
3. Configure the parameters in the dialog as desired. For more information on the available parameters, see the next section, "The Digital Release Dialog."
4. Click OK. The files are generated.

THE DIGITAL RELEASE DIALOG

Parameters for the files generated by the Digital Release option are set in the Digital Release dialog:

- Tracks: A list of all tracks in the Project. All boxes are checked by default; uncheck the boxes for tracks you do not want to export as files.
- Location: To set the location to which the audio files will be written, click the button with the legend "…" (ellipsis), and navigate to the desired destination folder. A folder will be created here for the files.
- The folder name will be <<Project metadata Artist>> – <<Project metadata Disc name>> if the Artist Name box is checked, and <<Project metadata Disc name>> if it is not. If no Disc name is entered, the Project name is used.

- File format: Click in this field and select the desired format for the audio files from the list that drops down. The available formats are: WAV, AIFF, FLAC, Ogg Vorbis, and MP3 (the default). Most of these formats display additional format parameters when selected. For more information on these parameters, see the section "Exporting Mixes" in chapter 3, "Mixing."

- Resolution: Click in this field and select the desired bit depth for the files from the list that drops down. The available options vary with the selected format, as described in the section "Exporting Mixes" in chapter 3, "Mixing."

- Samplerate: Click in this field and select the desired sample rate from the list that drops down.. The available options vary with the selected format, as described in the section "Exporting Mixes" in chapter 3, "Mixing."

- Tracknumbers box: When checked, the Tracknumbers box causes the name of each track to start with the number describing its position in the Track Column.

- Artist Name box: When this box is checked, the Project and Track Artist metadata fields are used. The Project Artist metadata field starts the name of the folder enclosing the exported files, and substitutes in track names where no Track Artist name has been supplied. The Track Artist name starts the name of the exported file for the track if the Tracknumbers box is not checked, or follows the track number, if it is.

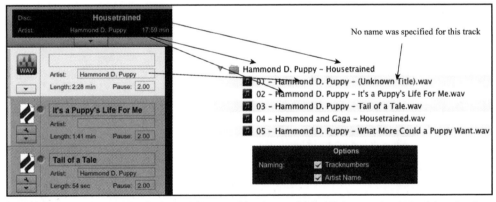

Fig. 6-6: The names of the folder and files resulting from a Digital Release export are determined by the Project and Track metadata fields, and the Tracknumbers and Artist Name checkboxes in the Digital Release dialog. When the artist field is blank for a track, the Project artist name is used in its place. When the Track name is blank, the phrase "(Unknown Title)" is substituted. If the Project artist field is blank, "(Unknown Artist)" is used, and if the Project Disc field is blank, the Project name is used in its place.

- Realtime Processing: This forces a real-time bounce to accommodate the use of outboard processors whose output needs to be captured in real time.

- Publishing options: This section contains three mutually exclusive options: Do not publish, Upload to Nimbit, and Upload to SoundCloud. Uploading to Nimbit or

SoundCloud can only succeed if you have set up an account and access to it has been established. Uploading to SoundCloud and Nimbit in a single pass is not possible from this dialog, but uploading to these services is easily accomplished using the Servers tab of the Project page Browser, as described in the next section, "The Browser Files > Servers Tab."

THE BROWSER > FILES > SERVERS TAB

The Servers tab of the Files pane in the Browser (on both the Song and Project pages) hooks directly into the internet from Studio One 2. The Servers tab provides immediate drag-and-drop access to both PreSonus Exchange and SoundCloud.

It's easy to access a server:

1. Click on a server in the list to select it.
2. Click on the login button at the bottom of the browser. The appearance of the login button will vary with the server selected.
3. If you have not logged into the server before, you will be asked to create an account. Clicking the Remember My Credentials box will eliminate the need to fill in the login form when you log in the next time; just click the login button and you'll be logged in.
4. Once you are logged in, the server structure will be visible, and content can be downloaded (and, in the case of SoundCloud, uploaded) simply by dragging from the Browser to your Song or Project.

Fig. 6-7: The Servers tab of the Files pane in the Browser provides access to SoundCloud and PreSonus Exchange.

Fig. 6-8: Each server displayed on the Servers tab has its own login button at the bottom of the Browser.

PRESONUS EXCHANGE

PreSonus Exchange is a rich resource in the Studio One 2 community. You can upload work of yours to Exchange for others to try, and download work others have posted to try in your own Songs and Projects. It is free to all registered Studio One users. Log onto Exchange using your regular PreSonus login and password information.

To access Exchange:

1. Click the Files button at the bottom of the Browser.
2. Click the Servers tab at the top of the Files pane.
3. Click the Exchange login button at the bottom of the pane and log in.
4. Once logged in, click the disclosure triangle to the right of Exchange in the Servers list. A list drops down, showing folders with the different kinds of data available.

Quite a few kinds of data are available on Exchange:

- Extensions posted by PreSonus, such as the Macro toolbar, Sound Set Builder, and international language packs.
- FX Chains.
- Groove templates.
- Macros.
- Pitch name sets.
- Presets (for VIs and plug-ins).
- Sound sets.
- Most recent additions to Exchange
- The top-rated (most downloaded) data.

Fig. 6-9: PreSonus Exchange provides access to presets, extensions, and much other useful data.

The Info Area and Preview Player

When a file is selected in Exchange, the bottom of the Browser will either show the Preview Player, if the selected file is a loop or other audio file, or it will show the Info Area. The Info Area contains a brief description, date and time the file was posted, and by whom.

Both the Info Area and Preview Player include an Install button on the right side.

Downloading and Installing Content from Exchange

The easiest way to download and install data from Exchange is to use the Install button:

1. Click on the file you want to download and install to select it. Information about it will appear below the list of files.

2. Click the green Install button in the info area and the data will be properly installed. The Transfers window will open to show you a log of what you have downloaded and installed.

It is also possible to download and install using drag-and-drop, but there are slightly different procedures for the various kinds of data available in Exchange. In most cases, downloading simply involves dragging the data from the Browser to an appropriate destination.

It's easy to tell when you have dragged a file over an appropriate destination. When a file being dragged is not over an appropriate destination, the cursor icon is the file's icon as seen in the Servers tab, but when the cursor passes over an appropriate place to drop the file,

Fig. 6-10: The Transfers window shows items you have downloaded from Exchange or SoundCloud and installed.

the icon changes to indicate that. There is enough variation among the various data types that I will describe proper installation for each kind:

- Extensions: These are the easiest of all. Just drop an Extension from the Servers tab anywhere on the Song or Project page and the extension will be installed.

- FX Chains: Drop a dragged FX Chain on a track in the Arrange view on the Song page, a channel in the Song page mixer, the insert area of a channel strip or Event FX in the Inspector pane, a track in the Track Lanes on the Project page, a track in the Track Column on the Project page, or the Inserts area of a Track Device Rack or the Master Device Rack. (Of course, it can be dropped in the Post area of the Master Device Rack, as well.)

- Groove templates: These must be dropped in the Groove Map area of the Quantize panel on the Song page to be loaded into the Song.

- Macros: Macros can only be installed using the Install button.

- Pitch name sets: These are dropped on the keyboard on the left side of the note area of the Music Editor for the Instrument track into which you wish to load the pitch names.

- Presets (for VIs and plug-ins): This works identically to dragging in a preset from the Instruments or Effects panes of the Browser. Drag to a track, channel, or insert area.

- Sound sets: Like extensions, sound sets can be dropped anywhere in the Song or Project page.

Uploading Data to Exchange

Uploading to Exchange is not done from Studio One 2, but from the Exchange web page, http://studioone.presonus.com/exchange/.

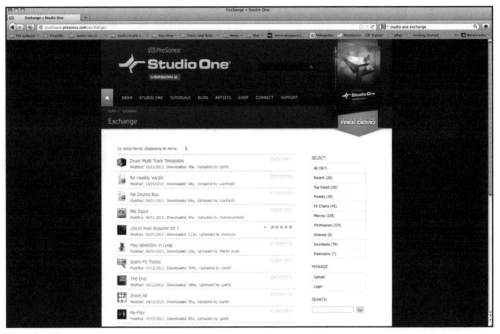

Fig. 6-11: The Exchange web page is where you will upload materials to Exchange.

1. Log in to the Exchange web page using your PreSonus account information.
2. Click the Upload button on the right of the window.
3. Browse to locate the content you want to upload.
4. On the next screen, enter a title and description.
5. Upload any additional materials: a logo, MP3 preview file, or PDF documentation.
6. Submit your content!

SOUNDCLOUD INTEGRATION

SoundCloud is an online community for exchanging music and sounds. Naturally, it would be nice to have this directly tied into your music-making environment. Pow! Studio One 2 has got it covered, and it's pretty easy.

First, you have to set it up:

1. Create a SoundCloud account for yourself.

2. Log in and SoundCloud will give you a confirmation code. You'll need this in a moment.

3. When you try to connect from Studio One 2, SoundCloud will ask you for that confirmation code. Enter it and you should be connected to SoundCloud.

Accessing SoundCloud from Studio One 2

Fig. 6-12: Clicking the SoundCloud icon on the Start page opens the SoundCloud client.

Access SoundCloud from Studio One 2 using either of two methods.

ACCESSING SOUNDCLOUD FROM THE START PAGE

1. Click the SoundCloud icon on the Start page. The SoundCloud client will appear.

2. If you have not entered the confirmation code you received, you will be asked to do so at this point.

3. If you have previously entered the confirmation code, click on the Connect with SoundCloud button and you will be logged in.

ACCESSING SOUNDCLOUD FROM THE BROWSER

1. Open a Song or Project.

2. Click the Files pane of the Browser.

3. Click the Servers tab and select SoundCloud.

4. Click the Connect with SoundCloud link at the bottom of the Browser pane.

5. If you have not entered the confirmation code you received, you will be asked to do so at this point.

6. If you have previously entered the confirmation code, you will be logged in and see the folders in your account appear.

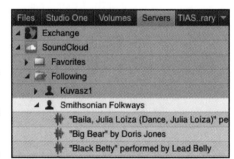

Fig. 6-13: When SoundCloud is accessed from the Browser, the Servers tab shows folders in your account.

Uploading to SoundCloud

UPLOADING TO SOUNDCLOUD FROM THE SONG PAGE

- To upload to SoundCloud from the Song page: Drag the audio content you want to upload and drop it on any part of the SoundCloud entry in the Servers tab of the Files pane of the Browser. As you drag, a pop-up tool tip will say, "Export to SoundCloud." When you drop the file, the SoundCloud client will open.

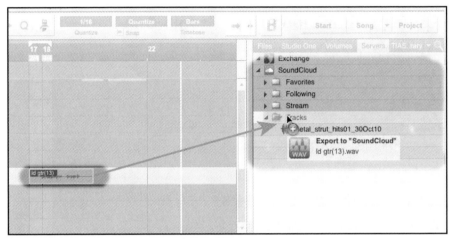

Fig. 6-14: Dropping content on a SoundCloud folder in the Servers tab opens the SoundCloud client.

UPLOADING TO SOUNDCLOUD FROM THE PROJECT PAGE

Uploading directly from Studio One 2 to SoundCloud is an option when your Project is exported for digital release. To export your Project and upload it to SoundCloud:

1. Click the Digital Release button in the Project page toolbar. The Digital Release dialog opens.
2. Make all export settings in the Digital Release dialog.
3. Check the Upload to SoundCloud box in the Publishing section in the lower right of the dialog. The SoundCloud client will open as soon as the export is complete. All metadata is automatically included.

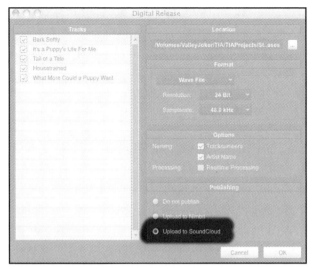

Fig. 6-15: Check the Upload to SoundCloud box in the Digital Release dialog and your tracks will be exported and then immediately uploaded.

THE SOUNDCLOUD CLIENT

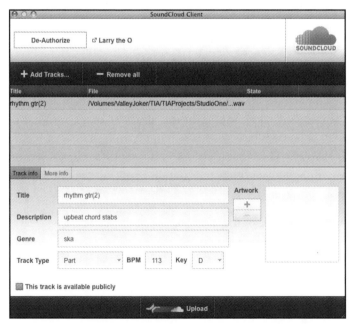

Fig. 6-16: The SoundCloud client is how content is uploaded to SoundCloud.

The SoundCloud client is very easy and intuitive. To upload content from the SoundCloud client:

1. Load your content into the SoundCloud client from the Start, Song, or Project page. You will see your tracks listed in the Track List portion of the client.

2. Tracks can also be added by clicking the Add Tracks…button and navigating through your computer's file system to the files you want to upload.

3. Tracks can be deleted from the list by selecting them and pressing the Delete key, or by clicking the Remove all button at the top of the client, which, of course, will remove all tracks in the list.

4. Fill out any metadata fields in the Track Info or More Info tabs that are not yet filled in.

5. Click the This Track Is Available Publicly button to make your track visible to all.

6. When all tracks are present and the metadata has all been entered, click the Upload button at the bottom of the client. The State column will show the progress of the upload in terms of the percentage of each track that has been uploaded.

Downloading from SoundCloud

Downloading audio from SoundCloud is simply a browser drag:

- To download an audio file from SoundCloud: Navigate to the file in the Server tab of the Files pane of the Browser, and drag it from the Browser to an audio track.

- Streams cannot be dragged into tracks.

NIMBIT INTEGRATION

Nimbit is a musicians' services company, a "one-stop shop" interface between an artist and his/her/their fans. Nimbit was bought by PreSonus with the idea very much in mind of integrating it with Studio One. Content can be uploaded to Nimbit from all three of Studio One 2's pages: Start, Song, and Project. The Nimbit extension is installed as part of version 2.5, so you don't have to do anything to get Nimbit integration happening in Studio One 2. You do have to set up Nimbit, however:

1. Click the Nimbit icon in the upper left of the Start page.

Fig. 6-17: The Nimbit icon on the Start page accesses the Nimbit client.

2. Create an account for yourself. A basic account is free, and there are two subscription plans that offer increasing quantities of services.

3. Log in. Check the Remember My Credentials box to make logging in easy. You should be ready to access Nimbit from within Studio One 2 now.

Uploading to Nimbit

When you upload the files from a digital release to Nimbit, the album that was your Project is now, in Nimbit, a "product."

Nimbit uploads are performed through the Nimbit client window. You can upload to Nimbit in any of these ways:

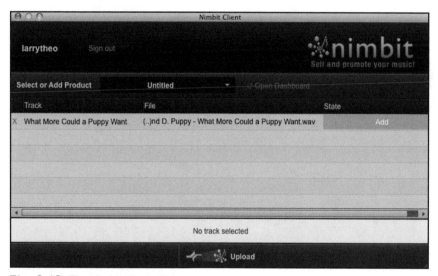

Fig. 6-18: The Nimbit client window.

- On any page, choose Studio One > Nimbit Client from the main menu bar. The Nimbit client window will open. Drag in 44.1 kHz/16-bit files from the Browser, Mac Finder, or Windows Explorer.

- On the Start page, click the Nimbit icon in the upper right. The Nimbit client window will open. Drag in 44.1 kHz/16-bit files from the Browser, Mac Finder, or Windows Explorer.

- If the Upload to Nimbit box is checked in the Export Mixdown dialog on the Song page, when the export finishes the Nimbit client opens with the exported mix file displayed in the client's track list.

- If the Upload to Nimbit box is checked in the Digital Release or Disk Image dialog on the Project page, when the mastered files are outputted, the Nimbit client opens with the mastered files displayed in the client's track list.

A Few More Features

- Select or Add Product field in the Nimbit client: Click on the arrow at the right of this field and select a product from the drop-down menu that appears, or click in the field and enter a name for a new product.
- Open dashboard link: Click this link to open your Nimbit dashboard web page.
- When you are filling out metadata for the tracks in your Project, don't forget that generating valid ISRC codes is an included service, even with a free Nimbit account.

Update: What's New Since Volume I

Things move fast in the world of Studio One 2, and much has happened since *Power Tools for Studio One 2,* volume 1 was written. The chapters in this book are written to be current as of version 2.5, but there have been many changes to the topics covered in volume 1, as well. This chapter is intended to bring that information up to date as of version 2.5, as well as to throw in a few items that probably should have been in volume 1 but somehow slipped the net.

The most substantial item in this chapter that was not previously covered is most likely the Macros feature. In terms of updates to volume 1 info, the single most significant updates may be comping and editing. But lots of other juicy items are worth noting, as well, such as the Song Notes feature. (Hey, I'm big on documenting things…but you knew that already.)

I gave Macros their own section, because I thought them significant enough to merit it. Everything else, I sorted into sections named for the chapters in volume 1 where the information would have appeared had it been current when volume 1 was written.

So, dig in and get up to date!

MACROS

Macros are one of the most powerful workflow enhancers I have ever come across. If keyboard shortcuts double your work speed, macros have the potential to double it again. Macros are sequences of commands that you repeat time and again. I find them most useful when recording, but as with key shortcuts, anytime you find yourself repeating the same sequence more than three times, you may find it useful to create a macro for it. Best of all, once a macro is created, there are a few different ways of triggering it quickly:

- Assign a key shortcut to it. Macros can be assigned key shortcuts, just as individual commands can.
- Place a button for it on the Macro panel.

- Click the Action button in the Macros panel and choose it from the menu that drops down.
- Assign a MIDI controller message to trigger it.

Here are a few other important points to know about macros:

- Studio One 2 macros are actually XML files, so they can be edited or easily transferred to your laptop running Studio One 2, or uploaded to PreSonus Exchange for others to use.
- To reveal the location where your Studio One 2 macros are stored, click the link labeled Show Macros Folder in Explorer/Finder at the bottom of the Macro Organizer window. For more about the Macro Organizer window, see the section "Creating and Managing Macros in the Macro Organizer" later in this chapter.
- Information about the Macros feature is available by choosing Help > Studio One Macro Toolbar from the main menu bar, or choosing Action > Help in the Edit section of the Macro panel.

Installing the Macro Toolbar Extension

The fastest and easiest way to install the Macro Toolbar Extension is to get it from PreSonus Exchange. For more information on PreSonus Exchange, see the section "PreSonus Exchange" in chapter 6, "Sharing Your Work."

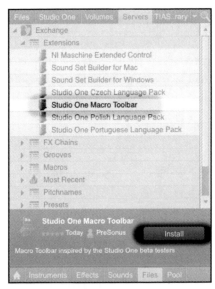

1. Log in to Exchange and navigate to the Extensions folder.
2. Click Studio One Macro Toolbar in the list of extensions in the folder to select it.
3. Click the Install button at the bottom of the Browser or drag the extension into the Song or Project page. The Transfers window will show the download, then the Extensions window will open for the installation. Click OK in the confirmation dialog and the extension will be installed.
4. Studio One 2 needs to be restarted before the Macros feature will be available. Click the blue Restart Now link that has appeared at the top of the Studio One Extensions dialog to restart the program.

Fig. 7-1: Locate the Macro Toolbar extension in Exchange and click the Install button at the bottom of the Browser to install it.

If your computer is not connected to the Internet, you can download the extension from the Exchange website (http://studioone.presonus.com/exchange), copy it to a flash drive, and "sneakernet" it to your studio computer.

Creating and Managing Macros in the Macro Organizer

Macros are built and managed in the Macro Organizer window. Every command shown in Prefs > Options > General > Keyboard Shortcuts is available to be used in a macro. Note that this does not cover every function in Studio One 2, but it sure covers most of them.

ACCESSING THE MACRO ORGANIZER

Open the Macro Organizer window using any of these methods:

- Choose Studio One > Macro Organizer from the main menu bar.
- Click the button with the Macro icon in the top left corner of the Start page.
- In the Macro panel, click the Setup button (with the wrench icon) in the Edit section of the panel and choose Macro Organizer from the menu that drops down.

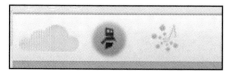

Fig. 7-2: Clicking the Macro button on the Start page is one way to open the Macro Organizer.

To close the Macro Organizer window: Click the close box in the upper left corner of the window.

The Macro Organizer dialog has the following components:

- A list of installed macros by name.
- The Group, if any, to which each macro is installed.
- Macro management buttons: New, Edit, Delete, and Refresh.
- The Show Macros Folder in Explorer/Finder link, which reveals the folder containing the actual XML Macro files.
- A close box in the upper left corner.

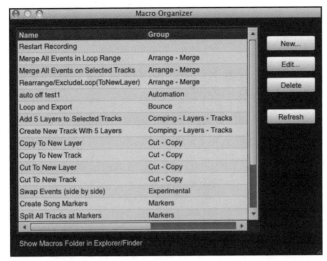

Fig. 7-3: The Macro Organizer window.

MAKING A NEW MACRO

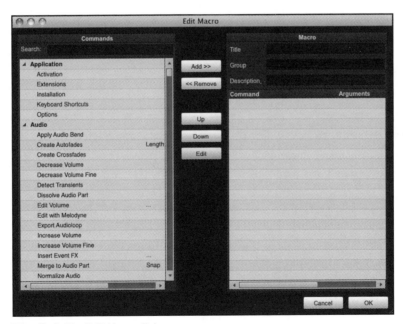

Fig. 7-4: The Edit Macro dialog.

1. Click the New button. The Edit Macro window opens.
2. Click in the Title field in the Macro pane on the right of the window and enter a name for the macro. Keep the name short and try to throw in one or two good keywords so the basic purpose of the macro can be gleaned without having to open it for editing.

3. If you want the macro to be part of a group, click in the Group field in the Macro pane on the right of the window and enter a group name. There is no drop-down list of existing groups, so type carefully if you are assigning a macro to an existing group. For more about macro groups, see the section "Adding, Renaming, and Deleting Groups" later in this chapter.

4. Enter a brief text description of what the macro does. This is the text someone will see in Exchange, if you choose to upload it.

5. Build and configure the macro by working in the Command List in the Macro pane on the right of the dialog. (The sections following detail working with commands.) Click OK when the macro is built as you want it.

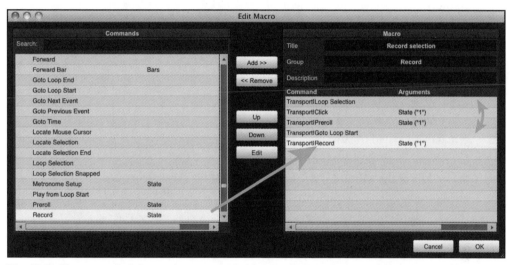

Fig. 7-5: Macros are built by moving commands from the Commands pane on the left to the Macro pane on the right, then configuring and reordering the steps as necessary.

6. Your new macro is immediately available in the Action submenu of the Edit section of the Macro panel. If you wish, you can assign a key shortcut to the macro as described in the section "Assigning Key Shortcuts to Macros" later in this chapter, place a button for the macro on the Macro panel as described in the section "Customizing the Macro Panel" later in this chapter, and/or assign a MIDI controller message to trigger the macro as described in the section "Triggering Macros with MIDI Controllers" later in this chapter.

EDIT MACRO DIALOG LAYOUT

Macros are edited or created from scratch by selecting commands, putting them in the right order, and setting values for any variable parameters the commands require. All of this work is performed in the Edit Macro dialog.

The layout of the Edit Macro dialog is quite simple:

- Commands pane: On the left is the list of all of the commands available in the Keyboard Shortcuts list. This includes many commands that don't appear anywhere in the UI, but it does not include everything the program can do. You may sometimes be faced with a need to be clever to make your macro accomplish its goal, and you might even occasionally just have to give up on a particular task that can't be kludged.

- Some commands have parameters that can be specified (Studio One 2 uses the programmer-speak term *arguments* for these). Available arguments are shown to the right of the command's name in the list. Most arguments are simple binary-state flags that can be set to either 1 or 0.

- Macro pane: The right side of the window is where your new macro is created, named, grouped, and generally prepared for use.

- Command management buttons: In the middle of the window is a handful of buttons that manipulate the commands in the Macro pane. More information about these buttons are given in the following sections.

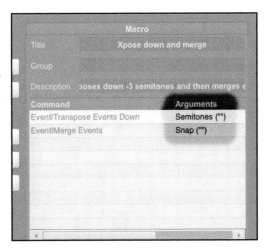

Fig. 7-6: If a command is available in the Keyboard Shortcuts pane, it will be available for use in a macro. Some commands have "arguments," or parameter values that can be set.

The Refresh button causes the Macros folder to be rescanned and the macros list to be updated.

ADDING AND REMOVING COMMANDS

- To add a command to a macro: Select a command in the Commands pane and click the Add button, or double-click the command in the Commands pane. The command will be added to the end of the macro.

- To remove a command from a macro: Select the command in the Macro pane and click the Remove button.

REORDERING COMMANDS IN A MACRO

Commands in a macro are executed in the order shown in the Macro pane of the Edit Macro dialog. The exact order is often critical to the macro's correctly executing the task for which it is designed. Thus, rearranging the order of the commands is a common need, which is easily met:

- To move a command higher in the order: Select the command in the Macro pane and click the Up button. The command will switch positions with the command immediately above it. Repeat as many times as desired to move the command to the desired position.

- To move a command lower in the order: Select the command in the Macro pane and click the Down button. The command will switch positions with the command immediately below it. Repeat as many times as desired to move the command to the desired position.

ASSIGNING ARGUMENT VALUES FOR A COMMAND

As already noted, some commands require arguments to make sense and be executed. These commands are identifiable in the Commands pane of the Edit Macro window by the argument description that appears to the right of the command name in the list. When a command has a single argument, the description is a brief text name, but when there are multiple arguments, the description is ". . ." (ellipsis).

1. Move the command from the Commands pane of the Edit Macro window to the Macro pane; argument values can only be edited for commands in the Macro pane.

2. Double-click the command in the Macro pane, or select it and click the Edit button. If no arguments are available for a command, nothing will happen. If arguments are available, a Command Arguments dialog opens. The name of the dialog window will vary with the command.

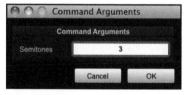

3. Set values for all of the arguments in the dialog that opens. The number and name of the arguments varies with the command. When all arguments are entered, click the OK button.

Fig. 7-7: The Command Arguments dialog is only available for commands that have parameter values.

EDITING AN EXISTING MACRO

- To modify an existing macro: Double-click the macro in the macros list in the Macro Organizer, or select the macro in the macros list in the Macro Organizer and click the Edit button. The Edit Macro window will open and commands can be added, removed, and reordered using the methods just described.

DELETING A MACRO

To delete one or more macros:

1. In the Macro Organizer window, select the macro(s) you want to delete.

2. Click the Delete button. A confirmation dialog will appear.

3. Click OK in the confirmation dialog to delete the macros. Note that this actually deletes the macro file from the Macros folder.

The Macro Panel

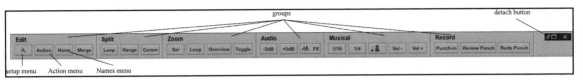

Fig. 7-8: The Macro Panel puts your favorite macros one click away, as well as providing access to special functions like naming macros and opening the Macro Organizer.

Studio One 2's Macro panel provides immediate access to the macros you like to click the most, grouped into different areas in the panel. (Studio One 2 calls this the "Macro toolbar," but it is accessed and behaves more like a panel.) The panel is reconfigurable, so that if the default macros do not suit you, you can replace them with ones that are more useful to you.

However, the Macro panel quietly houses considerably more functions than buttons that trigger macros. Tucked away in the Edit section is the ability to instantly rename an item from an editable list of names, a drop-down menu of all available macros, and access to the Macro Organizer window.

Access and configure the Macro panel using any of these methods:

Fig. 7-9: The Macros button in the Song page toolbar.

- To open or close the Macro panel: Click the Macros button in the Song page toolbar, or choose View > Additional Views > Macros from the main menu bar.
- To detach the Macro panel from the Song page: Click the Detach button (which shows an arrow pointing up) in the upper right corner of the panel.

  Fig. 7-10: The Detach button makes the Macro toolbar mobile.

- To reattach the Macro panel when it has been detached: Click the Detach button (which shows an arrow pointing down) in the upper right corner of the panel.
- To change the orientation of the panel when it is detached: Right-click (Ctrl-click in Mac) anywhere in the panel and choose Vertical from the contextual menu that drops down. A checkmark is added next to the command when the orientation is vertical; the command is unchecked when orientation is horizontal.
- To compact the button layout of a group on the Macro panel: Right-click (Ctrl-click in Mac) in the Group area in the Macro panel, but not on a button, and check the Compact box in the contextual menu that drops down.

- To set the alignment of the row of buttons in the layout of the Macro panel: Right-click (Ctrl-click in Mac) in the Macro panel outside of any Group area and choose the desired alignment (Left, Center, or Right) from the contextual menu that drops down.

CUSTOMIZING THE MACRO PANEL
ADDING, RENAMING, AND DELETING BUTTONS

- To add a button to the Macro panel: Right-click (Ctrl-click in Mac) anywhere in the Group area in which you want to add a button and choose New Button from the contextual menu that drops down. New buttons are blank, so the button will need to be renamed, as well as assigned.
- To rename a button: Right-click (Ctrl-click in Mac) on the button, then double-click on the button name in the gray field at the top of the contextual menu that drops down, and enter the desired name.
- To remove a button from the Macro panel: Right-click (Ctrl-click in Mac) on the button and choose Remove Button from the contextual drop-down menu that appears.

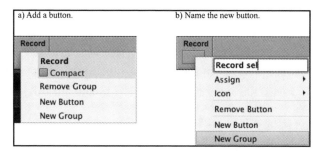

Fig. 7-11: a) Right-click on the Macro panel where you want to add a button, then b) Right-click on the button to give it a name.

ASSIGNING BUTTONS TO COMMANDS OR MACROS
To assign a button to a command:

1. Right-click (Ctrl-click in Mac) on the button and choose Assign > Assign Command from the contextual menu that drops down. A Select Command dialog appears.
2. The dialog contains the same list of commands that appears in the Keyboard Shortcuts list, plus a search field at the top to make it easier to find a specific command.
3. Locate the command which you want to assign to the button and click the OK key to complete the assignment.

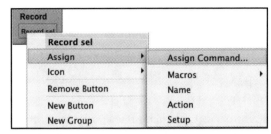

Fig. 7-12: Right-click (Ctrl-click in Mac) on a button and choose Assign Command or Assign Macro to link the button to a command or macro.

To assign a button to a macro:

1. Right-click (Ctrl-click in Mac) on the button and choose Assign > Macros from the contextual menu that drops down.

2. Choose a macro from the list that drops down.

ADDING A CUSTOM ICON TO A BUTTON

Each button can be assigned a custom icon. Any 22 x 22 pixel .png or .jpg file can be used as a button icon.

1. To add a custom icon to a button: Right-click (Ctrl-click in Mac) on the button and choose Icon > Select Image from the contextual menu that drops down.

2. Navigate to the image file you want to use, select it, and click the OK button.

SPECIAL MENU BUTTONS

Three button assignments are actually menus. Assigning a button to one of these simply means that clicking on the button drops down the menu. All three of these buttons exist on the Macros panel by default. However, these selections enable you to place them where you wish, or even to have duplicate menu buttons on the Macros panel, if you can possibly think of a reason you would want them there.

To assign a button to a menu:

1. Right-click (Ctrl-click in Mac) on the button and choose Assign > Name, Assign > Action, or Assign > Setup from the contextual menu that drops down.

2. The button will now drop down the selected menu.

For more information on the functions of these menus, see the section "Edit Section" later in this chapter.

ADDING, RENAMING, AND DELETING GROUPS

Macro groups are for organizing the display of macros. Groups are used for display in two places: grouping buttons on the Macro panel, and in the list of macros in the Action submenu of the Edit group on the panel.

- To create a new group: Right-click (Ctrl-click in Mac) anywhere in any Group area and choose New Group from the contextual menu that drops down.
- To rename a group: Right-click (Ctrl-click in Mac) in the Group area (but not on a button), then double-click the Group name in the header of the contextual menu that drops down and enter the new name.
- To remove a group: Right-click (Ctrl-click in Mac) in the Group area (but not on a button), then choose Remove Group from the contextual menu that drops down.

RESETTING THE PANEL

Maybe you got a little carried away, or perhaps you don't want the Macro panel configuration stored in a template. The panel can be restored to the default setup.

Fig. 7-13: Right-click (Ctrl-click in Mac) in the Macro toolbar and choose New Group from the contextual drop-down menu to make a new toolbar group.

- To reset the Macro panel to the default setup: Click the Setup button (with the wrench icon) and choose Reset Toolbar from the menu that drops down.

EDIT SECTION

Although the Edit group can contain buttons like any other group, it also contains three buttons that drop down important menus when they are clicked.

THE ACTION SUBMENU

The Action button drops down a list of all of the currently loaded macros, arranged by group. Any macro shown can be executed by selecting it in the list.

Fig. 7-14: The Action menu in the Macro panel.

THE NAME SUBMENU

If you have any consistency in the instrumentation you usually work with, time can be saved by using the renaming macros in the Name submenu to apply names to selected Audio Events and Instrument Parts. The list of names can be edited in any text editor, so customizing names is easy. This also makes it easy to use a different set of names for each project, for example.

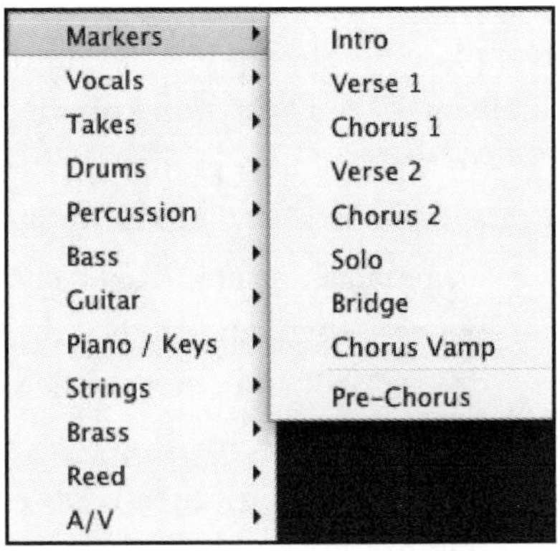

Markers ▶	Intro
Vocals ▶	Verse 1
Takes ▶	Chorus 1
Drums ▶	Verse 2
Percussion ▶	Chorus 2
Bass ▶	Solo
Guitar ▶	Bridge
Piano / Keys ▶	Chorus Vamp
Strings ▶	Pre-Chorus
Brass ▶	
Reed ▶	
A/V ▶	

Fig. 7-15: The Name menu (and the Markers submenu).

To rename one or more Events or Parts:

- Select the item(s) you want to rename.
- Click the Name button in the Edit group of the Macro panel and choose the desired name from the list that drops down. All selected items will be given the same name. When multiple items are renamed together, numbers will be appended to the names.
- To edit the list of names, choose Edit Names from the Setup menu (with the wrench icon). This will open the file <<user data>>/Macros/EventNames.txt in your default text editor for editing, where <<user data>> is the location named in the Preferences > Options > Locations > User Data Location field.
- To load a previously saved set of names into the Names menu, choose Reload Names from the Setup menu (with the wrench icon). It will load the names in the EventNames.txt file mentioned in the last step.

SETUP

This button drops down a short but powerful menu. I have already discussed all of the commands in this menu, so I will simply list them here, and information on them can be found earlier in this chapter.

- Help: Opens Help document on the Macro Toolbar.
- Macro Organizer: Opens the Macro Organizer window.
- Edit Names: Opens the EventNames.txt file.
- Reload Names: Reloads previously saved names files to the Name submenu.
- Reset Toolbar: Restores the default button layout on the Macro panel.

DEFAULT BUTTONS IN THE MACRO PANEL

Following is a list of the default macros. Any of these can be opened for study and/or editing, as we will discuss in just a moment.

THE SPLIT SECTION

The three buttons in the Split section provide "quick click" access to three commands, listed here with their key shortcuts:

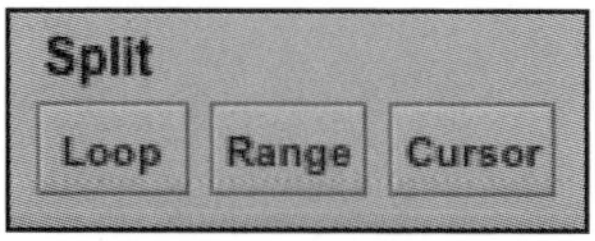

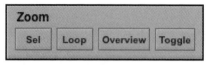

Fig. 7-16: Default buttons in the Split section of the Macro toolbar.

- Loop button: Split Loop (Cmd + Shift + X [Ctrl + Shift + X in Windows])
- Range button: Split Range (Cmd + Option + X [Ctrl + Alt + X in Windows])

Cursor button: Split at Cursor (Option +X [Alt + X in Windows])

ZOOM SECTION

As with the Split section, the Zoom section provides one-click execution of four zoom functions, listed here with their key shortcuts:

Fig. 7-17: Default buttons in the Zoom section of the Macro toolbar.

- Sel button: Zoom to Selection (Shift + S)
- Loop button: Zoom to Loop (Shift + L)
- Overview button: Not Zoom Full, this macro selects everything in the Song and then zooms to the selection.
- Toggle button: Toggle Zoom (Z)

AUDIO SECTION

The Audio section lets you change the Event volume of one or more selected Audio Events with button clicks.

Fig. 7-18: Default buttons in the Audio section of the Macro toolbar.

- -3dB: Decreases the Event Volume of selected Audio Events by 3 dB. If a range is selected, rather than one or more Events, this macro splits the selected range into a new Audio Event, decreases the Event Volume by 3 dB, and creates crossfades to meld it back in.
- +3dB: Increases the Event Volume of selected Audio Events by 3 dB. If a range is selected, rather than one or more Events, this macro splits the selected range into a new Audio Event, increases the Event Volume by 3 dB, and creates crossfades to meld it back in.
- Render Event FX (with the waveform and "FX" label): Renders Event FX on one or more selected Events. If Event FX are not enabled for the Event, this command will have no effect.

MUSICAL SECTION

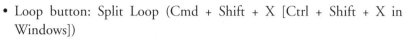

- 1/16: Sets the length of all selected notes in the Music Editor to sixteenth notes. If an Instrument Part is selected in the Arrange view, all notes in the Part will be set to sixteenth notes.

Fig. 7-19: Default buttons in the Musical section of the Macro toolbar.

- 1/4: Sets the length of all selected notes in the Music Editor to quarter notes. If an Instrument Part is selected in the Arrange view, all notes in the Part will be set to quarter notes.

- Humanize: Invokes the Humanize command.

- Vel–: Decreases the velocity of all selected notes in the Music Editor by 10. If an Instrument Part is selected in the Arrange view, the velocity of all notes in the Part will be decreased by 10.

- Vel+: Increases the velocity of all selected notes in the Music Editor by 10. If an Instrument Part is selected in the Arrange view, the velocity of all notes in the Part will be increased by 10.

Assigning Key Shortcuts to Macros

1. To assign a key shortcut to a macro: Open the Preferences > Options > General pane and choose the Keyboard Shortcuts tab.

2. Locate the Macros folder in the commands list on the left.

3. Inside the Macros folder, select the macro to which you want to assign a key shortcut.

4. Assign a key shortcut to the macro, as described in the section "Keyboard Shortcuts" of chapter 1, "On Your Mark" in *Power Tools for Studio One 2*, volume 1.

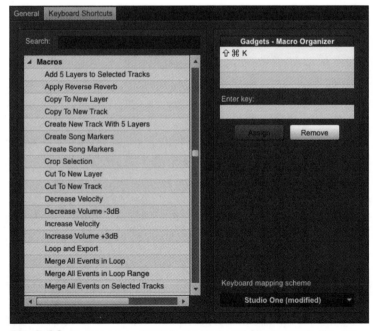

Fig. 7-20: Macros are available in the Keyboard Shortcuts tab, like any other command.

Triggering Macros with MIDI Controllers

Macros can be triggered by standard MIDI continuous controller (CC) messages. Generally, a button is used to trigger a macro, but other controls could be used. To assign a macro to be triggered by a MIDI CC message:

1. Open the Device Controller Map for the control surface or other external device you want to use to trigger a macro.

2. Right-click (Ctrl-click in Mac) on the control in the Device Controller Map that you want to use for the trigger and choose Assign Command from the contextual menu that drops down. The Select Command dialog opens.

3. Locate in the list of commands the macro you want to assign to the control. It will be listed under Macros.

4. Click OK to complete the mapping.

Fig. 7-21: Assigning a physical control to trigger a macro is done by right-clicking (Ctrl-clicking in Mac) on a button or switch control in the Device Controller Map for the control surface. When the Assign Command dialog appears, macros will be available in the list, along with the rest of the commands.

ON YOUR MARK

Studio One Free

On the whole, free is good. In the case of Studio One Free, PreSonus probably thinks it's good marketing. And they could hardly be more right. Studio One Free is an unabashed ploy to make converts early, when musicians are just learning how to work with software, knowing they'll grow into more powerful (and profitable) versions of the software.

It is possible PreSonus did too good a job, because Studio One Free, while missing a lot of the fireworks of the other versions, is still a quite viable tool. Yes, a few basic tools are missing, such as MP3 compatibility, and hosting of third-party plug-ins; and there are limitations, such as only two inputs and outputs, and eight bundled plug-ins.

But Studio One Free still has many of the core features that make Studio One 2 such a great program, such as drag-and-drop, comping, and automatic delay compensation. Plus, whatever limitations there might be, Studio One Free has some important areas with no limits: the number of Audio and Instrument tracks, number of FX channels, and number of inserts and sends on each channel. Oh, and I didn't say there weren't *any* fireworks included: real-time time-stretching, Track Transform, and multitrack MIDI editing.

You don't need Studio One Free, because you already have Studio One 2 Artist, Producer, or Professional…don't you? But your friends, who are afraid to spend any money to find something new and different…well, you can turn them on to Studio One Free at http://studioone.presonus.com/free.

Song Notes

One thing that had been missing from Studio One 2 was a place to make text notes about a Song, such as documenting mic assignments, take evaluations, or outboard processor presets. The Song Notes field now provides a place for that documentation.

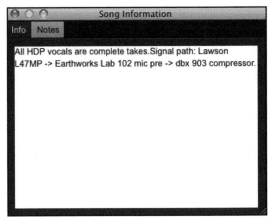

Fig. 7-22: The Song Notes field enables settings, comments, and other useful text to be entered into the Song document.

- To add text notes to a song: Choose Song > Song Information from the main menu bar. When the Song Information dialog appears, click the Notes tab. The window can be resized if you are entering a large amount of text.

Attachments in the Pool

Items in the Pool can now have attachments, which are data files linked to the item. For instance, when you render Event FX, the original file (before rendering) appears in the Pool as an attachment to the rendered file.

An attachment shows up as a gray badge with a paperclip icon next to an item's name.

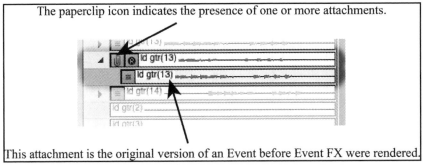

The paperclip icon indicates the presence of one or more attachments.

This attachment is the original version of an Event before Event FX were rendered.

Fig. 7-23: An attachment is a data file associated with a file in the Pool. it can be accessed and used independently of the file to which it is attached.

- To see attachments to an item: Click the disclosure triangle to the left of its name.
- Attachments can be dragged from the Browser for use in the Arrange view independently of the item they are attached to.
- To delete an attachment: Right-click (Ctrl-click in Mac) on the attachment you wish to delete and choose Delete from the contextual menu that drops down. Warning: You can't undo this!

Here are some examples of attachments you may encounter in the Pool:

- Music Loops imported to tracks will show the musical performance as an attachment.
- Audio clips edited with Melodyne will show the detected notes as an attachment.
- Audio clips with transformed Event FX will show the original event as an attachment.

Transport Bar

Fig. 7-24: New Transport bar features include a secondary time display, so a location can be viewed in two time bases simultaneously.

The Transport bar has three new features:

- Secondary time display: To the left of the original counter is now a smaller counter that can display different units than the larger one. This lets you see a location in bars and beats, and, at the same time, in absolute time.
- To change horizontal alignment of the Transport bar: Click the Alignment button (with the verrry small wrench icon) in the upper right corner of the Transport bar and choose Align Left, Center, or Right from the menu that drops down. If the icon is not visible, grow the Studio One 2 display wider. In fact, unless the display is stretched pretty wide, the alignment makes only a little difference.
- To see how much recording time is remaining at any given time: Find the Remaining Record Time indicator, labeled Record Max, between the secondary counter and the sample rate display, or choose View > Remaining Record Time from the main menu bar to open a larger display window.

Templates

Templates can now store tempo, time signature, and sample rate.

In the New Song dialog, templates listed on the left are now organized into three tabs: Styles (application-based templates, for example "Rock Band" and "Singer/Songwriter"), Interfaces (templates optimized for PreSonus interfaces, including the StudioLive mixers), and User (templates you have created and stored in the folder <<user data folder location>>/ Studio One/templates/).

Open TL Compatibility

Open TL (Open Track List) is an EDL (Edit Decision List) file format created by Tascam for its HD recorders. Because it was easy to implement and included support for several audio file formats and both Mac and Windows file systems, it has seen a fair degree of acceptance, and several DAWs are able to read and write Open TL files. Tracks and the location of audio regions in them are the only information that is transmitted. No plug-in or automation data is carried over.

- To export a Studio One Song as an Open TL file: Choose Save As from the main menu bar, click the file format field near the bottom of the dialog, and choose Open TL (.tl) from the menu that drops down.
- To import an Open TL file: Choose File > Open from the main menu bar, navigate to the file you want to import, and click the OK button. If for some reason, the .tl file is grayed out, try clicking the file format field near the bottom of the dialog and choosing Open TL (.tl) from the menu that drops down.

GET SET TO RECORD
Add Tracks Dialog

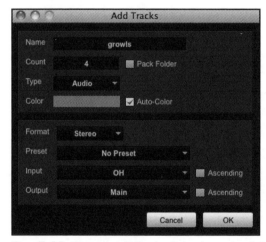

Fig. 7-25: The new Add Tracks dialog in version 2.5.

Several useful options related to creating multiple tracks at once have been added to the Add Tracks dialog:

- Pack Folder box: When this box is checked, a Folder track will be created with the name shown in the Name box above it. All tracks will be created in the folder and given the same name with a sequentially numbered suffix. That is, if the Name field says "oobydooby" and you create four Audio tracks, they will be named oobydooby 1, oobydooby 2, and so on This is great for making drum tracks, setting yourself up for double- or triple-tracking vocals, or prepping tracks for a wall o' guitars.

- Track Type and Format menus: The New Tracks dialog used to have a Format menu with four choices: Mono, Stereo, Instrument, or Automation. This mixed track type and format in the same menu. Version 2.5 adds a Track Type field to the dialog (choices: Audio, Instrument, Automation, Folder), and only displays the Format field (choices: mono, stereo) when Audio is selected as the Track Type.

- Input select (Audio and Instrument tracks): When Track Type is set to Audio or Instrument, click on the Input field and choose the desired input from the list that drops down. For a mono audio track, the list will contain the available mono inputs; for a stereo track, the stereo inputs; and for an Instrument track, the available keyboards and other controllers defined as external devices.

- Input Ascending box: When more than one track is specified to be created by the Count field, checking this box causes inputs to be assigned successively, in ascending order. Fig. 7-26 illustrates this.

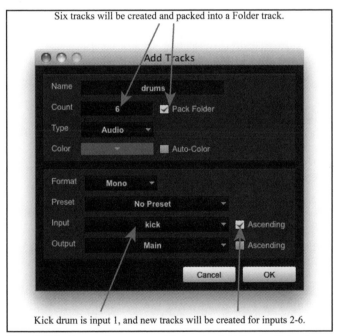

Fig. 7-26: New options were added to the Add Tracks dialog in version 2.5. In this example, mono drum mics have been connected to inputs 1 through 6, and new tracks can be created for all of them in a single gesture.

- Output select (Audio and Instrument tracks): When Track Type is set to Audio or Instrument, click on the Output field and choose the desired output from the list that drops down. For mono or stereo audio tracks, the list will contain Bus channels,

Output channels, FX channels, and sidechains. For an Instrument track, the list contains available VIs and external devices, as described in the next point.

- New Instrument/Existing Instrument Output radio buttons: When the Existing Instrument option is selected, the drop-down list of outputs for an Instrument track will contain VIs and external devices already instantiated in the Song. When the New Instrument option is selected, the list contains all available VIs and external devices, as shown in the Browser's Instruments pane.

- Output Ascending box: When more than one track is specified to be created by the Count field, checking this box causes the Instrument tracks being created to be assigned to successive MIDI channels on the instrument named in the Output field, in ascending order.

Arrange View

Fig. 7-27: You can keep an Event but replace the audio file it references just by Option-dragging (Alt-dragging in Windows) the new file from the Browser and dropping it onto the Event.

- To replace the audio file used in an Event: Option-drag (Alt-drag in Windows) an audio file from the Browser and drop it on the Event. Note that the dropped file is replacing the file (in the Song, not on disk) on which the Event is based. This means that any other Events based on the same file will also be replaced.

- To insert multiple files from the Browser to a single track: Select the files and Cmd-drag (Ctrl-drag in Windows) them to the track. The files will be inserted end to end.

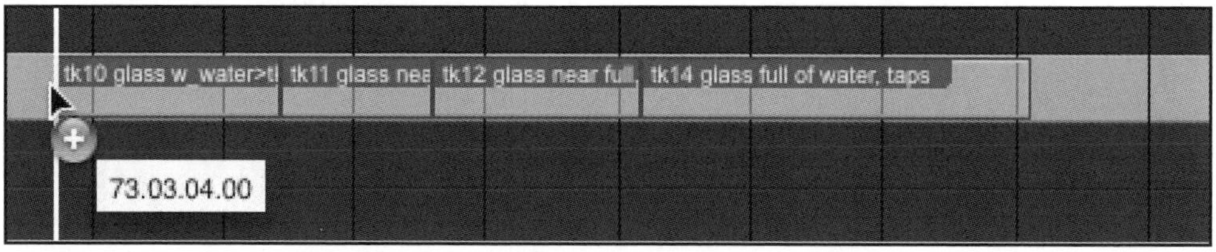

![tk10 glass w_water>t| tk11 glass nea tk12 glass near full tk14 glass full of water, taps | 73.03.04.00]

Fig. 7-28: Cmd-dragging (Ctrl-dragging in Windows) a group of files from the Browser to a track imports them all to the one track, placed end to end.

GO! RECORDING WITH STUDIO ONE

Editing and Comping with Layers

- It is no longer necessary to double-click a selected range on a layer to move it to the comp on the current layer. Merely selecting a range on a layer now moves it to the comp.
- When comping, you can select an Event on the track, then double-click or Cmd-click (Ctrl-click in Windows) in the same range on a layer, and that range of the layer will be comped to the track.
- When tracks are grouped, soloing a layer on one of them solos the corresponding layers on the others in the group.
- When multiple Events are selected, as would be the case with grouped tracks, using the Unpack Takes command unpacks all takes in all selected Events.
- The Options > Record Takes to Layers command now puts each take on a new layer, regardless of whether or not you are loop recording. This makes it easy to record multiple takes to different layers when you prefer to stop between takes, instead of looping.
- Layers Follow Events box (Track inspector): When this box is checked, any Event that gets copied, pasted, or moved to another location on the same track carries all layers with it. This means you could duplicate a comp several times, then modify the copies to create variations.

Fig. 7-29: With the Layers follow events box in the Track inspector checked, all layers move together when an Event is copied, pasted, or moved on the same track.

TAGGING EVENTS IN LAYERS

Working with layers, you are dealing with so many Events it is difficult to keep information about them straight. Tagging Events by name and/or color makes it much easier to, for example, mark a particular passage with your evaluation of it after auditioning it. Perhaps green is the best take, and others are yellow or red, depending on their quality. Comping is quick once you have rated all of your source material and marked it.

- To set the name for an Event on a layer; Right-click (Ctrl-click in Mac) on the Event in a layer, double-click in the name field and enter the desired name.
- To set the color for an Event on a layer: Right-click (Ctrl-click in Mac) on the Event in a layer, click on the color bar, and choose the desired name from the palette that drops down.
- You can also delete the Event from this menu.

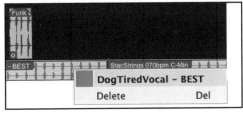

Fig. 7-30: Events on any layer can be named and colored. This is useful in tagging which Events are keepers and which flawed.

EDITING COMPS IN AUDIO PARTS

The process of comping often ends with the finished edit getting merged into an Audio Part. A few new capabilities make it easy to do further edits to the comp, even once it has been made into an Audio Part:

- Selecting an Audio Part made from a comp highlights all of its source ranges on the track's layers.

- Portions of layers added as comps to an existing Audio Part automatically get merged into the Audio Part.

- To trim the start or end of an Event in an Audio Part from its source layer: Select the Audio Part in the track, and move the cursor over the edge of the highlighted range in the source layer that represents the Event in the Audio Part you wish to edit. The cursor turns to an arrowhead with a line and you can drag left or right to trim the edge.

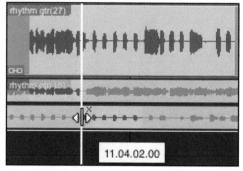

Fig. 7-31: In an Audio Part created by comping, you can trim an Event from the source layer.

Pre-Record

We love the precision of computers, but now and then that same precision can be a pain. Say you start recording with a count-in, but your very first note is just a tad ahead of the beat. Feels good, but recording was set to start right on the downbeat, so your note is cut off. Pre-Record is here to help. The idea behind Pre-Record is that each track has a small buffer that is recording continuously in the background. When Studio One 2 actually enters Record, there is already an additional amount of time (determined by the buffer size) that has been recorded. If you were on top of the beat on that first note, you can have the whole thing. The buffer is managed intelligently to enable seamless recording when you do punches on a single track. Pre-Record is a global feature, applying to all tracks.

- To enable Pre-Record: Click the Pre-Record audio input box on the Preferences > Options > Advanced > Audio tab. Click in the field to the right of the checkbox label and enter a buffer time up to 1 minute (60 seconds).

- When Pre-Record is enabled, background recording is happening as long as the physical inputs are connected.

- To reveal the audio captured by Pre-Record: Simply drag the Event start earlier with the arrow tool.

Markers

MARKER INSPECTOR

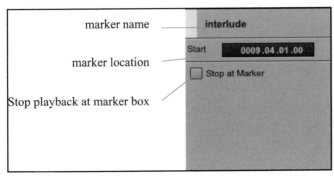

Fig. 7-32: The Marker inspector.

There is now a small inspector for markers:

- To open the Marker inspector: Press F4 to make the Inspector pane appear and click any marker to select it. The Marker inspector will appear.

There are three settings in the Marker inspector:

- Marker name: Double-click in this field and enter a name for the selected marker.
- Start: The marker location, not a start point for anything. To set the marker location, position the cursor over any units field and drag up or down to increase or decrease the value, click on any units field and use the arrow up and down keys to increment value, or click on any units field and enter a value directly.
- Stop at Marker: When checked, playback will start whenever it reaches this marker. For more information on this, see the next section, "Stop Playback at Marker."

STOP PLAYBACK AT MARKER
- To set a marker to stop playback: Right-click (Ctrl-click in Mac) on the marker in the Marker track and click the Stop at Marker box in the header of the contextual menu that drops down, or click the marker to select it and check the Stop at Marker box in the Marker inspector. Playback will stop whenever that marker is reached.

Instrument Track Record Modes

- Note Repeat mode is independent from Note Erase mode and cannot be combined with it.
- Note Erase mode is available only when recording is set to Record Mix.
- Studio One 2 switches off Note Repeat and Input Quantize when it starts (or restarts).

For more information on Record modes, see the section "Instrument Track Record Modes" of chapter 4, "Virtual Instruments and MIDI" in *Power Tools for Studio One 2*, volume 1.

Record Offset

The Record Offset preference is a mechanism for compensating for constant latency in your system. I'm not talking about monitoring latency here, but latency in the record signal path, such as A/D conversion time. Such sources create small delays that are constant and global, and Record Offset is a fixed, global time offset to deal with it. Set Record Offset once and you should never need to touch it again unless something changes the fixed latency in your system.

To set a Record Offset:

1. Open Preferences > Options > Advanced >Audio.
2. Position the cursor over the Record Offset field and drag up or down to the desired offset value in samples, or click in the field and enter a value directly. The maximum offset is 100,000 samples.

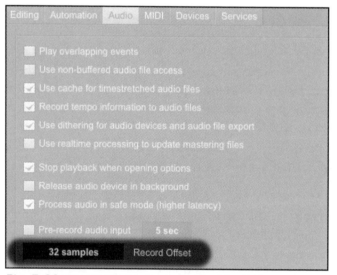

Fig. 7-33: Record Offset in the Audio tab of the Preferences > Options > Advanced pane is a fixed, global time offset intended for compensating for constant system latency.

MIDI AND VIRTUAL INSTRUMENTS

Previewing MIDI Files in the Browser

Standard MIDI Files (.mid files) can now be auditioned in the Preview Player using any instrument being used in the Song.

1. Select the Instrument track in the Arrange view that is playing the instrument you want to use for auditioning MIDI files. It can be a VI or an external device being played from the Instrument track.
2. Select the MIDI file you want to audition.
3. Click the Play button in the Preview Player and the MIDI file will be played by the selected Instrument track.
4. To audition different sounds with the MIDI file: Click the Loop button in the Preview Player and select another Instrument track or another sound on the selected instrument while it is playing. Some changes might cause artifacts, such as two different sounds playing the MIDI file while the file is playing, but when it loops back to the beginning, things usually get sorted out properly.

Fig. 7-34: Standard MIDI files can be auditioned in the Preview Player using any Instrument channel/track in the Song. This MIDI file is being played by the channel DimensionPro.

TIP: If you want to audition a MIDI file contained in a Musicloop file, select just the .mid component of the Musicloop file. Selecting and auditioning a Musicloop file directly will always play the audio file contained in the Musicloop file, rather than the MIDI file.

Selecting Reason Modules by Name

- When an Instrument track is playing Reason as a ReWire instrument, instead of a drop-down list of MIDI channels for the track output field of the track header, there is now a drop-down list of all modules in the currently active Reason document, so you can choose the target module by name.

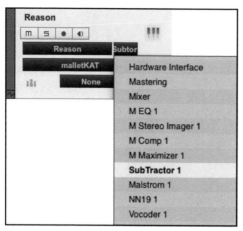

Fig. 7-35: Working with Reason in Studio One 2 is easier now that you see module names instead of channel numbers.

Legato and Overlap Handling in the Music Editor

New features have been added to correct for overlap and legato issues. The new features appear as a new section at the bottom of the Length command dialog. For more information on the Length dialog, see the section "Advanced MIDI Editing" of chapter 6, "Advanced Editing" in *Power Tools for Studio One 2*, volume 1.

When the Length command is invoked on selected notes or Parts, you will find four settings in the new bottom section, three radio buttons and a value field:

- Legato: When selected, this button causes notes to be lengthened until they overlap the next note by the duration (in bars and beats) specified in the Overlap field. Note lengths are never shortened.

- Overlap Correction: This does the opposite of Legato: when selected, this button reduces the lengths of overlapping notes until the overlap is eliminated and the notes are separated by the duration specified in the Overlap field.

- Legato + Overlap Correction: Wait…Legato and Overlap Correction do opposite things; isn't this like combining matter and antimatter? Well, if it was, this book would no longer exist, and neither would you, so we can surmise that's not quite the case. In fact, this particular duality is more like two ends of a spectrum, with Legato at one end and Overlap Correction at the other.

    When the Legato + Overlap Correction box is selected and the Overlap field is set to 0, this option acts more like "Fit Note Lengths," because what it does is adjust the lengths of selected notes so that each one ends at the start time of the following note. No overlap, no gaps.

Move the Overlap slider to the right of zero and you get legato, with notes overlapping by the Overlap duration. Move the slider to the left and it is Overlap Correction, leaving a gap between notes of the Overlap duration (which is a negative value when the slider is moved left).

- Overlap field: To set the duration used by the Legato and Overlap radio buttons, move the slider to a desired value in the range +/−1 bar, or click in the field and enter a value directly.

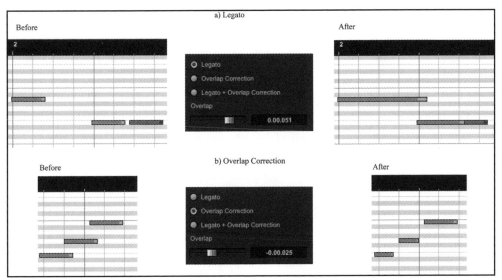

Fig. 7-36: Legato and Overlap Correction. a) Legato stretches notes until they overlap each other by the specified duration. b) Overlap Correction performs the complementary action, shortening overlapping notes until there is a gap between notes.

Viewing Controllers as Percentage or MIDI Value Range

Studio One 2 often uses percentage as the value range for many parameters. Everyone would be fine with that if MIDI had not gotten there a quarter-century earlier, using that good ol' 7-bit number range of 0 to 127 for controllers. Lots of us got very used to thinking that way, so a MIDI value range option has been added to the Controller Lanes at the bottom of the Music Editor.

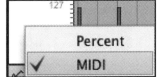

- To choose between percentage and MIDI value range for the controller lanes: Right-click (Ctrl-click in Mac) in the value scale on the left side of a controller lane and choose Percent or MIDI from the contextual menu that drops down.

Fig. 7-37: Right-click (Ctrl-click in Mac) on the left side of a controller lane to switch between viewing the values as percentages or the 0 to 127 MIDI value range.

ON THE CUTTING ROOM FLOOR: BASIC EDITING

Nudging

- When Snap is active, the nudge increment is the value in the Quantize Value field. When Snap is not active, the nudge increment is one millisecond.
- To nudge one or more selected items later in time: Press Option + Right Arrow (Alt + Right Arrow in Windows) or choose Edit > Nudge > Nudge from the main menu bar.
- To nudge one or more selected items earlier in time: Press Option + Left Arrow (Alt + Left Arrow in Windows) or choose Edit > Nudge > Nudge Back from the main menu bar.
- To nudge one or more selected items later in time by one bar: Press Option + Cmd + Right Arrow (Alt + Ctrl + Left Arrow in Windows) or choose Edit > Nudge > Nudge Bar from the main menu bar.
- To nudge one or more selected items earlier in time by one bar: Press Option + Cmd + Left Arrow (Alt + Ctrl + Left Arrow in Windows) or choose Edit > Nudge > Nudge Bar Back from the main menu bar. (Anybody who's spent too many late nights packing up in a club after a gig knows what a "bar back" is.)

Fade Fields in the Event Inspector

- To set the fade-in or fade-out time to zero, Cmd-click (Ctrl-click in Windows) on the fade-in or fade-out field.
- When dragging up or down over the fade-in or fade-out field, hold down the Shift key to get finer increments.

Folder Tracks

- Clicking on the Folder icon in the header of a Folder track expands and collapses display of the tracks in the folder.
- Basic editing operations (cut/copy/paste/duplicate, and so on) can now be performed directly on the track waveform overviews in the Folder track (Oh, did I mention that waveform overviews have been added?).
- Record-enable and input monitor buttons have been added to Folder track headers. Clicking one of these affects all tracks in the folder, regardless of whether they are in a group or a submix (or both).
- The Track area of a Folder track now displays a waveform for each track in the folder. Of course, if there are more than just a few tracks in the folder, these displays are rather teensy, so after collapsing a Folder track, you may want to grow it vertically to be able to make out any of the waveforms.

Track List Presets

Track List presets do for the Arrange view track area what Console Scenes do for the mixer. In the Track List you can hide and show tracks. Once you have a useful configuration, you can store it in a Track List preset. So, you might have one preset for drums and bass, one for guitars, and so forth. This lets you quickly reduce the track layout to those tracks you want to edit or work with at a given time.

- To store a Track List preset: Click the + (plus sign) button in the preset area at the bottom of the Track List and enter a name when the Store Preset dialog appears.
- To recall a Track List preset: Click in the Preset Menu (with the downward-pointing arrowhead) to the right of the + button and choose the desired preset from the menu that drops down.
- Track List presets can be edited, but the original preset cannot be overwritten. You must save the edited preset and then delete the original preset. Note that the Track List allows saving multiple presets with the same name, so you cannot overwrite an old version by entering the same name for the new version.
- To delete a Track List preset: Be sure that the preset you want to delete is currently active and click the – (minus sign) button in the preset area at the bottom of the Track List.
- To assign a key shortcut to one of the first five presets in the list: Open the Preferences > Options > General > Keyboard Shortcuts pane and navigate to Track > Select Scene 1 through Select Scene 5. These commands recall the first five Track List presets.

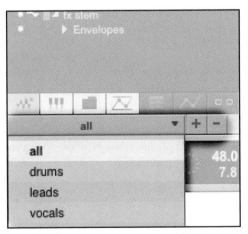

Fig. 7-38: Track List presets provide the Arrange view with the same visual configurability as Console Scenes provide in the mixer.

Listen Tool

Fig. 7-39: The Listen tool button in the Arrange view toolbar selects the Listen tool for fast auditioning.

- The Listen tool now behaves the same on a layer as on a track: as long as the mouse button is held down, the track or layer plays.
- The Listen tool plays from the position where it was clicked.
- To loop and solo an Event: Shift-click the Event and hold down the mouse button. The loop start and end points are set to the Event start and end times for as long as the mouse button is held down, returning to their previous positions when it is released.
- Holding down the Option key (Alt in Windows) while the cursor is over an Event in a layer temporarily selects the Listen tool. This makes it easy to audition Events or specific spots on a layer.

A SNEAK PEEK AT VERSION 2.6

By the time you read this, version 2.6 won't be too awfully far away. Not a lot can be said at this point…but there are a few things! However, everything here is subject to change before version 2.6 is actually released. Hey, that's the nature of sneak peeks!

- The Nimbit extension will be updated to add a small Nimbit dashboard to the Start page. The dashboard will show information about your Nimbit account and Nimbit will update it in real time.
- StudioLive integration will be enhanced with the ability to import mixer scenes from a StudioLive 32.4.2AI mixer. Mixer scenes will get stored along with audio in a session recorded in the Capture software that comes with the mixer. Studio One can import Capture sessions. To fully reproduce the session in Studio One as it existed in the StudioLive mixer, Studio One will gain a Fat Channel plug-in that provides the same processing and sound as the Studio Live's Fat Channel processing.
- Mackie HUI/Mackie Control support will be enhanced with such features as bidirectional communication of channel names, better bank handling, and more. In general, HUI/MCU will be more complete.

Appendix A
When Things Go Wrong

Troubleshooting sucks. It's frustrating and distracting. The highly analytical, linear thinking required for troubleshooting is at odds with the nonlinear leaps associated with creative thinking. It's a general pain in the patootie. Worst of all, many problems are so simple we feel like idiots when we figure it out and realize the whole hassle was because of something dumb we did and forgot about.

But troubleshooting is an unavoidable reality, and as long as we use advanced technology to make music and sound, it will continue to be so. Our only choice, then, is to just try to get it done as expeditiously as possible so we can get back to having fun as soon as possible.

Which brings us to this appendix. There's no way to do any real tech support in a book like this, so my idea is just to try and give you a fighting chance. I'll start with a section on how to approach solving problems, then follow with some suggestions that might help you figure out the root of your Studio One 2 problem.

HOW TO TROUBLESHOOT

Troubleshooting is all about logical thinking, taking a methodical approach, and keeping straight what you do and do not know. The heart of troubleshooting comes down to two steps: isolate and diagnose. First, narrow down where the problem actually lies, and then, with a reduced scope to consider, figure out exactly what the root cause is.

Most problems encountered using a DAW come down to something wrong in the signal path, usually an assignment or mute function. Something is turned off that should be on, something on that should be off, or something is not routed correctly. The next most common kind of problem is configuration: a setting that has not been made, that was made incorrectly, or that did not get changed when it should have. Look for these things before thinking something exotic, such as that a program bug or hardware failure is at fault.

Isolating Problems

Isolation is accomplished by finding somewhere in the signal chain at which things are working, and then moving toward the end of the signal path until you encounter a place where things are not working. (Of course, if no spot in the chain is working, that narrows things pretty sharply right there.)

Here are some pointers for isolating:

- You can't be certain you are on the right track unless you actually prove whether things are working at any given point. Metering and auditioning are two good ways of confirming that things are or are not working. Metering can prove that a signal is present at a given point in the signal chain, whereas auditioning can tell you whether it is the right signal and whether the signal sounds as you would expect at that point.

- Make a document to log each test you do, and its outcome. The most vexing problems can become clear instantly when you look at the results of a number of tests. Also, keeping a record of your tests saves your repeating tests and getting into a tail-chasing mode. Finally, there have been times when simply documenting a description of a problem has led me to an idea of what the cause was.

- As much as possible, try to only change one variable at a time between tests. This leads to a *lot* more tests and what seems like more time, but tests with several variables can easily lead you astray, with the result that you spend a good deal of time on a premise that was flawed from the start. In the end, by juggling too many variables, you spend more time chasing down the wrong track than a lot of valid, single-variable tests would have taken. When only one variable is changed, you can be definite about the impact of each variable.

- When trying to establish the last place in the signal chain where things are working correctly, it is often a good strategy to try the middle of the signal chain first. The result of a test there immediately cuts the size of the job of diagnosis in half. This is particularly valuable when starting in on a long or complex signal path.

Diagnosing Problems

Once a problem has been isolated to a small functional area, diagnosing is usually not as hard.

- If it is a signal path problem, once you have got some indication of where the failure is occurring, you know that the problem must lie with signal's getting into that part of the signal path, getting through it, or getting out of it. Check these one at a time: routing, on/off functions, level controls.

- It you suspect a configuration problem, consider exactly what is broken and what settings affect that feature. For example, if you solo a track then select another track and don't hear it, you might have unchecked the Solo follows Selection option.

- Devise tests designed to exercise the feature and give you more information.

- If you have done something successfully in the past that is similar to what you are now trying to do without success, try to reproduce the successful setup, then try to modify it to the setup you are after. Remember, just change one thing, then test again.

Getting Help

We all need to reach out sometimes and get a little help from our friends. Well, you have this book, which I hope can give you some information that could be useful in working out your issue. There is always the manual, too, of course.

- To open the Studio One 2 Reference manual from within Studio One 2: Press Option + F1 (Alt + F1 in Windows).

Beyond this book and the manual, community can be a beautiful thing. PreSonus Tech Support is great, but they have a heavy load, and sometimes going to the community for help with an issue is faster than the Tech Support front door.

- The PreSonus Studio One forum is a great place to try and find answers, and, if you cannot find any, post your question: http://forums.presonus.com/forums/list.page.
- PreSonus also has quite a few video tutorials posted, and these can be useful in figuring out problems as well: http://Studio One 2.presonus.com/tutorials/.
- YouTube has multiple channels devoted to Studio One, and many assorted videos relating to it.

WHY CAN'T I HEAR ANYTHING?

The most common problem of all is not hearing something you should be hearing. It's such a common problem because there are so many possible causes, depending on the specifics of the situation. Here's a handful of the most common offenders:

- A channel is muted or soloed. Check the global Solo indicator and you can immediately see whether any channel in the mix is soloed. Click the global Solo button to disable all soloing. The global Mute indicator is of less use because, although it similarly tells you whether any channel is muted, it is not unusual for some channels to be constantly muted in a mix.
- A fader is set all the way to the bottom.
- There is volume or mute automation on the track that blocks the signal.
- A channel output is not properly assigned.
- Main Out is set to the wrong interface outputs.
- Input monitoring is not engaged on a record channel.
- If an audio interface cannot be set to the sample rate of a Song or loses an external clock it is set to follow, there will usually be no output.
- No audio interface is found by Studio One 2. In this case, an icon replaces the Performance monitoring meters on the Transport bar. Click the icon to open Preferences and look at the interface settings.

HUH? NOTHING GOT RECORDED!

You're singing your heart out or playing your butt off (and perhaps should be keeping a tighter hold on your body parts), but when you play it back, you hear nothing. Oops. Check these things:

- The correct input is not selected for the channel.
- The interface input has not been connected to the virtual input in the Preferences > Song Setup > Audio I/O Setup pane.
- There is a problem in the signal chain before the interface: a condenser mic receiving no phantom power, a cable unconnected or connected to the wrong input, a bad cable, even a bad mic, an active DI box getting neither phantom nor battery power, the mic preamp gain is down.
- The channel is not record-enabled. Maybe the channel next to it is record-enabled instead!
- Confirm signal on the Input channel strip. If you don't see it there, look at any metering your audio interface offers.
- Confirm that Studio One 2 is actually recording.

IT SOUNDS WEIRD

Clicks and Pops

- If you are hearing clicks and pops while recording or on playback after recording: Try increasing the buffer size. This will, of course, increase latency. If you have interface-based low-latency monitoring, that won't matter, however.
- Reduce the number of virtual instruments (VIs) and high-CPU plug-ins that are running by transforming tracks, rendering Event FX, and so on.
- Watch the Performance Monitor meters and see whether there is any momentary spiking in the CPU demands. If so, try to reduce CPU demand until it stops spiking. There may be times when you remove something for testing purposes that you actually cannot work without. If you do that and the problem stops, you will either have to get clever and figure a way around it, or you just might not have the hardware "oomph" you need to do what you want to do.

Other Gremlins

- If the entire mix has a metallic sound, check that no tracks are playing mixdown files from earlier exports. The Export Mixdown dialog has an option for importing the bounced file to a new track; if that track is playing along with the Song, cancellations will occur.

- If there is distortion, look for clipping. Check more than just the Main Out meters: look at channels, buses, even meters in plug-ins. Although it is difficult to clip plug-ins internally, there are ways it can happen sometimes, so it is worthwhile to try kicking a plug-in into Bypass or reducing the level going into or coming out of it to determine whether the plug-in is causing the distortion.
- If audio has a highly filtered sound, check that no plug-ins are set to audition their sidechains.

THE CONTROLLER WON'T PLAY THE INSTRUMENT

The MIDI Monitor is a very effective tool in solving these problems.

- The controller is transmitting on a MIDI channel other than those specified for it in the Preferences > Options > External Devices pane.
- The Instrument track Input is not set to All Inputs, or is set to the wrong controller.
- The Instrument track is not set to Input Monitor, so the controller signal is not being sent to the instrument.
- The instrument is multitimbral and the track is set to play the wrong channel.
- The Instrument track is muted.
- The Instrument channel is muted.
- The Instrument channel Output is set incorrectly.
- An Instrument track is playing an external device that is not correctly set up. Try loading a factory preset on the instrument.
- The audio or MIDI system is set up or configured incorrectly, either at the system level or in the interface(s).
- The note range of the controller is out of range for the instrument. This can happen when playing in the octaves above middle C on a controller that is playing a drum machine with its sounds assigned to the lower octaves.

MONITORING

Monitoring problems can happen both in the control room (main) mix and in Cue mixes.

Things Sound Late

- Check the buffer size. If your system will run with a smaller buffer, try it. Remember that VI returns are subject to latency, as well.

Cue Mix Problems

- The Cue mix box is not checked for the Output channel in the Outputs tab of the Preferences > Song Setup > Audio IO Setup pane.
- The Cue mix Output channel is not assigned to the right interface output.
- The Cue mix Output channel is muted.
- There is a problem with your interface's onboard low-latency monitoring (probably muting or misassignment).
- The Cue mix Output fader is all the way down.
- The channel Cue mix send is not enabled, or the level is all the way down.

I Hear It, but I Don't See It

- The channel is hidden.
- The track is hidden and the Arrange view and Mix views are linked.
- The track is in a Folder track that is collapsed.

WHERE ARE MY EFFECTS?

Using a plug-in:

- A channel send to the effect was not added.
- The channel send has been muted.
- The FX or Bus channel with the effect return is muted.
- The Output assignment for the FX or Bus channel with the effect return is incorrect.
- A parameter in the plug-in is preventing output.
- A wet/dry mix control in the plug-in is set to all dry.

Using an outboard processor, things are a little more complicated because of the need to interface with the world outside the computer. If you look at the meter on the outboard device and see no input level, you know the problem is probably before the device.

If simple troubleshooting does not reveal the problem, you need to eliminate the device itself as being the cause of the problem. This is best done by connecting a source directly into the jacks on the back of the device, rather than through any patching or cabling that is already in place. Similarly, the output should be taken directly from the device's output jacks. A small test set can help you establish at least that signal is passing through the device. Once that is established, then you know the problem is in the signal path, not the device itself. Here are some possible problems in an effects setup that uses an outboard processor:

- The Output channel being used as a send is not assigned to the correct interface output. In this situation, you will see level on the Output channel meter, but not on the interface meters.

- The interface output is not correctly connected to the outboard processor. In this case, you would see output level on the interface meters, but no input level on the processor meters.

- The device's input or output level is turned down.

- The device is not on.

- The device output is not correctly connected to the interface. If the device has output metering, you will see signal there, but not on the interface meters.

- If using the Pipeline plug-in, the Pipeline Send or Return is not properly assigned.

- Rendered Event FX do not include outboard processing incorporated using the Pipeline plug-in.

Automation

If automation is not playing back, check these things:

- Automation is not in Read mode.

- The automation envelope has been disabled.

- The automation is on the wrong envelope.

Control Surfaces

If there is no control from the surface:

- The surface is not properly connected to the computer.

- An internal setting on the control surface is preventing it from properly sending messages.

- The control surface is not correctly defined in the Preferences > Options > External Devices pane.

- Controls are not mapped to parameters.

- Control is working on a parameter that is off-screen. This can happen with HUI controllers, which control the first eight channels in the mixer, whether or not they happen to be onscreen.

Burning Issues

If a disk came out blank:

- If the Pipeline plug-in is used in master processing, check that it is functioning correctly.
- Check that the correct output is selected when the Project is burned.

If the bounce comes out in mono:

- Check that the Channel Mode of Main Out is set to stereo. It is possible to forget to restore the setting after checking the mix in mono.

LOOPING

If a loop is not following tempo changes:

- No audio file tempo has been set.
- The Track Tempo mode is set to Don't Follow.

I MADE CHANGES TO MY MIX, BUT I DON'T HEAR THEM IN THE PROJECT

- The mastering file needs to be updated.

Appendix B
PreSonus Audioloop

FILE FORMAT SPECIFICATION VERSION I.0
© 2012 PRESONUS SOFTWARE LIMITED

INTRODUCTION

The PreSonus Audioloop format is a container for storing audio together with musical meta data, such as tempo and slicing information in a unified way, independent of the actual audio encoding. It is solely based on other widely adopted open standards, which makes it straightforward to implement.

A special flavor of this format called PreSonus Musicloop adds the benefit of preserving musical performance data together with instrument and effect preset data used to generate the sound, making it a universal media object that can be used either as pure audio or reimported into the original software instrument for further editing.

For easier differentiation and assumptions on how the file should be handled by an application without having to scan its content, Audioloops and Musicloops carry different filename extensions.

Audioloop:

- Content: tempo-tagged and optionally sliced audio
- Filename Extension: .audioloop
- Internet media type: application/x-presonus-audioloop

Musicloop:

- Content: tempo-tagged audio, musical performance and instrument/effect preset data.
- Filename Extension: .musicloop
- Internet media type: application/x-presonus-musicloop

Audioloops and Musicloops have been introduced by PreSonus with Studio One 2.0. This document describes the logical and the physical structure of Audioloops in more detail. It is mainly intended for developer audience already familiar with the underlying technologies.

CONTAINER FORMAT

Numerous multimedia container and audio file formats already exist, and each file format provides a more or less extensible foundation for auxiliary data. Instead of defining ways to embed musical data into multiple formats, the Audioloop specification wraps an audio file into a general-purpose file container and imposes a logical file structure on it. It uses a subset of the well-known ZIP container format, meaning that each .audioloop and .musicloop file is a valid .zip file, but of course, not vice versa.

Rules for using ZIP as container for Audioloops:

- The compression methods are limited to None (0) and Deflated (8).
- Filenames have to be encoded with the historical DOS-Encoding (IBM Code Page 437) or UTF-8 with the Language Encoding Flag set to 1.
- Files larger than 4GB have to use the ZIP64 Extra Fields.
- ZIP version is 20 in general, or 45 when ZIP64 is used.

More in depth information on the ZIP format can be found at:
http://www.pkware.com/documents/casestudies/APPNOTE.TXT.
Compression/decompression can be implemented using zlib: http://zlib.net/.

To allow direct playback and sample-accurate seek of the audio stream, the audio file entry inside the ZIP container must not be compressed. To enable playback of Audioloops from remote storage locations via Internet transfer protocols, such as HTTP, the order of file entries inside the container is important. All relevant metadata required for playback must precede the actual audio data. The local file headers defined by the ZIP container format serve as markers between file entries in this scenario, and the central directory at the end of the file can be ignored.

META INFORMATION

The first entry in the Audioloop container has to be the metainfo .xml file. This entry is mandatory. It contains a simple XML dictionary with key-value-pairs defining attributes like tempo, time signature, creator, and generator of the file.

Example:

```
<code>
<?xml version="1.0" encoding="UTF-8"?>
<MetaInformation>
<Attribute id="Document:MimeType" value="application/x-presonus-audioloop"/>
<Attribute id="Document:Creator" value="Username"/>
<Attribute id="Document:Generator" value="Studio One/2.0.0.15986"/>
<Attribute id="AudioLoop:AudioFile" value="Audio.flac"/>
```

```
<Attribute id="Media:Tempo" value="110"/>
<Attribute id="Media:TimeSignatureNumerator" value="4"/>
<Attribute id="Media:TimeSignatureDenominator" value="4"/>
</MetaInformation>
</code>
```

- AudioLoop:AudioFile: This field defines the name of the audio file entry in the container. It defaults to Audio .flac.
- Media:Tempo: Original tempo of the Audioloop in BPM.
- Media:TimeSignature Numerator and Media:TimeSignature Denominator: Time signature of the Audioloop.

The meta information fields may be extended in future versions of this specification.

AUDIO FORMATS

In general, an Audioloop contains a WAV-format audio file when uncompressed or a FLAC-format file for lossless compression. Bit depth, sample rate and channel setup are depending on the capabilities of the audio format in use. These attributes are not repeated in the Audioloop meta information file. To recognize the exact sample format and length of the audio stream, the header of the embedded audio file has to be parsed.

AUDIO SLICES

Even though timestretching algorithms provide good quality when adjusting the tempo of audio material, there are situations where slicing might be a better choice, especially for percussive material and for the use in sampler instruments. The audio material for all slices is saved in a continuous audio stream, accompanied by a map that indicates the slice points in sample offsets and in musical time. The source length of a slice can be longer than the audible length at the original tempo. Therefore, playing back the raw audio stream of a sliced Audioloop file does not necessarily reproduce the intended musical timing. A simple slicing engine needs to be implemented that stitches together the audio for rendering at the requested tempo. It is heavily recommended to crossfade between slices while rendering. A good guess for the fade length is 5 milliseconds, whereas the fade-in might be shorter than the fade-out.

Slice information is saved in the audioslices.xml file.

Sample positions always refer to full sample frames; that is, independent of the channel count, at the original sample rate of the audio stream. Musical time is expressed as normalized PPQ values where 1.0 equals one quarter note. Converting between sample positions and musical time is always subject to rounding errors. Therefore, the slice entries carry both value domains as calculated by the generating application.

Example:

```
<code>
<?xml version=“1.0” encoding=“UTF-8”?>
<AudioLoopSlices sampleLength=“384873” ppqLength=“16”>
<AudioLoopSlice sampleOffset=“0”
sampleLength=“6263”
ppqPosition=“0”
ppqLength=“0.26035156250000002”
sourceLength=“9658”/>
<AudioLoopSlice sampleOffset=“6263”
sampleLength=“5717”
ppqPosition=“0.26035156250000002”
ppqLength=“0.23769531249999998”
sourceOffset=“9658”
sourceLength=“8818”/>

. . .

</AudioLoopSlices>
</code>
```

The attributes “ppqLength” and “sampleLength” in the <AudioLoopSlices> tag describe the full length of the loop in musical time and in audio samples at the original tempo and sample rate.

Each <AudioLoopSlice> item has the following fields:

- sampleOffset: Position of the slice in samples within the loop at the original tempo and sample rate as rounded by the generating application. This value can be recalculated from ppqPosition.

- sampleLength: Length of the slice in samples at the original tempo and sample rate as rounded by the generating application. This value can be recalculated from ppqLength.

- ppqPosition: Musical start position of the slice within the loop.

- ppqLength: Musical length of the slice within the loop.

- sourceOffset: Start of the audio material for the given slice within the audio stream. The value can be different to sampleOffset in case slices overlap.

- sourceLength: Maximum length of the audio material in samples for the given slice. This value can be different to sampleLength, in case more audio material is available than needed for playback at the original tempo, which allows to slow down the loop without dropouts between slices.

Any field can be omitted if its value is zero.

Please note that slices do not support any further instructions for processing, such as volume, mute, transient shaping, and so on. All effect processing needs to happen when the Audioloop container file is created. This reduces complexity and ensures compatibility between different systems. However, gaps between slices are allowed and need to be handled correctly when rendering.

MUSICAL DATA

Musical performance data is saved as a Standard MIDI file (SMF), either type 0 or type 1 with a single track.

For more information on the MIDI specification please refer to: http://www.midi.org

PreSonus Studio One additionally saves the musical performance in a proprietary XML-based format as a .music file. This representation preserves automation data for software instruments other than standard MIDI controllers.

Musicloops have the following additional meta information fields:

- Media:Length: Length of the musical performance in seconds.
- Media:PpqLength: Length of the performance in musical time.

This allows determination of the length of the performance without reading the whole MIDI or .music file, and notes inside the performance can be longer than the intended boundaries of the musical building block.

PRESET DATA

Instrument and effect preset data is saved in the native format of the relevant plug-in API.

- Apple AudioUnit: .aupreset
- Steinberg VST2:   .fxb
- Steinberg VST3:   .vstpreset
- PreSonus native: .fxpreset

Because PreSonus native plug-ins are supported by Studio One only, Musicloops containing preset data for these instruments and effects cannot reproduce the exact same sound when opened for editing in third-party music software applications. However, the rendered audio and the musical performance data can be accessed anyway.

Presets are organized in a file named presetparts.xml, where each <PresetPart> item refers to the preset data file by its name inside the container.

Example:

```
<code>
<PresetParts>
<PresetPart>
<Attribute id="Class:ID" value="{3713E26C-2FCA-4024-9F25-17E9D2BE2B9A}"/>
<Attribute id="Class:Name" value="Presence"/>
<Attribute id="Class:Category" value="AudioSynth"/>
<Attribute id="Class:SubCategory" value="(Native)/Sampler"/>
<Attribute id="Class:Vendor" value="PreSonus"/>
<Attribute id="AudioSynth:IsMainPreset" value="1"/>
<Attribute id="MusicLoop:InstrumentPort" value="0"/>
<Attribute id="Preset:DataFile" value="Presence 3.fxpreset"/>
<Attribute id="Preset:DataMimeType" value="audio/x-fxpreset"/>
</PresetPart>
<PresetPart>
<Attribute id="Class:ID" value="{073C4094-E062-4FB5-8328-74608DD1A3A4}"/>
<Attribute id="Class:Name" value="Pro EQ"/>
<Attribute id="Class:Category" value="AudioEffect"/>
<Attribute id="Class:SubCategory" value="(Native)/Mixing"/>
<Attribute id="Class:Vendor" value="PreSonus"/>
<Attribute id="AudioSynth:PortIndex" value="0"/>
<Attribute id="Preset:DataFile" value="Presence 3/1 - Pro EQ.fxpreset"/>
<Attribute id="Preset:DataMimeType" value="audio/x-fxpreset"/>
</PresetPart>
. . .
</PresetParts>
</code>
```

The first item in the list always describes the preset data of the software instrument. It is marked with the attribute AudioSynth:IsMainPreset.

For multitimbral instruments, the attribute MusicLoop:InstrumentPort defines which input should be feed with the musical performance. Because plug-in APIs have different bussing and channel architectures for musical events, this address is the absolute position when all busses and channels are collected into a flat list.

The following items refer to effect processors inserted into the audio outputs of the instrument. The AudioSynth:PortIndex attribute defines the relevant output. Effects are inserted in the order they appear. If the application supports on-demand activation of instrument outputs, any output mentioned in the list should be activated.

Each <PresetPart> item must have the following additional fields:

- Class:ID: String representation of the16 Byte GUID defining the plug-in class. A direct mapping is possible for PreSonus native plug-ins and for VST3 only. For VST2, the mapping between 4 Byte identifiers and GUIDs is described in the VST Plug-in SDK. The mapping for AudioUnit identifiers follows.
- Class:Name: User-readable name of the plug-in.
- Preset:DataFile: Filename of the actual preset data inside the container.
- Preset:DataMimeType: Internet media type of the preset data file.

For Apple AudioUnit plug-ins, the component description is mapped to a 16-byte GUID with the following C++ function:

```
<code>
void AudioUnitID_to_GUID (const ComponentDescription& desc, GUID& guid)
{
guid.data1 = desc.componentType;
guid.data2 = (short)((desc.componentSubType >> 0) & 0xFFFF);
guid.data3 = (short)((desc.componentSubType >> 16) & 0xFFFF);
guid.data4[0] = (unsigned char)((desc.componentManufacturer >> 0) & 0xFF);
guid.data4[1] = (unsigned char)((desc.componentManufacturer >> 8) & 0xFF);
guid.data4[2] = (unsigned char)((desc.componentManufacturer >> 16) & 0xFF);
guid.data4[3] = (unsigned char)((desc.componentManufacturer >> 24) & 0xFF);
guid.data4[4] = 'B';
guid.data4[5] = 'A';
guid.data4[6] = 'L';
guid.data4[7] = 'K';
}
</code>
```

Appendix C
Video Extras

Give a man a fish and he'll eat for a day, but give him a video on how to fish and he'll be able to generate enough tweets on his Twitter account to last a lifetime. I don't really care how much you fish, but I've tried to capture a few of the most important concepts in the book in videos that I hope will give you a faster grasp of some of Studio One 2's best features. Although the Macros feature is covered in *Power Tools for Studio One 2,* volume 2, I included a video about Macros with volume 1, so go back there to check out macros on video. For volume 2, here's what you get:

- Musicloop and Audioloop Files: PreSonus' new proprietary file formats are easy to create and hold great creative possibilities. I look at both sides of the equation in this video.

- Stems and Stem Mixing: Studio One 2's Export Stems command performs the eminently useful task of exporting each track in a Song to a separate file, including all processing. But this is not stem mixing. Stem mixing is easy enough to do in Studio One 2, however, and this video shows you both the Export Stems command and how to do what I call "true stem mixing."

- Song/Project Integration: In some ways, the integration of the Song and Project pages strikes me as the single most powerful production tool in all of Studio One 2. A big statement, but once you have experienced being able to shape individual mixes with the benefit of being able to instantly hear them in the context of the entire album, you will find it frustrating to produce an album in any other DAW.

- Project Page Overview: No other DAW has an entirely separate dedicated mastering environment like the Project page. I'll walk you down its components and how the Project page works.

- Integrating External Processors with Pipeline: While other DAWs provide mechanisms for bringing outboard equipment into your mixes, Pipeline goes a step further by providing measurement tools that enable you to optimize the setup.

- Metering: Mix with your ears, but let your eyes help. Studio One has excellent metering capabilities, including powerful metering plug-ins. I'll let you see metering on both the Song and Project pages, plus take a look that plug-ins.

Index

ABOUT THE AUTHOR

Larry the O has been working with sound and music for so long his ears are permanently stained with them. Production is the name of his game, and he has played it in live performance, music recording, film, network TV, video games, magazines, industrial sound design, oh, and books. Composition, sound design, engineering, producing, writing, marketing…this boy has no idea where the bus stops. It's nearly frightening.

Not a Forrest Gump by a long shot, the O has nonetheless managed to traverse some interesting times in the audio industry, everywhere from manufacturers such as Lexicon and Meyer Sound; to production houses such as LucasArts, Electronic Arts, and the late, lamented San Francisco studio, Russian Hill Recording; to periodicals such as *Mix* and *Electronic Musician* magazines.

An innocent-looking outbuilding in Vallejo, California, the gateway to Northern California's wine country, houses Studio Faire la Nouba, the O's production facility. There are no windows there, but there are orange and peach trees just outside the door.